Beyond
Boundaries

MUSIC AND THE EARLY MODERN IMAGINATION

Massimo Ossi, editor

Beyond Boundaries

Rethinking Music Circulation in Early Modern England

Edited by

LINDA PHYLLIS AUSTERN, CANDACE BAILEY,
and AMANDA EUBANKS WINKLER

INDIANA UNIVERSITY PRESS

Bloomington and Indianapolis

This book is a publication of

Indiana University Press
Office of Scholarly Publishing
Herman B Wells Library 350
1320 East 10th Street
Bloomington, Indiana 47405 USA

iupress.indiana.edu

© 2017 by Indiana University Press

All rights reserved

No part of this book may be reproduced or utilized in any form or by any means, electronic or mechanical, including photocopying and recording, or by any information storage and retrieval system, without permission in writing from the publisher. The Association of American University Presses' Resolution on Permissions constitutes the only exception to this prohibition.

♾ The paper used in this publication meets the minimum
requirements of the American National Standard for Information Sciences—
Permanence of Paper for Printed Library Materials,
ANSI Z39.48-1992.

Manufactured in the United States of America

Cataloging information is available from the Library of Congress.

ISBN 978-0-253-02479-4 (cloth)
ISBN 978-0-253-02482-4 (paperback)
ISBN 978-0-253-02497-8 (ebook)

1 2 3 4 5   22 21 20 19 18 17

We dedicate this book to our contributors.

Contents

Acknowledgments   ix
Note on Transcription   xi
List of Abbreviations and Library Sigla   xiii

Introduction: Rethinking Boundaries in Musical Practice and Circulation / Linda Phyllis Austern, Candace Bailey, and Amanda Eubanks Winkler   1

1. Tudor Musical Theater: Sounds of Religious Change in *Ralph Roister Doister* / Katherine Steele Brokaw   13

2. English Jesuit Missionaries, Music Education, and the Musical Participation of Women in Devotional Life in Recusant Households from ca. 1580 to ca. 1630 / Jane Flynn   28

3. The Transmission of Lute Music and the Culture of Aurality in Early Modern England / Graham Freeman   42

4. Thomas Campion's "Superfluous Blossomes of His Deeper Studies": The Public Realm of His English Ayres / Christopher R. Wilson   54

5. Oyez! Fresh Thoughts about the "Cries of London" Repertory / John Milsom   67

6. "Locks, Bolts, Barres, and Barricados": Song Performance, Gender, and Spatial Production in Richard Brome's *The Northern Lass* / Katherine R. Larson   79

7. "Lasting-Pasted Monuments": Memory, Music, Theater, and the Seventeenth-Century English Broadside Ballad / Sarah F. Williams   96

8. The Challenge of Domesticity in Men's Manuscripts in Restoration England / Candace Bailey   114

9. A Midcentury Musical Friendship: Silas Taylor and Matthew Locke / Alan Howard   127

10. Music and Merchants in Restoration London / Bryan White   150

11. Daniel Henstridge and the Aural Transmission of Music in
Restoration England / Rebecca Herissone   165

12. Courtly Connections: Queen Anne, Music, and the Public Stage /
Amanda Eubanks Winkler   187

13. Disseminating and Domesticating Handel in Mid-Eighteenth-
Century Britain / Suzanne Aspden   207

14. From London's Opera House to the Salon? The *Favourite* (and Not
So "Favourite") *Songs* from the King's Theatre / Michael Burden   223

15. Education, Entertainment, Embellishment: Music Publication in
the *Lady's Magazine* / Bonny H. Miller   238

Selected Bibliography   257
List of Contributors   299
Index   305

Acknowledgments

This book would not have been possible without the assistance of many. We would especially like to thank Raina Polivka, sponsoring editor from Indiana University Press, for her encouragement and support from the beginning. We are also indebted to the two anonymous readers who provided such incisive comments. Special thanks go to Northwestern University musicology PhD student and fellow member of the North American British Music Studies Association, Jason Rosenholtz-Witt, for tackling the onerous task of compiling and checking the master bibliography for the volume. We are grateful to our contributing authors for writing such interesting and varied essays for this collection. We also recognize that our work would not be possible without the assistance of the staff working in the institutions cited in the individual essays, and we sincerely appreciate their help in locating and making available resources for this book. Finally, it has been a pleasure to work with one another from early discussions about the circulation of music in early modern England through the final stages of preparing this study. We are most grateful to our families, who, as usual, have put up with us working through nights, weekends, and summer vacations.

Note on Transcription

Quotations from early modern sources retain original spellings, capitalization, and punctuation with these exceptions: the *y* used as a thorn has been changed to *th* and the use of *i, j, u,* and *v* have been modernized for ease of reading.

Abbreviations and Library Sigla

Abbreviations

BDECM	*A Biographical Dictionary of English Court Musicians 1485–1714*
DNB	*Dictionary of National Biography*
ECP	Eighteenth-Century Periodicals
GMO	*Grove Music Online*
OED	*Oxford English Dictionary Online*

Library sigla

B (Belgium)

Bc	Brussels Conservatoire

D (Germany)

Hs	Staats- und Universitätsbibliothek Carl von Ossietzky, Musikabteilung

GB (Great Britain)

AB	Aberystwyth, National Library of Wales
Cfm	Cambridge, Fitzwilliam Museum
Ckc	Cambridge, King's College, Rowe Music Library
Cssc	Cambridge, Sydney Sussex College
Cu	Cambridge University Library
ERO	Essex Record Office
Eu	Edinburgh, University Library, Main Library
Ge	Glasgow, Euing Music Library
GL	Gloucester, Cathedral Library
Lbl	London, British Library
Lcm	London College of Music
Lg	London, Guildhall Library
Ob	Oxford, Bodleian Library

Och	Oxford, Christ Church
TNA	The National Archives, Kew

J (Japan)

Tn	Tokyo, Nanki Music Library

US (United States)

NH	New Haven, Yale University, Music Library
NYp	New York, New York Public Library for the Performing Arts, Music Division

Beyond Boundaries

Introduction: Rethinking Boundaries in Musical Practice and Circulation

Linda Phyllis Austern, Candace Bailey, and
Amanda Eubanks Winkler

The fifteen essays in this collection reconsider ways in which musical practice and circulation in early modern England negotiated boundaries, demonstrating how music and musicians fluidly moved between social and professional hierarchies, oral/aural and written traditions, and sacred and secular contexts.[1] From the mid-sixteenth century to the end of the eighteenth century, musical spaces were elided among home, stage, court, church, and street, and musical collaborations triumphed over national, vocational, and confessional differences. Gender norms were relaxed and reconfigured, and labor and leisure overlapped for the performance and consumption of music. Through patterns of circulation and use, the public became private, the private public, and the musical dicta of etiquette and pedagogical manuals were suspended.

This book began as a series of conversations among several contributors. It became increasingly evident that many of the categories applied to seventeenth-century English music making are anachronistic. Most immediately questionable, we found, were hard divisions between the public and the private and "amateur" and "professional" musicianship. Actual patterns of practice, especially as evident in manuscripts and eyewitness accounts, were far more nuanced than theoretical bifurcation allows. As our discussions expanded into the sixteenth and eighteenth centuries, we realized that other widely accepted oppositions such as female and male, Catholic and Protestant, oral and written, high art and popular, and creator and consumer were more set in modern scholarship than in historical practice. Even the clean division of institutional music making into court, church, theater, and chamber so beloved by introductory textbooks became murky as we considered the contents of manuscripts, title pages and dedications of print collections, mass-market circulars such as broadsides and magazines, and performance practices for anything classified as dramatic or theatrical. The picture was further complicated by subtle and changing notions of gender, class status, social circulation, and networks of friendship and patronage; even the inherent inequality and power dynamic between teacher and student varied across time and according to instructional context.[2]

As we looked from Tudor England to Georgian Britain, we recognized the extent to which changes in media technologies, architectural space, and institutions—including court and theater—influenced musical practice. National and familial politics, especially during the seventeenth century, redefined performance spaces and associated repertories as well as distinctions between amateur (or recreational) and professional (or occupational) musicianship.[3] The years covered by this book—between ca. 1550 and 1800—were particularly tumultuous ones for the English/British political and related social systems. They witnessed a transition between absolute and constitutional monarchies with a period of commonwealth government. They also saw multiple redefinitions of official state religion and plural patterns of change to family structures, educational programs, and notions of community. Each of these influenced the circulation and consumption of music. The first permanent playhouses and spaces designated as "theaters" arose during this period, as did a culture of public concerts; these coincided with the explosive growth of a native music-printing industry that enabled the spread of standardized content from one point of origin and one sort of musician or consumer to a multiplicity of others. Above all, musical practice emerged as a complex social process that united and divided individuals and groups across space, place, and even time. The contents of this book reflect these nuances.

One of the thorniest concerns from which many of these essays arose is the fluid interplay between "public" and "private." From long before the sixteenth century and into our own, the two have mostly been theorized as oppositional binaries in which each implicitly delimits the other. Throughout the period covered by this book, and even in the current century with its revealing tweets, mass-media fixation on celebrity secrets, and virtual socializing enabled by Instagram and Facebook, the two domains overlap in practice. Hannah Arendt reminds us that "even the twilight which illuminates our private and intimate lives is ultimately derived from the harsh light of the public realm."[4] The essays by Flynn, Wilson, Bailey, Eubanks Winkler, Aspden, Burden, and Miller highlight ways in which a firm binary between the two terms is misleading for studies of sixteenth-, seventeenth-, and eighteenth-century English culture. Those by Brokaw, Milsom, Larson, and Williams feature creative works that span spaces and places often theorized as "private" or "public," but which stand apart from either notion. The ease by which music and its materials cross physical and social barriers, especially as a communal or sociable process, makes it a particularly effective medium for reevaluating slippage between these historically vexing categories. In fact, Harold Love has argued that music was central to the creation of a "public" during the eighteenth century, when lines became more firmly drawn between avid listener, amateur performer, and professional musician.[5] Flynn, Wilson, Williams, Bailey, Howard, and White show in this book that musical performances and commodities had already paved the way earlier by creating communities of shared taste and consumption.

England stood at the forefront of radical change to Western social and political constructions of private and public during the years covered by this book. Philippe Ariès considered it "the birthplace of privacy" based on the practice of keeping diaries and memoirs beginning in the 1590s when Flynn's recusant Catholics were bending official (public) religious practices of their faith and their nation-state in (private) households.[6] Jürgen Habermas seminally connected the emergence of a "bourgeois public sphere"—"the sphere of private people come together as a public"—to the rise of capitalism and the modern political state first fully evident in eighteenth-century Britain.[7] More recent scholars, including Bailey, Flynn, and Eubanks Winkler in this volume, continue to acknowledge English innovation as they interrogate Habermas's definition, either explicitly or implicitly.[8] Indeed, various "publics" figure prominently in all four eighteenth-century essays in this collection, each of which is concerned with the repackaging and movement of music between physical locations and those imagined communities in which consumers are brought together through shared access to material.

Overlapping concepts of the public and the private spanned the social and political loci of domestic and national governance, patronage, and friendship throughout the early modern era, and the relationship between the two terms changed over time. The English word *public* derives from classical Latin *publicus* through the Anglo-Norman term indicating "official" as well as authorized by or representing the community. In 1559, not long after our book begins, the term was applied to the nation-state. By 1751 and through the remaining half century covered by our book, it came to include a collectivity of audience and/or spectators.[9] The word *private* derives from classical Latin *privatus* (past participle of *privare*), meaning "deprived," specifically of public office and the civic status that went with it.[10] For most of the period covered by this book, the "private" person was tied to an extended family bound through designated officials to a "public" nation-state and to one religion. All three of these—family, state, and church—were public social institutions reflecting cosmic order and hierarchy. Each had a designated head and each member had a prescribed role.[11]

This political understanding of private and public gradually acquired social and spatial connotations during the early modern era.[12] In the sixteenth and early seventeenth centuries, the public and the private were most often constructed as a flexible axis on which individual positions could shift by circumstance, and whose points of contact were continuously transformed. Essays by Flynn and Wilson illuminate contrasting ramifications of this process, in which the former shows how practice could shift individuals and locations across domains, and the latter why such transformation was not always desirable.[13] By the mid-eighteenth century, "public" and "private" had emerged as spheres of influence. The former was not only a consuming audience but also a discursive community organized around shared ideas. Individuals could participate from any space. Yet the "public" sphere continued to encompass service to the state, and the "private" still indicated what stood apart from state purview. So there came to be many publics, ways to engage with them, and new means (and places) to obtain at least a semblance of privacy.[14] This led to an endless variety of overlap between spaces, practices, communities, and the materials that bridged them, as Aspden and Burden especially show. By the 1770s and 1780s, for London diarist Anna Lampert, "publick" activities designated those to which purchase of a ticket granted access while admission to private ones was by invitation.[15] The most fashionably select musical performances of Lampert's century, which we also see in Aspden's essay—ticketed subscription concerts priced for the elite and held in highly visible spaces—reflect the fine historical nuance of these terms.[16] The final three essays of this book demonstrate how commodification of such "public" music, especially for use at home, muddies the waters still further.

It is therefore no surprise that millennia of legal, political, and social theory have strongly disagreed about where to position the domicile, family, and household authority within a system in which "public" and "private" are often defined by mutual exclusion yet also in relation to church, state, and community service.[17] Flynn, Bailey, and Miller particularly demonstrate ways in which a simple binary between the public and the private is inapplicable to domestic life during the sixteenth, seventeenth, and eighteenth centuries. It is no coincidence that each of these authors also questions assumptions about the gendering of space and genre, or that Flynn focuses on the home in its ancient role as a place of Christian worship bound to global practice. The dwelling overlapped in function with designated places for prayer, entertainment, social bonding, and statecraft, multiples of which are brought together in the essays by Brokaw, Flynn, Milsom, Aspden, and Miller. Households were situated within physically proximate and wider communities, through which ideas, materials, and visitors flowed. More or less restricted spaces could be repurposed to signify favor or status, because architectural constructs are as much social as physical. We see this in the essays by Flynn, Williams, Aspden, and Burden, all of which challenge the idea of the domicile as a space apart from public concerns.

Trends in residential architecture across the centuries covered by this book support the notion that awareness of "public" and "private" spaces changed over time with the attendant ramifications for perceptions about music. Evidence indicates a gradual shift from multipurpose rooms to single-function ones starting at upper social echelons and in urban areas.[18] During the sixteenth and early seventeenth centuries, rooms were mainly communal and lacked connecting hallways. Metaphors of interior spaces show that they were generally understood as public. Family members, visitors, and any resident servants or apprentices moved throughout, allowing no clear distinction between domestic and community affairs. There was no space set aside for the performance of intimate bodily business.[19] However, during the seventeenth century, a new English house plan developed partly out of desire for "privacy" and "convenience." By then, aristocratic heads of household had already begun to stage withdrawal into more secluded space set aside for their personal use.[20] The invention of back stairs in country houses late in the century enabled segregation of servants from family and guests even as the latter two occupied more spacious and isolated apartments. It was not until interior hallways became common toward the end of the eighteenth century that British houses offered dependable separation of inhabitants, a necessary condition for more modern notions of privacy that we begin to see in all their complicated reality in the essays by Aspden and Burden.[21] Royal houses retained their "public" position as centers for policy and nation-building in which the monarch's whereabouts were always known. Yet their architecture had helped restrict access to him or her at least since Tudor times.[22] Brokaw and Eubanks Winkler show how works performed before royalty carried national concerns between court and wider populace during the sixteenth and early eighteenth centuries.

In *Beyond Boundaries: Rethinking Music Circulation in Early Modern England*, music joins a nexus of social actions that both united and transcended persons and places, sometimes in unexpected ways. Such transformative encounters help to generate space, an interactive practice in which boundary constructs such as walls offer less actual separation than indefinite continuity.[23] Michel Foucault reminds us that space is fundamental to communal life and to the exercise of power.[24] Music is especially suited by its physical and sociable properties to this dynamic process. Spaces for musical performance during the early modern era mutually interpenetrated or superimposed themselves, as we see in the essays by Flynn, Herissone, Eubanks Winkler, Aspden, and Burden.[25] Much of music's social meaning is also derived from its ability to provide people with means to recognize identity and place, as argued by Flynn and Aspden.[26] Sometimes, as in Milsom's contribution, this process reconfigured a single performance site into an ingenious multiplicity of others. As in Brokaw's and Howard's, it helped forge relationships across confessional divides. And, as Williams demonstrates, the mental faculties of memory enabled reflective elision of discrete spaces as music moves from place to place.

It is no coincidence that the spaces most often referenced in this book are residential and/or theatrical, realms for the imaginative reconfiguration of space and social norms. In the theater, men and boys were accepted as women, and, starting somewhat later, women as men. Choirboys, as Brokaw and Milsom remind us, became actors. Even before the development of specifically theatrical structures in the early modern era, open urban space had been used for the performance of drama and ritual.²⁷ We also see the opposite process enacted in this book. As Larson and Eubanks Winkler emphasize, the stage could transform into a London street or royal court. For Milsom and Williams, street music is mediated for indoor performance. For Flynn's recusant Catholics, as for conforming members of the Church of England, home overlapped with church, and women could perform genres and styles otherwise denied them.²⁸ Musical practice additionally complicated early modern spatial plans and designations. Within the home, rooms used for music frequently served several purposes. Functional spaces such as nursery, kitchen, parlor, and garden served as sites of musical activity, as famously did the banqueting rooms of the nobility. Seventeenth-century antiquarian John Aubrey recalls learning from the ballads of his old nurse and fireside romances of family maidservants, scrambling conventional lines of gender, class, authority, orality/aurality, and literacy as well as place. When musicians such as Giovanni Battista Draghi played for salon audiences, they probably did so in space that functioned at other times in nonmusical ways. Similarly, Thomas Britton repurposed the loft in his Clerkenwell house into a concert hall by adding two keyboard instruments. Newspaper advertisements from the late seventeenth and eighteenth centuries indicate that dancing schools and academies were also used as concert spaces, and Aspden describes concerts in pleasure gardens.²⁹

In this book, the residence is a polyvalent space. For Freeman, it is a place for creative revision of music between teacher and student, and for Bailey among acquaintances making music. For Miller, it is a site for decorous consumption of music repackaged from other times and places, and for Williams a stage in the circulation of a richly intertextual and multimedia repertory. For Herissone and Burden, it is one of a number of locations in which to rethink performance practices of widely circulating music. For Larson, it becomes part of a multidimensional London street- and sound-scape represented in the theater. For Brokaw and Eubanks Winkler, royal residences provided performance spaces for national propaganda that reached outward during troubled times with messages of unity. These two authors, plus Milsom, Larson, Williams, and Burden, also remind us that the fluid nature of theatricality during the two-century-plus establishment and rise of the commercial English entertainment industry enabled multidirectional encounters among stage, page, home, and other sites for dramatic representation. Brokaw and Milsom recollect the stylistic proximity between court and especially church and theater as venues for musical spectacle during the sixteenth and early seventeenth centuries, while Herissone calls our attention to the range of spaces in which Restoration cathedral musicians practiced music and Flynn to the domestic community as a unit of Christian worship.³⁰

Even before the establishment of England's first theaters or designated concert spaces, Brokaw demonstrates how one musical court drama unified a diverse audience while further evoking sites of religious ritual, the fluid position of choristers between church and stage, and debates over ongoing liturgical reform. An intermingling of sacred and secular music gently suggests and urges religious compromise during the turbulent 1550s as the Catholic Mary succeeded the reformist Edward. Milsom brings us to slightly later material that shifts between some of the same venues through one of the least easily categorized repertories of early modern England: the "Cries of London" from around 1600, which paradoxically unified jingles from the streets of London with a sophisticated musical style often considered "courtly." His essay suggests that these "Cries" remained in dialogue with each other; with church, home, and theater as well as public urban spaces; and with repertory associated with choirboys, singing men, and possibly London's municipal waits. In parallel to Brokaw and Milsom, Larson shows a multiplicity of contemporary musical practices and locations brought together, in this case on the stage of the Globe and Blackfriars Theatres. Here, music making spatially delimited and defined social relations among a community of fictionalized Londoners in and outside of the home, largely in gendered terms. Like Brokaw's, Eubanks Winkler's essay straddles court and stage during an unsettled time—one in which conditions of the monarchy, theater, and circulation of music as commodity had changed radically. Here, music that transcended performance sites also becomes a means to bring about unity at a critical juncture in national politics, in this case through encomia for Queen Anne that moved among court, public theater, print collections, and any space into which the latter could be brought. Burden presents the case of the operatic aria, which he follows from performers and copyists employed in the mid-eighteenth-century London King's Theatre through the printing house, through consumers with a variety of intentions, and into the range of spaces to which any of the individual or collective contents could wander as commodities or part of the continuum of performance. All of these essays, plus Williams's, Aspden's, and Miller's, not only connect theater (or theatricality) to other locations, but they also serve as a reminder that, for much of the early modern era, the term retained its older meaning as a tangible compendium of knowledge as well as its newer sense as a space to engage with performance.[31]

A number of essays in this book examine the fluid performance conditions of early modern England in which musicians of various backgrounds came together in a range of spaces to play, sing, and exchange music. Music thus became a powerful force for building what lexicographer John Bullokar defines as "*Communitie. Fellowship in partaking together,*" sometimes across class, national, religious, and gender boundaries.[32] Such practices demonstrate the dynamic nature of "community" between the sixteenth and eighteenth centuries, a concept even more slippery than "public."[33] Physical space and place were less important to early modern theories of community than shared relations to a Christian God, and, especially later in the era, civic leadership. Conflict was inherent to the system. Rhetorical ideals of community made use of ritual, boundary, and standards of inclusion and exclusion as we see to different effects in Brokaw's, Flynn's, Eubanks Winkler's, and Aspden's essays. Yet, as Flynn and Milsom demonstrate to contrasting ends, practice diverged from the more rigid bounds of political rhetoric.[34] Musical "partaking together" enabled membership in multiple communities, often in different spaces. It also defies, as Bailey especially shows, rigid lines between musical recreation and kinds of "professionalism," not only in terms of remunerated status but also ability and choice of material.[35] Herissone demonstrates how Daniel Henstridge (ca. 1646–1736), a provincial Restoration cathedral organist, moved through multiple musical communities and locations as teacher, performer, collector, and especially copyist, frequently retaining in his manuscripts material traces of each. For Brokaw, music becomes a means to call for unity as a national community in the face of religious division, anticipating Samuel Johnson's later definition of "community" as "The commonwealth; the body politick."[36] In contrast, for Flynn, membership in the community of true faith trumps nationhood, while for Milsom, disjunct communities of musical practice are imaginatively unified by clever writing. Miller, too, presents rearranged music carefully selected from an astonishing range of spaces and communities. The late-eighteenth-century *Ladies Magazine* enabled women to take their appropriate place each month among "the commonwealth; the body politick" through carefully selected music without leaving home. Howard shows how one mid-seventeenth-century "great friendship" between two musical men from opposite sides of multiple personal, professional, and political boundaries brought them together as participants in the exchange and practice of music through a growing culture of "music meetings." Their association may also have had profound benefit for both in another era of rapid multidirectional political and religious change. White brings us to a community of Restoration merchants and businessmen who used their increased wealth and social standing to learn, consume, and patronize music and musical products, influencing wider national taste through concerts.

Contents of this book also draw attention to the material media that facilitated music's circulation among individuals, places, and communities. The mid-sixteenth through eighteenth centuries witnessed extraordinary change to the physical formats of music and to the social and cultural meanings of music as paper commodity. Williams and Burden show contrasting ways in which print items from both ends of the price spectrum were valued as material objects, and Miller's conclusions depend on general-interest periodicals that included notated music. As Aspden, Burden, and Miller demonstrate, printed music functioned similarly in concert venues and domestic spaces at least through the eighteenth century. Williams investigates the most popular and widely circulating musical commodity of the entire era—the broadside ballad—an endlessly reimagined multimedia commodity suited for nearly any space and also connected to aurality and memory.

Manuscripts offer a particularly complex view of music in the seventeenth and early eighteenth centuries, a period often thought to be dominated by print.

Nonetheless, as essays by Bailey, Freeman, Herissone, and Burden especially show, manuscripts remained crucial to musical practice. From the 1650s onward, London music publishers and booksellers added new dynamics to the interplay among print, manuscript, and performance by offering a range of formats aimed at target market segments.[37] Freeman and Wilson discuss contrasting manifestations of the ambivalence toward print as a medium for the circulation of lute music even earlier in the century. Burden considers how print volumes could contribute to the creation of utilitarian manuscripts for a variety of purposes and consumers. Herissone's investigation of the case of Henstridge illuminates the range of reasons for which people continued to copy music into manuscript in an era of print, which include attempts to learn styles of composition, compiling teaching pieces for students, collecting favorite tunes, and preserving major works by leading composers.[38] Scholarship over the past century has tended to apply the misleading terms *amateur* and *professional* to manuscript sources as well as the musicians who compiled them. But these lines were blurred in practice, as Bailey and Burden especially demonstrate.[39] Bailey further challenges assumptions about the gendered and professional performance-style typographies of late-seventeenth-century keyboard manuscripts associated with domestic settings, and Freeman questions why most of the tremendous amount of lute music from the late sixteenth and early seventeenth centuries circulated in manuscript when relevant print technologies were available and in use, as Wilson further notes. Freeman makes a persuasive case that manuscripts permitted more flexible performance practice in an era that still valued aural transmission, especially for the dialectics of pedagogy that Bailey links to keyboard use. Oral practice features prominently in Brokaw's and Larson's essays, in which musical information is entirely presented through words. Collectively all of these, plus Milsom's, Williams's, Aspden's, and Miller's, also raise questions about hard divisions between "elite" and "popular" practices.

Taken as a whole, this volume reconsiders assumptions that early modern English musical "works" belonged to specific locations, practices, or sorts of performers. Musical form and structure altered as pieces and performances moved between places, uses, and (kinds of) consumership; and music created new alliances, sometimes against otherwise rigid social or political strictures. Relationships between the public and the private, as well as the understanding of the concepts themselves, were remarkably fluid in the late sixteenth through eighteenth centuries, and the social and professional interactions between musicians of any status were more complicated and varied than conventional labels suggest. Music helped to (re)define spaces in which it was used even as it suggested other places and performances. It also relied on remembrance while enabling the imagination of possibilities to come. Each essay in this collection encourages readers to situate music in ways that push against modern binary formulations, complicating theories that do not accurately reflect historical patterns of participation or circulation.

Notes

1. Throughout this book, "aural" refers to the sense of hearing, and "oral" to speech and the transmission of verbal text.
2. See Marsh, *Music and Society*, 198–201 and 211; *Calendar of State Papers Relating to English Affairs in the Archives of Venice, Volume 5*, 531–567 (accessed April 19, 2014), which reports that Mary I had taught "*molte sue damigelle*" to play the lute and spinet. For more general studies of musical education in early modern England, see Harris, "Musical Education in Tudor Times," 108–139; Starr, "Music Education and the Conduct of Life in Early Modern England," 193–206; Nelson, "Love in the Music Room," 15–26; and Westrup, "Domestic Music under the Stuarts," 19–53.
3. See, for instance, Bailey, "Blurring the Lines," 510–546; Evans, *Henry Lawes*, 212–213; Jocoy, "The Role of the Catch in England's Civil War," 325–334; Kerr, "Mary Harvey—The Lady Dering," 23–30; Marsh, *Music and Society*, 215–221; Spink, *Henry Lawes*, 94–95; and Herrisone, *Musical Creativity in Restoration England*, 3–116 and 260–314.
4. Arendt, *The Human Condition*, 51.
5. Love, "How Music Created a Public," 259–260, 263. For more on the consumer of "elite" music during this period, see Hume, "The Economics of Culture in London," 487–533.
6. Ariès, "Introduction," *A History of Private Life*, vol. 3, 5; and Mackenzie, "Introduction," *Sir James Melville*, x.
7. Habermas, *Structural Transformation of the Public Sphere*, 31–79.
8. See, for example, Hauser, *Vernacular Voices*, 64; Lake and Pincus, "Rethinking the Public Sphere in Early Modern England," 1–22; and McKeon, *The Secret History of Domesticity*, 70–76.
9. "public, adj. and n.," *OED* (accessed May 13, 2014).
10. "† private, adj.2," *OED* (accessed May 13, 2014); and Spacks, *Privacy*, 1–2.
11. Amussen, *An Ordered Society*, 36; and West-Pavlov, *Bodies and Their Spaces*, 23–24, 28–29, and 42.
12. Orlin, *Locating Privacy in Tudor London*, 11.
13. Castan, "The Public and the Private," 403; Chartier, "Introduction," 399–401; Lake and Pincus, "Rethinking the Public Sphere in Early Modern England," 1–12; McKeon, *The Secret History of Domesticity*, xix–xx; and Orlin, *Locating Privacy in Tudor London*, 9–10.
14. Hauser, *Vernacular Voices*, 64; Knowles, "'Infinite Riches in a Little Room,'" 10–11; McKeon, *The Secret History of Domesticity*, 70–76; McMullan, "Preface: Renaissance Configurations," xviii–xix; and Vickery, "Golden Age to Separate Spheres?," 383–414.
15. Vickery, "Golden Age to Separate Spheres?," 412.
16. See Baldwin and Wilson, "The Subscription Musick of 1703–04," 29–44; and McVeigh, "The Professional Concert and Rival Subscription Series," 1–135.
17. Elshtain, *Public Man, Private Woman*, 9–11 and 102–114; and Habermas, *Structural Transformation of the Public Sphere*, 5–6.
18. See Gowing, "The Freedom of the Streets," 135; Johnson, "Meanings of Polite Architecture," 45 and 50; and Mertes, *English Noble Household*, 169.
19. Flather, *Gender and Space in Early Modern England*, 68–71; Fumerton, "Secret Arts," 62; Gowing, "The Freedom of the Streets," 134–136; Mertes, *English Noble Household*, 169; Pollack, "Living on the Stage of the World," 78–79; Stone, *Family, Sex and Marriage*, 253–254; and West, "Social Space and the English Country House," 110.
20. Bold, "Privacy and the Plan," 107–119; Chartier, "The Practical Impact of Writing," 134–140 ; Fumerton, "Secret Arts," 62; Girourard, *Life in the English Country House*, 56;

Mazzola and Abate, "Introduction: 'Indistinguished Space,'" 3–4; Orlin, *Locating Privacy in Tudor London*, 297 and 306–313; and Rambuss, *Closet Devotions*, 103–104.

21. Girourard, *Life in the English Country House*, 11 and 138; and Spacks, *Privacy*, 6–7.
22. Thurley, *Royal Palaces of Tudor England*, 1.
23. Lefebvre, *Production of Space*, 87; and Certeau, *Practice of Everyday Life*, 117–118.
24. Foucault, "Space, Knowledge, Power," 252.
25. Lefebvre, *Production of Space*, 86–87.
26. Folkestad, "National Identity and Music," 151; Stokes, *Ethnicity, Identity and Music*, 5; and Turino, *Music as Social Life*, 93–94 and 106.
27. Carlson, *Places of Performance*, 14–15.
28. Austern, "'For Musicke Is the Handmaid of the Lord,'" 89–102; Temperley, "'If Any of You Be Mery Let Hym Synge Psalmes,'" 90–99; Temperley, *Music of the English Parish Church*, 71–75.
29. See, for example, Aubrey, *Remaines of Gentilisme and Judaisme*, 68, 70; Evans, *Henry Lawes*, 212–214; Lipsedge, *Domestic Space* 22; McVeigh, "The Professional Concert and Rival Subscription Series," 1; Schwegler, "Oral Tradition and Print," 436 and 438–439; and Tilmouth, "Calendar of References to Music in Newspapers," 1–107.
30. Arendt, *The Human Condition*, 53–54 and Mertes, *English Noble Household*, 139.
31. West, *Theatres and Encyclopedias*, 43–78.
32. Bullokar, *English Exposito[u]r*, s.v. "communitie" sig. D8 (1621) and C3 (1684).
33. "community, n." *OED* (June 2015). Oxford University Press. http://www.oed.com.turing.library.northwestern.edu/view/Entry/37337?redirectedFrom=community (accessed August 3, 2015).
34. Shepard and Wirthington, "Communities in Early Modern England," 6–8; and Spierling and Halvorson, "Definitions of Community," 21–23.
35. The term *amateur* for "one who cultivates anything as a pastime, as distinguished from one who prosecutes it professionally," along with the implicitly derogatory meaning inherent in it, only emerged in English usage in the 1780s, following slightly earlier German use of the similar term *Liebhaber*; see "amateur, n.," *OED* (accessed July 3, 2014); and Bach, *Sechs Clavier-Sonaten für Kenner und Liebhaber*, title page.
36. Johnson, *Dictionary*, vol. 1, sig. T6.
37. See Thompson, "Manuscript Music in Purcell's London," 613–616.
38. Herissone, *Musical Creativity in Restoration England*, 89–101; and her essay in this volume.
39. See Milsom, *Christ Church Music Catalogue*, http://library.chch.ox.ac.uk/music (accessed May 29, 2014); Woolley, "English Keyboard Sources," 139–141; Herissone, *Musical Creativity in Restoration England*, 101–102; and Bailey, "Blurring the Lines," 510–546.

1.

Tudor Musical Theater: Sounds of Religious Change in Ralph Roister Doister

Katherine Steele Brokaw

When she acceded to the throne in July 1553, the Catholic Mary Tudor hoped to reverse the damage her reformist brother Edward VI had done to church music in his preceding six-year reign.[1] Contemporary records indicate that upon the reading of the proclamation that Mary was Queen,

> suddenly a great number of bells was heard ringing.... And shortly after the proclamation, various Lords of the Council went to St. Paul's... and had there sung the "Te Deum laudamus," playing organs and thanking the Almighty, which displays were not customary with them and had altogether been put aside of late.[2]

There are multiple accounts of nationwide singing, bell ringing, and organ playing to celebrate the proclamation and procession of Mary I, and a "Vox Patris Caelestis" for six voices was composed for her October coronation.[3] In 1553, such music had not been heard publicly in England for several years, as Edward VI's administration had drastically changed the sounds of English religious experience in official churches. In the early months of her reign, Mary was still deciding what form England's newly revived Catholicism would take, and in particular the sound of its musical rituals.

In the months after Mary's coronation, Nicholas Udall presented at least two plays for her at court: *Respublica*, a political morality play, and *Ralph Roister Doister*, an English play in the style of Roman comedies.[4] *Ralph Roister Doister*, performed by boys from a London choir school, represents and parodies the kinds of religious music that were being debated at the time, while appealing variously to a range of confessional dispositions.[5] I argue that the music of *Roister Doister* petitions the new queen to adapt a hybridized musical liturgy, combining elements of Roman Catholic ritual and Edward's evangelical reforms.[6] Such a petition was only possible in the early months of Mary's rule, and only a playwright as canny and adaptable as Udall could have suggested such a musical-religious compromise in this historical moment.

In December 1553, a few months after her coronation, Mary issued a proclamation that forbade the playing of "interludes . . . ballads, rhymes, and other false treatises in the English tongue concerning doctrine in matters now in question and controversy touching the high points and mysteries of Christian religion."[7] Udall—a favorite playwright of Mary's—thus needed to avoid overt reference to "mysteries of Christian religion" and the surrounding "controversy."[8] *Roister Doister* uses music to create a multivalent play that presents itself as entertainment while obliquely commenting on the "matters now in question." The musical play's interpretive complexity comes from a number of factors: that it was performed by choirboy actors during the period of the most complex and dynamic religious changes of the sixteenth century; that music was central to this religious dynamism; and that early Tudor dramas took on charged political and religious meanings because of the varying sacred, secular, and pedagogical spaces in which they were performed.

Udall's extant writings sketch out some of the complexities of navigating rapid religious changes while keeping favor with royal patrons, religious powers, and academic administrations. When Mary became queen, the most zealous reformers were forced into exile to save their heads and stay faithful to their beliefs.[9] Udall, however, adapted to the new religious, dramatic, and musical contexts of Marian England.[10] In the 1530s and 1540s, he had been a reformist playwright and educator: his plays were performed for Henry VIII's evangelical adviser Thomas Cromwell. In 1541, Udall had been fired from his post at Eton on charges of "buggery" (sodomy) with an older male student. However, his disgrace was surprisingly short lived; soon afterward, he had a steady stream of commissions by the likes of Catherine Parr (Henry VIII's final wife, a reformer) and then-princess Mary Tudor to write and translate, and he was given a lucrative rectorship in Calborne under Edward. He translated humanist texts written by the moderate Catholic Erasmus and by the zealous Italian reformer Peter Martyr Vermigli; and he was patronized and employed by the Henrican reformer Thomas Cromwell and Edward VI in addition to Parr and Mary.[11] Spanning four Tudor reigns, Udall's work and life transcended categories of sacred and secular, Catholic and reformist.[12] Critics have therefore viewed him as a timeserver or a moderate, but his slippery religious identity is consistent with early Tudor religious politics, and demonstrates the way Tudor subjects often elided categories of religious confession.[13]

The audience for Udall's plays was similarly complex. Several historians warn against thinking of members of Mary's court, and of England as a whole, in terms of categorical Catholics who supported the Queen and reformers who opposed her.¹⁴ In the early years of Mary's reign, the continued presence of reformist members of Edward's government in her court meant that the audience for Udall's plays was doctrinally diverse. Ahistorical categories like "Catholic" and "Protestant" are inadequate to describe the audience members of Mary's court, and they are also inadequate descriptors of sixteenth-century religious music.

The same music was often used interchangeably in traditional and reformist services.¹⁵ Since Henry's dissolution of the monasteries and many choir schools, traditional Catholic musical liturgy had been in decline. Edward's 1552 *Book of Common Prayer* and a series of injunctions banned organs and reduced parish church music to unaccompanied psalms sung by the congregation in English.¹⁶ While Mary was eager to return to the Latin musical polyphony of the pre-Reformation church, official change to doctrine came more slowly. Nicholas Temperley explains that "there was a period of more than eighteen months at the beginning of Mary's reign in which it was possible to conduct worship according to the [Edwardian] 1552 prayer book, and even to hope for some compromise in the future."¹⁷ One cannot assume that the religious music this queen heard early, or at any point, in her reign was strictly "Catholic." The fact that a play like *Roister Doister* includes sacred music within a context of courtly and pedagogical entertainments, and that the play includes popular music alongside parodies of religious music, makes categories like "sacred" and "secular" insufficient to describe this music.

Although these religious and musical historical contexts complicate the interpretive possibilities of *Roister Doister*'s music, its particular performance context for Mary—in the space of the court and with choirboy performers—defies tidy categories. As Greg Walker explains, we cannot speak of "theater history" in discussing these Tudor plays, which were "precisely not theatrical, in the sense of taking place in a building designed for drama."¹⁸ Early Tudor choirboy actors performed in their schools and at court, as well as in cathedrals, churches, and chapels; the playwrights' careers as educators, courtiers, scholars, and priests overlapped in these spaces.¹⁹ Such drama, therefore, "lived in the spaces in which the real events which they allegorized also took place, and it drew rhetorical and symbolic strength from that fact."²⁰ The choirboy performers, in moving from school to ecclesiastic spaces, demonstrate the problems of categorizing drama and musical performance according to performance space. And as young performers who were still in training, the choirboy performers of *Roister Doister* and similar plays also defy neat categories of recreational or occupational.

It is for this multivalent performance context and climate of religious and political uncertainty that the once-avowedly reformist Udall wrote *Roister Doister* for the boys of a local choir school.²¹ These performers inhabited the domains of religion, music, drama, and education, thus helping to expose how the controversies regarding each subject are related and mutually constitutive. And performance in a household, even when that household was the court, blurs the distinction between private and public. These performers of *Roister Doister* were given audience by the most powerful decision makers in the land.[22] And that audience heard them sing the very kinds of music that were the source of much contention.

Music is sung or discussed at length in nine scenes in *Roister Doister*; it is integral to the play's structure, its plot, and the characterizations of everyone from Ralph (as a "roister" he is a loud braggart) to the servants. The (mock) hero Ralph spends the play unsuccessfully trying to woo the widow Christian Custance, often by means of music. Custance finds Ralph despicable and is also engaged to one Gawayn Goodluck. Ralph is described by his servant Dobinet Doughtie as one who keeps everyone awake with his musical practice, who plays several instruments as well as composes, and who coerces his servants into joining him in song. For Ralph, music is an emotional experience, tied to several failed attempts at courtship:

> With every woman is he in some loves pang,
> Then up to our lute at midnight, twangledome twang ...
> Of Songs and Balades also he is a maker,
> And that can he as finely doe as Jacke Raker ...
> Then when aunswere is made that it may not bee,
> O death why commest thou not? By and by (saith he) (2.1.19–20, 27–28, 35–36)[23]

Indeed, Ralph demonstrates throughout the play that he and his freeloading companion, Matthew Merrygreek, are well versed in ballads, love songs, and also music of the Catholic liturgy.

After a prologue on the merits of mirth, the play begins with a song for which no words are given. The wandering and wily Merrygreek sings, and then gives an exposition on music's ability to make one's life "longer by a day" (1.1.2). The immediate presence of music makes the play seem like mere entertainment, a sort of musical comedy. The fact that the performers were boys—innocent of adult religiopolitical machinations and too young to have been fully inculcated to Edwardian reformism—would have made the play seem particularly unlikely to touch on Christian controversy.[24] Although their youthful innocence may have made them seem less politically charged than adult performers, the boys' association with a local choir school was a reminder of their religious duties. Not only did they move from classroom to chapel to court, but their audiences would have been constantly reminded of their religious affiliations when they sang with recognizably church choir–trained voices.[25]

Their musical skills were on display especially in scenes 1.3 and 1.4 of *Roister Doister*. The first of several featured songs is a solo by Custance's female servant Tibet Talkapace, who is spied on by Ralph in hopes of gathering information about Custance from her servants (stage direction after 1.3.16). After her solo, Tibet is joined by her fellow servants Madge Mumblecrust and Annot Alyface for a song, presumably sung in three-part harmony. Annot proposes that singing while working will make the time pass more quickly, and they interrupt their singing to comment on their work (1.3.56). During the final refrain, the servants articulate their decision to give up their work entirely:

> *They sing the fourth tyme.*
> Pipe Mery Annot. etc.
> Trilla. Trilla. Trillarie.
> When Tibet, when Annot, when Margerie.
> I will not, I can not, no more can I.
> Then give we all over, and there let it lye.
> *Lette hir caste down hir worke.* (1.3.72–76)

Thus, early in the play, music is shown as unproductive, leading the women to abandon their work. Reformist audience members might not have been surprised by this; in evangelical morality plays of the 1530s and 1540s, idle vice characters are almost always characterized as singers.[26] The following scene shows more musical idleness, as Ralph's servants Dobinet and Harpax engage in a botched attempt to serenade Custance, and are joined by Madge to sing and dance to "Whoso to Marry a Minion Wyfe," the lyrics of which are printed along with other songs in an appendix at the end of the unique copy of the play (appendix 1-12). The songs of act 1 not only expose Ralph's social ineptitude but also show music to be fruitless, if entertaining, vanity. While reformist audience members might have thought this musical context referred to the equation of music with idle distraction, Udall, who had tutored the young Princess Mary, would have been aware of her fondness for, and skill in, secular music.[27] By including so much music in his play, and having it voiced by young choirboys whose very purpose was to be church singers in training, Udall's comedy appeals to the queen's love of music, both sacred and secular, even while evidently pleasing his former constituency, the reformers for whom music represented vanity and idleness.

In act 2 scene 3, Ralph's servant Dobinet is stranded at Custance's house while he awaits a response from her. Custance's lone male servant, Tom Trupenie, asks Tibet and Annot, "Shall we sing a fitte to welcome our friende . . . ?" (2.3.53). Dobinet is then welcomed into the household by joining Tom, Tibet, and Annot in a song about music's ability to inspire people, as the refrain says, "lovingly to agree." Music's ability to incorporate new members into the community resonates with Tudor ideas about the sympathetic relationship between musical harmony and social concord.[28] The trajectory of the play's first few songs, then, moves music from a solitary activity for a wayfarer, to idle entertainment, to social activity to unite new acquaintances in literal and figurative harmony.

The three- and four-part harmonies of these songs had religiopolitical consequences, as they highlighted the way in which the musical talents of choirboys across the country could be put to more use under Mary's religion than under her brother's. While polyphonic compositions were written under Edward, polyphonic singing in choir schools had diminished considerably. In fact, composers like John Sheppard who wrote masses during Mary's reign often wrote them for only four parts because cutbacks in choral provisions from Edward's reign had not been fully restored.[29] The harmonious theatrical singing of the actors here is an embodied reminder to Mary that these choirboys, like her Children of the Chapel (for whom Udall likely wrote *Respublica*), were being trained to restore complex harmonies to church services.[30] Instruction in counterpoint and polyphony had been reestablished in the chapel during Mary's first year, and the plays these boys performed likely served a pedagogical function to further musical skills.[31] Records indicate that Mary financially rewarded the dean of St. Paul's choir school because the teachers trained their choristers to sing Catholic liturgy; she likely would have been pleased by the abilities of the *Roister Doister* cast to perform harmony.[32] Religious and musical pedagogy is thus an implicit theme of the play presented by a career educator.

In act 3 scene 3, Ralph almost makes good on his frequent promise to die from the pain of Custance's rejection. With the help of Merrygreek and his servants, he stages a mock funeral with music from Catholic rites for the dead. As the scene begins, Merrygreek returns with the news that Custance has refused Ralph's love yet again. After Merrygreek mocks Ralph for his failure, the two have the following exchange:

> ROISTER: Well, what should I now doe?
>
> MERRYGREEK: In faith, I cannot tell.
>
> ROISTER: I will go home and die.
>
> MERRYGREEK: Then shall I bidde toll the bell?
>
> ROISTER: No.
>
> MERRYGREEK: God have mercie on your soule, ah good gentleman [. . .] How feele your soule to God?
>
> ROISTER: I am nigh gone.
>
> MERRYGREEK: And shall we hence straight?
>
> ROISTER: Yea.
>
> MERRYGREEK: *Placebo dilexi*.
>
> Maister Royster Doyster will straight go home and die.
>
> (3.3.47–49, 52–54)

Merrygreek then begins to intone an entire funeral sequence for Ralph, who periodically interrupts the ritual, usually to agree that it is warranted: "Heigh how, alas, the pangs of death my hearte do break" (3.3.55). Merrygreek begins with the *Placebo dilexi*, the start of Office of the Dead at vespers in the Catholic Sarum

Rite. He moves on to the *Nequando*, an antiphon from the burial service, then to the *Dirige* and several other antiphons, including the *Requiem aeternam* from the Office of the Dead. Merrygreek's liturgy—in Latin with English commentary—quotes directly from all parts of the Catholic funeral and burial rites. Since Edward's 1553 primer had no *Dirige*, the play reproduces rites newly restored under Mary.[33] As critics of *Roister Doister* have pointed out, the play almost faithfully re-presents Catholic ceremony, which makes the performance of these rites somewhat of a crux.[34]

In literary and performative terms, the funeral mass at this dramatic moment is a parody, whose purpose, in the later definition of Ben Jonson, is "to make it absurder than it was."[35] By juxtaposing the solemnity of the religious text and the frivolity of Ralph's love life, the mock funeral becomes ironic comedy.[36] While many polemical evangelical playwrights had parodied Catholic rites in the 1530s and 1540s, most had decimated those rites by reducing them to scatological gibberish instead of requoting them verbatim as Udall does.[37]

As a performance of Catholic rites intoned anew by the next generation of believers, *Roister Doister*'s funeral demonstrated the resilience of traditional religious musical forms. Performed by choirboys in the multivalent space of the court, this representation of Catholic musical rites was able to comment obliquely on changing doctrinal policies without causing offence to members of the court who were less fond of such changes. Whether he was a moderate reformer or a timeserver, the Udall who served Mary instead of fleeing into exile with other evangelicals was perhaps in favor of reinstituting some musical rites in the re-reformed church. In his drama, Udall intentionally invited the sort of audience aporia that likely saved his life. Carla Mazzio claims that this sequence in the play exemplifies "the double sense where abuses of English come head to head with anti-Catholic Latin satire."[38] However, I would argue that the sounds of music—the melodies of the requiem, as sung by trained choirboys—was as important to the parody's doubleness as its Latinity.

A theatricalized funeral mass in any form could be heard as ridiculous by reformers who hoped that Mary's church would retain some of the musical elements for which they had advocated, hearing a mockery of musical rites no longer relevant to the liturgy. But many auditors—including Mary herself—who desired a return to complex Latin liturgical choir music, could hear in this music an acknowledgment of the cultural cachet the rites continued to have. The parodic mass is actually "too light" to please a true reformer.[39] The joke is on Ralph, who looks silly for taking part in such a ritual while still alive. He, and not the rite, comes off looking foolish. The faithful citation of the musical rites may therefore prove that such extra-theatrical rituals survived and held their own against misuse.

The performance of a funeral for a (fake) boy corpse would also have called to mind a recent real funeral: that of Edward VI in August 1553. Windsor Herald Charles Wriothesley's account of the events explains how Mary arranged her brother's funeral and burial:

> The 9th of August, in the afternone, the Quene helde an obsequy for the Kinge within the church in the Tower . . . , and had a solemne dirige songe in Latine. The morrow . . . the Quenes highness had a solemne masse of Requiem songe within the chappell in the Tower for the Kinge.[40]

This private mass had public consequences: it was not only documented but also replicated throughout the country.[41] That week in Melton Mowbray, for example, the altar stones that had been removed during Edward's reign were returned so that a mass could be said for the deceased monarch, and 8d. had been paid to the "ryngers at the dyryge for the king."[42] Thus, Mary orchestrated a nationwide Catholic funeral to mark the death of her brother, in whose reign those very funeral rites had been abolished.[43]

The day after she heard her "private" Latin Requiem Mass, Edward was buried in the abbey in a reformed service conducted by Thomas Cranmer. The queen had compromised by allowing a two-part sequence including both a traditional requiem and reformed rites from the 1552 *Book of Common Prayer*.[44] Wriothesley's account indicates that the burial "was all in Englishe, without any copes or vestments . . . accordinge to the Booke of Common Prayer last sett forth by Act of Parliament."[45] Thus, it seems that Mary was open at the start of her reign to mixing conventional Catholic and reformist elements in religious rites, allowing the sort of denominational hybridity usually associated with her younger sister, Elizabeth I.[46]

Early in the funeral sequence of *Roister Doister*, Merrygreek comments in Latin and English on the kind of service he will conduct: "*Dirige*. He will go darklyng to his grave, /*Neque lux, neque crux, neque* mourners, *neque* clinke" (3.3.58–9). That is, Merrygreek says Ralph will be buried without the usual props and actors of a Catholic requiem: without candles (lux), without a crucifix (crux), without mourners, and without the traditional passing bells (clinke). This macaronic language mirrors reformist language about eschewing popish props for funerals.[47] Indeed, candles, crucifixes, and bells were objects of scorn for most reformers. While Merrygreek is somewhat silly here—they won't have these elements because the event takes place in a house and not a church—he also suggests that they conduct a sort of hybridized rite, one combining Catholic musical liturgy with some reformist restraint. Merrygreek's funeral sequence thus mirrors the one Mary had just orchestrated for her brother. By parodying it (and doing so gently), Udall's play reified it, making it seem as though the kind of funeral sequence that drew from both Catholic and reformist practice could become the new standard; the mirror of Edward's funeral became a model for the future.

While the mock service never uses candles, crucifixes, or traditional vestments, Merrygreek changes his mind at the end of the service and *does* call for bells, which he orders Ralph's servants to ring:

MERRYGREEK: Pray for the late maister Royster Doysters soule,
  And come forth parish Clarke, let the passing bell toll.
Ad servos militis [to the soldier's servants]. Pray for your mayster sirs, and for
  hym ring a peale:
  He was your right good maister while he was in heale.
The Peale of belles rong by the parish clark, and Roister Doister's foure men.
The First Bell A Triple
  When dyed he? When dyed he?
The Seconde.
  We have hym, We have hym.
The Thirde.
  Roister Doyster, Roister Doyster.
The Fourth Bell.
  He commeth, He commeth.
The Freate Bell.
  Our owne, Our owne. (3.3.81–84, appendix 24–28)[48]

The props here must have been real handbells and were probably brought into the court from the chapel or cathedral in which the choirboys usually performed, or from the nearby Chapel Royal. That Merrygreek changes course to end the funeral sequence with this traditional musical practice is politically important. Edward had banned all bells except one to signal the beginning of a sermon, and many sixteenth-century evangelicals had requested burial without bells.[49] Although many bells were too large to destroy, most handbells were so small that they were demolished under Edward. In her first year, Mary required parish churches to buy several kinds of service bells, including handbells for funerals.[50] Repurchasing bells, including large outdoor ones, was expensive for churches, but the process of fund-raising and rebuilding was under way the year *Roister Doister* was likely performed. The bells used for this play would, therefore, either be new bells or preserved ones from Edward's reign. By staging the traditional summoning prayers for the dead complete with handbells, even in jest, the play brings sacred objects into the "secular" space of the court to remind Mary of the funeral bells' nationwide resurrection.

In a conservative reading of the parodic funeral mass, it models the rites that will soon be restored; in a reformist interpretation, the parody mirrors the supposed emptiness of the rites themselves.[51] This feature of parody—its double-edged voice—is exactly what makes this scene work so well. By gently parodying an issue of great contention between reformers and Catholics, Udall sends varying messages to audience members of different strokes but also pushes both resistant, reformist courtiers and the Catholic queen toward a middle ground,.

In the final scene, the play's sworn enemies—Ralph and Gawayn—lead the whole company (described as a "quier") in a final song. Gawayn appears to be something of a fuddy-duddy, arguing against music and sport in a way that recalled, most recently, the attacks on music by ardent reformers like John Bale, Thomas Becon, and others who had self-exiled under Mary.[52] When the play ends, Gawayn's protestations turn to almost regret, and he is reminded that "melodie" is in fact something he once enjoyed:

> ROISTER: I wyll be as good friends with them as ere I was.
>
> MERRYGREEK: Then let me fet[ch] your quier that we may have a song.
>
> ROISTER: Goe.
>
> GAWAYN: I have hearde no melodie all this yeare long.
>
> MERRYGREEK: Come on sirs quickly.
>
> ROISTER: Sing on sirs for my frends sake.
>
> DOBINET: Cal ye these your frends?
>
> ROISTER: Sing on, and no mo words make.
>
> *Here they sing.*
>
> GAWAYN: The Lord preserve our most noble Queene of renowne
>
> And hir vertues rewarde with the heavenly crowne. (5.6.41–47)

We do not know what song was sung here, or if the song was in fact part of the prayer for the queen led by the newly reconciled Gawayn. Whether there was a sung prayer, a song and then a spoken prayer, or a song and then a sung prayer, in any scenario a representative of a more extremist antimusic position has chosen to join in harmony with the group and to praise the new queen.[53] Musical harmony, a hallmark of Catholic ritual, was thought to be community forming not only for the way, as humanists said, it subsumed the individual into the larger whole, but also because, as the Marian administration emphasized, it was symbolic of the community's unity with one another and God.[54] In the final line of the (sung or spoken) prayer, the entire company ("omnes") pleads, "God graunt the nobilitie hir [the Queen] to serve and love, / With all the whole commontie as doth them behove" (5.6.58–59). History, of course, proved such a plea to be in vain, as Mary soon stopped trying to please the "whole commontie": heresy laws were restored and burnings began in 1555.[55]

Although the play's music seems to suggest social and spiritual harmonizing, at least on the surface, there may be resistance and complaint on the part of Custance, who is left out of the song called for by Ralph; her servants, who sing earlier of their tedious lives, are also excluded here.[56] Musical harmonies may therefore conceal social dissonance. In these final moments, Ralph does not *exactly* want to be Gawayn's friend; the song allows him to evade Dobinet's question, "cal ye these your frends?" To join hands and sing seems unifying in the moment, but is at best a temporary fix to more complex societal ills and tensions. While Udall's play may present a model of compromise, the strains of resistance at which the play finally hints will prove to be more fracturing than flexible. In Mary's reign, at least, theatrical-musical urging did not result in real social compromise.[57]

Defying simple categories of "Protestant" and "Catholic," the once-reformist Udall remained in England to write musical plays for Mary's court. Some critics have called it "timeserving," but he was not alone in his ability to shift or sublimate his religious identity. Mary herself was something of a timeserver in the years before 1553, reconciling with her father and Jane Seymour, for example. Her decision as queen to restore the church to the pope's authority was not immediately obvious to everyone; as David Loades writes, "it may be deduced that she had always, and for good reason, dissembled about the papacy."[58] Mary therefore understood the slipperiness of identity, hiding or professing her personal faith depending on her political position, and befriending and collaborating with people whose religious views she opposed.[59] Such hiding of one's private thoughts while operating in the public sphere is another challenge to tidy divisions between "public" and "private."

Henry VIII's last (and reformist) wife, Catherine Parr, was so influential with the Princess Mary that in 1545 she persuaded her to translate Erasmus' paraphrase of the Gospel of St. John into English.[60] Mary needed a Latin tutor to help her with this project and hired one Nicholas Udall. She never finished it herself, but when Udall published his own version in 1548, he dedicated it to her in acknowledgment of their early work on it together. Perhaps Udall taught his pupil Mary about timeserving; perhaps he learned from her model. In any case, Udall seems to have been optimistic about people's ability to adapt to doctrinal vagrancies.

During Edward's reign, authorities employed Udall as a public spokesman for the new state religion. When a group of Catholic rebels argued that they did not want to use the reformed Christmas service but preferred to "have our old service of matins, mass, evensong, and procession in Latin, not in English, as it was before," Udall responded that

> after ye shall have well used it one Christmas, ye shall find such sweetness and ghostly comfort in it, that all days of your life after ye will curse, abhor, detest, and defy all such pernicious ringleaders of mischief as will attempt or entice you to make any more such midsummer games as ye have now at this present time played.[61]

It is possible that Udall's confidence in people's ability to change their minds, his own shape-shifting, and his relationship with Mary led him to write a play that presented the kinds of musical changes Mary was making alongside a model for religious compromise on matters musical and doctrinal. *Ralph Roister Doister* presents embodied musical metaphors for the social problems of and potential solutions for religious difference. The musical productions of this entertainment at court, which used choirboy actors and church bell props for a private performance before a Catholic monarch and her partially reformist council, demonstrate the fluidity of several kinds of musical spaces and categories: court and church, sacred and secular, Catholic and Protestant, public and private. These very complexities in the courtly performance context for the music of *Ralph Roister Doister* allow it to make varied dramatic meanings at once. The slipperiness of two Tudor identities—Udall's and Mary's—reveals the sense to which musical and dramatic producers and consumers elided spatial categories as they played and sang and listened to the dramatic rituals and ritual dramas of their lives.

Notes

1. Lincoln Cathedral's 1548 injunctions, for example, forbid Latin music and organ accompaniment (LeHuray, *Music and the Reformation in England*, 9). While some polyphonic compositions continued to be written under Edward, Edward's reformist advisers increasingly stressed congregational unison singing over complex choir music, and Edward's 1552 *Book of Common Prayer* drastically reduced the amount of music sung in official services. For outlines of the differences among official church musics under early Tudor monarchs, see Page, "Uniform and Catholic," passim.; Leaver, "The Reformation and Music," 379–384; and Bray, "England I, 1485–1600," 487–508. For a summary of the religious changes between Henry, Edward, and Mary, see, for example, Haigh, *English Reformations*, 105–234.

2. *The Accession and Coronation and Marriage of Mary Tudor*, 20.

3. For more on the *vox patris*, see Milsom, "William Mundy's 'Vox Patris Caelestis,'" 1–38. Henry Machyn writes of *Te Deums*, bells, and organs throughout London in *The Diary of Henry Machyn*, 37 and in 1553 Richard Taverner writes about ringing of bells and other mirth throughout England and Wales in *An Oration Gradulatory*, Aiir-v.

4. *Respublica* was likely presented during Mary's first Christmas by the Children of the Chapel Royal. For an analysis of this play in the context of Mary's new queenship, see chapter 4 of Hunt, *The Drama of Coronation*, 111–145.

5. The play was first printed in 1566, but its original performance date is a matter of debate. I agree with critics such as David Bevington, who proposes the play's courtly performance under Mary in *Tudor Drama and Politics*, 124; he is echoed, for example, in Walker, *Politics of Performance*, 165; and Shapiro, "Early Boy Companies," 124. Some scholars, however, advocate for a 1552 date, for example, Hornback, "A *Dirige* and Terence 'In the Briers,'" 22. Evidence for Udall's involvement in the 1554–1555 Christmas season can be found in Streitberger, *Court Revels, 1485–1559*, 212.

6. In preferring the terms *reformist* and *evangelical* to *Protestant* to talk about the early and mid- sixteenth century, I follow several recent historians who see *Protestant* as an anachronistic term for this early period. See Marshall, "The Reformation, Lollardy, and Catholicism," 21. The word *Protestant* was not used to refer to reformers in England until the 1560s, and then only rarely.

7. In *Tudor Royal Proclamations*, 6. Mary was not alone in wanting her court entertainments to be uncontroversial. Her father, Henry VIII, issued a statute in 1543 indicating that

entertainments were lawful as long as the "songes playes or enterludes medle not with interpretacions of scripture." Quoted in Gair, *The Children of Paul's*, 3.

8. Mary enjoyed Udall's plays enough to write in 1554 that "our welbeloved Nicolas Udall hath at soondrie seasons convenient heretofore shewed ... dialogues and interludes before us for our regell disport and recreacion" (Feuillerat, *Documents Relating to the Revels at Court*, 159–160). Records from 1520–1521, for example, indicate the young Princess Mary's fondness for revels (Streitberger, *Court Revels, 1485–1559*, 165).

9. For more on Marian exiles, see Haigh, *English Reformations*, 190–197, and Zagorin, *Ways of Lying*, 108–223.

10. For an outline of Nicholas Udall's biography and output, see Edgerton, *Nicholas Udall*.

11. See Edgerton, *Nicholas Udall*, 23–59 as well as his article "Nicholas Udall in the Indexes of Prohibited Books," 247–252 and Juhász-Ormsby, "The Books of Nicholas Udall," 507–512.

12. Hunt makes a similar point: "Udall's successful bridging of three Tudor reigns reinforces this need for a subtle understanding of divisions and slippage between 'Catholic' and 'Protestant' confessionalization," 134.

13. Peery argues that Udall was a "timeserver" in "Udall as Timeserver I" and "Udall as Timeserver II," passim. Edgerton, however, views him rather as a moderate in "The Apostasy of Nicholas Udall," 223–226.

14. See, for example, Haigh, *English Reformations*, 252–257; Wooding, "The Marian Restoration and the Mass," 230; Hunt, *The Drama of Coronation*, 112–116; and Duffy, "The Conservative Voices in the English Reformation," 87–97.

15. Leaver, "The Reformation and Music," 371–372.

16. LeHuray's *Music and the Reformation in England* remains a useful source for documenting these changes, particularly 9–29.

17. Temperley, *Music of the English Parish Church*, 27.

18. Walker, *Politics of Performance*, 1.

19. McCarthy, "The Sanctuarie Is Become a Plaiers Stage," 56–86. Gair also discusses how St. Paul's playhouse was identified as part of the cathedral in *The Children of Paul's*, 54. For more on the use of chapels, churches, and cathedrals as playing spaces, see also Stevens, *Music and Poetry in the Early Tudor Court*, 242–276; Lennam, "The Children of Pauls, 1551–1582": 20–36; and White, *Theater and Reformation*, 130–162.

20. Walker, *Politics of Performance*, 1.

21. Bevington proposes Bishop Gardiner's choir school in Southwark (*Tudor Drama and Politics*, 120). Udall had brought boy performers to court before, including during his time at Eton, and he used the boys of the Chapel Royal for *Respublica*. A choir school offered him a larger pool of actors than the Chapel Royal. See Shapiro, "Early Boy Companies and Their Acting Venues," 125.

22. For more on Tudor child performers, see Gair, "The Children of Paul's," 1–78; Lamb, *Performing Childhood in Early Modern Theater*, passim.; Shapiro, "Early Boy Companies," passim.; Austern, *Music in English Children's Drama*, 1–6; and Lennam, "The Children of Pauls," passim.

23. Quotations and line numbers come from Nicholas Udall, "Royster Doyster," in *Tudor Plays: An Anthology of Early English Drama*, ed. Edmund Creeth, 215–314. I also consulted G. Scheurweghs's edition of the play, reprinted in *Materials for the Study of the Old English Drama*, vol. 16, 1–68; and John S. Farmer's edition in *The Dramatic Writings of Nicholas Udall*, 1–113.

24. Jensen discusses the disguise inherent in the acting of boy players in "The Boy Actors: Plays and Playing": 6–7, and McCarthy discusses the "ill-fitting mask" of the boy player who plays against type and its political advantages in "Disciplining 'Unexpert People'": 153.

25. See Gair, *The Children of Paul's*, 57.
26. See, for example, John Bale's *King Johan* and *Three Laws* (both 1538); a discussion of the tradition can be found in Giles-Watson, "The Singing 'Vice'": 57–90. While Bale and his contemporaries adapted the singing vice figures of earlier Catholic moralities, in their reformist drama the singing vice takes on a new valence, representing the musical vanity of the Catholic Church. For more, see Simpson, "John Bale, *Three Laws*," 109–114, and Watkins, "Moralities, Interludes, and Protestant Drama," 789–792.
27. See Helms, "Henry VIII's Book," 129–131, and Austern, "Women's Musical Voices in Sixteenth-Century England": 136–137.
28. For example, Sir Thomas Elyot's *The Boke Named The Governour* (1531), which tells tutors to "commende the perfecte understanding of musicke, declaring howe necessary it is for the better attaynynge the knowledge of a publicke weale"(p. 28). See also Helms, "Henry VIII's Book," 126–135, and Stevens, *Music and Poetry*, 270–275.
29. Bray, "Sacred Music to Latin Texts," 79.
30. Leaver ("The Reformation and Music," 382–383) explains that Henrican polyphonic masses were used under the 1548 prayer book but were not usable under the 1552 prayer book. The increasing concern during Edward's reign was with simplifying music into unified melodies to be sung by congregations, or with eradicating it altogether. Reformers like Thomas and Edward's chaplain William Turner railed against Catholic music in, respectively, *Jewel of Joye* (1553) and *A Worke Entytled of ye Olde God & the Newe* (1534) and Page ("Uniform and Catholic," 125) writes about how the polyphonic style of composers like Tallis, Sheppard, and Tye became the "explicit emblem" of the queen's restoration of Catholicism.
31. Page 131.
32. Gair, "The Conditions of Appointment for Masters," 117.
33. Duffy, *Fires of Faith*, 537. David Cressy (*Birth, Marriage, and Death*, 398) also describes how funeral rites reformed under Henry and Edward were restored under Mary.
34. Miller's "*Roister Doister*'s 'Funeralls'" explains the reproduction of the rites. Bevington (*Tudor Drama and Politics*, 124) and Doring (*Performances of Mourning*, 167–168) both remark on the oddness of the ritual's fidelity to actual rite.
35. The *OED* cites this Jonson quotation, from his play *Every Man in His Humour*, as an early use of the word.
36. Doring (*Performances of Mourning*, 168) defines Ralph's mock mass as parody according to more recent literary definitions.
37. Bale's *King Johan* is an example. For more on the tradition of anti-Catholic ritual mockery, see Shell, *Oral Culture and Catholicism*, 59–67. See also John Milsom's essay in this volume for discussion of another, later, moment when (perhaps) choirboy performers created a bathetic parody of religious music in the "Cries of London" repertory, "Oyez!"
38. Mazzio, *The Inarticulate Renaissance*, 77.
39. Bevington, *Tudor Drama and Politics*, 124.
40. Wriothesley, *A Chronicle of England during the Reigns of the Tudors*, 96.
41. Hunt (*The Drama of Coronation*, 130) also comments on the public nature of Mary's private funeral mass for Edward.
42. Scarisbrick, *The Reformation and the English People*, 104.
43. Duffy, *Stripping of the Altars*, 527. See also Hunt, *The Drama of Coronation*, xii, 130.
44. Whitelock, *Mary Tudor*, 198.
45. Wriothesley, 97.
46. See Marshall ("The Reformation, Lollardy, and Catholicism," 26–30) for an excellent overview of Elizabethan religion. For music and ritual in Elizabethan Protestantism, see Willis, *Church Music and Protestantism*, 39–160.

47. See, for example, Strype, *Annals*, vol. 1, pt. 2, 45; and Farmer, 136.
48. The direction *"ut infra,"* referring to the bell passage that is printed with the other songs at the end of the quarto, comes before these lines, but I agree with Scheurweghs's assessment that the bell pealing sequence likely follows these lines that clearly cue it. Scheurweghs, 102, n990.
49. Cressy (*Birth, Marriage, and Death*, 422) quotes the dean of Wells, who ordered communities to "abstain from such unmeasurable ringing for dead personas at their burials." See also chapter 9 of Marsh, *Music and Society*, 454–501, and his article "'At It Ding Dong,'" 151–153.
50. Marsh, *Music and Society*, 459; Duffy, *Fires of Faith*, 545.
51. The language of "models" and "mirrors" is inspired by Handelman, *Models and Mirrors*, passim.
52. See Leaver, "The Reformation and Music," 397 and n. 30 above.
53. In Mazzio's (*The Inarticulate Renaissance*, 76) words, the ending "privileges musical harmony over the play's verbal and textual ambiguities."
54. For more on Cardinal Pole and Bishop Bonner's strategies and Duffy's assessment of Catholic ritual as community forming, see Duffy, *The Stripping of the Altars*, 531–535.
55. While many reformers had been arrested in earlier years, 1555 was a turning point when burning began and more moderate reformers (but not Udall) who had stayed in England hoping for compromise fled into exile once hope for that compromise was lost.
56. Mazzio, *The Inarticulate Renaissance*, 79.
57. While choirboys may have failed to urge compromise in 1553, they were crucial to religion and social community building after 1558. Marsh (*Music and Society*, 425) points out that Marian choirboys were essential to the Elizabethan settlement, when they were employed to teach reformist psalms from the new *Book of Common Prayer* to congregations.
58. Loades, "The Personal Religion of Mary I," 18.
59. See also Richards, *Mary Tudor*, 188.
60. Loades, "Personal Religion," 13.
61. Reprinted in Doring, *Performances of Mourning*, 170.

2.

English Jesuit Missionaries, Music Education, and the Musical Participation of Women in Devotional Life in Recusant Households from ca. 1580 to ca. 1630

Jane Flynn

This essay examines the first fifty years of the Jesuit mission in England and its influence on the public and private lives of the Catholic gentle- and noblewomen who actively supported it. The Society of Jesus had been given special authority by the pope in 1540 to promote the Catholic reformation, and its highly educated members vowed to go wherever he sent them "into the whole world, and preach the gospel to every creature."[1] While on their apostolic mission, their "way of proceeding" was to adapt according to the circumstances they encountered.[2] Thus, in England where practicing the Roman Catholic faith had been a treasonable offense since 1571, their main approach was to convert the gentry and nobility in their own houses and secretly print and distribute "seditious" materials.[3] Out of necessity, they worked closely with several women who aspired to live as Jesuits. From about 1580 to 1630, these women negotiated new boundaries between their domestic and public lives, and tested traditional gender-assigned roles: they had received a good humanist education, underwent the Ignatian *Spiritual Exercises* with the intent of leading an apostolic way of life; they harbored and accompanied priests as they traveled around the country; they disputed theological points with men; and they provided a Catholic education (including Latin and music) for children, either in private houses or in Jesuit colleges on the continent.[4]

The imprecise markers between reformed and Catholic devotional materials meant that these women sang and played some of the same repertory for spiritual recreation as that of gentlewomen (and gentlemen) of other religious beliefs, but their interpretation of it was very different.[5] Much of it helped prepare them, their children, and/or other members of the household for performing music at clandestine liturgies. Their private houses became venues not only for the celebration of such masses—theoretically open to all Catholics and as such the public worship of the church—but also for the kind of education available in pre-Reformation choir schools.[6]

The Importance of Education and Music to the Jesuit Mission

Teaching was integral to the Jesuit mission, with curricula designed to train priests (and Catholic laymen) how to bring about conversion by instructing the young, and preaching and disputing persuasively.[7] Because the educational program was based on the *Spiritual Exercises*, students were actively involved in the learning process, which included extensive repetition but prioritized the creative application of the subject matter over rote learning.[8] Such approaches to education were particularly suited to the arts, which, according to Ignatius, "dispose the intellectual powers for theology."[9] The study of practical music was also beneficial because singing musical settings of texts helped students learn Christian doctrine, and performing music, if properly regulated, was a worthwhile activity for recreation.[10] Even though Ignatius resisted efforts by the pope to have Jesuit priests sing in choir, he accepted that singing and playing music was necessary for students. Furthermore, when students sang even simple plainsong or falsobordone (harmonized plainsong) at masses and vespers, more people were attracted to the services and more men encouraged to join the Society. Liturgical music that consisted of, or was based on, plainsong was particularly useful in the mission because it was easily adaptable, especially during this period in which musical performance practice was so flexible.[11] Thus, in the mission in the New World, plainsong, pricksong, and playing indigenous musical instruments formed part of the curriculum so that the converts could participate actively in the Mass.[12]

Music appears to have been equally integral to the Jesuit mission in England, perhaps because, as Katherine Steele Brokaw points out in this volume, "musical harmony" had been emphasized by the Marian administration as "symbolic of the community's unity with each other and God."[13] The Jesuits' way of proceeding—by converting the gentry in their private houses—made it appropriate that at liturgies celebrated there, family members, their servants, and friends would participate in the music. They used the traditional instrument of the church, the organ, when available, as well as instruments available in domestic settings, especially other keyed instruments and viols.

The Jesuit Mission and Women in England

Often disguised as gentlemen under assumed names, or circulating among their own gentry families and friends, English Jesuits were usually able to preach, hear confessions, and celebrate the liturgy for about three years only before they were captured, imprisoned, and (unless they could escape) executed for treason. Edmund Campion and Robert Persons were the first to arrive from the English College in Rome in 1580; they were followed by Jasper Heywood and William Holt in 1581; William Weston in 1584; Henry Garnet and Robert Southwell in 1586; and John Gerard in 1588.[14] Some of the women who came into contact with them were attracted by the Ignatian model of self-examination and vocation, and expressed the wish to join them, even to the extent of welcoming martyrdom.[15] However, Ignatius, who had experienced problems with two influential women who became Jesuits, had made the decision not to establish an order for women.[16] This decision was in line with the Tridentine decrees that directed all women's religious orders to be cloistered, including tertiary and teaching orders.[17]

Nevertheless, many women supported the mission in an active way. Gerard reported that Elizabeth (Roper) Vaux, having "complained that our priests were forbidden to receive vows [from women] ... was ready to set up house wherever ... I judged best for our needs."[18] Her sister-in-law, Anne Vaux, who never married, even made private vows to Garnet: he reminded her shortly before his martyrdom that after his death, she would no longer be bound by them.[19] Her contribution to the mission was widely acknowledged; indeed, Michael Walpole dedicated his translation of Pedro Ribadeneira's biography of Ignatius to her, describing her as one of Ignatius's children.[20] She and her widowed sister Eleanor (Vaux) Brookesby rented White Webbs in Warwickshire for use as a secret Jesuit center; Garnet described it as the refuge of "many holy women consecrated to God."[21] Like Jesuits, they used aliases as protection against discovery: Anne's was Mrs. Perkins, sister to Mr. Meysey/Meaze (one of Garnet's aliases), and Eleanor's was Mrs. Edwards.

In 1616, Mary Ward attempted to renegotiate the boundary between women and men engaged in the English mission, explaining to Pope Paul V why women should be allowed to participate (officially):

> As the sadly afflicted state of England, our native Country stands greatly in need of spiritual labourers, and as priests both religious and secular, work assiduously as apostles in this harvest, it seems that the female sex should and can in like manner undertake something more than ordinary in this same common spiritual necessity ... we also desire ... to embrace the religious state and at the same time to devote ourselves according to our slender capacity to the performance of the works of Christian charity towards our neighbour that cannot be undertaken in convents.[22]

Nevertheless, the pope held to the Tridentine position that all women's orders should be enclosed. Moreover, many (covert) English Catholic priests disapproved of the Jesuits' interactions with women.²³ In *A Decacordon*, William Watson complains that Gerard not only led men in the *Spiritual Exercises*, but also "In like manner he dealeth with such Gentlewomen, as he thinketh fit for his turne, and draweth them to his exercise," such as "Mistresse Wiseman now prisoner."²⁴

Jane (Vaughan) Wiseman (a close friend of Elizabeth and Anne Vaux and Eleanor Brookesby) and Wiseman's son, William, who had rented a house in London for Gerard's use, were arrested in 1594 for harboring him. Also arrested during the raid was the musician John Bolt, perhaps a former deputy to the recusant Sebastian Westcott, master of the choristers at St Paul's Cathedral.²⁵ Bolt had some seditious material on him, including Southwell's *Saint Peters Complaint* and Richard Whitford's *Jesus Psalter*. Whitford was a monk of Syon Abbey, the Bridgettine convent where Wiseman's eldest daughters, Anne and Barbara, were professed.²⁶ At his arrest, Bolt also "confesste that certeine leaves conteynenge lines and many verses beginninge Why do I use my paper penne and inke . . . is all of his owne hand wrytinge"; this refers to a poem on the martyrdom in 1581 of Campion (attributed by Garnet to Henry Walpole, who became a Jesuit martyr in 1595).²⁷ Bolt escaped, but "Widow Wiseman" spent several years in prison before being condemned to be crushed to death. She was eager to be martyred, but Elizabeth stayed the execution, and eventually Wiseman was pardoned by James I.

Another friend of the Vauxs and Wisemans was Anne Howard, Countess of Arundel, who sheltered Southwell from 1586 to 1592 and Gerard in 1594; she took a vow of chastity after the death of her husband in 1595.²⁸ Watson considered her behavior inappropriate:

> [She] was brought into such a forwardnesse of following these holy fathers & taught withal her lesson how to use the art of dissembling, according to the Jesuits rule.²⁹

Catholic Education in Latin and Music

During Elizabeth's reign, it became progressively more difficult to provide a Catholic education for children. Wealthy parents hired private unlicensed tutors or arranged for their children to be educated on the continent, both options being illegal.³⁰ William Bell, suspected of assisting Campion and Persons in the 1580s, described in his *Testament* the kind of education he hoped would be given to his children after his death. Significantly, it refers to skills taught to pre-Reformation choristers, not only for his sons but also for his daughter:

> I would that Marguerite my daughter should, so soone as thee [sic] is able to goe to schoole, and be applied in her bookes, and with her neelde [needle], so farre forth as shee be of capacitie, and if it may be, that shee be also taught her pricksong, and plainesong, and to play on the virginalls.³¹

Bell's children were subsequently brought up by Edward Sheldon and his sister Elizabeth Russell, whose father, Ralph Sheldon, was a friend of Persons, as well as of William Byrd and Thomas Paget.[32]

Because the subjects of Latin, music, and Catholic doctrine were so intertwined, some Catholic priests were able to disguise themselves as music teachers. For example, in 1586, an informer reported that one George Lingam was staying at Francis Perkins's house, Ufton Court, and that "under collor of teaching on the virginalls, goeth from papist to papist, is thought also to bee a priest, so made in Queen Marie's tyme."[33] Likewise in 1605, it was reported

> [t]hat there are in the Lord [Henry] Mordant's house certain persons suspected to be very dangerous, in regard of their own obstinacy and their Popish superstition, and also for labouring to seduce others from the truth; namely Tutfield, tutor to the Lord his son, and late tutor to the Lord Vaux [Elizabeth Vaux's son, Edward]; and Gregory Hill, a musician who teaches the daughters of the said Lord in that art.[34]

Music teachers like Hill were considered "very dangerous" because of their potential influence as religious educators. During the 1594 raids organized by Richard Topcliffe on known Catholic households (including the Wisemans'), at the house of a Mrs. Marchant the pursuivants found "a very bad man and by report one that doth great [word omitted] in the country, for under the colour of teaching the childer music it is thought that he doth teach them worse matters. For he is a notable recusant and was taken when Campion was taken."[35] This was John Jacob, a friend of Gerard's, imprisoned again in 1593 and described as "a syngyng man and . . . a goar from one recusante's houwse to another undar the colar to teche mewseke."[36] Even so, it was possible for a few Catholic musicians (favored by Elizabeth) to follow their own conscience of faith in positions supporting the state church. For example, Westcott was still teaching choristers at St. Paul's in 1582, even though, in 1563, he had been accused by Bishop Edmund Grindal of instilling "corrupte lessons of false Religion into the eares and myndes of those children committed unto him."[37]

Some women following the Jesuit model acted as tutors, even though it was unusual for women to teach music and Latin (except in some convents).[38] Several of Mary Ward's "English Ladies," having trained on the continent, returned to England, and "[i]n a manner similar to that of the missionary priests . . . would typically live with a family, under the guise of a member of the household."[39] One of them, Sister Dorothea, taught the curriculum of Ward's Institute to children in their parents' houses.[40] Ward's plan of 1612 for her school refers to "liberal arts, singing, playing musical instruments" including "playing the organ."[41] Ward based her curriculum on those of English Jesuit schools for boys, one of which gives a detailed description of music instruction. According to the *Constitutiones* for St. Omer, founded by Persons in 1592, students were to be taught the organ and harpsichord, which "greatly adorn and are well suited to ecclesiastical chant" (*cantum ecclesiasticum valde ornant et decent*), and viols, the music for which was especially distinguished (*Honorata est Musica mere ex violis*).[42]

The use of viols at St. Omer presumably stems from their importance to pre-Reformation English choir schools. Since the 1540s at the latest, choristers played on viols at least some of the liturgical music that they sang (with men), such as motets, and to substitute for the organ or regals for accompanying a solo voice (or voices) in the moralistic songs written by their masters for their recreation, some of which were included in choristers' plays.[43] They may have used viols (in addition to the keyboard) for practicing other skills, such as various ways of improvising descant (counterpoint) on plainsong. During Elizabeth's reign, choristers continued to play viols in the larger institutions of the established church, such as St. Paul's Cathedral.[44] In his will of 1582, Westcott bequeathed his "cheste of vyalyns and vialles to exercise and learne the children and Choristers."[45] Presumably, Westcott had continued to educate his choristers the way he had during Philip and Mary's reign, producing apprentices such as Peter Philips.[46] However, as Thomas Whythorne commented ca. 1576:

> When the old stor of the miuzisians be worn owt, the which wer bred when the miuzik of the chiurch waz maintained . . . yee shall hav few or non remaining, exsept it be A few singing men, and plaierz on miuzikall instriments, of the which ye shall fynd A very few or non that kan mak a good lesson of deskant.[47]

The progressive decline in music education at choir schools may have helped create a market for printed music treatises in English. Such treatises, combined with musical training provided by tutors, would help Catholic households to maintain skills useful for the liturgy, such as making "a good lesson of deskant," and make it practical to collect and preserve old as well as newly composed Latin liturgical music.[48] *A Briefe Introductione to the True Art of Musicke* by William Bathe (who became a Jesuit in 1595) includes the rules of making descant on a plainsong, and his *Briefe Introduction to the Skill of Song* demonstrates notational methods of "Musitions in old time."[49] Thomas Morley's *Plaine and Easie Introduction to Practicall Musicke*, dedicated to Byrd, includes instruction on "obsolete" musical practices used in Latin "pricksong," noting their utility for singing old music.[50] Morley's *Introduction* is also a mine of information on the teaching methods of the "old descanters."[51]

Women's Use of Music for Spiritual Instruction and Recreation

Educated women and men of the gentry were expected to have the ability to appreciate music and to sing and play musical instruments for recreation. Musical repertories favored by reformed and Catholic households are not always clearly distinguishable: the selection might depend as much on musical tastes and ambition as on religious belief. However, the devotional songs favored by many reformed households, especially for teaching children, were simple settings of psalms, such as Sternhold and Hopkins's *Whole Booke of Psalmes* (also sung in church) or *Whole Psalmes in Foure Parts*.[52] In contrast, the Catholic recusant Elizabeth (Bernye) Grymeston chose texts of a different nature, and accompanied herself on an unusual instrument, the organ.[53] Her *Miscelanea*, published posthumously in 1604 by her husband, Christopher, includes religious texts written by her "cousin," the Jesuit Southwell (whose "seditious" texts were found on Bolt when he was arrested). Chapter XI is entitled "Morning Meditation, with sixteene sobs of a sorrowful spirit, which she [Elizabeth] used for mentall prayer, as also an addition of sixteene staves [stanzas] of verse taken out of [Southwell's] Peters complaint; which she usually sung and played on the winde instrument."[54] Elizabeth sang them to her son, Berny, who demonstrated that he understood her teaching by writing a verse of his own (an "active" way of learning): chapter XII, "A Madrigall made by Berny Grymeston," uses the image of her playing the organ and singing the penitential stanzas while looking lovingly at him.[55]

Grymeston's *Miscelanea* also includes verses from *Odes in Imitation of the Seaven Penitential Psalmes* printed by Richard Verstegan, a supporter of the Jesuit mission.[56] Verstegan dedicated this publication "To the vertuous Ladies and Gentlewomen readers of these ditties" in hopes that their "sweete voyces or virginalles may voutsafe so to grace them, as that thereby they may be much betrered."[57] Verstegan's dedicatees may have been the English nuns at the Benedictine Convent at Brussels founded in 1598 by Mary Percy (with the assistance of Holt and Persons).[58] These nuns were reportedly famous for their music by the time Bolt went to their convent (sometime between 1608 and 1611) "to help their music."[59] Grymeston's copying of selections from Verstegan's *Odes* demonstrates that repertories of devotional song suited to English nuns—the well-educated daughters of English gentry living on the continent—were also suited to their sisters and cousins, who were educating their children in England.[60]

Several generations of women, including female servants, in the "firmly Jesuit-supporting" Petre household (in which Bolt taught intermittently from 1586 to 1589) took an active role in music and music education.[61] The household accounts for the period 1558–1560 include a reward for one of the senior female servants, Mrs. Persey, for "teaching the gentlewomen to play on the virginalles."[62] In 1605, a Tom Boult (perhaps a relative of John Bolt) was paid for viol strings and for teaching viol to Besse Hatch, the daughter of a servant.[63] Catherine Petre (wife of William, 2nd baron Petre) was the daughter of Edward Somerset, 4th earl of Worcester, to whom Byrd dedicated his *Cantiones sacrae* (1589). She was the person who handed over the instruments and music books (including Byrd's *Gradualia*) in 1608 to Richard Mico, who was to teach the children to play the viol. The receipt signed by Mico (GB-ERO MS D/DP E2/1) includes a "Chest of violls wch are in number 5"; keys to "the wind Instrument" (an organ installed in

1590) and to "the greate virginales."⁶⁴ Mico also bought another pair of virginals for their daughter, Mary, then aged eleven.⁶⁵

Women in the Paston household were similarly much involved in music making. Margaret (Berney) Paston was given a miscellany entitled "Preciosas Margaritas" by her musically gifted husband, Edward Paston. The gift of these fifty-three compositions (GB-Lcm MS 2036, comprising three partbooks) suggests that she, too, was musical.⁶⁶ Thirty-three of the pieces are liturgical (fifteen by Byrd), and many have text incipits or titles only, therefore belonging to the category of textless polyphony, or sol-faing songs (for playing on viols and/or for singing using sol-fa syllables).⁶⁷ One assumes that Margaret herself would have taken part in singing and/or playing these and similar pieces for recreation, perhaps with her daughters Catharine, Francisca, and Anne, cousin Helen Draycott, and niece Mary Berney when they were old enough.⁶⁸

Sol-faing songs straddled the boundaries between different faiths: they were acceptable to non-Catholics who could enjoy the "absolute" music without problematic texts, but for Catholics, an incipit would be sufficient to remind them of some or all of the text of a Latin motet or mass setting, which they could either sing from memory or meditate on while sol-faing or playing the viol.⁶⁹

Catholic Household Performances of Festal Liturgies

The preservation and cultivation of musical skills suited to Catholic liturgies in wealthy households lie behind the few surviving descriptions from this period of solemn masses. All but one refers to instruments being played, as well as to singing. From July 15–23, 1586, a Jesuit conference was held at Hurleyford Manor, the house of Richard Bold (a relative of Gerard), to welcome Garnet and Southwell to England. According to Weston, Bold's house, which was remote,

> possessed a chapel, set aside for the celebration of the Church's offices. The gentleman was also a skilled musician, and had an organ and other musical instruments, and *choristers, male and female, members of his household* [i.e., including servants]. During those days it was just as if we were celebrating an uninterrupted octave of some great feast. Mr. Byrd, the very famous English musician and organist, was among the company.⁷⁰ [italics mine]

"Some gentlewomen" who had gone there "to hide" (presumably nuns) likely participated in the music, and perhaps also Bold's wife, Jane (Mordaunt), a relative of Henry Mordant, whose daughters studied music with Gregory Hill.⁷¹ Garnet himself "had a fine singing voice" and was "very skilful in music and in playing upon musical instruments."⁷²

Southwell, referring to the same conference in a letter to Claudio Aquaviva, general of the Society of Jesus in Rome, mentions that "choice instrumental and vocal music was to be performed" (*et insigni, variorum instrumentorum et vocum symphonia decantatum*) for a festal mass.⁷³ He does not mention anyone by name (letters could be intercepted, as this one was) or that women sang in the chapel choir, perhaps because Aquaviva, in Rome, would not have approved, and/or possibly even because it was usual practice in England for women to participate.

On November 21, 1604, the feast of the Presentation, "High Mass was sung" at White Webbs, the house rented by Anne Vaux and Eleanor Brookesby. Garnet refers to several Jesuits being there: Gerard, Richard Blount, John Percy, Thomas Strange, and Thomas Cornforth, chaplain of Edward Vaux.[74] The "holy women" taking refuge there presumably attended the mass: they most likely led a relatively public (unenclosed) life, like Sister Dorothea, and like the three Bridgettine nuns who attended the mass celebrated by Campion at Francis Yate's house, Lyford Grange, but were "disguised in Gentlewomans apparrell" the following day when the house was raided.[75]

In 1605, the feast of Corpus Christi was described by three different people at (Owen Rees suggests) the same unidentified location.[76] One account is by the Spanish widow Luisa de Carvajal, who, according to one of Watson's followers, was persuaded by Michael Walpole (and other Jesuits)

> to go from Valladolid, through France, into England, in order to convert (or rather pervert) our English Females.... For they persuaded her, she should be called the Apostoless, or She-Apostle of England.[77]

According to Carvajal:

> The Masses were numerous [with] ... music of diverse, finely tuned voices and instruments (*las músicas de diversas voces y instrumentos en extremo acordadas*); and this same music [of voices and instruments], after the lunches and dinners, with spiritual and moving motets, delighted the soul.[78]

Garnet, who had arranged for Carvajal to be escorted there from Douai, gives a similar description of the music in a letter to Elizabeth Shirley at St. Ursula's, and mentions that twenty-five people left the following day: "We kept Corpus Christi day with great solemnity and music, and the day of the octave made a solemn procession about a great garden."[79] Charles de Ligny reports that Garnet and other Jesuits were there, and that *Monsieur Willaume Byrd ... sonnait les organes et plusiers aultres Intrumens* ("Mr William Byrd ... played the organ and several other instruments").[80] Byrd's *Gradualia I*, which includes a Corpus Christi Mass proper, was published that year; it also includes a setting for one voice (medius) and four instruments (presumably viols) of *Adoramus te*. This could have been one of the "moving motets" performed after meals, but the reference to "organs and other instruments" at Mass suggests that it could have been performed liturgically, especially because its text is proper to the office of the Invention of the Cross, which occurred during Carvajal's visit.[81]

The "organ and other instruments" used at clandestine liturgies would most likely be small and portable.[82] It is notable that sometime between 1623 and 1639, in Petre's chapel at Ingatestone a "frame for a payr of harpsicorne virginals" was installed, bearing in mind that at St. Omer the harpsichord as well as the organ was used to accompany voices in the liturgy.[83] Viols were even more portable, provided excellent accompaniments to and substitutes for voices, as well as having the long-standing association with training liturgical musicians. Music appropriate for consorts of viols in particular blurred the boundaries between spiritual recreation and the liturgy. The professional musicians discussed in this essay—Westcott, Bolt, Byrd, and Mico—all played the viol as well as keyboard instruments.[84]

Conclusions

The descriptions of music performed at clandestine liturgies celebrated in English Jesuit-influenced households stress the beauty and solemnity of the occasions, as if a fully functioning form of the public mass were still available to all Catholics. However, several compromises in the musical practices were necessary, contrary to those advocated by Tridentine reformers: in masses celebrated at Bold's house, women sang in choir with men, and instruments other than the organ may have been played. Carvajal's reference to the same musicians playing at liturgies and for recreation is significant because of the possible implications for women's participation in instrumental music. The women discussed in this essay may well have sung and/or played the viol, organ, or harpsichord in liturgies as well as for spiritual recreation. Moreover, the descriptions bear a resemblance to liturgies celebrated at Jesuit educational institutions, such as St. Omer, as well as to liturgies performed in the mission to the New World. The resemblance is understandable if we bear in mind that private English houses served not only as places of clandestine worship but also in lieu of choir schools. And because gentlewomen, whose domain was the house, were among the most active supporters of the Jesuits, the Jesuits in turn gladly accepted their contributions to the mission and assisted them in founding Jesuit-style women's institutions on the continent. Unfortunately, this did not last: Gerard's support of Ward's *Institute* led to his being forced to resign his rectorship of Liège Abbey.[85] In 1631, Ward was imprisoned as a heretic and Pope Urban VIII suppressed "the pretended she-Jesuites."[86] The inclusion of women as active musical participants in Mass may for a brief period have been an extraordinary result of the English Jesuits' "way of proceeding."

Notes

1. Bible, Douai-Rheims: Mark 16.15. *Constitutions of the Society of Jesus*, 130.
2. See McCoog, *Society of Jesus*, 267–272.

3. Carrafiello, "English Catholicism," 771–774; Scully, "Trickle Down Spirituality?," 285–299. The pope excommunicated Elizabeth in 1570.

4. The *Spiritual Exercises* consist of four "weeks" of directed meditation. Ignatius, *Spiritual Exercises*; Lux-Sterritt, "Virgo Becomes Virago"; McBride, "Recusant Sisters."

5. Austern, "For Musicke Is the Handmaid," 77–91; Brokaw, "Tudor Musical Theater," this volume.

6. Southern, *Elizabethan Recusant House*, 29–30: Magdalen Montague "hindered none from hearing Masse in her house." Dolan, "Gender and 'Lost' Spaces," 652–658; Hodgetts, "Godly Garret," 38–44; McGrath and Rowe, "Elizabethan Priests."

7. *Constitutions of the Society of Jesus*, 154. This paragraph is based on information given in Culley and McNaspy, "Music and the Early Jesuits," 213–245; Kennedy, "Jesuits and Music," 15–60.

8. *Ratio Studiorum*, 1586 (revised 1599); Whitehead, "To Provide for Learning," 109–143; Loach, "Revolutionary Pedagogues?," 67.

9. *Constitutions of the Society of Jesus*, 179.

10. Forney, "Proper Musical Education," 91–101; Willis, *Church Music*, 164–174.

11. Westrup, "Domestic Music," 25–26, lists titles that refer to flexible performance options.

12. Bermúdez, "Urban Musical Life," 177.

13. Brokaw, this volume.

14. *Monumenta Angliae I*, lx–lxiii. Seminary (non-Jesuit) priests, trained at Douai, began arriving in 1574.

15. Rhodes, "Join the Jesuits," 33–49.

16. Simmonds, "Women Jesuits?," 120–135 and Rhodes, "Join the Jesuits," 40–45, discuss Isabel Roser and the Spanish Infanta Juana of Austria.

17. *Council of Trent, Twenty-Fifth Session*, 240. Beales, *Education*, 203; Walsham, "Translating Trent?" discusses the implementation of Tridentine reforms in England. Tertiaries lived in communities and bound themselves to a mendicant order; Culpepper, "Our Particular Cloister," 1017–1037.

18. Caraman, [Gerard] *Autobiography*, 148.

19. Caraman, *Garnet*, 422–423.

20. Ribadeneira, *Life of B. Father Ignatius*, A2r-v.

21. Eleanor and Edward Brookesby had earlier sheltered Persons; Lux-Sterritt, *Redefining Female Religious Life*, 160.

22. "Memorial to Pope Paul V," in Rowlands, "Recusant Women," 169.

23. Marotti, *Religious Ideology*, 32–65.

24. Watson, *Decacordon*, 90.

25. Mateer, "William Byrd, John Petre," 32–33; Murphy, "Music and Post-Reformation English Catholics," 43–47.

26. Cunich, "Brothers of Syon," 60. Two of Wiseman's sons, Thomas and John, entered the Society of Jesus but died young, and her younger daughters, Jane and Bridget, professed at St. Ursula's, Louvain; Connelly, *Women of the Catholic Resistance*, 88.

27. Kilroy, *Edmund Campion*, 59–88; see Murphy, "Music and Post-Reformation English Catholics," 252–260, on Byrd's setting of the first stanza and two newly written stanzas.

28. Southwell dedicated his *Epistle of Comfort* to Anne, having based it on letters he wrote to her husband, Philip Howard, who spent the last ten years of his life in the Tower. It was printed at her secret press, probably in her house at Spitalfields; Monta, "Anne Dacre Howard," 65.

29. Watson, *Decacordon*, 39.

30. Beales, *Education*, 28–87.

31. *The Testament of William Bel*, 38–42. Flynn, "Education of Choristers," 141–145. Most masters of choristers' indentures dating from after 1560 refer to "singing" instead of

"plainsong"; Flynn, "A Reconsideration of the Mulliner Book," 252–254. "To goe to schoole" can mean going to another household; Charlton, *Women, Religion*, 126.

32. Harley, *The World of William Byrd*, 171, 205–207.
33. Sharp, *The History of Ufton Court*, 95. In 1599, Ufton Court was described as "a common receptacle for preistes, Jesuytes, Recusantes" (ibid., 99).
34. *Calendar of the Manuscripts*, vol. 17, 528. Mordant's men included "one Tuttfeilde, bred an Oxford scholar and supposed a priest" (ibid., 626).
35. Hodgetts, "*Loca secretiora*," 391.
36. Petti, *Recusant Documents*, 81–82.
37. A letter from Grindal to Robert Dudley in Strype, *Edmund Grindal*, 113–116. In 1563, schoolmasters were required to take the oath of allegiance; Beales, *Education*, 36.
38. In 1621, when Ward was setting up her Institute at Liège, some of the skeptical Jesuits asked whether a man would teach the girls music and language; Ward answered that the nuns themselves would teach both; Peters, *Mary Ward*, 228–230; Lux-Sterritt, *Redefining Female Religious Life*, 93.
39. Lux-Sterritt, *Redefining Female Religious Life*, 124. According to Bicks, "Producing Girls," 144–145, "By 1624 Ward had made numerous trips back home to oversee the 30 known Jesuitesses of her Institute who were at work in London."
40. See Gallagher, "Ward's 'Jesuitresses,'" 199–218.
41. Lux-Sterritt, *Redefining Female Religious Life*, 63.
42. Ward, "Sprightly & Cheerful Musick," 105; Iribarren, "Anthony Poole," 87–102; Beales, *Education*, 60–71, 158–173.
43. Woodfield, *The Early History of the Viol*, 206–227; Flynn, "Education of Choristers," 151–160.
44. Payne, "Provision of Teaching on Viols," 3–15; Milsom, "Oyez!," this volume.
45. Gair, *Children of Paul's*, 21.
46. Iribarren, "Anthony Poole," 39–41.
47. Whythorne, *Autobiography*, 245.
48. For example, GB-ERO MS D/DP Z6/1, a partbook bearing the name of John Petre, includes motets by Fairfax, Tallis, Taverner, and Byrd, among others; Brett, "Edward Paston," 58. On Byrd's "publishing drive" between 1588 and 1591 of his older liturgical music, see Brett, "Blame Not the Printer," 17–66. See Smith, *Thomas East*, 56, 157–158 on East's printing of almost all of Byrd's new liturgical works, including the masses à 3, 4, and 5 (ca. 1593–1595), *Gradualia I* (1605, dedicated to Henry Howard) and *Gradualia II* (1607, dedicated to John Petre).
49. Ó'Mathúna, "William Bathe, S. J.," 47–61; both texts are edited by Karnes in Bathe, *Briefe Introduction*.
50. Morley, *A Plaine and Easie Introduction*, 183. Morley's religious faith appears equivocal; Murray, *Thomas Morley*, 14–19.
51. Morley, *A Plaine and Easie Introduction*, 90–92; Flynn, "To Play upon the Organs," 30–31; Flynn, "Musical Knowledge," 178–180.
52. Harris, "Musical Education," 131–134.
53. Snook, *Women, Reading, and Cultural Politics*, 83–114. The organ was the instrument most associated with liturgical music in church, and therefore not usually played by women (apart from nuns in their convent). Like Grymeston, Mary Skidmore, may have been taught to play the organ in England. The seminary priest Arthur Pitts (a former chorister at All Souls, Oxford, who may have been her teacher) contributed £30 toward an organ for her to play when he and Eleanor Brookesby escorted Mary to Louvain to join St. Ursula's; *Chronicle of... St Monica's* [vol. 1], 36, 65, 68, 118; Cichy, "Parlour, Court and Cloister," 182–183.

54. Grymeston, *Miscelanea*, D4. Southwell, himself, had intended *Saint Peters complaint* to be sung, according to the dedicatory Epistle addressed to his (unidentified) "loving Cosen" [A2v]. Organs were often referred to "the wind instrument"; see Bicknall, *The History of the English Organ*, 75, and below.

55. Grymeston, *Miscelanea*, E4v.

56. Snook, *Women, Reading, and Cultural Politics*, 85. Verstegan fled to the continent in 1582 after printing Thomas Alfield's *True Reporte of the Death & Martyrdome of M. Campion Jesuite*, to which was "annexid certayne verses," including "Why doe I use"; Kilroy, *Edmund Campion*, 60.

57. [Verstegan] *Odes*, A2.

58. Arblaster, *Antwerp & the World*, 78. Mary was the niece of Henry Percy, 9th earl of Northumberland (whose daughter Lucy at about nine years old studied with Byrd) and the daughter of Thomas Percy, 7th earl, whose inventory of 1570 includes virginals and viols; "Humberston's Survey," 154. When Henry Percy was imprisoned in 1585 for treason (with Philip Howard, mentioned above), Byrd was also under suspicion; Harley, *The World of William Byrd*, 131.

59. See *English Benedictine Nuns in Flunders*.

60. Cichy, "Parlour, Court and Cloister," 188–190; Murphy, "Music and Post-Reformation English Catholics," 53–58.

61. On the Petres' links to the Jesuit mission, see Kelly, "Kinship and Religious Politics," 332–334.

62. Price, *Patrons*, 86.

63. Ibid., 90.

64. Facsimile on plate 5, Hanley, "Mico."

65. Bennett and Willetts, "Richard Mico," 29.

66. Brett, "Edward Paston," 54, 60. Margaret was a relative of Elizabeth Grymeston, daughter of the recusant Martin Bernye.

67. *Census-Catalogue of Manuscript Sources*, vol. 2, 121. On sol-faing, see Edwards, "The Performance of Ensemble Music," 113–123.

68. According to the *Chronicle of St. Monica's* [vol. 2], 35, Helen Draycott, orphaned at the age of three, was "left to be brought up by a cousin-german of hers (Mr Paston), who was also a Catholic, and so she had good education." Catharine and Franciska Paston professed at Mary Percy's convent, and Draycott and Berney at St. Monica's; Sequera, "House Music for Recusants," 11–15; Arblaster, "The Infanta and the English Benedictine Nuns," 520, 526. At St. Monica's, Bolt "set up all our music to the honour of God, teaching our sisters to sing and play on the organ"; Cichy, "Parlour, Court and Cloister," 179–180.

69. Flynn, "The *In nomine* as a Jesuit Emblem," further discusses sol-faing song, demonstrating the *In nomine*'s connections to music education and to Jesuit symbolism and meditative practices.

70. Weston, *Autobiography*, 71; Harley, *The World of William Byrd*, 175–176.

71. Weston, *Autobiography*, 71.

72. Comments by Thomas Stanney; Caraman, *Garnet*, 33.

73. Strype, *Annals*, vol. 3, part 2, 418.

74. Brett, *Gradualia I*, ix.

75. Ellyot, *Very True Report*, B4b. On other Bridgettine nuns who led a missionary life, see Walker, "Continuity and Isolation," 171–175.

76. Rees, "Luisa de Carvajal," 270–280.

77. *Authentic Memoirs*, 45–46.

78. Rees, "Luisa de Carvajal," 272–273.

79. Caraman, *Garnet*, 320; Rees, "Luisa de Carvajal," 274.
80. Rees, "Luisa de Carvajal," 279, 275.
81. Ibid., 280.
82. Most Tudor organs were free-standing, single-manual instruments (with no pedal board), which could be carried by two or three men, and set in place for performance; Bicknall, *The History of the English Organ*, 26–68.
83. Bennett and Willetts, "Richard Mico," 33.
84. Ibid., 35.
85. Simmonds, "Women Jesuits?," 125.
86. Peters, *Mary Ward*, 569.

3.

The Transmission of Lute Music and the Culture of Aurality in Early Modern England

Graham Freeman

Despite the popularity of the lute in sixteenth- and seventeenth-century England, there was very little printed solo music for it in England, at least when compared with that printed on the continent.[1] Despite the fact that Petrucci had published the first printed lute music in 1507, English lutenists did not begin publishing their music in print tablature until William Barley's *A New Booke of Tabliture* in 1596, after which time the only significant publication of English lute music from before the middle of the seventeenth century was Robert Dowland's *Varietie of Lute Lessons* from 1610.[2]

A number of excellent studies have recently shed light on the place of the lute in early modern England, including Julia Craig-McFeely's *English Lute Manuscripts and Scribes 1530–1630*, Matthew Spring's *The Lute in Britain: A History of the Instrument and Its Music*, and Elizabeth Kenny's "Revealing Their Hand: Lute Tablatures in Early Seventeenth-Century England."[3] Additionally, Kirsten Gibson has undertaken a reconsideration of the lute songs of John Dowland and their place in the musical and print culture of the sixteenth and seventeenth centuries.[4] The main difficulty in assessing the solo lute music of this period is its ephemeral nature. Much of it was surely transmitted aurally, and what manuscripts remain must represent only a small fraction of what was once in circulation. Yet the relationship between aurality and manuscript transmission for this repertoire has thus far been underexamined.[5]

There were many practical considerations that required lutenists to transmit their solo music aurally and through manuscript, such as avoiding the expense and complexity of print or because of the greater availability of popular pieces in aural and manuscript circulation. However, what if, in addition to these considerations, aural and manuscript transmission were so profoundly interwoven with the aesthetic and cognitive processes involved in the creation and transmission of lute music as to make printed editions simply unnecessary? In other words, what if both aural and manuscript transmission were so much an effective part of the working methods of both the recreational and occupational lutenist in England that lutenists were reluctant to let them go in favor of printed music because they had become a vital element of the way they worked? My contention in this chapter is that aurality and manuscript transmission were not simply practical requirements, but were also part of an organizing system that relied on these methods to achieve maximum throughput of musical material in the community of English lutenists.

The Lute and Its Sources in Early Modern England

Julia Craig-McFeely has determined that the extant lute music of England is distributed among eighty-five manuscript and five print sources.[6] She places these into three categories: (1) fragmentary sources of ballad settings and Italian lute music from between 1530 and 1580; (2) those containing the elaborate fantasias and dances of such figures as John Dowland, Daniel Batcheler, and John Johnson from the "Golden Age" of lute music between 1580 and 1615; and (3) the predominantly French music in the sources after 1615. Within these sources, Craig-McFeely identifies four additional categories: (1) fragments that were at one time associated with a larger work, (2) teaching fragments, which were loose exemplars likely used for copying by students; (3) professional books used by waits or court musicians; and (4) pedagogical books prepared by a student learning the lute under the guidance of a tutor. In total, there are 3,330 pieces, of which 2,100 are different and 1,230 are concordances, with the vast majority appearing during the period 1580–1615.[7] Of these, only five are printed books. This is despite the fact that, as John Milsom has demonstrated, music printing in England was under way by the 1520s, with the patent for music printing being granted by Elizabeth I to William Byrd and Thomas Tallis in 1575.[8]

Most of these manuscripts contain several scribal hands and are what are more commonly referred to as "miscellanies," in which scribes at least once removed from the author copied music from various composers into a blank book, usually for the purposes of self-study or archival preservation.[9] This is in stark contrast to the manuscript collections of other repertoires, such as for viol, which, as Harold Love describes, were often published in scribal editions written by the composers or hired scribes and sold directly to players.[10] Love calls this "scribal publication," a procedure in which the composer disseminated the music in manuscript form from which additional copies were made by music lovers and performers.[11] Although the books themselves were sometimes passed around as exemplars, often only individual pages were circulated.[12] Moreover, lute manuscripts usually did not originate with the composers and were often meant for private consumption.[13] The varied contents of the lute manuscripts, containing works from many different composers, demonstrate that they are also commonplace books in which the scribe collected the music that either appealed to them or that their teacher thought best suited to them.[14]

English lute manuscripts share some features in common with literature disseminated according to the parameters of scribal publication. Much like the works of Donne and Rochester, lute music often exists in versions that differ from one another considerably. John Dowland's *Lachrimae* is a good example of this, as it exists in many different versions for solo lute in addition to consort and vocal arrangements by both Dowland and his admirers. Like much of the English lute repertoire after 1580, *Lachrimae* is a tripartite dance consisting of three separate strophes, each of which is followed by virtuosic divisions on the previous section. While the main strophic statements tend to remain similar if not identical throughout the various sources, the divisions often show extreme variation, indicating that the compiler of the book chose to include his own divisions in place of those provided by the teacher or found in the exemplar. *Lachrimae*, in all its many incarnations, therefore tends to consist of the three relatively simple strophic statements composed by Dowland followed by virtuosic divisions provided by the student, teacher, or other lutenist.

Lachrimae is one of the many pieces found in the collection of manuscripts from Cambridge known as the "Mathew Holmes Lutebooks." Holmes was a singing man and precentor at Christ Church Cathedral, Oxford from 1588 to 1597, after which time he took up a similar post at Westminster Abbey until 1621.[15] He was therefore an individual of considerable musical knowledge, and though he likely did not play the lute for a living, there is a strong likelihood that he provided instruction in ensemble playing to the members of the choir at Christ Church.[16] The technical range of the works in his manuscript collection indicate that he was a skilled lutenist, and his manuscripts are often those to which modern editors go in order to find the works most likely representative of the apex of technical and compositional accomplishment in English lute music of the period.[17] This collection of four manuscripts—GB-Cu MS Dd.2.11; Dd.5.78.3; Dd.9.33; and Nn.6.36—towers above all others as the most important collection of English lute music surviving today, with over seven hundred pieces represented, of which five hundred are found only once in the manuscripts. In the case of Dowland's *Lachrimae* pavane, there are three versions in Dd.2.11: one in G minor and one in A minor, each for solo lute, and one for bandora. The two versions for solo lute have quite different variations, and the fact that Holmes would have gone to the trouble to write out two drastically different versions gives us some idea of the unique existence he granted each one: less that they were variations of the same piece as much as they were unique pieces unto themselves.[18]

Lute music in England, therefore, remained circulating in manuscript long after it had begun to appear in print on the continent and long after the means for disseminating it in print had appeared. Lutenists seem consciously to have avoided print, opting instead to allow their music to be disseminated freely in a hybrid collaborative form in which the student or performer altered and amended the music to suit his own abilities and aesthetic tastes. So why did they not adopt print technology? To answer this question, we must look more deeply into the role of aurality and manuscript culture in sixteenth-century England.

Aurality, Cognition, and Organizing Systems

Despite the advance of the printing press, early modern England maintained a complex interrelationship between aurality, chirography, and typography. Rising literacy rates and the steady increase in the production and consumption of print materials meant that many in England could either read and write reasonably well or had access to someone who could.[19] Print and literacy therefore went hand in hand. However, both chirography and aurality continued to play an important role in the everyday lives of many people, as was the case with broadside ballad production, in which the printed ballad text would carry no musical notation but would instead contain instructions to sing it to a popular tune, thus relying on a combination of printed text and aurally transmitted music.[20] Although print was making headway in English society in the sixteenth century, aural and manuscript transmission remained a vital, if not dominant, medium of communication.[21]

For many Protestants, *Fides ex auditu*, or "faith by hearing," was a fundamental element of religious practice.[22] Preachers rarely wrote down their sermons, using instead a wide assortment of rhetorical devices more commonly associated with the theater than with the pulpit, and it was only with encouragement that preachers were persuaded that there might be a market for printed sermons.[23] Laurence Chaderton's printed preface to his sermon at St. Paul's Cross in 1578 contains a preface in which he assures his reader that "I have set downe, not in the same words I spake (for the Lord knoweth I never writ it, and therefore could not) but in other, so plainly as I could for the capacitie and understanding of all."[24] For many English Protestants, it was the word spoken that represented the word of God, while the word read represented Catholicism and, thus, idolatry.[25] Many sermons survive in manuscripts transcribed by the congregation. Given the emphasis on the reception of the spoken word from the pulpit, many members of the congregation took extensive shorthand notes on the structure, argument, and scriptural proofs of the sermon for the purpose of studying it, memorizing passages of scripture, and incorporating these ideas into their lives and prayers.[26] These sermons often show extreme variation among the manuscripts, as several people would often note the same sermon, and they show even greater deviation from the authorized printed versions that appeared later. Variation among these manuscripts does not necessarily represent error as much as it does the different methods and preferences of those doing the copying.[27]

By writing down the sermon, students created a personalized physical map of its structure for analysis, classification, and recombination into new material. Arnold Hunt describes how these physical maps made clear the structure of individual doctrines and sections in each sermon.[28] These sections could then be assigned a place in a sort of mental filing system for retrieval and application, either individually or rearranged in combination with other sections, in a commonplace book. Writing the sermon heard from the pulpit therefore not only played an important role in reinforcing the structure and detail of the material but also provided a source of modular material the listener could study and incorporate into additional texts, sermons, or conversations of their own.

The metaphor of these documents as "maps" is derived, in part, from the work of Evelyn Tribble, who sees a different but complementary use for similar types of documents. In her work on the working methods of the actors of the Globe Theatre in Elizabethan England, Tribble draws our attention to the use of "plots," which were large sheets of paper containing what was essentially a schema of the entire production: entrances, exits, props, and musical cues.[29] These plots represent a step in a process that begins with capturing aurally transmitted information on paper, creating a schematic or layout of that information in a way that allows for visuospatial cognition to retrieve that information by memory, and culminates in the execution of an action that involves the use of that retrieved information either through restatement or as raw material for the creation of new texts or works.

Why can print not serve this same purpose? If this system was to be constructed simply on the organization of information, or what we might consider content management, then certainly a printed version of that information could work just as well. However, I contend that the predetermined presentation and structure of information on a printed page negates some of the most important steps in this particular system, especially that of content creation. To demonstrate this point, I point to Robert J. Glushko's concept of the "organizing system."[30] Glushko defines the organizing system as "an intentionally arranged collection of resources and the interactions they support." A printed document is one in which the graphical and visuospatial decisions have been made according to the organizing system of the printer or editor, not necessarily the end user. As a result, printed documents may not be designed according to the organizing principles most important to the end user, which negates the potency of the organizing system.[31]

To summarize, the critical value of aural transmission and manuscript transmission in scribal communities lies in their pivotal roles in a complex organizing system that incorporates both physical elements (the creation of the manuscript document) and abstract elements (the structuring and organization of the information as a schema or map that reflects the cognitive priorities of the end user). There is no suggestion here that the possibility of such a system is unique to England or to the lute community. Instead, I contend that this instance of the organizing system among English lutenists was unique as a result of the particular set of constraints within which that community operated.

The Transmission of Lute Music in Early Modern England

This final section weaves together the previous threads to answer the following questions: (1) How does the issue of aurality and its role in an organizing system change our perceptions of the transmission of lute music in England?; (2) Why did the innovation of print not have a significant impact on lutenists in England?; and (3) Why does the system proposed here apply only to English lutenists and not to communities of other musicians both in England and on the continent?

Much of the iconography of lute performance shows lutenists performing without music, even in consort, suggesting that much of their repertoire was improvised over memorized structures familiar to the musical community. Many of the lute manuscripts support this idea. Perhaps the best example of this would be the Ballet lutebook dating from ca. 1593–1603.[32] Ballet contains approximately thirty simple and unadorned ballad tunes, many of which are the earliest examples of tunes that later found their way into the publications of folksong scholars like William Chappell.[33] Tunes such as these would have served as a familiar basis for improvisation by the lute player, perhaps in a social or theatrical setting in which the audience would be familiar with the tune.[34] Variations and improvisations on well-known ballad tunes were an important aspect of the English lute repertoire, and manuscripts such as Ballet represent a collection of maps or plots that served as the basis for these improvisations. They are therefore not the finished product but simply a framework for the execution of complex variations and improvisations.[35]

The aural nature of lute performance provides us a different perspective on the workflows and practices of lutenists in England, especially concerning pedagogy. Traditional assumptions about English lute pedagogy have focused on the idea, summarized by Craig-McFeely, that lute teachers provided students with loose leaves containing musical examples from which the students would make copies into their own books, or that the teachers wrote down the music themselves for the student to learn.[36] This is the case with the Board lutebook, in which John Dowland made a number of additions to the work of his student Margaret Board.[37] By placing greater emphasis on the importance of aurality in the transmission of lute music, I am suggesting that perhaps this music was not transmitted, at least not entirely, in writing during the pedagogical process but was, in fact, transmitted aurally by the teacher and transcribed by the student either during the lesson or at a later time. Elizabeth Kenny has noted that the Mynshall lutebook is an example of a book that was created for the express purpose of recording the pedagogical procedure Craig-McFeely describes. Kenny points to the "Flat Pavan" by John Johnson as a piece in the manuscript that has many concordances. She notes that it demonstrates elements of both attention and carelessness in the inscribing of the music on the page, and a change of ink and rhythmic signs as indications that the piece was copied from an exemplar during at least two different sittings. She suggests that the errors would probably have been of secondary consideration to the beautiful presentation of the music and that the performer would likely have known the music and would have been able to improvise on it well enough to play it from memory without needing to refer to the book. As Kenny writes, the work is "a stimulus to a performing text, not a representation of one."[38] Yet we should not discount a third possibility: that it is an imperfect transcription of one. John Ward suggests this possibility when he writes, in reference to amateurs' miscellanies: "Lack of skill in notation, not in playing, is what the manuscripts record; the one skill is independent of the other . . . [scribes] must have known how most, probably all, of the music was supposed to sound, may first have learned the pieces 'by ear' and later written them down as best they could. The Folger MS . . . is full of what look like *aides-mémoire*."[39] In place of the concept of the *aide-mémoire*, however, I would substitute instead the concept of the map or schema that provides a visual representation of the path the lutenist will follow and a repository of the modular musical material they will vary and recombine as they improvise. Though the music in many manuscripts might suggest careless copying from an exemplar, such errors are typical of ethnographic field transcriptions, in which the transcription is done with paper and pencil as the performance takes place or perhaps later from memory. Such transcriptions usually require repeated performances in the field, and until the advent of recording technology in the early part of the twentieth-century, many tunes were preserved using only this imperfect method.[40] In this sense, lute manuscripts may represent what ethnomusicologist Charles Seeger referred to as "prescriptive" music writing, in which only the broad outline of the music is provided before a formal and detailed "descriptive" transcription can be provided after repeated listening and study.[41] In the case of the lute manuscripts, however, the descriptive notation never arrived and was likely realized only through the improvisation of each performance.[42] This sort of aural transmission is a common practice in many non-Western musical cultures and is often a required part of their musical pedagogy regardless of the complexity of the music.[43] As we have seen in other media, such as the noting of sermons, one was not considered to have embraced and mastered the material until one had heard it delivered and noted the structure and detail in one's own hand. If one wanted to be truly able to absorb and reapply the material, one needed to hear it, write it, analyze its structure, and repeat and recombine it without any access to a written intermediary.

Having proposed the pivotal importance of aurality to the manuscript culture of English lutenists, it is worth further speculating on a scenario that represents the end-to-end workflow for the typical English consumer of lute music. In this scenario, the lute student is possessed of some musical talent but is not an occupational musician. A lute teacher visits the student once a week to provide instruction on the fundamentals of playing the lute. During the course of this lesson, the teacher performs a number of pieces that the student must copy into her workbook either during the performance or to the best of her ability after the conclusion of the lesson. The purpose of copying down the music in her own hand is for the student to create her own personalized cognitive map of the music, which means that the visuospatial representation of the music is memorized and becomes a schema that can be used for further composition or improvisation. Further, the music on the page, particularly the improvised variations, becomes raw modular material that can be mentally accessed and applied to new musical situations. Essentially, therefore, each piece in manuscript is a map containing modular musical material, and this map both contains musical material that can be accessed according to the student's personal preferences and also represents a schematic vessel into which musical material from other maps can be placed to create new pieces of music. This entire process represents the student's organizing system, a system that is intentionally designed by the student to be an efficient and practical manifestation of her musical abilities and preferences. While these manuscripts still contained entire pieces that could be performed verbatim, they also served as vessels that provided access to organized musical materials and maps to which musical materials from other maps could be applied.

Why, then, could this system not accommodate printed music? Building on the organizing system described above in relation to aural and manuscript culture, I propose that lute culture in England was largely process-driven and not product-driven. The goal of this process was not simply to have a piece of music on paper from which the musician could play—a goal that could easily have been satisfied by printed music—but to engage in the entire process from beginning to end. This process was an organizing system in which the lack of printed music essentially operated as a constraint that generated the innovative communication channels that supported England's extensive aural and manuscript cultures.[44] Lutenists effectively broke the constraint by working around it with this organization system.

Does this, then, mean that the system simply could not accommodate print or that the lute community was hostile to print? No, but it does highlight three significant reasons that printed lute tablature was slower to catch on in England than it was on the continent. First, as suggested above, lutenists had an innovative process for capturing and assimilating aural performances of lute music that was supported by extensive communication channels, making the initial forays into print potentially redundant. The second reason may be best explained by the idea in which the nature of an innovation such as print, the communication channels by which that innovation travels, the amount of time it takes for an innovation to travel such channels, and the constitution of the social system in which the innovation is planted all represent constraints that can inhibit and retard the diffusion of even the most vital innovations in a society.[45] Those such as innovators, early adopters, and change agents must contend with various constraints on innovation such as those that inhibited printed lute music in England, including printing technology that cannot readily adapt to the demands of lute tablature, small addressable markets, and competing processes that would have to be displaced by the innovation, such as the organizing system defined above. Finally, if time were required to allow the innovation of printed music to diffuse through the community of English lutenists, that was something that the lute in England simply did not have on its side. While by the seventeenth century the most fashionable lute music in England was French, by 1660 the lute in general, even in France, was beginning to cede territory to the harpsichord, and between 1610 and 1676, there are only three sources of lute music printed in England: Robert Dowland's *Varietie of Lute Lessons* (1610), Richard Mathew's *The Lutes Apology for Her Excellency* (1652), and Thomas Mace's *Musick's Monument* (1676).[46] After the Restoration in 1660, while the theorbo continued to be a popular continuo instrument, the influence of the lute in England diminished, thus further decreasing the size of any addressable market for printed lute music.[47]

Conclusions

My proposal that English lute manuscripts are components of a process-driven organizing system does little to disrupt our notions of manuscript culture or the aural tradition in England. What it does do, however, is cast it in a somewhat different light, as it provides some insight into a particularly inventive way in which the community of lutenists in England selected resources according to the needs of their communications channels and organizing system. It also shows us that while innovations like print can produce seemingly miraculous changes in some social systems, they can flounder in others that have already created competing and effective systems of communication and invention.[48]

Notes

1. The term *solo* used here is not meant to be exclusive to music for a single lute but merely to exclude songs and other ensemble music in which the lute might have played a role. Lute duets, of which there are several in the manuscripts, are included in the category defined here.

2. Printed music in England had a less-than-glorious beginning, something that Joseph Kerman has attributed to the oppressive and chaotic printing monopoly Elizabeth I granted to William Byrd and Thomas Tallis in 1575. D. W. Krummel has suggested that the lack of printed lute music in England could be attributed to Byrd himself, and that his lack of sympathy for the lute led him to avoid printing any music for it. See Krummel, *English Music Printing*, 103 and Kerman, *The Elizabethan Madrigal*, 267. For more on English printed music, see Smith, *Thomas East and Music Publishing*, 19–37.

3. Craig-McFeely, "English Lute Manuscripts and Scribes," 70–102; Spring, *The Lute in Britain*, 96–148; Kenny, "Revealing Their Hand," 112–137.

4. Gibson, "'How Hard an Enterprise It Is,'" 43–89; "'So to the Wood Went I,'" 221–251; "'The Order of the Book,'" 13–33.

5. Kenny, for example, asserts that lutenists frequently memorized both complete pieces and harmonic patterns for the purpose of improvisation or creating a unique version of the piece suited to the technique and tastes of the player, but the possibility of aural transmission remains conspicuously absent in such accounts ("Revealing Their Hand," 201).

6. Craig-McFeely, "English Lute Manuscripts and Scribes," 35.

7. Ibid., 35–36.

8. Milsom, "Songs and Society in Early Tudor London," 235–293 and Krummel, *English Music Printing*, 15. Elizabeth I granted the printing privilege to Tallis and Byrd on January 22, 1575. The Elizabethan monopolies were devised as a means of encouraging the English economy by providing protectionist measures that would prevent English markets from being colonized by foreign producers and would promote English ones. As far as this strategy went with printed music, it must be considered a dismal failure. When the patent expired in 1596, there was a brief period during which there was no printing patent in force before Thomas Morley renewed it in 1598. Krummel asserts that the period during which there was no patent was one of the most lucrative for printed music, as it allowed printers such as William Barley, Peter Short, and Thomas East to publish music at will, thus making 1597 a high point in the history of English music publishing. Unfortunately, that success did not translate into any significant publications for the lute. The sole publication of music for solo lute was Barley's *A New Booke of Tabliture* from 1596. Subsequent to this, the only significant publication of music for solo lute came in 1610 with Robert Dowland's *Varietie of Lute Lessons*.

9. Personal miscellanies could contain any number of items, regardless of genre. Many miscellanies include transcriptions of music and lyric from print literature, recipes, lists of prominent public figures, transcriptions of ideas about theology and history, or family histories. If it was worth preserving, it could be found in a personal miscellany. See Marotti, *Manuscript, Print, and the English Renaissance Lyric*, 17–22.

10. Love, *The Culture and Commerce of Texts*, 27–28.

11. Ibid., 36.

12. Ibid., 79–83.

13. Love describes such sources as "weak user" scribal publications. Ibid., 36.

14. Ward, "The Osborn Commonplace-Book," 22–36.

15. Harwood, "'A Lecture in Musick,'" 19–20.

16. Ibid., 19.

17. Poulton (*John Dowland*, 97), for example, considers them the most important of the English lute manuscripts.

18. Gale, "John Dowland," 213–216. Perhaps one of the most intriguing examples of the personal anthology is the Brogyntyn lutebook (GB-AB Brogyntyn MS 27), which contains ornate decorations and was copied with obvious care. These are qualities that Craig-McFeely describes as those that set these sources apart from the hurried and practical presentations of

professional and pedagogical lute books. Curiously, Brogyntyn features the titles of each piece in a ciphertext, an additional element that testifies to the obvious private or limited circulation of the manuscript. See Craig-McFeely, "English Lute Manuscripts and Scribes," 99.

19. Fox, *Oral and Literate Culture in England*, 19.
20. Watt, *Cheap Print and Popular Piety*, 39–73.
21. Smith, *The Acoustic World of Early Modern England*, 128.
22. Hunt, *The Art of Hearing*, 22.
23. Crockett, "'Holy Cozenage' and the Renaissance Cult of the Ear," 50. For a parallel musical scenario involving the lute ayre, see Wilson, this volume.
24. Chaderton, *An Excellent and Godly Sermon*, Aiii.
25. The debates concerning the merits of preaching over reading were widespread in England, even among Protestants, with many believing that the written word of the Bible was simply the foundation upon which oral transmission and preaching rested. For a more thorough examination, see Hunt, *The Art of Hearing*, 19–59.
26. Hunt, *The Art of Hearing*, 72.
27. Marotti suggests that the dissemination of poetry by means of memorization and oral transmission, followed later by its inscription into various manuscripts, was not only an integral aspect of literary life in early modern England but also an explanation for the incredible diversity of texts, with variants representing not errors of transmission but emendations and expressions of creativity on the part of the persons copying them down. Readers during this period therefore had a much more dialogical relationship with the text than we might imagine today, and our modern idea of the "work" is anachronistic compared to this very different idea of each manifestation or performance of the text being a unique event. See Marotti, *Manuscript, Print, and the English Renaissance Lyric*, 143–144. For a discussion of this idea in relation to a slightly later period of English music, see Herissone, *Musical Creativity in Restoration England*, particularly chapter 4, 209–260; and Herissone, this volume.
28. Hunt, *The Art of Hearing*, 99.
29. Tribble, "Distributing Cognition in the Globe," 144–147.
30. Glushko, *The Discipline of Organizing*, 47–93.
31. Walter Ong's theory of "presence" offers some alternative insight into the importance of the manuscript and its relation to orality/aurality. Presence is the concept of the human subject behind the medium of communication. Oral communication is rich with the concept of presence because it is an ephemeral means of communication, one that cannot exist without a vocal subject and a hearing recipient. Manuscript retains the presence of orality/aurality by virtue of being the product of direct human agency. For an excellent summary, see Love, *The Culture and Commerce of Texts*, 142.
32. Spring, *The Lute in Britain*, 126.
33. Ibid.
34. This was, of course, not unique to England. For anecdotes about the improvisation of Francesco da Milano, see Coelho, "The Reputation of Francesco da Milano," 49–72.
35. Bailey explores a similar issue in relation to manuscript collections of keyboard music in Restoration England in this volume.
36. Craig-McFeely, "English Lute Manuscripts and Scribes," 78.
37. Ibid., 214.
38. Kenny, "Revealing Their Hand," 125–127.
39. Ward, "The Osborn Commonplace-Book," 24.
40. For more on folk transcription, see Ellingson, "Transcription," 110–152.
41. Seeger, "Prescriptive and Descriptive Music-Writing," 184–195.
42. For an examination of the importance of prescriptive transcription of aurally transmitted material later in the seventeenth century, see Herissone, this volume.

43. Daniel Neuman (*The Life of Music in North India*, 49, n7) provides an excellent example from his study of Indian music: "The medium for the guru's message is not a written system (notations are considered ineffective for any but the most rudimentary lessons) but his own disciples, their message and remembrance . . . ustads typically feel that notations are either harmful or at best useful only as mnemonic devices for learning basic structures, and that real learning must be received orally." See also Haynes, *The End of Early Music,* 204–205.

44. The most famous exploration of the ways in which organizing systems find innovative ways around constraints is the Theory of Constraints of Eliyahu Goldratt and Jeff Cox in their book *The Goal: A Process of Ongoing Improvement*. Although designed for large-scale business organizations, they effectively identify the important roles that constraints play in forcing innovation in the creation of ways of working around and breaking those constraints.

45. This idea is based on the theory given in Rogers, *Diffusion of Innovations*. As an example of his assertion that "innovations do not sell themselves," Rogers relates how a preventative method against scurvy was not officially instituted in the British Royal Navy until 1795 despite having been identified and documented in 1601. See Rogers, *Diffusion of Innovations*, 7–8.

46. Spring, *The Lute in Britain*, 343.

47. For a thorough examination of the decline of the lute in England, see Spring, *The Lute in Britain*, 400–450.

48. This also provides a speculative contribution to the questions concerning John Dowland's ventures into printed music. Dowland must correctly have determined that lutenists, at least those of the English variety, were not yet sympathetic to the idea of "authoring" lute music in print, despite the fact that his considerable reputation rested on his skill in this area. Through the creation and promotion of the genre of the lute song, a genre that would appeal to musicians beyond simply lutenists, Dowland found a way to access a more extensive network of communal domestic music making in his quest for self-promotion. For more, see Gibson, "'How Hard an Enterprise It Is,'" 52, and Wilson, this volume.

4.

Thomas Campion's "Superfluous Blossomes of His Deeper Studies": The Public Realm of His English Ayres

Christopher R. Wilson

The works of Thomas Campion (1567–1620) were published during his lifetime in five books of ayres, three masque "Discriptions," a treatise on prosody, a treatise on "counterpoint" (*recte* four-part harmony), two large collections of Latin poetry,[1] and a group of elegies set to music by John Coprario.[2] In all of these genres, Campion was and is recognized as a major exponent. Defensive tropes on being reluctant to commit his work to publication are found in the prefaces and dedicatory epistles to several of his English works. There is nothing exceptional in this. Similar disclaimers occur variously and frequently in both English and continental prefaces to published books. What makes Campion particularly unusual is that he asserts it was his Latin poems that he regarded confidently as his major work suited for public dissemination and that his English ayres—his "superfluous Blossomes"—were subsidiary, apt for private consumption. This essay interrogates that assertion.

Between 1596 and 1622, William Barley's *A New Booke of Tabliture* and John Attey's *The First Booke of Ayres,* thirty-two collections of English ayres were published. This print phenomenon has never been satisfactorily explained,[3] given that the lute song together with instrumental lute music,[4] had been a manuscript genre since the 1560s.[5] It is noticeable that its start coincided with Byrd's relinquishment of his printing patent to Thomas Morley.[6] What is certain is that it released into the public domain a music-poetry genre hitherto confined to esoteric circles of readers and authors. Among the most prolific contributors to this culture were John Dowland, Thomas Campion, and Robert Jones.[7] Prestigious folio books of lute ayres usually comprised eighteen to twenty-eight leaves or pages accommodating a corresponding number of ayres either for solo voice with lute and/or viol (sometimes orpharion), or arranged in parts for three or four voices.⁸ The majority contains twenty-four leaves following the precedent set in Dowland's first book of 1597.⁹ The vogue for the lute ayre was at its most intense between 1597 and 1610, comparable with the madrigal, whose popularity, according to publication statistics, can be identified to have been at its height between 1588 and 1600, falling off slightly to 1610 and more markedly to 1620 and finishing in 1632.¹⁰

The comparatively narrow time span, the generic similarities of the music/poetic form, and the fact that several composers issued three or four collections of ayres has led modern commentators following the empiricist advocacy of Edmund Fellowes and his pioneering editions of his so-called school of English lute-song composers and Peter Warlock's influential *The English Ayre* (1926) to identify the English ayre as a generic whole.¹¹ Performative issues could reinforce this approach; the ayres are intended to be performed as solo voice pieces with instrumental accompaniment. About two hundred of the six hundred ayres in the printed collections contain alternative part-song versions, presumably made by the composer of the original solo ayre.¹² But a reexamination of the intended audience for the ayre and its artistic purpose as defined by its author would reveal divergent tendencies within the genre.

The differing artistic personae of the three most prolific composers of lute ayres, namely Dowland, Campion, and Jones, provide insights into publication motivation beyond William Barley's commercial cynicism.¹³ In his dedicatory epistle in *A New Booke of Tabliture* (1596) to the Ladie Bridgett, Countesse of Sussex, Barley asserts that

> bookes ... that are compiled by men of divers gifts, are published by them to divers endes: by some in desire of a gainefull reward: some for vaine ostentation, some for good will & affection, and some for common profit which by their works may be gotten.¹⁴

John Dowland was in today's terminology a professional musician¹⁵—composer, instrumentalist, and teacher—keen to parade his professional music qualifications in his publications. On the title page of his *The First Booke of Songes or Ayres* (1597), and subsequent books, he is styled "Batcheler of musicke in both the Universities."¹⁶ His prefaces advertise his musical expertise and prowess. Why he published his books of ayres accords with his career development, or rather his professional aspirations. Diana Poulton suggests the reason "he chose the year 1597 in which to publish his first collection probably resulted from the realization that, after the second failure to secure an appointment at Court, his career had reached a critical point, and that some special effort was needed to maintain himself in public favour after his absence abroad."¹⁷ That he chose lute ayres and not solo lute music, Poulton contends, was because he could reach a wider audience, although the inclusion of a galliard for lute duet in the first book may undermine the legitimacy of this assertion.¹⁸ Or it may unashamedly advertise his potential as a teacher.¹⁹ The audience Dowland, or rather his publisher, targeted, was diverse. Some years later, his son, Robert, justified the contents of *A Musicall Banquet. Furnished with Varietie of Delicious Ayres* (1610) according to the potential recipients of the collection:

> Some [ayres] I have purposely sorted to the capacitie of young practitioners, the rest by degrees are of greater depth and skill, so that like a carefull Confectionary, as neere as might be I have fitted my Banquet for all tastes.²⁰

Those tastes varied among aristocratic households and the fast-emerging mercantile gentry, for their own amusement, for their family's entertainment and erudition, or for their music servants to perform. In his dedicatory epistle to "the Honourable the Ladie Arbella,"²¹ Michael Cavendish offers his *14. Ayres in Tabletorie to the Lute* (1598) "whereby I can best express my service to you, and you may (if it please you) make use of them at your idlest houres."²² Thomas Ford wishes to express his gratitude to "The Worthie and vertuous Knight, Sir Richard Weston" in his *Musicke of Sundrie Kindes* (1607) for his continuing patronage:²³

> I shall not neede to make an Apologie in defence of these musickes, since none are so much in request nor more generally received then of these kindes, which with all hartie affection I offer to your favorable judgement not as a worke whose merit or worth deserves so judicious a patron, but a manifestation of my worthlesse affection bound unto you by many particular favours.²⁴

William Corkine similarly acknowledges his debt to Sir Edward Herbert²⁵ and Sir William Hardy in his *Ayres, To Sing and Play to the Lute* (1610) for their support for his musical education: "that I might shew my humble duetie, and gratefull minde to you my two Honourable Masters, whose bountie bestowed on me that knowledge (whatsoever it is) that I have attain'd in Musicke."²⁶ In his discussion of patronage and the "private encouragement of musicians," David Price cites the case of a certain John Ramsey, a gentleman of Mount in Surrey, whose diary records his library list, compiled over more than twenty years, which included music books by Dowland, Byrd, Robert Jones, Philip Rosseter, Michael Cavendish, Thomas Morley, and a number of Elizabethan madrigalists.²⁷ Price contends that this list reveals a certain conservatism in taste, an "appreciation for the more restrained moral and musical atmosphere of Elizabeth's court."²⁸ By all accounts, it also reflects a norm of interest typical of an educated gentleman of the period.

Robert Jones was a composer and performer who "professed Musicke" to earn his living. His professional qualification was the BMus he received from Oxford University in 1597. He published five books of ayres between 1600 and 1610. It seems his ayres attracted a mixed reception if his defensive preface "To all Musicall Murmurers" in his fourth collection, *A Musicall Dreame* (1609) has meaning:

> Thou, whose eare itches with the varietie of opinion, hearing thine owne sound, as the Ecchoe reverberating others substance, and unprofitable in it selfe, shewes to the World comfortable noyse, though to thy owne use little pleasure, by reason of uncharitable censure.[29]

Jones's popularity and esteem do appear to have suffered a decline during the first decade of the seventeenth century (and thereafter). An ayre in his first collection, *The First Booke of Songes or Ayres* (1600), by all accounts was "one of the most successful of all the English lutenist songs" together with some of Dowland's ayres, and perhaps Campion's.[30] In addition to instrumental arrangements for lute, cittern, mandora, and virginals, "Farewel Deare Love" was rearranged as vocal-lute parody in several sources and published as far distant as Scotland and the Netherlands.[31] It was used by Shakespeare in *Twelfth Night* (act 2, scene 3) shortly after its publication in Jones's book, and later by Beaumont in his *Knight of the Burning Pestle* (ca. 1609) (2.470–471). Its appearance in a theatrical context attests both to its further appeal and to Jones's connection with the theater. On January 4, 1610, Jones was granted a patent to "practice and ex'cise [boys] in the quality of playing by the name of Children of the Revells of the Queene within the white ffryers," together with Philip Kingham, Philip Rosseter, and Ralph Reeve.[32]

Unlike Dowland and Jones, Thomas Campion did not "profess" music and boasted no professional qualification until he made public his medical "Doctor of Phisicke" on the title page of the *Description of the Lord Hayes* masque in 1607.[33] There is no evidence he received any specialist music education and yet his musical output is at least comparable with most English lute-song writers and more inventive and assured than Robert Jones. However, in his first publication, *A Booke of Ayres* (1601), his joint author and associate, Philip Rosseter, makes plain he regarded his English ayres as second best to his Latin poetry, "superfluous blossomes of his deeper Studies."[34]

Like Jones, Campion published five books of ayres. They were issued between 1601 and 1618. Unique among the lutenist songwriters, Campion composed both music and poetry for all these collections. That seems to have afforded Campion a special control over the contents. All his books were printed as paired volumes (i.e., two volumes in one publication) and, with the exception of the first *A Booke of Ayres*, undated. The first book contains twenty-one ayres by Campion in the first part and an equal number by Rosseter in the second, possibly suggesting an acknowledged qualitative presentational preference. The second and third books are arranged according to poetic and musical content, the "first are grave and pious; the second amorous and light." The fourth and fifth books are characterized not so much by subject matter as by the supposed relationship of the ayres to the respective dedicatees, Sir Thomas Mounson and his son, Mr. John Mounson, following the example set in his *Two Bookes of Ayres*, the first dedicated to Francis, Earl of Cumberland, the second to his son and heir, Henry Lord Clifford.[35]

That Campion was seemingly reluctant to commit his ayres to print can possibly be explained both by his special circumstances and the print culture surrounding the ethos of the English ayre in the early seventeenth century.[36] Several composers make the point that their ayres were "made" for private consumption and have been released for public display grudgingly at the behest of others. Thomas Morley expresses his gratitude to a worthy backer, Ralph Bosville, Esq, by publishing a book of lute ayres, his *The First Booke of Ayres* (1600), "In recompence therefore of my private favours, I thought it the part of an honest minde, to make some one publique testimonie and acknowledgement thereof."[37] Aware, like Morley, of adverse criticism, Robert Jones attempts to defend his stance on making public his private ayres. In his address "To The Reader" in his *The Second Booke of Songs and Ayres* (1601) he states:

> The trueth is, although I was not so idle when I composed these Ayres, that I dare not stand to the hazard of their examination: Yet I would be glad (if it might be) that thy friendly approbation might give me incouragement, to sound my thankefulnes more sweetely in thine eares hereafter. If the Ditties dislike thee, 'tis my fault that was so bold to publish the private contentments of divers Gentlemen without their consents, though (I hope) not against their wils: wherein if thou find anie thing to meete with thy desire, thank me; for they were never meant thee.[38]

The passage from private to public ayre and its consequences are expressed by John Danyel in his dedicatory verse to "Mrs Anne Grene the worthy Daughter to Sir William Grene"[39] in his *Songs for the Lute Viol and Voice* (1606):

> That which was onely privately compos'd,
> For your delight, Faire Ornament of Worth,
> Is here, come, to bee publikely disclos'd:
> And to an universall view put forth.
> Which having beene but yours and mine before,
> (Or but of few besides) is made hereby
> To bee the worlds: and yours and mine no more.[40]

John Maynard finds himself in a similar position with regard his *The XII. Wonders of the World* (1611) in his apology to his hoped-for patron, "the Lady Joane Thynne, of Cause-Castle in Shropshire":[41] "What at first privately was entended for you, is at last publickely commended to you."[42] Secure in the patronal favors of Sir Richard Weston, Thomas Ford intimates in his *Musicke of Sundrie Kindes* (1607) his ayres were thrust in the public domain by "the perswasion of some private friends, together with the general good of such as take delight therein."[43] Aware of peer approbation or criticism, William Corkine acknowledges in his dedicatory epistle in his *Ayres, To Sing and Play to the Lute* (1610) the increasing number of composers who have released their ayres to the wider public: "Among so many [musitians], I have now made one, yeelding my private inventions subject to publicke censure."[44]

In keeping with other lute-song composers, Campion claims his ayres were originally intended for private consumption and only subsequently did he permit them to be made public.[45] In the preface "To the Reader" to *Two Bookes of Ayres* (ca. 1613) he opens with a disclaimer that only at the behest of others were his ayres, many composed a number of years earlier, released to a wider audience: "Out of many Songs which partly at the request of friends, partly for my owne recreation were by mee long since composed, I have now enfranchised a few, sending them forth divided according to their different subject into severall Bookes."[46] Uniquely among the lute-song composers, Campion offers two exceptional reasons why his English ayres were his private property. In the dedicatory epistle to Sir Thomas Mounson in *A Booke of Ayres* (1601), Philip Rosseter observes that Campion's ayres were "made at his vacant houres, and privately emparted to his friends, whereby they grew both publicke, and (as coine crackt in exchange) corrupted: some of them both words and notes unrespectively challenged by others."[47] The special circumstances of Campion's authorship, that he wrote both words and music, give this statement added potency. The same point is made by Campion himself, with less vehemence, in his preface "To the Reader" to *The Fourth Booke of Ayres* (ca. 1617) where he says, "Some words are in these Bookes, which have beene cloathed in Musicke by others, and I am content they then served their turne: yet give mee now leave to make use of mine owne." He also recycles "three or foure Songs [of his own] that have beene published before."[48] The second explanation why Campion's ayres were not primarily made public was due to his status as a (neo-)Latin poet, as Rosseter intimates in *A Booke of Ayres*: "In regard of which wronges, though his selfe neglects these light fruits as superfluous blossomes of his deeper Studies, yet hath it pleased him upon my entreaty, to grant me the impression of part of them."[49] Campion's "light" offerings are his (rhyming) English ayres; his "more serious studies" are his Latin poems and Classical learning, as the dedicatory epistle to the Lord Buckhurst in his *Observations in the Art of English Poesie* (1602) attests.

Campion's Latin poems outweigh his English in quantity produced. His first substantial work was his collection of Latin poems, *Poemata*, published in 1595. It contains the epic fragment, *Ad Thamesin*, celebrating the defeat of the Armada (1588)—the first of its kind; what turned out to be the first part of a neo-Ovidian epic, the *Fragmentum Umbrae*; a book of 16 elegies, and a book of 129 epigrams. Although many were fanciful and often erotic "youth-borne" poems of indeterminate quality, according to Percival Vivian, *Poemata* "won him a considerable reputation almost immediately."[50] Among a number of approbatory references in contemporary sources, Francis Meres, for example, in his *Palladis*

Tamia, Wits Treasury (1598), praises Campion as a Latin poet in the company of Walter Haddon, Nicholas Carr, Gabriel Harvey, Christopher Ocland, Thomas Newton, Thomas Watson, and others, many of whom were also distinguished writers of English poetry, in august comparison with Sir Philip Sidney, Spenser, Samuel Daniel, Drayton, Warner, Shakespeare, Marlow and Chapman, who Meres cites.[51] Notable Latin poet and a prominent member of the circle around Campion, which included the Mychelburnes, Laurence, Edward, and Thomas, was Charles Fitz-Geffry who accords Campion second place as a writer of Latin epigrams behind Sir Thomas More, whose *Epigrammata* was published in 1520. Fitz-Geffry supports Campion's claim in his *Elegeia I* (1595) to be the best English writer of Latin elegies in an epigram addressed to Campion, "O cujus genio *Romana* Elegia debet," in *Affaniae* (1601).[52]

Toward the end of his life, the second substantial collection of Campion's Latin poems was published, the *Tho. Campiani Epigrammatum Libri II Umbra Elegiarum liber unus* (London, 1619). It comprised 453 epigrams, the large majority of which were new though many only a couple of lines long; 88 were reworkings of epigrams originally published in 1595, the completed *Fragmentum umbrae* from 1595; and 13 elegies, most of which were derived from earlier poems. The majority of Campion's Latin poems, therefore, as Davis points out,[53] effectively represent his early work, before he started publishing English ayres and before he published his treatise advocating quantitative meters in English poetry, his *Observations in the Arte of English Poesie* (1602).[54]

Despite his exhortations to Edward Mychelburne and reminder to Fitz-Geffry to publish, it is probable not all Campion's Latin poetry was in fact published. In *Epigrammatum liber primus* (1619), Campion writes to Mychelburne:

> Haec quorsum premis? ut pereant quis talia condit?
> Edere si non vis omnibus, ede tibi.[55]

In *Epigrammatum liber secundus* (1619), to Fitz-Geffry he writes:

> Carole, si quid habes longo quod tempore coctum
> Dulce fit, ut radijs fructus Apollineis,
> Ede, nec egregios.[56]

Campion's long epic panegyric, *De puluerea conjuratione* (*On the Gunpowder Plot*) survives in a manuscript copy in the library of Sidney Sussex College, Cambridge.[57] Clearly a "public" poem dedicated to King James, its two books intend a historical narrative rather than a *laudator temporis acti*, yet it is not certain why it remained unpublished. Its most likely date of composition in its completed state, possibly after revision, Lindley argues, is 1615–1618.[58] If that is the case, then its lack of publication is curious given the number of Latin poems by Campion published in 1619.

The relationship between Campion's Latin poems and his English is characterized not so much by his long poems as by the short, pithy epigrams. In both *A Booke of Ayres* (1601) and *Two Bookes of Ayres* (ca.1613), he compares his ayres to epigrams:

> Short Ayres if they be skilfully framed, and naturally exprest, are like quicke and good Epigrammes in Poesie, many of them shewing as much artifice, and breeding as great difficultie as a larger Poeme.[59]

This confirms his earlier apology in 1601:

> What Epigrams are in Poetrie, the same are Ayres in musicke, then in their chiefe perfection when they are short and well seasoned . . . as *Martiall* speakes in defence of his short Epigrams, so may I say in th'apologie of Ayres, that where there is a full volume, there can be no imputation of shortnes.[60]

Short lyrical poems possess a quality longer ones are incapable of sustaining—that is, personal reflection and intimacy. This quality presents a dilemma to the early modern author who wishes to present his private thoughts and sentiments in public. Unlike overt forms of "public" display such as masques and plays, in which certain kinds of ayres were included, the ayres of the song books often reveal an individuality and introspection not found for example in madrigals and theater songs. As Daniel Fischlin observes,

> the ayre presented an alternative form of theatricality or performativity, one in which overt codes of social and political hierarchy were displaced by the humanist concern with monody, the affective yoking of words to music in a manner that does not undermine the focus on the words. Implicit in such an aesthetic is a turning away from the use of art to idealize power or the powerful (as in the masque) or of art to create a public spectacle that represents the dialogical interplay of a particular extended narrative (as in the theatre).[61]

Campion wrote music and words for four courtly masques, decidedly a public statement of his art in contrast to many of his lute ayres. Fischlin goes on to assert that the performative and receptive relationship between author and audience emphasize its "private" status:

> the ayre, by virtue of its internalized theatricality, rejects many of the conventions of public spectacle to stage something quite different: the highly accomplished "individual" singing carefully wrought words and music as an expression of the very power of words and music to stage that individual's voice. . . . The ayre as a performance genre implicitly repudiates mass spectacle, whether musical or theatrical, cultivating instead the staging of introspection, solitude, and dialogical intimacy as part of its aesthetic appeal, even if it does so in public.[62]

A number of Campion's ayres (as poems), however, are expressly public. His *Songs of Mourning: Bewailing the Untimely Death of Prince Henry* (1613), "worded" by

Campion and set to music by John Coprario,[63] are collectively public, albeit moving from formal statement in the poems addressed to the king and queen to more personal recollection in the poem "spoken" to Princess Elizabeth, as Lindley notes, "further dismantling the distance between poet and addressee, [which] allows for the first time a sense of the poet speaking as grieving individual, rather than public spokesman."[64] The balance between distance and intimacy is most sensitively achieved by Campion in his *Two Bookes of Ayres*, published around the same time as the *Songs of Mourning*. The division of the collection into two books, the first "contayning divine and morall songs," the second "light conceits of lovers" sets up an apparent opposition between public and private statement. The first book represents a public face of the poet, notably in no. 1, "Author of Light";[65] no. 3, "Where Are All Thy Beauties Now?" on the death of Queen Elizabeth; no. 6, "Bravely Deckt Come Forth Bright Day" on the Gunpowder Plot; no. 7, "To Musicke Bent Is My Retyred Minde"; no. 8, "Tune Thy Musicke to Thy Hart" on the affective power of music; and no. 21, "All Looks Be Pale," an elegy on Prince Henry's death. Whereas the second book of "amorous and light" ayres constitutes an "idealized private space as its performative context, one in which whispering, dreaming, pleasure, and intimacy [are] part of the aesthetic values reflected in both the lyrics and their musical settings," especially in the ayres where "lovers cares" are expressed.[66]

Campion was not unusual among the lute-song composers in claiming that his ayres were originally intended for private consumption. In the first book of the lute-song series, *The First Booke of Songes or Ayres* (1597),[67] Dowland makes the point in his preface "To the courteous Reader": "How hard an enterprise it is in this skilfull and curious age to commit our private labours to the publike view."[68] Composers make similar observations in subsequent publications, as has been noted. No other authors, however, claim their English ayres were overshadowed by Latin poetry and their publication inhibited as a consequence. Moreover, as author of both words and music, uniquely among the lute-song composers, Campion presents a special aesthetic in that his ayres retain their artistic integrity with or without their musical setting. Hoping to deflect adverse criticism he acknowledges the variable qualitative worth of the ayres in the preface to *Two Bookes of Ayres*. In contrast to all other lute-song writers, he also advises that his ayres may be either sung or read.

> Omnia nec nostris bona sunt, sed nec mala libris;
> Si placet hac cantes, hac quoque lege legas.[69]

In his dedicatory verse to Francis, Earl of Cumberland, in the same book, he similarly proclaims:

> These Leaves I offer you, Devotion might
> Her selfe lay open, reade them, or else heare
> How gravely with their tunes they yeeld delight
> To any vertuous, and not curious eare.[70]

Evidence that at least some of Campion's ayres were read without their music can be deduced from their inclusion in printed verse miscellanies and manuscript commonplace books. Three poems were included in Francis Davison's *Poetical Rapsody* (London, 1602), namely "A Hymne in Praise of Neptune," "When to Her Lute Corinna Sings," and "Blame Not My Cheeks." Campion's "What If a Day" enjoyed especial popularity. It is first found in the commonplace book of John Sanderson (GB-Lbl Lansdowne MS 241 fol. 49) and subsequently in a number of sources.[71] "The Man of Life Upright" appears in a manuscript mistakenly attributed "Sir John Harrington's Poems, Written in the reign of Queen Elizabeth" (Oxford Bodleian Rawlinson MS. 31). The verse miscellany, GB-Lbl Harley MS 6910 (ca.1596), contains transcripts in sonnet form of "Thou Art Not Faire, for All Thy Red and White" and "Thrice Tosse These Oaken Ashes in the Ayre." Without their music, as Campion intimates, reading may lead to increased intimacy and privacy, beyond the innate privacy of ayres "enfranchised" in public.

Notes

1. The long and ambitious Latin poem, *De Puluerea Coniuratione* exceptionally survives in manuscript: GB-Cssc MS 59. See below.

2. There are two collected editions: Vivian, *Campion's Works*; Davis, *The Works of Thomas Campion*. For a brief review of secondary literature see Wilson, "Words and Notes Coupled Lovingly Together," 1–10 and "Campion," *GMO* (accessed August 15, 2015).

3. Doughtie (*Lyrics from English Ayres*, 10) argues that the songbooks could be considered a continuation of the poetical miscellanies of the sixteenth century. This does not account for the music.

4. See above, Freeman, "The Transmission of Lute Music." As Freeman discusses, lute music continued to be a manuscript genre.

5. See Greer, *Songs from Manuscript Sources*.

6. According to Stanley Boorman, Byrd's royal patent expired in 1596 at which date the London booksellers and printers Peter Short and William Barley began printing music. In September 1598, Thomas Morley secured a patent; Barley became his associate (Boorman et al., "Printing and Publishing of Music," *GMO* (accessed June 20, 2013). The patent is reproduced in Steele, *Earliest English Music Printing*, 27–29. Graham Freeman notes in his essay (fn7) Krummel's assertion that 1597 marked a high point in English music printing while the patent was in abeyance. Following Morley's death, probably in 1602/3, Short and Thomas East developed the business. Subsequent reasonably successful printers of music books include John Wyndet (1607), Humfrey Lownes (1604–1613), and Thomas Snodham (1609–1624). For a reference work on music publishing, see Krummel, *Literature of Music Bibliography*. For a more specific discussion of later sixteenth- and early seventeenth-century English music publishing, see Price, *Patrons and Musicians*, 180–189 and Smith, *Thomas East and Music Publishing*.

7. No critical overview of the so-called English lute song exists but the subject entries in *GMO* under individual composers provide references to seminal secondary literature. Campion has attracted a possibly disproportionate amount of critical attention.

8. This diverse accompaniment possibility distinguishes and differentiates the so-called lute song from instrumental lute music so that the two genres cannot be regarded as interchangeable.

9. On the role of John Dowland in the Elizabethan musical world and print culture, see Gibson, "'How Hard an Enterprise It Is.'" See also Gibson, "'The Order of the Book.'" Freeman refers to these sources in "The Transmission of Lute Music."

10. Although it is included in Sternfeld and Greer's revised edition of *English Madrigal Verse* (1967) under "Lute Songs," Walter Porter's *Madrigales and Ayres* (1632) contains no lute ayres and therefore can only be categorized as a madrigal book, albeit of a late kind. For a still-pertinent comparative study of the two genres and their contextual significance, see Ruff and Wilson, "The Madrigal, the Lute Song and Elizabethan Politics," 3–51.

11. Fellowes, *English School of Lutenist Song Writers*; Warlock, *The English Ayre*.

12. These are available in Greer, *Collected English Lutenist Partsongs*, Musica Britannica, vols. 34 and 35. For a discussion on the compositional status of the part-song version see Wilson, "Thomas Campion's 'Ayres Filled with Parts' Reconsidered," 3–12.

13. In fact, as Price (*Patrons and Musicians*, 184–187) points out, publication "gave very little financial encouragement to prospective composers." Printers/publishers like William Barley made the profit.

14. Barley, *A New Booke of Tabliture* (1596), Part I, sig. A2.

15. For a discussion of this possibly misleading terminology, see Bailey, "The Challenge of Domesticity," this volume.

16. According to Poulton (*John Dowland*, 49), by 1597, Dowland had been awarded BMus degrees from both Cambridge and Oxford because he describes himself as "Lutenist and Bachelor of musicke in both the Universities." See also, Ward, "A Dowland Miscellany," 9–10.

17. Poulton, *John Dowland*, 48–49.

18. In fact, Dowland's publication catalyst may have been the printing in 1596 of Barley's two "plagiarising primers," *A New Booke of Tablature* and *The Pathway to Musicke*. See Price, *Patrons and Musicians*, 183.

19. On Dowland as instructor, see Gale, "John Dowland, Celebrity Lute Teacher," 205–218.

20. R. Dowland, *A Musicall Banquet*, unpaginated.

21. Lady Arabella Stuart (1575–1615). Warlock (*The English Ayre*, 111) notes that several music books were dedicated to her.

22. Cavendish, *14. Ayres in Tabletorie to the Lute*, unpaginated dedication. The madrigal was also intended as a leisure activity for the nobility. In his dedicatory epistle to Arthur, Lord Chichester, in his *The Second Set of Madrigals* (1618), Thomas Bateson, for example, made it clear that his madrigals were "solely entended for your Honours private recreation."

23. Sir Richard Weston (1577–1635) received his knighthood in 1603 and became first Earl of Portland in 1633. Brian Quintrell, "Weston, Richard, First Earl of Portland (bap. 1577, d. 1635)," *DNB* (accessed November 21, 2013).

24. Ford, *Musicke of Sundrie Kindes*, sig. A2.

25. The gentleman of letters, Sir Edward Herbert (1583–1648) was the first Baron Herbert of Cherbury and brother of George Herbert.

26. Corkine, *Ayres, To Sing and Play to the Lute*, sig. A1v.

27. GB-Ob Douce 280, fol.120 in Price, *Patrons and Musicians*, 187.

28. Ibid., 188.

29. Jones, *A Musicall Dreame*, sig. A2[v].

30. Greer, "Five Variations on 'Farewel Dear Loue,'" 214. See also Greer's insightful brief summary, 225–227.

31. See further, Greer, "Five Variations," 215–222.

32. See Brown, "Jones, Robert (ii)," *GMO* (accessed November 21, 2013).

33. It is not certain when and where Campion qualified. Shapiro, "Thomas Campion's Medical Degree," 495, made a convincing case for Caen in 1605.
34. Rosseter, *A Booke of Ayres*, unpaginated dedication to Sir Thomas Mounson.
35. For further discussion of this point, see Davis, *The Works of Thomas Campion*, 128–129, where he argues that the "difference between the two [books] is . . . a distinction in tone, between rather bitter and hard-headed songs on the one hand and lighter frothy ones on the other. Youth and age here signify innocence and experience. Surely one reason for the peculiar form of the distinction is that these two books are occasional in a way that none of the other songbooks are: in his epistle, Campion is at great pains to specify the way he feels about Monson and his relation to him in this book."
36. For a discussion of a wide range of aspects of print culture, and one that interrogates its meaning and significance in the early seventeenth century, see Raymond, *The Oxford History of Popular Print Culture*, vol. 1. On music and printing, see Krummel, *English Music Printing*. On the decline in music printing after 1612, see Pattison, "Notes on Early Music Printing," 416–418. For a general comparison with literary works, see Miller, *Professional Writers* and Saunders, *Profession of English Letters*.
37. Morley, *The First Booke of Ayres*, sig. A2. Ralph Bosville of Bradbourne, Kent, was a militia officer and was knighted by James I on July 23, 1603 (Doughtie, *Lyrics from English Ayres*, 493).
38. Jones, *The Second Booke of Songs and Ayres*, sig. A2[v].
39. Doughtie (*Lyrics from English Ayres*, 549) records that Sir William Green acquired the manor house at Great Milton in Oxfordshire by 1588 and was still living there in 1611. He was knighted by James I on July 9, 1603.
40. Danyel, *Songs for the Lute Viol and Voice*, unpaginated dedication.
41. Lady Joan Thynne was the wife of Sir John Thynne of Longleat and daughter of Sir Royland Hayward, sometime Lord Mayor of London (Doughtie, *Lyrics from English Ayres*, 596).
42. Maynard, *The XII. Wonders of the World*, unpaginated dedication.
43. Ford, *Musicke of Sundrie Kindes*, sig. A2.
44. Corkine, *Ayres, To Sing and Play to the Lute*, unpaginated dedication.
45. Campion's social status, like his father's, was "gentleman." His career at Peterhouse, Cambridge and Gray's Inn attests to a person of private means and family support. See Vivian, *Campion's Works*, xvii, xxv–xxxi. For a gentleman to publish for an audience of unequal social rank was regarded indecorous in Elizabethan and Jacobean society. Price (*Patrons and Musicians*, 192), argues that "it was at least possible, if not strictly advisable, that some artistic gentlemen of proven pedigree could risk criticism by appearing in print. . . . This acceptance was made easier if a publishing composer could claim that his work, previously circulated in manuscript, had been abused in some way."
46. Campion, *Two Bookes of Ayres*, unpaginated. Poems and/or music appearing earlier include First Book: no. 2, "The Man of Life Upright" in *A Booke of Ayres*, 18; no. 18, "Seeke the Lord" in *A Booke of Ayres*, 4; Second Book: no. 7, "Give Beauty All Her Right" compare the second stanza of "Now Hath Flora" in *The Lord Hayes Masque* (1607); no. 10, "What Harvest Halfe So Sweet Is?" part derived from *A Booke of Ayres*, 7. The ayre "Bravely Deckt Come Forth Bright Day" l.6 refers to the Gunpowder Plot (November 5, 1605) in the first stanza and the death of Prince Henry (November 6, 1612) in the last.
47. Rosseter, *A Booke of Ayres*, unpaginated dedication.
48. Campion, *The Fourth Booke of Ayres*, sig. G[1]. For the identity of "others" and Campion's parodies see Sternfeld and Greer, eds., *English Madrigal Verse*, 732–733.
49. Rossiter, *A Booke of Ayres*, unpaginated dedication.
50. Vivian, *Campion's Works*, xxxvi.
51. Meres, *Palladis Tamia* (1598), fol. 280r.

52. Fitz-Geffry (FitzGeofridi), *Affaniae* (1601), 56.
53. Davis, *The Works of Thomas Campion*, 359.
54. For one of the best discussions of Elizabethan verse in classical meters, see Attridge, *Well-Weighed Syllables*. On theory in Campion's treatise, see Fenyo, "Grammar and Music in Campion's *Observations*," 46–72.
55. Campion, *Thomas Campiani Epigrammatum libri II, Epigrammatum liber primus*, no. 192, "Why do you censor these [Latin poems]? Who creates such things so that they may wither? If you wish not to publish for all, publish for yourself" (translation by the author with advice from Dr. David Bagchi).
56. Campion, *Epigrammatum liber secundus*, no. 70, "Charles, if you have anything that, by long ripening, has become sweet, as fruit are by the rays of Apollo [the sun], then publish . . . " (translation by the author with advice from Dr. David Bagchi).
57. GB-Cssc MS 59. Lindley, *Thomas Campion: De Puluerea Coniuratione*.
58. Lindley, *Thomas Campion*, 4.
59. Campion, *Two Bookes*, unpaginated.
60. "To The Reader," *A Booke of Ayres*, sig. A2v.
61. Fischlin, *In Small Proportions*, 21.
62. Ibid., 21.
63. On the working relationship and artistic interactions between Campion and Coprario, see further Wilson, "A New Way of Making . . . Counterpoint," 7–10 et passim.
64. Lindley, *Thomas Campion*, 5.
65. For a compelling analysis of this ayre, see Mellers, "Words and Music in Elizabethan England," 404–408.
66. Fischlin, *In Small Proportions*, 253–254.
67. This book set the format for most successive publications. It went into five "newly corrected and amended" editions: 1597, 1600, 1603, 1606, and 1613.
68. Dowland, *The First Booke of Songes or Ayres*, sig. A1.
69. Campion, *Two Bookes of Ayres. The First*, "To the Reader," sig. A1v. "Not all things in our book are good, but neither are they all bad. If it pleases [you], you may sing them, or, accordingly, read them" (author's translation with advice from Dr. David Bagchi).
70. Campion, *Two Bookes of Ayres. The First*, sig. A1.
71. See further, Greer, "'What If a Day,'" 316–318.

5.

Oyez! Fresh Thoughts about the "Cries of London" Repertory

John Milsom

From time to time, a recording appears or a performance takes place of one of those strange English works called the "Cries of London."[1] These pieces, composed by Thomas Weelkes, Orlando Gibbons, Richard Dering, and others during the decades 1590–1620, and scored for a mix of voices and instruments, deserve to be called "strange" because they surprise on so many counts. Most obviously, their vocal content is borrowed from elsewhere—from the cries of urban street vendors such as fishwives, fruit sellers, dairymaids and tinkers, chimney sweeps, oarsmen, town criers, and night watchmen; but these calls have been embedded in instrumental polyphony, remote from the culture of the streets, and the resulting works evidently speak to a sophisticated audience. Clearly, all manner of boundaries are being crossed here. Mercantile noise becomes artwork; oral becomes literate; outdoors becomes indoors; social classes are traversed; and there could even be some bending of genders. The works are strange, too, for being so overtly dramatic. A singer who urges her audience to "buy my quarter of good smelts" must draw her audience into a world of make-believe: momentarily, she is a fishwife, even though seconds before she had tried to sell "four ropes of onions." Being medleys without story or narrative, these pieces are remote from the condition of opera, but nonetheless, they beckon their singers into character acting, and in places, they do possess brief moments of drama. And as a final twist: the performance fishwife who mimics her street equivalent may find it a hard act to follow, for a real fishwife can be a skilled performer in her own right, highly persuasive and memorable to those who witness her. A performance of a "Cries of London" that fails to catch or match the spirit of the streets might be deemed to have fallen flat.

Modern performances and recordings, the portals through which most people today access the "Cries of London" repertory, may add significantly to the perceived strangeness of these works. Ponder, for instance, two recordings of Thomas Weelkes's "Cries of London" made in 2004–2005. On paper, this work is a string of street cries notated on a single stave under treble clef, accompanied by four instruments. In the first recording (Fretwork), a solo tenor sings the cries an octave below Weelkes's written pitch, making this a firmly masculine performance.[2] He adopts a modern cockney/estuary accent that identifies him as a working-class Londoner of our own time; clearly, this singer has listened to some current street vendors. He performs in a resonant building (actually a church), but he moves around it as if to imply that the criers walk as they call, or that we the listeners are passing through the streets. Supporting him are four stationary viols, soft-voiced instruments linked with interior spaces. In almost every respect, this performance differs from the second (Les Sacqueboutiers).[3] Here, Weelkes's vocal line is sung at notated pitch by a female soprano using modern standard English. Her delivery is lively but abstract; as an evocation of street life, it does indeed fall flat. She, too, is recorded indoors but accompanied by cornetts and sackbuts, instruments linked either with ceremony and spectacle or, when played by city waits, with performance out of doors. In only one aspect of production do these two recordings align: the imaginary streets they portray are eerily silent, and the only listeners are the microphones and ourselves.

Do these productions in any way touch on the realities of performance Weelkes himself would have had in mind? That question in turn unlocks a host of others. Where exactly were these "Cries of London" performed when they were new? Who sang them, who played them, and to what audience? What were the genders and ages of the musicians who took part? What instruments were played? How were the works meant to be received? Why were they composed in the first place? Their only extant sources are manuscript copies seemingly made for domestic use, perhaps by amateur musicians for their own recreation. So were these "Cries" written with that use in mind, or have they crossed boundaries from one performance context to another? Modern performers can sidestep these questions, but the historian bent on time travel needs to face them head-on. The following remarks therefore pursue them as far as the evidence allows.[4]

Some of these questions have been asked before. Most obviously, they were tackled by Philip Brett in his edition of *Consort Songs*, which includes an exemplary critical edition of most of the "Cries of London" repertory. (This volume is cited below as *CS*.)[5] Brett knew well that the only surviving sources for these "Cries" were compiled for domestic use, but he suspected that the pieces themselves had indeed crossed boundaries in order to end up in these particular manuscripts.[6] Remarking on the relative popularity of the "Cries," some of which circulated quite widely, he has this to say:

Their vogue may perhaps be explained in terms of the increased sophistication of a court audience bored with the grandiloquent madrigal and eager to share vicariously in the rough-and-tumble of common life: a patronizing tone is never far from the surface.[7]

How Brett arrived at that image of a "court audience bored with the grandiloquent madrigal" is not explained, but the notion has taken root. See, for instance, the following expansion of it by Philippe Canguilhem:

> this music, with its working-class inspirations, is nevertheless coming to us directly from the rarified milieu of the King's court, whose members were in a position to appreciate the ironic juxtaposition . . . between these echoes of urban life and the elaborate musical language borrowed from the fantasia genre.[8]

David Pinto's booklet notes for Fretwork seems more inclined to connect the "Cries" repertory with what he calls the "parlour," as implied by the domestic origins of the extant manuscript sources. But he agrees with Brett that the criers themselves are "portrayed with some condescension."[9] These views need to be tested, and that means looking afresh at the works themselves.

The casual reader of CS will reckon there are four pieces in the "Cries of London" repertory: one by Thomas Weelkes, one by Orlando Gibbons, one anonymous, and one by Richard Dering. A more careful reading of Brett's edition shows that the situation is in fact much more complex. The setting by Weelkes (CS no. 66) survives in two quite different states, one considerably shorter than the other; they are designated below as Short Weelkes (recorded by Les Sacqueboutiers) and Long Weelkes (recorded by Fretwork). Brett himself makes no judgment as to which version is the prototype. Loosely related to them is an autonomous third work, unattributed in its only known source, which Brett describes briefly in his Textual Commentary but excluded from CS itself. This rejected work is, in his view, "modelled closely" on Short Weelkes, "except that the cries are not restricted to one voice. It is of inferior workmanship and may possibly be by William Cobbold, whose 'New fashions' is the next item in the MS."[10] This rejected piece, designated below as Anon/Weelkes, is not currently available in a modern edition or recording; it is also incomplete, one partbook being missing from its only known source.[11] Collectively, the three pieces mentioned so far constitute the Weelkes group. Turning next to the setting by Orlando Gibbons (CS no. 67), Brett's edition gives it as a long work in two halves, each built on a statement of the *In nomine* cantus firmus. Brett's textual commentary, however, explains that this is an unstable piece; its two halves circulated independently and sometimes in reverse order, making it unclear whether this is in fact one piece or two. In the discussion below, its two halves are designated as Gibbons A and Gibbons B. Fretwork, following Brett's lead, present them successively as Gibbons A/B; Les Sacqueboutiers give us Gibbons A alone. Allied to Gibbons A/B in the sense that it usually circulated with them is the anonymous "Cries of London" (*CS* no. 68). However, this piece is not based on the *In nomine* cantus firmus, and on stylistic grounds is unlikely to be by Gibbons himself. For reasons explained later, it is cited below as the "Winter Cries"; there is a recording by Les Sacqueboutiers. Last comes the setting by Dering (*CS* no. 69), the longest and probably the latest of the group. It is cited below as Dering, and is recorded by Fretwork. *CS* presents the pieces in what Brett reckoned to be their possible chronological order. In his view, Long/Short Weelkes is the earliest, dating from "around 1599," and all the works were probably written "before 1615."[12]

Our best point of entry into this thicket is Long Weelkes. On paper, it looks like a song for solo voice with instruments, and Fretwork treat it that way. But there is a discrepancy here: the melodic line is inherently multivocal, a medley of cries by many different vendors and tradespeople. Fretwork transpose the line down an octave and make use of spatial effects to break up the chain of cries, but the solo tenor never varies his accent or delivery, and he ends up sounding like a jack-of-all-trades. No heed is paid to the closing words of the text, which point to a radically different solution. "White lettuce, white young lettuce!" sings the last of the vendors, followed by this coda: "Now let us sing, now let us sing; and so we make an end: with alleluia, with alleluia." There is an air of schoolboy humor about the pun on "lettuce"/"let us," but it also allows the coda to speak in the plural: "now let us sing." Then come the last two words, "with alleluia," which are incongruous and unexpected. Why are they there? One possible explanation is that the notation is misleading: not a song for solo voice, but rather, music for a cohort of singers who perform singly for the individual cries, then in unison for the coda. If so, then the words "with alleluia" allow the singers to unmask themselves: they are no longer street vendors; they are probably choirboys. Thomas Weelkes, composer of this piece, worked with boys throughout his adult career, first as organist of Winchester College (a school) from 1598, then as master of the choristers at Chichester Cathedral from 1601/2, and perhaps also as a Gentleman Extraordinary of the Chapel Royal, whose choristers were famous boy actors.[13] In any of those capacities, Weelkes would have been ideally placed to devise and even stage an entertainment in which choirboys impersonated vocalists of a quite different kind: the community of street traders.

Anon/Weelkes and Short Weelkes now need to be brought into play. Philip Brett reckoned Anon/Weelkes to be "modelled closely" on Short Weelkes and "of inferior workmanship," but he does not justify those views nor probe the reasons why these three interconnected works should coexist, so some pressing issues remain unexplained. Under what circumstances would somebody take the unorthodox step of either pruning or expanding an existing polyphonic work? Why would a wholly new piece then be "modelled closely" on the short version, giving rise to music "of inferior workmanship"? Exactly how do the members of the Weelkes group relate to one another?

Full responses to these questions must await an edition of Anon/Weelkes, but in the interim, the following points can be made. First, Anon/Weelkes differs from the other "Cries of London" in an important way: at least six of its street cries are passed imitatively from voice to voice in the manner of a catch or round.[14] This is how older polyphonic pieces based on street cries had behaved; each vendor is mimicked by two or more singers rather than by a solo voice.[15] But the later "Cries of London" for voices and consort do not do this. In Short/Long Weelkes, the street cries unfold sequentially on a single notated line, to be sung either by one solo voice or by a chain of soloists who unite at the end; Gibbons, Dering, and the "Winter Cries" avoid any polyphonic sharing of individual calls. If the imitative polyphony of Anon/Weelkes seems to take a step backward from Short/Long Weelkes, then we must ask if Anon/Weelkes might actually be earlier than them, and perhaps even the prototype of the whole genre. Not only are some of its cries delivered polyphonically, but the whole piece is also densely textured, giving it the effect of a consort fantasia that just happens to be studded with some street cries.

At this point, the relationship of Anon/Weelkes to Short Weelkes needs to be assessed. These two pieces are copied side by side in GB-Lbl Add. MSS 18936–9, which is their only extant source; the manuscript is cited below as Aldhouse. One of these settings must indeed be "modelled closely" on the other, because their selection of street cries is almost identical, and delivered in virtually the same order. Brett assumed that one composer borrowed from another, which is indeed possible, but there is also a chance that both settings are actually by Weelkes himself; Aldhouse is a significant source of Weelkes's music, containing early states of some pieces he subsequently revised for publication.[16] Either way, however, it is tempting to reverse Brett's chronology, and to view the semimadrigalian fantasia of Anon/Weelkes as having been radically refashioned to create the more declamatory Short Weelkes—which, in turn, was expanded into Long Weelkes by adding two new passages of further calls, including that of the town crier. Such reworkings, if that is what they are, look very much like a project in progress, as if someone were refining and developing a successful concept, such as a choirboy entertainment.[17]

The three members of the Weelkes group have one thing in common: they are all medleys without inbuilt elements of drama. No real attempt is made to evoke the nature of a street-vending scene, and instead, the cries are delivered in tidy groups arranged by genre: first the fishmongers, then the fruit vendors, then the pie sellers, and so on.[18] Anon/Weelkes ends by signaling nightfall with the words of the night watchman ("Maids in your smocks, look well to your locks, your fire and your light, and so goodnight"), but Long Weelkes actually steps away from the streets for its punning coda, and Short Weelkes probably did the same. (In Aldhouse, its final words have been deliberately missed out, as if unwanted for the purpose this copy was meant to serve.) If the "Cries of London" were indeed conceived as semidramatic works, then we might reckon the composer(s) of the Weelkes group to have missed a trick. What, then, of their successors?

There is much to ponder in the setting(s) by Gibbons. Echoes of the Weelkes group are to be heard everywhere, most obviously in the selection of street cries: a large number of them were used by Weelkes, sometimes with identical words and melodies, to the extent that one wonders if Gibbons is sometimes intentionally quoting from Weelkes, not from the streets.[19] A major departure, however, is that Gibbons A and B are both built on the *In nomine* cantus firmus, which is played continuously in long notes in the middle of the texture. This might have been done to show the composer's dexterity in combining street cries with plainchant; but it is equally possible that the *In nomines* are there to remind us of that genre's long association with choirboy pedagogy, a link that would be especially apt if Gibbons A/B too were written with boy performers in mind. Unlike Weelkes, Gibbons has put street cries into all five of the polyphonic parts, so that low broken voices are needed as well as high trebles. The cries are now largely jumbled together rather than grouped by type, and they also sometimes sing over one another, as if to mimic the reality of the streets; thus one vendor will sell salt while another sells a dish of eels, and so on.[20] But Gibbons has also struck on the bright idea of what David Pinto calls "tracing the passage of dawn to dusk."[21] The outcome, though not exactly drama, adds structure and form where Weelkes had none.

That being said, the effectiveness of Gibbons partly depends upon performance decisions reached about its unstable text. Not only are the two halves reversible and separable; hands other than Gibbons's have tampered with this piece, changing or adding extra street cries, and even extending Gibbons A with a large chunk of new music that has no right to be there—the "Chandler insert" transcribed by Brett in *CS* page 126. The performance by Fretwork accepts almost all of these contaminations, and also presents the two halves in what is arguably their less successful order (A/B); the results may be remote from what Gibbons had in mind. The performance by Les Sacqueboutiers, which is of Gibbons A only, without Chandler or the spurious extra cries, sidesteps the question of how A and B might interrelate. In the absence of a recording, words alone must serve to present a different reading.

If Gibbons B is placed before Gibbons A and the spurious material excised, then there are several definite gains to be had. First, the piece begins with one of the best jokes in early music: the start of what seems to be an earnest *In nomine* is plunged into bathos as a solo treble sings the immortal words "A good sausage, a good, and it be roasted." There follows a medley of street cries, ending as Anon/Weelkes had done with the call of the night watchman. Its first three lines are sung solo, watchman-like, after which the other voices join in for the last line, "and so goodnight." Here the piece might have ended, inviting applause—but not if it plunges quickly into Gibbons A. The watchman now announces daybreak with the words "God give you good morrow, my masters, past three o'clock and a fair morning," and a new medley of street cries unfolds, with no repetition of those already heard in Gibbons B. The last of them is a different watchman's call: "Lanthorn and candlelight, hang out, maids, for all night." There follows a formal close, sung by all five voices in madrigalian fashion: "And so we make an end, and so we make an end." As in Long Weelkes, the singers might remove their masks here and become themselves.

Where, when, and for whom could Gibbons have composed this work? Its polyphony is unsophisticated—little effort was needed to combine street cries with the *In nomine* plainsong, the notes of which are often divided—and this, plus its alliance to the *In nomine* genre, might imply that Gibbons was or had recently been a chorister when he wrote this piece. Gibbons was of humble birth. His father, William Gibbons, was a municipal and university wait, employed variously in Cambridge and Oxford, and seems to have played wind instruments, specifically the "tenor hoeboye" or shawm.[22] The link with the waits is interesting, but the main issue here is that of class: Orlando Gibbons's origins as the son of a city wait did not place him significantly higher in the social order than the street vendors he portrays in his "Cries of London." So the question arises: need Gibbons's "Cries" have been made for the eyes and ears of a "court audience bored with the grandiloquent madrigal and eager to share vicariously in the rough-and-tumble of common life," as Philip Brett suggests, or might it derive from another facet of Gibbons's career? Is a "patronizing tone ... never far from the surface" in this work? These are guesses, and they could be far from the truth.

No composer's name is attached to the "Winter Cries" (*CS* no. 68)—a regrettable loss, because this fine and fascinating work might have been more easily understood within the frame of a biography. It opens with a spoof on the call of the town crier, a figure who features prominently in Long Weelkes and Gibbons A but not in their likely predecessors Anon/Weelkes and Short Weelkes. Normally, the crier seeks news of a lost horse, but this time, his quest is for "a little maiden child about the age of six, or seven ... and forty," for which there is a reward of fourpence, "and that's more than she's worth." Street cries follow; they include vendors of "fine Seville oranges," which are in season in winter, and of "white Saint Thomas onions" (the feast of St. Thomas the Apostle falls on December 21), but there is no mention of summer fruit such as strawberries. At the center of the piece, something happens that has no equivalent in any of the other settings: some of the criers briefly interact with one another. The scene is the river; boatmen vie for trade, and a customer chooses between them. This exchange invites action, perhaps even the theatrical use of space:

[first boatman]: Will you go with oars, sir, will you go with oars?
[second boatman]: Will you go with a sculler, sir?
[first oarsman]: I am your first man, sir, will you go with oars?
[customer]: I will go with oars.
[first boatman]: George, George, George, George, bring the boat to the stairs.

The work's crowning glory, however, is its ending. "Wassail, wassail, jolly wassail!" sings the treble; "Master and mistress, if you be within, call for some of your merry men to rise and let us in, with our wassail, our jolly wassail." A five-voice chorus then closes the piece: "Joy come to our jolly wassail, our jolly wassail!" The intended function of this ending is unclear. Does it merely evoke a wassail, or do the singers here cast off their masks (as at the end of Long Weelkes) and address the audience as themselves, as part of a midwinter entertainment? Either way, there are two important details to note here. First, the wassailers are by implication outside while the company they address is "within"; this again invites the use of theatrical space. Second, the company is headed by a "master and mistress." There is no suggestion here of a "court audience." So for whom could such a work have been made?

Possibilities abound. One of them emerges from the text of an entertainment made for use at St. John's College, Oxford, on Twelfth Night 1603; it brings to an end a sequence of dramatic entertainments in rhyme composed specifically for that year's Christmas festivities, and it would have been performed in the college hall before an audience comprising the president, fellows, and their guests. The task of introducing the wassailers fell to the college porter, who spoke the following words to the assembled company:

> If youl have any sporte, then say ye woord
> Heere come youths of ye parish yat will it affoord
> They are heere hard by comminge alonge
> Crowning their wassaile bowle with a songe . . .
> I am your porter & your vassaile
> Shall I lett in ye boyes with their wassaile
> Say: they are at doore to sing they beginne
> Go to then, ile goe & lett them in. /
>   Enter ye wassaile, two of them bearinge ye bowle, & singinge ye songe & all of them bearing ye burden[23]

A different kind of context was documented forty years earlier by Henry Machyn, parish clerk at the church of Little Trinity in the City of London, who compiled a detailed chronicle of civic events in the central decades of the sixteenth century. It refers to a midsummer festivity, and is therefore seasonally remote from the "Winter Cries," but its explicit mention of musicians playing and singing before one of London's foremost livery companies (the Grocers) and their guests is relevant and noteworthy:

> The xvj day of June was the masters the Grossers fest; there dynyd my lord mare, [then a list of named men], and mony worshephull men and mony lades and gentyll women; and grett chere; boyth the whettes [waits] and clarkes syngyng, and a nombur of vyolles playhyng, and syngyng. . . .[24]

Here is rare documentation of apparently two different vocal/instrumental ensembles performing at a feast: first, the waits and parish clerks (loosely equivalent to the forces used by Les Sacqueboutiers but all male), then a consort of voices and viols (as used by Fretwork, and again likely to be all male). Records such as this and the one from St. John's alert us to the fact that there were many different types of performing context where the "Cries of London" repertory might have been welcomed. The royal court was only one of them.

After the "Winter Cries," Richard Dering's "Cries of London" offers meager fare to the historian, partly because the piece contains so little that is not present in the other settings, partly because its composer's life is too thinly documented to hint at the work's origin and function. Dering seems to have taken most of his street cries from the Weelkes group or Gibbons A/B, and bulked the piece out with street songs in rhyming verse that more probably come from his own imagination than from the streets themselves.[25] The following is representative:

> Garlic, good garlic, the best of all the Cries;
> it is the only physic against all maladies;
> it is my chiefest wealth good garlic for to cry,
> and if you love your health, my garlic then come buy![26]

Similar tableaux are found in Dering's matching "Country Cries" (*CS* no. 70), and they give the impression that Dering has tried to develop the picturesque genre established by his elders by means of extension. But otherwise, he attempts little real novelty, and his London "Cries" remains a medley, with barely any marking of the passage of time, no dialogue, and no implied actions. Thus the last of the "Cries of London" tells us nothing we did not already know. Here, the repertory runs out; as the final chorus of Dering puts it, "and so goodnight."

What exactly has the present study achieved? Little by way of locating hard facts. It hazards some guesses at questions posed at its start, but frankly, we remain in the dark about the *why*, *where*, *when*, and *to whom* of every piece in the "Cries of London" repertory, and probably always will, unless explicit documentary evidence should come to light. Its main achievement is therefore to have muddied the waters, by cautioning against linking these works too securely with any single function or context or place of origin. Nothing in them demands that they be connected with royalty, nobility, or court, and in truth, they could have been written for all manner of unsuspected uses. The "Cries of London" repertory could well have appealed to a "court audience bored with the grandiloquent madrigal and eager to share vicariously in the rough-and-tumble of common life," but its true roots may lie elsewhere.

Who would have first performed these works? This study makes a case for boy choristers, at least for Short/Long Weelkes and possibly for the entire repertory. London's choirboys were among the most trained and talented actors in England,

and the "Cries" themselves invite acting, movement, masking, and disguising. As for instruments, the extant manuscript sources imply viols, a view promoted by modern opinion, and viols were definitely played by choirboys; however, these soft-toned instruments might have been too quiet for larger spaces with rowdier audiences. In addition, viols have implicit links with education, gentility, and refinement, making them strange bedfellows with street cries. The same is not true of shawms, cornetts, sackbuts, and violins, which are the instruments of the waits, and therefore the instruments of the streets and theaters.[27] To perform the "Cries of London" with viols, as Fretwork do, may be true to the spirit of the surviving manuscripts, but if these works did indeed cross boundaries from origins elsewhere, then the sound world of Les Sacqueboutiers may in fact come closer to hitting the mark.

Finally, some thoughts about intentions: How were these works meant to be received when they were new? Is "a patronizing tone . . . never far from the surface"? Do Weelkes, Gibbons, and the rest really portray their street criers "with some condescension"? An alternative view is that these works are really burlesques of genres, not of people. They take the genres of the verse anthem and the consort song and eject their usual vocalists, replacing them instead with raucous vendors and tradesmen—a carnivalesque travesty that is cleverly reversed at the end of Long Weelkes by the words "with alleluia." Perhaps, then, these "Cries of London" ask their audiences to laugh with the criers rather than at them. The street cries themselves are never parodied (though the town crier does say some ridiculous things), and even the putative street songs in Dering are neither patronizing nor condescending.[28] The instrumental parts carry their polyphony lightly—so lightly, in fact, that we might ask if the juxtaposition of fantasia with street cries is really so much ironic as incongruous. Thus the real wit of these works, at least from an early listener's perspective, may have lain in the fact that so many boundaries are being crossed here. Noise becomes art; outdoors becomes indoors; social classes are traversed; and the genres of consort song and verse anthem, conventionally sites for serious thoughts, are quite literally dragged down to the level of the streets.

Notes

1. In their earliest sources, these works bear titles that do not necessarily emanate from the composers themselves; they include "The Crie of London," "Cryes of London," "The [second etc.] London Crie," and "The Citty Cryes." The works are here collectively called the "Cries of London" repertory.

2. *The Cries of London*, performed by Theatre of Voices and Fretwork (Harmonia Mundi HMU 907214; rec 2005); booklet notes by David Pinto.

3. *The Cries of London*, performed by Les Sacqueboutiers (Ambroisie AMB 9965; rec 2004); booklet notes by Philippe Canguilhem.

4. Many of the ideas explored in this chapter were first aired in oral presentations delivered in 2008 to the Viola da Gamba Society of Great Britain in Oxford, United Kingdom, and at the York Early Music Festival in York, United Kingdom. I am grateful to members of the audiences on these two occasions for their comments and suggestions, several of which have been incorporated and developed here.

5. Brett, ed., *Consort Songs*.

6. For details of the manuscripts, their copyists, owners, and functions, see Monson, *Voices and Viols in England*.

7. *CS*, xvi.

8. Booklet notes for Les Sacqueboutiers, 21.

9. Booklet notes for Fretwork, 5.

10. *CS*, 184.

11. A reconstruction by the present author is in preparation, to be published by Fretwork Editions.

12. *CS*, xvi. None of the pieces can be dated more precisely than this. Estimated dates of 1599 for Weelkes and Dering, 1614 for Gibbons, and ca. 1614 for the "Winter Cries" by Smith in *The Acoustic World*, 64, are unexplained and misleading.

13. Katherine Steele Brokaw also addresses the fluidity of performance between choirboy and actor from the mid-Tudor era in "Tudor Musical Theater," this volume. By 1600, the renowned troupe of boy actors that had emerged from the Chapel Royal choir had become a commercial venture with a rather loose relationship to the actual chapel and its choristers; see Austern, *Music in English Children's Drama*, 7–10; Gibson, *Squeaking Cleopatras*, 161–173; Lamb, *Performing Childhood*, 61–65; Shapiro, *Children of the Revels*, 24–29; and Wallace, "Children of the Chapel at Blackfriars."

14. This number is calculated on the basis of the four extant voice parts of Anon/Weelkes. Tentative reconstruction of the missing voice part suggests that it, too, shared street cries with the other voices.

15. Distant precedents would include Clément Janequin's "Les Cris de Paris," in which four singers deliver the words but not obviously the melodic contours of street vendors. Models closer to home would include (1) the anonymous and fragmentary St. Cuthbert's Day song from Durham, discussed in Milsom, "Cries of Durham"; (2) the anonymous three-voice round "New Oysters," first recorded in the Lant roll of 1580 (GB-Ckc Rowe MS 1), edited in Morehen and Mateer, *Thomas Ravenscroft: Rounds, Canons and Songs*, 7; (3) the anonymous four-voice "Cony Skines Maydes," copied by John Sadler in GB-Ob Mus. e. 1–5; no modern edition.

16. GB-Lbl Add. MSS 18936–9; discussed in Monson, "Thomas Weelkes: A New Fa-la," 133–135.

17. Short/Long Weelkes include a component that is absent from Anon/Weelkes: a "street song" that may actually derive from the theater rather than the streets. "Have you any boots, maids" in Short/Long Weelkes (*CS* no. 66, mm. 148–155) is a cognate of the song delivered by the character Conscience in R[obert] W[ilson], *A Right Excellent and Famous Comoedy Called the Three Ladies of London* (1584), sig. D4r; this connection was first noted in Bridge, *The Old Cryes*, 27.

18. It is possible that the order of the criers in the Weelkes group broadly corresponds to the daily timetable of street vending, though the settings themselves do not specify this.

19. This raises a vexed question: did early modern street vendors and traders use fixed and invariant calls, or did the composers of the "Cries of London" repertory borrow from one another? The first interpretation is preferred by Bridge, *The Old Cryes*, 25. For a useful tabulation of all quoted material in the "Cries of London" repertory, arranged by category of crier, see Sargent, *Oyez! Elizabethan and Jacobean Street Cries*; its transcriptions derive from Brett's *CS* editions.

20. The same effect is achieved in the four-voice round "Brooms for Old Shoes," the earliest source of which dates from 1611; modern edition in *Ravenscroft: Rounds, Canons and Songs*, 104.

21. Booklet notes for Fretwork, 6.

22. Harley, *Orlando Gibbons*, 5–14.

23. Elliott, Nelson, Johnston, and Wyall, *Records of Early English Drama: Oxford*, vol. 1, 269.

24. Machyn, *The Diary of Henry Machyn*, 260.

25. For an alternative view, see Bridge, *The Old Cryes*, 46–51, which assumes that the tradesmen's songs in Dering have their origins in oral culture. The truth may never be known.

26. *CS* no. 69, mm. 145–146.

27. For summary information about waits, see most recently Marsh, *Music and Society*, 115–130. Collaborations between the waits and London's companies of child actors are discussed in Austern, *Music in English Children's Drama*, 24–25 and 61–76.

28. The same is true of the various etched and woodcut images of street vendors that were published in single-sheet format during the seventeenth century; they represent the criers in a neutral way, without caricature or comment. The target market for these sheets is unknown. None of them can be dated precisely; all extant copies seem to belong to the second half of the century. Images of a selection of them can be accessed on the British Museum's website, via the tags "Research" and "Collections," using the search term "cries." One of these sheets, "Made and Sold by Richard Newton," includes verses that loosely resemble the street songs featured so prominently in Dering. For a reproduction of the top of this sheet, see Shesgreen and Bywaters, "The First London Cries for Children," 228; the lower portion of the sheet can be viewed on the British Museum's website using the search term "Richard Newton."

6.

"Locks, Bolts, Barres, and Barricados": Song Performance, Gender, and Spatial Production in Richard Brome's The Northern Lass

Katherine R. Larson

Song is integral to Richard Brome's *The Northern Lass* (1629), which was performed to great acclaim by the King's Men at the Globe and Blackfriars theaters, and restaged and reprinted into the eighteenth century.[1] The play is not unique among Caroline dramatic works in featuring song as a structural device.[2] It stands out, however, for its attention to the spatial dimensions of early modern song performance and, in particular, to the question of how gender shapes the settings framing—and framed by—the songs sung by Brome's musical protagonists. As he charts the movements of his characters through the streets and households of London, Brome both elides and reimagines ostensible architectural and sociocultural boundaries. In doing so, he establishes a vital interplay between musical self-expression and spatial production.

The Northern Lass hinges on a mix-up between two women named Constance, both of whom are singers: Brome's titular heroine and Constance Holdup, introduced in the dramatis personae as a "cunning Whore."[3] When the virtuous Constance sends a letter to her presumed betrothed, Sir Philip Luckless, soliciting his favor, he assumes the missive is a request from Holdup seeking support for her "Bastard" (1.4.246). He denounces Constance and expedites his marriage to the widow Mistress Fitchow to avoid further entreaties. In response, Brome's lovesick northern lass falls into a melancholy-induced madness. The comic denouement again relies on the confusion of these characters as Holdup's impersonation of the melancholic Constance paves the way for Luckless's divorce from

Fitchow and his reunion with his beloved. Musical settings of three of the songs performed by Constance and one by Holdup are extant, attributed to John Wilson.[4] The play's popularity is also attested to by the songs composed for new print editions and by several ballads centering on the northern lass.[5]

The Northern Lass repeatedly enacts song's ability spatially to construct social relationships. As such, it constitutes a useful case study for considering music's role in negotiating and even dissolving seemingly fixed boundaries in the early modern context. This essay will explore these issues by focusing on three pivotal scenes that use song to reconfigure the domestic spaces framing them and that depict musical boundary making (and unmaking) in explicitly gendered terms: Constance's first song performance in act 2, scene 3; Holdup's impersonation of Constance in act 4, scene 4; and the misogynist song performed by Widgin and his friends in act 3, scene 3. Song emerges in *The Northern Lass* as a powerful mechanism for spatial and sociocultural mediation, one that holds particular ramifications for Brome's female protagonists.

Sounding Space in Early Modern England

The interrelationship between sound and space is dynamic and potentially transformative. Location and setting tend to determine the nature and the scope of the sounds produced within particular boundaries. If space holds a powerful capacity to delimit sound, however, sound likewise can alter spatial and social parameters. Spaces—and the perceived boundaries between them—are shaped moment by moment by their inhabitants even as those inhabitants are shaped by the spaces they occupy.[6] Sound, however, is a tricky spatial phenomenon. It overflows the boundaries that seemingly delimit it and penetrates walls and bodies in unexpected ways. Judith Butler has traced the "insurrectionary" force of non-normative sounds and gestures introduced into spatial and social settings.[7] Such interventions, she argues, can "jam the machinery" of those sites, thereby redrawing their boundaries.[8] Butler locates a similarly disruptive force in the excess of the sounding body, accentuating the inability wholly to command the signification and impact of one's gestures and language: "No act of speech can fully control or determine the rhetorical effects of the body which speaks."[9] Her approach provides a valuable lens through which to consider how song—the product of the body as instrument—might create and reconstitute seemingly fixed boundaries.

Song's affective potential was certainly recognized in early modern England. Sound was believed to act directly on the body as the vibrating air generated by singer or instrument penetrated the vulnerable ear of the listener.[10] Song was understood to be an especially powerful medium, its union of text and tune equally capable of seducing hearers or elevating them to the divine. This rhetorical spectrum underscores the cultural ambivalence associated with song performance, an ambivalence regularly articulated in gendered terms. On one level, music was lauded as a marker of good breeding, integral to educational precepts aimed at preparing young gentlemen for public roles and gentlewomen for the marriage market. At the same time, its association with seduction, sensuality, and effeminacy posed risks for performer and listener alike.[11] The conflation of the female singer with the siren, a paradoxical figure represented in the period as a celestial deity responsible for the music of the spheres and as a singing seductress, exemplifies this tension.[12] If music was understood as an emblem of universal, sociopolitical, and physiological harmony—that is, a marker of well-ordered boundaries—the performing body activated music's "insurrectionary" force.[13]

Sixteenth- and seventeenth-century spatial practices likewise resist straightforward—and straightforwardly gendered—demarcation. Recent work in literary studies has helped to trouble the limiting binaries of private/feminine and public/masculine space in the period, charting the movements and rhetorical interventions of men and women within and through an array of indoor and outdoor settings.[14] Early moderns recognized the moderating effects of spatial boundaries on acoustic production. The sonic and gestural rules touted by prescriptive writers were carefully tailored to setting: "I know not," declares Castiglione's Unico, "who is so fonde to go about his fence, whan the rest be in their musicke: or to go about the streetes daunsing the Morisco, though he could do it never so well."[15] Other documents suggest a correlation between location, choice of musical activity, and even musical genre. Samuel Pepys, whose musical proclivities were such that he converted his "Wardrobe" into a "room for Musique," includes tantalizing spatial details in his accounts of his musical pastimes.[16] He describes singing catches and other songs at clubs and taverns, and retiring to his bedchamber to sing psalms, record songs in manuscript notebooks, and dabble in music theory. He also frequently gathered with family and friends to sing after dinner, both in his own house and when visiting others.[17] Thomas Morley provides further evidence of the centrality of song in dining spaces in *A Plaine and Easie Introduction to Practicall Musicke*, when Philomathes recounts his embarrassment at being presented with a partbook at a dinner party and being unable to sight sing.[18]

In practice, however, songs moved fluidly across spatial boundaries, obscuring divisions of gender and class. Men and women came together in the home to sing part-songs and lute songs made popular by commercial theater performances and court entertainments. Psalms were sung in churches, streets, and closets.[19] Ballads and bawdy catches were hawked in urban and rural areas and performed in taverns as well as in domestic settings across the social spectrum. Vocal genres also evinced a powerful capacity to complicate and even reshape the boundaries of their settings, as recent interventions in musicology and literary studies are beginning to illuminate. Linda Austern, for instance, has shown how all-male musical gatherings within the home fostered communal identity and reinforced masculine authority within and beyond the household.[20] Sandra Clark and Bruce Smith, meanwhile, have explored how the ballad's flexible "I" enabled women to experiment with new subject positions and critique gender and social hierarchies.[21]

Such musical acts—and the resultant spaces they generated or reshaped—were often short-lived. Yet song's transience does not detract from its performative force. It is precisely the fleeting and untamable elements of music, so often overlooked in formal analysis, that account for its affective impact.[22] If early modern song was shaped by the contexts of its production and circulation, it also constituted a rhetorical medium that, in performance, held the capacity to disrupt, dissolve, and shift—however briefly—the seemingly rigid boundaries of those sites. In so doing, song laid claim to new spaces of social encounter.

The Musical Spaces of Richard Brome

Richard Brome's extant dramatic works reveal a level of interest in space and location unusual even within what has been termed the "place-realism" vogue of the Caroline period.[23] Writing from the unique perspective of a former servant (Brome worked for Ben Jonson), he also interrogates the relationship between social and geographical positioning. In *The Antipodes* (1638), for instance, Brome imagines an *"AntiLondon"* that satirizes early modern English hierarchies through a fantastical travel narrative.[24] Above all, Brome was "fascinated by the dynamic possibilities of space and place and the ways in which geography can be contested and manipulated."[25] If drama constituted a key mode whereby early moderns expressed and experimented with spatial practice, Brome's works exemplify this phenomenon.[26]

Song is central to Brome's crafting of social and architectural space. In *A Jovial Crew* (1641–1642), the last of his plays printed during his lifetime, Brome uses song as a sonic framework for the barn the beggars occupy on Oldrents's estate. The beggars' music provides ironic commentary on early modern class divisions, at once romanticizing their antics and masking their hardship. In one memorable scene, the crew sings loudly to cover up the screams of a beggar woman in labor: "'tis their Custome," Randall explains to Oldrents as they hover anxiously outside the barn, "With songs and shouts to drown the woman's cries. / A Ceremony which they use, not for / Devotion, but to keep off Notice of / The Work, they have in hand."[27] *A Jovial Crew* remained popular into the eighteenth century in large part because of its singing beggars; it was adapted into a comic opera in 1731.[28]

This musical-spatial interplay is most fully realized in *The Northern Lass*, one of Brome's early triumphs and a work that has received surprisingly little critical attention.²⁹ Audiences were enamored with the music of the northern lass's voice, understood both terms of her songs and her northern dialect:

> Shee came out of the cold North, thinly clad. But *Wit* had pitty on her; *Action* apparrell'd her, and *Plaudits* clap'd her cheekes warme. Shee is honest, and modest, though she speake broad: And though *Art* never strung her tongue; yet once it yeelded a delightfull sound, which gain'd her many Lovers and Friends, by whose good liking she prosperously lived. (sig. A2r-v)

Brome's commendation of the lass's "delightfull sound" in this dedicatory epistle signals the play's preoccupation with the singing and speaking voice as a marker of location and identity. The northern lass's voice is a remarkably consistent signifier in the midst of the play's mix-ups and disguises. It is her singing which prompts her uncle to recognize her in act 2, when she appears as a masque performer: "The Womans voice had much in't like my Neece" (2.6.1207). Holdup's impersonation of Constance hinges on her ability to mimic her sound, exemplified by Fitchow's confident "recognition" of Holdup-as-Constance: "I know it is shee by her tongue, though I never heard her before" (5.7.2668).

Brome's conflation of Constance's musicality and her geographical dislocation also invites her audience to read her as a potentially contradictory character, intensifying the ambivalence registered by the female singer and by musical performance in the period. Northern English registered a fraught relationship between language and national identity.³⁰ Constance's dialect situates her as pure and honest—she is introduced as a "Virgin, of a most hopefull goodnesse" (1.5.320–321)—but also as Other. Her foreignness, however, also contributes to her sexual appeal. Before Constance makes her first appearance in act 2, Mistress Fitchow, hoping to secure a match between Constance and her brother Widgin, commends the lass in precisely these terms: "[She] sings, and speakes so pretty northernly they say" (2.1.714). Widgin's eager reply, meanwhile, transforms Constance into an acoustic commodity as he imagines her as a new addition to his ballad collection: "I have a great many Southerne songs already. But Northern ayres nips it dead. *Yorke Yorke* for my money" (2.1.731–732). By using dialect and song to accentuate Constance's displacement and attractiveness, Brome places the question of how spatial boundaries, musical expression, and gender inform each other at the heart of his play.

Brome's portrayal of his northern lass is complicated by the sonic and geographical slippage between the two Constances. For the audience, Fitchow's approbation of the virtuous northern lass would be difficult to dissociate from Sir Luckless's act 1 tirade against Constance, whose letter he has mistaken for Holdup's. Luckless does not refer explicitly to Holdup's singing voice here, but he clearly has music on his mind as he laments her exclusion from a satirical ballad, "Cupid's Muster": "*Constance!* shee had a Bastard tother day too. What a mischievous Maw has this shee Caniball that gapes for mee! Slight a common trader, with I know not how many! I marvell she was left out of *Cupids* Muster. Sure shee bribd the Ballat-maker" (1.1.246–249). Positioned alongside a ballad that likely offered a musical catalog of London prostitutes, the threat of Holdup's gaping "Maw" evokes both her genitalia and the open mouth of a singer.[31] Before either Constance appears on stage, therefore, Brome uses music—and the ballad genre in particular—to trouble the boundaries that normally would render them distinct foils: north/south, rural/urban, virgin/whore. The line between "pretty" singing and the threatening "Maw[s]" of "Cupids Muster" could be dangerously thin.

Relocating Song in *The Northern Lass*

Constance's acoustic presence is substantiated immediately after Fitchow and Widgin's interchange about her voice. Her first appearance, in act 2, scene 3, also features her first song performance. The scene takes place in the home of Constance's uncle Squelch, where she is living. At this point in the play, Beavis (a servant to Constance's governess) has tricked Anvil (Widgin's governor) into visiting the house by implying that it is in fact the brothel out of which Holdup operates. As he enters, Anvil's assumptions about the space shape his first impressions, comically revealing the disparity between Constance's residence and the places of ill repute Anvil has visited in the past:

> A place of fair promising! How have I liv'd that never discover'd this place before? This place royall! But sought my recreation in by-lanes, and sluttish corners, unsavory Allies and Ditch-sides? when here the whole house is perfum'd: An Earle might thinke it his owne lodging. (2.3.818–822)

The arrival of Constance's governess, Mistress Trainwell, does nothing to dispel his illusions. Ironically, her horrified response only serves to highlight the power that his preconceptions have to shape his interpretation of the building he has entered: "If you can imagine what you are, where you are, what you would have, or where you would be, I pray tell mee sir" (2.3.840–842).

Constance's singing at first seems to reify these imagined boundaries. She appears above in her "Chamber" (2.2.813), confiding her feelings for Luckless in what, she assumes, is a musical soliloquy. This is the first of several moments in the play that testify to the importance of song as a privileged mode of self-expression for Constance. Here, however, Brome's spatial positioning of Constance relative to Anvil—although both are visible to the audience, she is in a separate room, and he overhears her from below—combined with Anvil's expectations about his location, transforms the impact of Constance's performance: "Sweet prologue to the insuing Interlude!" (2.3.913), he proclaims, "Shee has rais'd my desire above her noates. Why am I thus ravishd, and yet delayd?" (2.3.916–917). Constance's musical disclosure of her love for Luckless results in double signification, as her lovesickness collides with Anvil's sexualized misinterpretation of her performance. Anvil figures her music as a quintessential seduction.

The effect is comic, but the scene is important not only in confirming the slippage between Constance and Holdup that has, to this point, been implicit, but also in underscoring the powerful—and powerfully gendered—interworkings of music and space in the play. Constance's song is spatially delimited from the rest of the scene. This is reinforced not only by her physical separation from Anvil but also by Anvil's verbal framing of the performance in terms of the imagined boundaries of the brothel. "There is no government under the Sunne, like the politique government of a Bawdy-house" (2.3.902–903), he pronounces before Constance begins to sing. Playing on early modern analogies that likened the structure of the household to the structure of the state, the statement ironically evokes the careful maintenance of domestic, physical, and civic boundaries; the word *government* last appeared in act 1 in reference to Constance's well-regulated upbringing (1.5.320). Anvil echoes himself at the end of the scene—"The politique government of this little common wealth!" (2.3.932)—placing spatial markers around Constance's performance.

Anvil's preconceived notions of "place"—the word appears three times in his speech that opens the scene—are crucial in shaping his reaction to the song, but Constance's performance literalizes the brief transformation of Squelch's home from place into space, house to brothel. Her song goes so far as to emblematize the sexual encounter Anvil came to the house to experience. Her ecstasy mirrors his as she is transported by the *"divine"* beauty of Luckless's *"shape"*: *"I can find more ods / 'Twixt him and others then I can, / find betweene him and Gods"* (2.3.904–912). John Wilson's musical setting (musical example 6.1) reinforces her naïve longing through its simple harmonies and predominantly major mode. Even in her melancholy, Constance's music remains remarkably hopeful, though the interesting tension in the piece between duple and triple time arguably hints at her inner torment.

From the audience's perspective, however, the scene showcases the manipulative and destabilizing potential of song. Witnessing Constance's performance, they experience multiple spaces at once—Squelch's house, as well as the imagined brothel—and a song that conveys Constance's yearning while also playing into every stereotype of the period concerning the sensuality of women's musical performances. These two levels of signification operate to some degree independently, but they cohere in the figure of Constance. Although Brome's lovesick heroine emerges from this scene still virtuous, her singing body is nonetheless marked by the sensual and erotic effects of Anvil's recontextualization and the articulation of her own desire.

Brome further capitalizes on song's ability to elide boundaries and reconstitute new spaces in his musical conflation of Constance and Holdup. Constance confides her feelings for Sir Luckless again through song later in act 2, witnessed

Some Say My Love is Butt a Man

Richard Brome
John Wilson

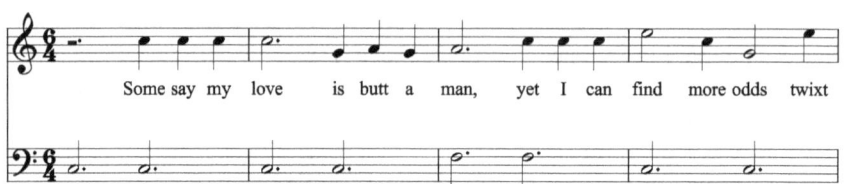

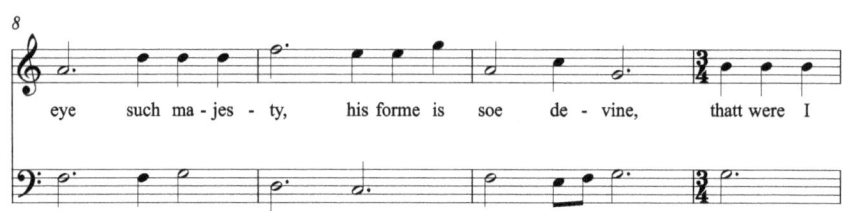

Musical Example 6.1 "Some Say My Love Is Butt a Man," by John Wilson. Transcribed from NYp Drexel MS 4041, fol. 10r.

by Luckless himself as she performs, disguised, in a household masque. As she descends further into melancholy, beginning in act 3, she turns increasingly to song to express her emotional deterioration.[32] Holdup's song performance in act 4, scene 4, taps into Constance's favored mode of communication and the musical manifestation of her melancholy as she strives to replicate her counterpart's "fit" (4.3.2179). Brome's conflation of Constance-as-singer and as-whore reaches its apex at this point. Structurally, the scene mirrors Constance's first musical appearance in act 2. It takes place in the house of one of Squelch's tenants, where Squelch is keeping Holdup (disguised as his niece) for his own pleasure. Once again, a man—Widgin in this case—enters under false pretenses, tricked into thinking that he is about to meet his hoped-for betrothed, the balladeering northern lass, to help heal her melancholy. Unlike Constance, however, Holdup is a knowing participant in this deception. The spatial workings of this scene play out very differently as a result, accentuating the performativity of her encounter with Widgin and his resultant humiliation.

In the brothel scene, Anvil remains distanced from Constance by his misinterpretation of the setting, Constance's song contained—even as it is transformed—by his commentary on the "government" of the supposed bawdy house. Holdup, too, is initially separated from her audience; the stage directions note that she is concealed behind a "*hanging*" (4.3.2180, stage direction). Here, however, spatial demarcation serves to accentuate the self-consciousness of her role-play. The house becomes, in effect, a theater. Before Holdup withdraws, she announces her transformation: "They come most fitly, and *I* must into my fit" (4.3.2178–2179).[33] She appears, as planned, first mimicking the throes of childbirth and then singing a lullaby, "Peace Wayward Barne," to her baby. At this point, Widgin actually enters Holdup's performance space, bringing the illusion created by her impersonation and his misperception of the situation into direct contact. Tapping into the notion that lovesickness could be cured by sexual intimacy with the beloved, Widgin addresses Holdup immediately after she has finished her lullaby, pretending to be Sir Philip and promising her marriage. The consummation of their relationship is confirmed in act 5, when Widgin boasts to his sister that he "phillipt her" (5.7.2694).

As in the brothel scene, song plays a crucial role in delimiting the space of their encounter. Most significantly, Brome makes music integral to the performative force of their marriage vows, as Holdup and Widgin woo each other with fragments of songs:

> **Hol.** *Marry mee, marry mee, quoth the bonny Lasse; and when will you beginne.*
> **Wid.** *As for thy Wedding Lasse wee'll do ewell* [sic] *enough in, spight o'the best o'thy Kinne.* (4.4.2258–2261)

Later, confiding the consummation of the relationship to his sister, Widgin again resorts to song to convey the "*delight*" of the moment (5.7.2698). Widgin, however, fails to recognize the spatial performativity of Holdup's songs, overestimating as a result his own ability to maintain control either of Holdup or of the presumed boundaries framing their musical exchange. He sees his impersonation of Sir Philip within the space created by Holdup's melancholy ballads as transient, and securely delimited by the circumstances: "Shee may perhaps, when shee comes to her selfe, and finds me to be no sir *Phillip*, be a little startled" (4.4.2311–2312). It is he, however, who is astonished to discover that he has in fact married a whore.

While the scene literalizes the sexualization and seductive potential of the female singing body introduced in the brothel mix-up, it is important to note that Holdup's songs, like Constance's earlier in the play, offer a poignant commentary on her own circumstances. As such, her impersonation further complicates the interplay between the domestic space in which Squelch maintains her and the boundaries established by the deliberate staging of her ballads, also situating her performance as private lament. Matthew Steggle persuasively reads Holdup's songs as evidence of Brome's sympathetic portrayal of his "cunning Whore" and, by extension, the overlooked affinities between the two Constances: "The Lass sings about men who desert women, and Holdup sings about the single-parenting which for her has been the consequence."[34] Holdup's second song, "As I Was Gathering Aprill Flowers," sung directly to Widgin after their vows have supposedly instigated the "cure" of her melancholy, offers an especially bitter example. Playing on Widgin's earlier acoustic commodification of Constance, Holdup offers the song as her dowry. The song is blatantly phallic, relating the speaker's encounter with a *"subtile Serpent"* in an arbor (4.4.2283): *"the Snake beneath me stir'd; / And with his sting gave me a clap, / That swole my belly not my lap"* (4.4.2290–2292). Wilson's relatively cheerful setting (musical example 6.2), which echoes Constance's earlier encomium to Luckless in its opening motive and overall harmonic and metrical structure, offers ironic commentary on the much darker text.[35] Even as Holdup's appropriation of the ballad's first-person perspective enables her to impersonate Constance, it simultaneously affords her a position from which to voice her own vulnerability to men like Squelch as well as the sexual vulnerability of all women. Holdup reinforces the multilayered function of her performance and its associated critique in her ensuing interchange with Widgin: "by my conscience, tis true, twere made i' *Durham*, on a Lasse of my bignesse" (4.4.2294–2295). Widgin's inane response, "By my troth 'tis pretty" (4.4.2293), highlights his obliviousness to his own role in such tales.

The ballads sung by Constance and Holdup draw compelling attention to the expressive significance of song as a mode of truth telling for women in *The Northern Lass*. As the framing of these scenes through Anvil's and Widgin's lustful eyes suggests, however, song is not a straightforwardly authorizing discourse for Brome's female protagonists. When produced by male characters, songs assume a very different—and arguably much less flexible—narrative and spatial function. Widgin's determination to possess Constance/Holdup musically and sexually

As I Was Gathering Aprill Flowers

Richard Brome John Wilson

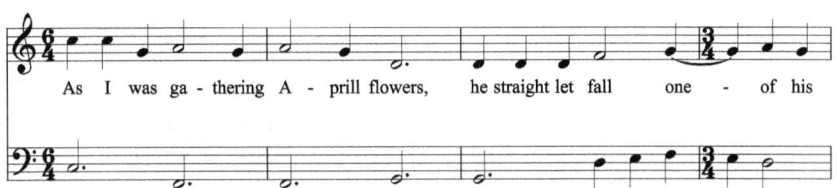

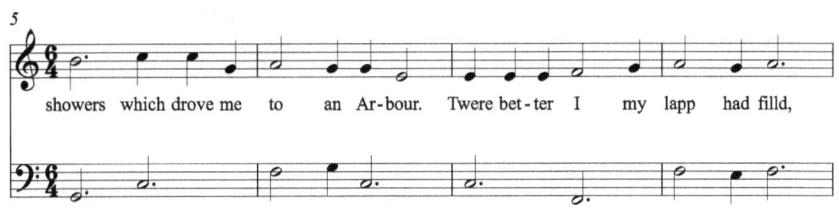

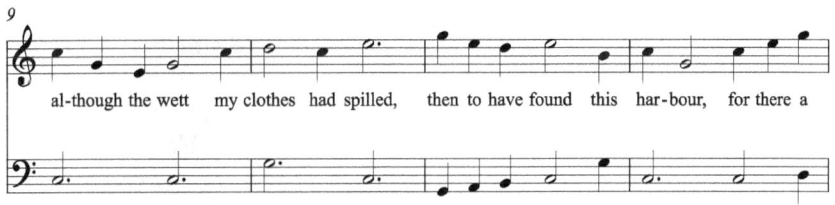

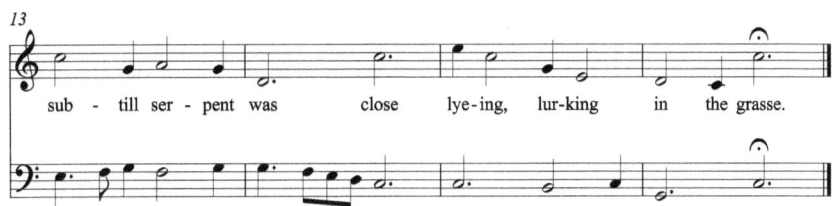

Musical Example 6.2 "As I Was Gathering Aprill Flowers," by John Wilson. Transcribed from NYp Drexel MS 4257, no. 47 and MS 4041, fol. 16v.

is ominously intensified in act 3, when he rebels against his domineering sister. Unlike the two Constances, Fitchow never sings, but she is a formidable speaker, memorably revealing in soliloquy her determination to "Controle, controvert, contradict, and be contraruy to all conformity" (1.6.417–419) after her marriage to Luckless. Her servant Howdee also testifies to her capacity for physical violence (2.5.1050–1065); Steggle likens her mourning ring to a "knuckleduster."[36]

As her relationship with Luckless progresses, Fitchow lays claim to her authority in both musical and spatial terms. In act 2, learning that revelers are arriving at her doorstep to present a masque, she positions herself as an exceptionally loud singer capable of overpowering the ensuing entertainment: "if they enter to make a Taverne of my house, ile add a voice to their consort shall drowne all their fidling" (2.6.1151–1153). The subsequent argument with Luckless figures marital authority as literal control of household boundaries:

Fit: Locke up the dores, and keepe them out.
Luc: Breake them open, and let them in.
Fit: Shall I not bee Master of my owne house?
Luc: Am not *I* the Master of it and you. (2.6.1155–1158)

Although Fitchow loses this particular squabble, she reclaims her domestic authority in act 3, locking Luckless out. "My sister," declares Widgin, "hath fortified her lodging with locks, bolts, barres, and barricados" (3.1.1398–1399). Control of the thresholds of the home becomes synonymous here with the sanctity of the thresholds of Fitchow's body.

When Luckless finally resigns his claim to the widow, he does so in terms that again highlight her sonic and spatial agency: "Oh I tremble to thinke on her; her presence shakes the house like an earthquake; the outrage of Prentizes is not so terrible to a Bawd or a Cutpurse, as her voyce is to me" (3.3.1779–1782). The audience immediately experiences the full force of that voice as Fitchow explodes onto the stage, again locking horns with Luckless as she seeks to bar him from her threshold. This time, however, Brome does not allow her railing to continue unchecked. Branded as a scold, Fitchow experiences the brunt of song's capacity not only to comment on but to delimit social relationships when she finds herself shut out of a moment of male musical bonding.

Tired of his sister's insults, Widgin calls his companions to help "Keepe her . . . off" (3.3.1852). They join hands and begin a circle dance, creating a site that functioned as an important mechanism of cohesion and segregation in the period. Dancing, like music, brought men and women together across boundaries of age and social class. It could also, however, exclude. Circle dances performed by men alone were a relatively rare occurrence; Christopher Marsh suggests that they tended to emphasize virility.[37] His hypothesis is consistent with the space created by the dancing men in *The Northern Lass*.

Here, though, song combines with dance to intensify the establishment of a distinctly gendered communal space.[38] The men mock Fitchow with a rendition of "Hee that marries a Scold," a misogynist song that pokes fun at the torments suffered by men who "*wed[] with a Roaring Girle / That will both scratch and bite.*" While the scold may dominate her husband verbally, he enjoys full control of her body: "*Though he study all day to make her away, / Will be glad to please her at night*" (3.3.1871–1874). When Bullfinch—who is, ironically, a justice of the peace—enters partway through the entertainment, he is physically and musically "*pull[ed] . . . into the Round*" (3.3.1865, stage direction). Joining the dance, he, like the other male participants, helps to "*bear the burden*" (3.3.1852, stage direction) of Widgin's song. The stage direction indicates that Fitchow, meanwhile, "*scolds and strives to be amongst 'hem*" (3.3.1852, stage direction).

If Fitchow's exclusion is reinforced spatially by the gleefully spinning bodies of Widgin and his friends, it is underscored musically by the song's refrain structure. In her discussion of women's singing in *Othello*, Heather Dubrow argues that song "establishes and strengthens gendered bonds" in part by laying claim to a ritualistic space that "resist[s] interruption."[39] The communal repetition demanded by the refrain, "*But he that marries a Scold, a Scold,*" exemplifies this phenomenon.[40] In a reversal of the sonic and spatial domination she hoped to achieve in act 2, Fitchow is quite literally drowned out—and shut out. Although the scene ends with her expelling Widgin and his companions from her home, the men exit the stage still singing, their masculine community intact—at least for the moment. As Katherine Steele Brokaw suggests in her essay in this volume, the harmony enacted by communal song and dance ultimately offers temporary respite from underlying social tensions. Widgin's performance nonetheless establishes song as a powerfully gendered tool for spatial control.

Fitchow's silencing anticipates Constance's surprising reticence in the last scenes of the play. Act 5 begins by again reminding the audience of her acoustic and musical presence. Echoing Fitchow's initial endorsement of the lass, Luckless's servant Pate notes that, "she prattles very prettilie" (5.1.2452). After Constance has been united with Luckless, however, we do not hear from her again, though she reappears on stage "disguis'd and Masqu'd" (5.9.2787, stage direction) in the final scene. That she remains silent on stage throughout these final machinations may have been in part a practical move; if the same actor played both Constances, he would have been needed in this scene to voice Holdup's final lines.[41] Introduced from the outset as a beautiful singer and speaker, however, Constance's silence cannot be taken as a straightforward cure of her melancholy. With the sounds of Fitchow's railing and Widgin's circle dance still ringing in the audience's ears, does this moment offer acoustic commentary on the subjugation of women within marriage? Julie Sanders sees it as "a performance of social containment that leaves a rather sour taste in the mouth."[42] Like other ambiguous depictions of silent women in early modern drama, however, such a reading would depend in part on the staging of the scene. It is also complicated by Hold-up's lucky release from her union with Widgin following the revelation of her identity and Tridewell's insinuations that he is not as excited about his impending nuptials with the seemingly unattainable Fitchow as he expected to be.

This is a strange conclusion to a play that has consistently emphasized Constance's musical voice. Perhaps, though, it ultimately works to underscore music's disturbing capacity to affect architectural and social spaces elsewhere in the play. The emphasis in the final scene is on the redrawing of relational boundaries. Brome continues to highlight the illusions of performance here, because nearly every character—including Constance—appears in disguise as they arrive at Squelch's home. "This is some inchaunted Place, and the people are charm'd. I have mistaken the house sure" (5.9.2807–2808), marvels a dazed Luckless. Brome's focus, however, is on visual, rather than musical, misinterpretation. As character after character throws off his or her disguise—a sequence that recalls the layered revelations underpinning the comedy in Jonson's *Epicoene*—boundaries begin to reestablish themselves. It is easier, it seems, to reverse the tricks of the eye than the ear in *The Northern Lass*.

Indeed, as the play achieves comic closure, Brome tacitly leaves the spatial and relational potency of musical sound that has dominated the play unchecked. In doing so, he continues to remind his audience of music's capacity both to shape individual sites of encounter and to trouble and exceed those boundaries. When Constance and Luckless leave the stage in act 5, scene 2, for instance, the quarto specifies that the music that plays throughout their reunion continues unabated into the next scene, refusing containment. Constance's "Masqu'd" appearance in the final scene, meanwhile, maintains her association with sensory manipulation. (Recall that one of Constance's early musical performances in the play occurs when she is similarly disguised for the household masque at Mistress Fitchow's.) Although the play's conclusion relies on the affirmation of her marriage to Luckless, who is revealed partway through the scene, nowhere do the stage directions indicate that she takes off her own disguise.

Confronting the interplay between sound and space in early modern culture is, ultimately, predicated on absence, a quest for silent traces of transient sound and the settings within which they echoed.[43] Constance's ambiguous reticence in this final scene evokes such methodological challenges. Still, it is difficult to imagine a character defined in terms of her voice remaining silent indefinitely. In the printed version of the play, Brome suggests that Constance is fully capable of a sonic return. Writing to his dedicatee Richard Holford, he insists that the "late long Silence" (sig. A2v) of the lass—the three-year gap between the play's initial staging and its publication—is temporary, and one she is eager to end. Audiences concurred; in at least one late-seventeenth-century production, Constance (played by the talented singer-actress Charlotte Butler) was responsible for an epilogue. It is likely, too, that some productions featured musical entertainments following the play's conclusion in which the actor playing Constance participated. Constance's final positioning, therefore, is not easily synonymous with either spatial or social containment. Even in silence, Brome's musical heroine offers an eerie reminder of the unruly potential of musical sound and of the singing bodies that affect spatial and sociocultural boundaries so powerfully in *The Northern Lass* and in early modern English culture.

Notes

1. For summaries of the play's early stage and print history, see Fried, *Critical Edition*, ix–xiii, xix–xxiv; and Bentley, *Jacobean and Caroline Stage*, vol. 3, 81–84. More recently, Julie Sanders has edited the play for *Richard Brome Online*, with the 1632 quarto text and a modern-spelling text viewable side-by-side; she is currently preparing a print edition for Oxford University Press. The *Richard Brome Online* edition also includes a helpful stage history of *The Northern Lass*, prepared by Elizabeth Schafer (http://www.hrionline.ac.uk/brome/history.jsp?play=NL).

2. Ingram, "Operatic Tendencies," 489–502.

3. Brome, *The Northern Lass*, sig. A1v. I follow the quarto text, edited by Julie Sanders, modernizing the long *s*.

4. Jorgens, *English Song*, vols. 9 and 10, facsimiles of US-NYp Drexel MS 4041 and MS 4257. The songs in question are "A Bonny, Bonny Bird I Have" (Drexel MS 4041, fol. 11r, and MS 4257, No. 45); "As I Was Gathering April Flowers" (Drexel MS 4041, fol. 16v, and MS 4257, no. 47); "Nor Love nor Fate Dare I Accuse" (Drexel MS 4041, fol. 10v, and MS 4257, no. 99); and "Some Say My Love Is but a Man" (Drexel MS 4041, fol. 10r). Although the survival of these settings helps to document the play's popularity, dramatic music often circulated only in performance; see Stern, *Documents of Performance*, 120–173.

5. See Fried, *Critical Edition*, xix. The English Broadside Ballad Archive (http://ebba.english.ucsb.edu) documents a number of "northern lass" ballads in the seventeenth century, testifying to the reciprocal influence between northern (especially Scottish) ballad culture and Brome's heroine. See Wales, *Northern English*, 79.

6. See Lefebvre, *The Production of Space*, esp. 142; and Certeau, *The Practice of Everyday Life*, esp. 117–118.

7. Butler, *Excitable Speech*, 145. Smith has also drawn valuable attention to the slipperiness of sonic experience in his archaeology of sixteenth- and seventeenth-century sound, *Acoustic World*. I emphasize Butler's work here, however, because of her attention to the transformative potential of this unruliness. For an excellent discussion of how gender shaped the sociocultural interventions of vocal sound in early modern England, see Bloom, *Voice in Motion*.

8. The phrase is Irigaray's, *This Sex Which Is Not One*, 78.

9. Butler, *Excitable Speech*, 155.

10. See Gouk, "Raising Spirits," 87–105, and "Some English Theories of Hearing," 95–113; Smith, *Acoustic World*, 101–106. See also Bloom, *Voice in Motion*, chapters 2 and 3, which trace the interplay between voiced breath and listening ear (66–159).

11. On the gendering of music and of musical sound, see Austern, "'Alluring the Auditorie to Effeminacie,'" 343–354; "'For, Love's a Good Musician,'" 614–653; "The Siren, the Muse, and the God of Love," 95–138; *Music, Sensation, and Sensuality*, 285–317; Dunn and Larson, ed., *Gender and Song*; and Wong, *Music and Gender*.

12. See Austern, "'Sing Againe Syren,'" 420–448; Austern and Naroditskaya, *Music of the Sirens*, esp. Calogero, "'Sweet Aluring Harmony,'" 140–175; and Larson, "'Blest Pair of Sirens,'" 81–106.

13. On the tension between music as philosophical ideal and performance practice, see Ortiz, *Broken Harmony*, and Minear, *Reverberating Song*, esp. 19–22.

14. See, for example, Chedgzoy, "Politics of Location," 137–149; Findlay, *Playing Spaces*; Kolentsis and Larson, *Gendering Time and Space*; Flather, *Gender and Space*; Larson, *Early Modern Women in Conversation*, 39–59; McMullan, *Renaissance Configurations*; Orlin, *Locating Privacy*, esp. 296–323; and Trull, *Performing Privacy and Gender*.

15. Castiglione, *The Courtyer*, sig. L.iii.v.

16. Pepys, *Diary*, vol. 5, 230.

17. For examples of these activities, see Pepys, *Diary*, vol. 1, 111, 194, 205, 302; vol. 3, 94, 99; vol. 8, 4, 206; vol. 9, 125, 151.

18. Morley, *A Plaine and Easie Introduction*, sig. B2r.

19. For a helpful introduction to the performance of psalms in domestic and church settings, see Temperley, "'If Any of You Be Mery,'" 90–100.

20. Austern, "Domestic Song," 123–138.

21. See Clark, "The Broadside Ballad and the Woman's Voice," 103–120; and Smith, "Female Impersonation," 284–301.

22. See Abbate, "Music: Drastic or Gnostic?," 505–536.

23. Steggle, *Richard Brome*, esp. 8–9. See also Miles, "Place-Realism," 428–440; Sanders, *Caroline Drama*, 43–55, and "Spaces and Sites in the Play," in her introduction to *The Northern Lass*; and Kaufmann, *Richard Brome*, 13–14.

24. Brome, *The Antipodes* (1640 text), sig. Ev.

25. Steggle, *Richard Brome*, 9.

26. On drama and spatial practice in the period, see Findlay, *Playing Spaces*; Hiscock, *The Uses of This World*; and Sanders, *The Cultural Geography of Early Modern Drama*.

27. Brome, *A Jovial Crew* (1652 text), sig. F2.

28. Kaufmann (*Richard Brome*, 36) describes *A Jovial Crew* as "something close to operetta or musical comedy." For an analysis of the songs in *A Jovial Crew*, see "Appendix 1: Songs" in Tiffany Stern's recent Arden edition (256–259).

29. On the music of the play, see Sanders, "Music, Song, and Ballad-Culture," in her introduction to *The Northern Lass*; and Shaw, *Richard Brome*, 40–41. Shaw notes that Brome "employs song in *The Northern Lass* with an ingeniousness rarely shown by his contemporaries" (40).

30. Blank, *Broken English*, 104–108, and Wales, *Northern English*, 77–88.

31. On the "promiscuity" of the ballad form, see Bruster, "The Jailer's Daughter," 293; and Ortiz, *Broken Harmony*, 207.

32. Brome draws on close associations linking melancholy and song in his treatment of Constance's later songs, reinforced by their overt allusions to Ophelia's ballads; Constance's penchant for ballad discourse also recalls the jailer's daughter in *The Two Noble Kinsmen*. See Bruster, "The Jailer's Daughter," 277–300. On the relationship between melancholy and song in the early modern context, see Dunn, "Ophelia's Songs," 50–64; and Eubanks Winkler, *O Let Us Howle Some Heavy Note*, 114–165. These echoes are reinforced in the workshop staging of act 3, scene 3, developed for *Richard Brome Online*. *The Northern Lass*, Videos (act 3, scene 2), *Richard Brome Online* (http://www.hrionline.ac.uk/brome).

33. The word *fit* playfully connects Holdup's staged melancholic lunacy with Widgin's well-timed appearance. *Fit* also denotes a section of a song or a tune, thus anticipating Holdup's musical performance.

34. Steggle, *Richard Brome*, 26.
35. On the potentially contradictory signification of ballad tunes and texts, see Marsh, "The Sound of Print," 171–190.
36. Steggle, *Richard Brome*, 22.
37. Marsh, *Music and Society*, 333–337.
38. On the importance of song for the creation of masculine identity in domestic settings, see Austern, "Domestic Song," 123–138.
39. Dubrow, *The Challenges of Orpheus*, 225.
40. Fitchow's musical humiliation would have been further intensified if the audience joined in singing the refrain.
41. This is purely speculative; there is no firm evidence for such a doubling. However, given the scripting of the two characters, the vocal requirements they demand, and the sonic slippage between them, their doubling is nonetheless an intriguing possibility to consider and one that was explored (though not ultimately used) during the staging workshops undertaken in conjunction with *Richard Brome Online*. I am grateful to Julie Sanders and Tiffany Stern for their insights into this issue. On the acting resources of the King's Men in the late 1620s and early 1630s, see Bentley, *Jacobean and Caroline Stage*, vol. 1, 16–26.
42. Sanders, "Introduction," para 24.
43. See Smith, *Acoustic World*, 110–114.

7.

"Lasting-Pasted Monuments": Memory, Music, Theater, and the Seventeenth-Century English Broadside Ballad

Sarah F. Williams

In William Congreve's Restoration-era comedy *The Old Batchelor* (1693), Heartwell, a "surly old pretended woman-hater," is tricked into marrying Silvia, the spurned lover of Vainlove. He laments that his downfall will be the talk of the town. He'll be "chronicled in ditty, and sung in woful Ballad."[1] The broadside ballads to which Heartwell refers were single sheet, folio-sized publications containing verse, a tune indication, and woodcut imagery that related cautionary tales, current events, and simplified myth and history to a wide range of social classes across early modern England. Broadsides had a very recognizable format and visual appearance, one that remained standard for over a century.[2] (See figure 7.1.)

They were sold, displayed, and sung in theaters, homes, streets, bookshops, marketplaces, fairs, and taverns—all manner of spaces.[3] New ballads often referenced old ones, and tunes were recycled for broadsides containing similar subject material.[4] By Congreve's time, the broadside was a well-established and venerable form attracting the notice of collectors such as Anthony (à) Wood and Samuel Pepys. In the above passage, Heartwell likens himself to both the print artifact itself and its aural form—that is, like the story of his experience, he will be a cautionary tale for all to remember, hanged in "Effigie" upon the wall. Heartwell then references several popular tunes to which his sad tale will perhaps be sung—"The Batchelors Fall," "The Superanuated Maidens Comfort"—though there is no record of these exact tune titles within the corpus of melodies employed by the early modern English broadside trade. Because Congreve is actually parodying

Figure 7.1 The Broadside Ballad *A Warning for Wives* (1629) to the Tune of "Bragandary." Pepys Library 1.118–119, © Magdalene College, Cambridge.

A Nother woman that was there,
   she out oth' doores did send,
And bad her fetch a Pot of Beere,
   oh then drew nere his end,
For ere the woman came againe,
This wife had her owne husband slaine:
         Oh women,
      Murderous women,
   whereon are your minds?

She long had thirsted for his blood,
   (euen by her owne confession)
And now her promise she made good,
   so heauen gaue permission
To Satan, who then lent her power
And strength to do't that bloody houre.
         Oh women, &c.

It seemes that he his head did leane
   toth' Chimney, which she spide,
And straight she toake, (O bloody queane)
   her Sisters from her side,
And hit him therewith such a stroake
Ith necke, that (some thinke) he nere spoke.
         Oh women, &c.

She hauing done that monstrous part,
   (was worth her for her labour)
No power had from thence to start,
   but went vnto a neighbour,
And told him, that she verily thought,
that she her husbands death had wrought.
         Oh women, &c.

The man amaz'd to heare the same,
   caught hold of her, and said,
Ile know the truth, and how this came,
   if such a part be plaid,
No sooner had he said the same,
But neighbours did her fact proclaime.
         Oh women, &c.

Then to New Prison was she sent,
   because it was so late,
And vpon the next day she went
   (through Smithfield to Newgate,
Where she did lye vntill the Session,
To answer for her foule transgression.
         Oh women, &c.

Where she condemned was by Law,
   in Clarkenwell to be burned,
Vnto which place they did her draw,
   where she to ashes turned.
A death, though cruell, yet too milde
For one that hath a heart so vilde.
         Oh women, &c.

Let all good wiues a warning take,
   in Country and in City,
And thinke how they shall at a stake
   be burned without pitty.
If they can haue such barbarous hearts,
What man or woman will take their parts.
         Oh women,
      Murderous women,
   whereon are your minds?

Printed at London for F. G. on Snow-hill.   FINIS.   M. P.

Figure 7.1 (*Continued*)

existing tune titles in this passage, as I will explore later, the success of this comedic lament depended upon seventeenth-century audiences' intimate knowledge of ballad culture, their recollections of these constantly reused melodies both within and outside of London's theaters, and the visually recognizable format of the broadside ballad artifact itself. Although twentieth- and twenty-first-century scholars often ignore the aurally circulating tunes associated with the broadside trade or dismiss them as ephemeral, theatrical references to ballad tunes and the common practice of intertexuality in the broadside trade throughout the seventeenth century depended upon the free circulation of ballads in early modern society, the collective memory of consumers, and a sense of musical permanence.[5] By analyzing how early modern thinkers believed memory worked, and its affinities with contemporaneous music and drama, I demonstrate how broadsides and their tunes could function as mementos, albeit unstable ones, and redefine our understanding of early modern theatrical space. Even though mnemonics was considered a learned art, the methods a practitioner employed to store and recall information resembled the intertextual processes in the broadside trade and their relationships early modern performance spaces as "memory theater," even beyond the public stage.[6] Memory mediates and complicates the liminal space broadside ballads occupied in early modern English culture as well as the circulation of their tunes through various places and social classes, further destabilizing the categories of public and private places for performance, preservation and unpredictability, material and ephemeral, music and text, and aural and written traditions.

Memory, Music, and Theater as Place (Locus)

Ars memoriae, or the memory arts as devised by Classical thinkers, and rendered into striking visual form by seventeenth-century Hermetic philosopher Robert Fludd, were designed to organize knowledge into memory systems by using images and places. To aid in categorization, storage, organization, and recollection of knowledge, most memory schemes were built around the mental practice of converting ideas into specific, fixed material objects such as pictures and architectural spaces. Originally conceived as a tool for the orator, this technique employs images and architecture as mental repositories through which one might train oneself to store and recall, for example, long passages of text. For early moderns, *memoria* describes the mental faculty that stores information, the site of that storage (the rear portion of the brain), the images stored, and the process through which storage occurs, or memorization.[7] Recollection is how these images and information are retrieved. While the individual definitions of *memoria*, recollection, and remembering are largely synonymous, their nuances hint at a continuum from individual, cognitive practice to cultural memory: "At one end, 'memory' is an internal, cognitive operation (as in 'the art of memory'), and at the other, it describes as set of material practices with an indeterminate relationship to that operation (as in rituals that are the expression of 'collective' or 'social' memory)."[8]

Theater as place, or *locus*, is intimately related to the memory arts. *Theater* or *theatrum*, first theorized by Greco-Roman, medieval, and later echoed by early modern humanist thinkers, was an ideological construct with linkages to learning, imagery and visual culture (sharing a stem with the word *theory* meaning "a looking"), and pedagogical tools. Classical writers such as Terence and Donatus, widely read by English humanists, imagined the theater an as "imitation of life" or the "image of truth" that could affect the character of society by mirroring didactic concepts such as morality.[9] Separate from the physical, performative space we associate with the early modern English dramatic tradition, early humanist writers perpetuated these concepts by defining *theatrum* as a "looking place," a monument upon which to meditate on the greatness of Roman culture, and a "large book that claimed to contain knowledge in a visual or visualizeable form."[10] Late sixteenth- and early seventeenth-century theater buildings were circular, a design with clear cosmological significance. Indeed, the Globe's name implies all that it represented: a self-contained mirror of the world, a circle of learning, a "wooden O," or *theatrum mundi*.[11] These humanist ideas informed how early modern writers on mnemonics constructed their memory theaters. Robert Fludd, believing one should not use fictitious memory places when devising mnemonic schemes, created his in the form of a theater now believed to have been modeled after a public amphitheater, or, more specifically, the Globe: "I call a theatre (a place [*locus*] in which) all actions of words, of sentences, of particulars of a speech or of subjects are shown, *as in a public theatre in which comedies and tragedies are acted.*"[12] Fludd designed his "memory theater" as constructed from a variety of distinct building materials with five doors or entrances opposite five columns that served as the memory loci. Jonathan Willis, in his seventeenth-century memory treatise *Mnemonica*, also created a repository, or memory scheme using an imagined architectural structure, fashioned after a theater which he defined thus: "A *Repository* is an imaginary fabrick, fancied Artificially, built of hewen stone, in form of a *Theater*."[13] Yet these static, imagined memory theaters stand in stark contradiction to the dynamic performative spaces that were first constructed in London during the 1560s. While the ideology of the theater explains its connections to the memory arts and as a powerfully efficacious "vehicle for displaying worldly knowledge" and social control, it is at the same time at odds with the *realization* of late sixteenth- and seventeenth-century theater as a constantly mutable experience in which the audience is diverted and entertained through music and acting. Analyzing these "diversions" through the *ars memoriae*, however, exposes the contradictions performed music, theater, and balladry presented in early modern English culture as they straddled oral/aural and written traditions, spatial and class boundaries, and material and performative formats.

Despite these contradictions, the similitudes among theater, music, and memory persist. Seventeenth-century playwrights consistently relied on their audiences' abilities to recollect fragments of song and passing mentions of balladry to create characters and allusion. Music is often literally and figuratively "in between" in drama; it opened and closed theatrical performances, announced the entrance of important characters, accompanied banquets, and sounded between acts. Music also bridged moments of fiction and reality, interiority and exteriority. One oft-discussed moment is Desdemona's "Willow Song" in act 4 of Shakespeare's *Othello*. Interrupted by her servants, Desdemona sings fragments of an "old song," or ballad, she recalls from her childhood. Music signals her introspection and a suspension of time, yet a knock at the door quickly draws her back to reality.[14] Erin Minear similarly notes the liminality created by musical memories such as Desdemona's. Music can be elusive, vanishing as soon as it sounds. At the same time, however, in drama

> it persists, haunting the memory with the reverberations of half-recalled and half-forgotten phrases. . . . Perhaps the most startling aspect of these musical memories is that the remembered music never remains fully in the past: recollection stimulates repetition and return, breaking down the distinction between memory and experience. To sing or hear a familiar song—or a fragment of song—makes memory experience, and vice versa.[15]

One of the most striking examples of elusive and fragmentary music in early modern drama is Ophelia's mad scene in *Hamlet* wherein she sings, frequently interrupted, snatches of popular and bawdy ballads. In her influential reading of this scene, Leslie Dunn views Ophelia's performance of broadside ballads that included laments, sexual innuendo, and phallic puns as indicative of disruptive feminine behavior.[16] Shakespeare's audience must stitch together their memories of these ballad fragments and allusions to understand the transgressive nature of the scene, Ophelia's mental state, and her ultimate demise.

Dramatists often present theater itself as a kind of memory—that is, a representation, or a recollection—one that intimately relies upon time and duration, much like music. Dialogues could be created between dramatist and audience with the actor as intermediary. Dramatists make reference to memory and forgetting as a kind of acknowledgment of the conditions of drama and the play-acting experience.[17] Early modern theatrical works also relied upon audience recollection for the purposes of not only allusion, as discussed above, but also communicating didactic exemplars. Thomas Heywood, in his *Apology for Actors*, notes that memories of a play or particular characters were so powerful they could affect positive behavioral changes in audience members through the presentation of exemplary traits:

> If wee present a forreigne History, the subject is so intended, that . . . by sundry instances, either animating men to noble attempts, or attaching the consciences of the spectators, finding themselves toucht in presenting the vices of others. If a morall, it is to perswade men to humanity and good life, to instruct them in civility and good manners, shewing them the fruits of honesty, and the end of villany.[18]

The early modern theater, in constant conversation with the broadside trade, functioned as a powerful mnemonic scheme, a real and imagined architectural space, a mirror of the world, a didactic tool, a repository of knowledge, and as a communal performative experience. The *playhouse*, as a public performance space and the street or home as "stageless" theater, reinforced and subverted the music and images present in the broadside trade, dynamic spaces that stood in stark contradiction to the static "monument" or *theatrum* upon which they were modeled.

Music and theater are also intimately related to early modern mnemonic systems in more concrete, practical ways. For example, drama and music are rhythmic, melodic, and temporal arts; ballad sellers and play actors performed from memory, many learning by rote. Additionally, musical and mnemonic systems share the common object of the image—that is, in the written tradition music relies on the spatial representation of pitch and duration in notation.[19] Scholars cite the pictorial nature of musical notation itself as akin to the theory of memory's transfer from the aural to the visual fields. The medieval pedagogical aid devised by Guido d'Arezzo to teach sight singing, the Guidonian hand, is another example of converting the immaterial to the material, or sound into spatial representation. Musicians adapted the systems of *ars memoriae* when learning music by affixing the order of pitches against a background scheme of "places" (or loci to use Fludd and Tinctoris's language), or the joints and fingertips, with each place corresponding to a letter or pitch.[20] Cicero explains this transfer—the imprint of music (abstraction) into figures (the material object)—in his *De Oratore* when he writes that

> perceptions received by the ears or by reflexion can be most easily retained in the mind if they are also conveyed to our minds by the mediation of the eyes, with the result that things not seen and not lying in the field of visual discernment are earmarked by a sort of outline and image and shape so that we keep hold of as it were by an act of sight things that we can scarcely embrace by an act of thought.[21]

Guido's medieval memory system, and its transference of the abstract to the material, was still very much present in the early modern consciousness at the turn of the seventeenth century. For example, Samuel Pepys, a ballad collector, delighted in visiting Bartholomew Fair in central London near the meat market and often entertained his friends by reading "new ballets," one in particular "made from the seamen at sea to their ladies in town."[22] There is also evidence he may have copied down the tunes he heard there—transferring the auditory memory of his experience to the visual through musical notation—perhaps to preserve these performances in the same way he meticulously collected broadsides themselves.[23] The famous music lesson scene in Shakespeare's *Taming of the Shrew* makes reference to this medieval spatial scheme as representation of sounding pitch when

Bianca recites the gamut, referencing the first and lowest pitch of the scale as closest to the earth: "'Gamut,' I am, the *ground* of all accord."[24] Western theories of memory focus on the visual, privileging it as the form of perception that grants stability to memory storage.[25] Yet this scene, like the practice of tune indications on broadsides and printed versions of plays, demonstrates a common trend in early modern culture—that is, the consistent tendency to translate acoustic material into visual forms. These translations, often fraught with complications, are akin to the liminal position broadside ballads occupied in early modern English culture when they circulated as, at any given moment, material objects, imagery, and domestic and public entertainments.[26]

Image

Like Guido's hand or musical notation, the ways in which ballads and their tunes were consumed and displayed position them as powerful forms of mnemonic imagery. The seventeenth-century fixation on the visual—emblematics, print culture, symbolism, and allegory—can be seen in not only the learned arts but also in popular prints, religious ceremonies, public spectacles, and of course broadside balladry.[27] In his 1631 *Whimzies: or, a New Cast of Characters*, Richard Brathwaite described ballad sellers in public houses and taverns, where their wares were displayed as "lasting-pasted monuments upon the insides of Country Alehouses."[28] Brathwaite's choice of words here—"monuments"—should not go unnoticed. Ballad sellers, as Braithwaite described, were frequent fixtures in the "Chimney corner[s]" of alehouses, drinking and singing, while their penny sheets were affixed to the walls. Decades earlier Nicholas Bownde commented on the "vain songs" that cottagers sing "though they cannot read themselves, nor any of theirs, yet will have many Ballades set up in their houses, that so they might learne them, as they shall have occasion."[29] There is a long tradition of displaying didactic text and images—including broadsides, emblems, scripture, and moral inscriptions—on the interior walls of early modern English public and private spaces.[30] A "national network of communications," taverns, inns, and alehouses in both city and country pasted "row[s] of Balletts" upon the walls for communal display and singing, while balladmongers sold their wares among the patrons.[31] As in Bownde's description, ballads were also a popular form of decoration in homes of modest means. "Artificers" and "poor husbandmen" papered their walls with broadsides. Abraham Holland also remarks in 1625 that in the "North-villages" "o're the Chymney they some Ballads have/ Of *Chevy-Chase*."[32] Surrounded by image, public display, and communal singing, a large and varied number of early modern English citizens from a diverse range of social classes had the opportunity to see and experience ballad performance and its standardized visual format.

The standardization of the broadside ballad as "image" occurred in the early decades of the seventeenth century, a phenomenon crucial to categorizing the broadside as a memento that could influence all those involved in its consumption. Instrumental in this shift was the creation of the "ballad partners." The ballad partners were formed on November 6, 1624, when the court of the Stationers' Company allowed Thomas Pavier and his associates John Grismond, Henry Gosson, and the brothers John, Cuthbert, and Edward Wright to register their ballads "heretofore disorderly printed without entrance or allowance."[33] The partners—and their subsequent generations—consolidated their inventory of popular stock ballads and other print items into shared warehouses with the goal to increase distribution and circulation of their product in "a familiar format."[34] The ballad partners were instrumental in shaping and standardizing the appearance of broadside ballads. Woodblock prints were "one of the best indications of a growing commercial sense in the ballad trade, and an awareness of the demands of the public . . . with the growing prevalence of the style which dominated for most of the seventeenth century: the two-part folio sheet with a row of woodcuts along the top."[35] Another addition to the standard visual appearance of the broadside ballad emerged in the early seventeenth century: indications of tune titles.[36] This information almost always appeared directly beneath the broadside title as a separate line of text that was expected and understood, if not completely intelligible, for semiliterate audiences. In his historical and structural analysis of the seventeenth century, José Antonio Maravall describes this manipulation of human conduct through formalized imagery as "guided culture":

> It was a matter of a statistical knowledge serving as the foundation for this "engineering of the human" that came to be baroque culture. The technification of political behavior in the prince . . . was not expressed in a mathematical formula but in symbols. These symbols may have been of very remote origin, but from Machiavelli to the individuals of the baroque they underwent a process that divorced them from their magical references, turning them into a conceptually formalized language.[37]

This same process is at work in the standardization of the broadside ballad format and imagery. The predictable appearance, or "language" to use Maravall's term, of the broadside—from the position of text and stock woodblock imagery to its appearance on walls in public and domestic spaces—helps to fashion them as efficacious memory images around which communal discussion, education, and indoctrination could occur.[38]

Greco-Roman and even early modern treatises suggest that auditory memory—which was temporal—was most efficacious when fixed to an image or a spatial scheme. The medieval philosopher and theologian Albertus Magnus wrote that "something is not secure enough by hearing, but it is made firm by seeing."[39] In the 1697 English translation of Marius D'Assigny's treatise on mnemonics, he agrees "That the Eyes of the Understanding, and consequently Memory, are carried more easily to the things that are seen, than to those that are heard."[40] Jonathan Willis espouses a similar opinion in *Mnemonica* when he writes:

Memory is quickened by *Idea's* [image/pictures] is thus manifest: No man is ignorant, that *Memory* is stronger conversant about sensible things then about insensible; and of sensible things, those which are visible make deepest impression; therefore things heard are more firmly retained in *Memory*, then those which are barely conceived in mind, & things seen better then those which are heard, according to the Poet:

> Things heard in mind no such impression make,
> As those whereof our faithful eyes partake,
> And whereof we our selves spectators are.⁴¹

The best images to use as memory aids, according to these early treatises, were active and striking, capable of arousing emotional affect through unusual imagery and aiding memory, from the comic and obscene, to the beautiful or grotesque.⁴² Broadsides also contain a diversity of visual information—from text size and font style, to woodcuts of human figures, landscapes, or scenes—in a very predictable, and recognizable, format. The woodcuts adorning the top third of the folio were often quite striking as well. To cite only one example, *A Warning for Wives* contains images that communicate the story in the text below, by picturing on one side a woman standing over a supine man and on the other a graphic image of, ostensibly, the same woman burning alive at the stake. (See again figure 7.1.) In early modern English society, a woman convicted of murdering her husband with a pair of shears, as Katherine Francis did in the ballad text version of this story, was sentenced to burn at the stake.⁴³ This was the same punishment bestowed upon those committing high treason, suggesting the crime for usurping the household hierarchy by murdering its "ruler" was akin to regicide. The pictorial images on *A Warning for Wives* are striking in their diversity—they contain figures relating the crime and its consequence—and also functioned in a didactic manner. While ballad tunes and their aural performances were ubiquitous, the visual presence of broadsides usually accompanied them in some way either in the hands of a seller, pasted to the walls, or on display in a shop window. In this sense, the broadside itself functions as a memento, or a mnemonic image, to remember the tune (the title of which was always clearly indicated in a predictable location, suggesting semiliterate consumers were capable of understanding the image and its implications), the didactic example, or the theatrical performance of its verses. Brathwaite's description of broadside ballads as "lasting-pasted monuments" speaks to their ability to function with some degree of permanence, impressing their visual and aural information upon a consumer, and aiding in the recollection, and sometimes the complication, of a particular tune or performance.⁴⁴

Theatrical Performance and Intertextuality

The common practice of changes in tune titles is another illustration of broadside authors relying upon, and stimulating, their audience's collective memory through sound and image. Several extremely popular seventeenth-century tunes illustrate the mutability of the broadside ballad in the public consciousness, and their close associations with theatrical works. The popular broadside trade melody "Fortune My Foe" was used at the end of the sixteenth century to accompany a ballad on the ill-fated magician Doctor Faustus.[45] Later in the seventeenth century, ballads employing the same poetic meter and stanza length appear, calling for their verses to be sung "to the tune of Doctor Faustus." Most of these later texts in some way recall the original subject material of the Doctor Faustus ballad—that is, witchcraft, the supernatural, the last testaments of criminals, warnings, and grisly murder narratives. Other tunes enjoyed these multiple iterations throughout the seventeenth century. The late-sixteenth-century tune "Bragandary" took at least two alternate titles—"Monstrous Women" and "O Folly Desperate Folly"—from the memorable refrains, or burdens, of the broadside texts with which it was paired.[46] (See table 7.1.) From a protocapitalist standpoint, these cross-references could be designed to aid in the recollection of a particularly popular broadside, and thus increase the sales of the new publication. This practice also suggests that while a ballad tune itself altered very little, at least in essential structure, these title changes indicate that the "image" of the tune indication on the broadside—a standard visual feature of the print form for over a century—was involved in some sort of extramusical communication to the consumer.

Intertextuality or cross-reference, a common practice in the broadside trade that relied upon collective memory, could also be reinforced through theatrical works.[47] The tune metamorphoses of "Fortune My Foe" and "Bragandary" were supported through not only the public circulation of ballads in theaters and the street trade but also in domestic spaces. In Margaret Cavendish's closet drama *The Comical Hash* (1668), the Lady Censurer recalls an instance in which she was implored by the ladies at court to sing "an old Song out of a new Ballad":

> I was to sing them a Song for my money; so I sung them an old Song, the burden of the Song, *Oh women, women, monstrous women, what do you mean for to do?* but because the Song was against women, they would have had me given them their money back again ... so then I sung them *Doctor* Faustus *that gave his Soul away to the Devill*; for I knew Conjurers and Devills pleased women best.[48]

The broadside ballad melodies the Lady Censurer mentions are well known to her courtly audience—that is, she references only the burden, or refrain, of an "old Song" by which she means a ballad. In commenting that the song "Oh Women, Women, Monstrous Women" is "against women," she implies her listeners would recollect the various broadside texts to which "O Women Monstrous Women/ Bragandary" was set—in this case, those describing female crimes and witchcraft trials. Settling on the tune "Doctor Faustus," she also demonstrates her audience would have been familiar with a century-old melody and could vividly recall the

Table 7.1 Selected Seventeenth-Century Broadsides Set to "Bragandary."

Ballad Title	Date	Catalog Number[1]	Tune Indication	Subject
The Unnatural Wife	1628	ESTC ID S116609	Bragandary	Demonic scold; murder
A Warning for Wives [contains the burden "O women, murderous women"]	1629	ESTC ID S126169	Bragandary	Demonic scold; murder
The Phantastick Age	1634	ESTC ID S115944	O women, monstrous, etc.	Monstrosity; vice
Bagnall's Ballet [contains the burden "O women, monstrous women"]	1658	ESTC ID R32937	[No tune indicated]	Vice; misogyny
The Salisbury Assizes, or the Reward of Witchcraft	1653?	ESTC ID R187381	Bragandary	Witchcraft
Wonder of Wonders	1662	ESTC ID R41805	Bragandary	Supernatural
The Careless Curate and the Bloudy Butcher	1662	ESTC ID R37465	Oh women, monstrous women	Murder; castration
A Prospective-Glass for Christians [contains the burden "O folly, desperate folly"]	1675	ESTC ID R227339	Monstrous Women	Moralizing advice
The West-Country Dialogue	1675?	ESTC ID R227468	O folly, desperate folly, etc.	Love; violence
The Country Parson's Folly	1690	ESTC ID R6887	Folly, desperate folly, etc.	Vice; religion
The Present State of England	1690	ESTC ID R234284	O Folly, desperate Folly, etc.	Injustice
The Country Schollar's Folly	1696	ESTC ID R174341	O folly, desperate folly	Vulgarity; vice
The Unconscionable Baker or, the Devil Correcting Sin	1697	ESTC ID R185853	O Folly desperate Folly	Devil; retribution

[1]English Short Title Catalogue.

dozens of murder and witchcraft broadsides with which it was paired. Another such instance of theatrical allusion occurs in Samuel Rowley and Thomas Dekker's drama *The Noble Souldier* (1634) when the character of the Poet is asked to write a libel on the subject of the King. The consequence of this treasonous act, the Poet fears, will be ballads "sung to the hanging tune" (i.e., "Fortune My Foe" or "Doctor Faustus") about his miserable end:

> The King! shoo'd I be bitter 'gainst, the King,
> I shall have scurvy ballads made of me,
> Sung to the hanging tune. I dare not, Madam.[49]

In these disparate dramatic works for courtly, domestic, and public audiences, playwrights rely on their listeners to recall the various broadside texts that the mention of a tune might evoke. The *ars memoria* and its affinities with music and theater help us expand our definition of the "theatrical space" in early modern English culture—that is, a ballad melody's mnemonic function and its circulation among staged and "stageless" spaces reconfigure the home, theater, and street as interrelated performative loci.[50]

Audiences could further reinforce their memories of ballad tune performances through the mnemonic device of *image* by purchasing a broadside set to the tunes they heard in the theaters from sellers both within and outside of the playhouse, or even one of the many broadside ballad versions of contemporaneous theatrical works including, for example, Shakespeare's *King Lear* and *Titus Andronicus*.[51] Broadsides and the theatrical performances thereof functioned as visual aids to memory—plastered upon walls in communal spaces both public and private, read at home, acted on a stage, or sold and collected as mementos sometimes within or directly outside of the amphitheater itself.[52] Broadsides moved fluidly between these performative venues and visual formats, and their reception both within and outside of London's theaters was complicated by performance and the intricate histories of the music accompanying their verses. These histories were, in turn, confused by the unruly and unpredictable memories of audiences. Standing in stark contrast to the controllability of humanist theater, seventeenth-century playwrights and ballad authors capitalized on these uncertainties when crafting their entertainments.[53]

In the passage from Congreve's *The Old Batchelor* that opened this chapter, Heartwell, for fear of being a cuckold undone by love, lamented that his story would be sung in ballad to tunes such as the "Superanuated Maidens Comfort" or the "Batchelors Fall." There is no record of tune titles such as these in the late-sixteenth- and seventeenth-century English broadside trade. More likely, these are puns on existing tunes such as "The Ladies Fall" or "The Poor Man's Comfort," melodies that had long been paired with narratives about unfortunate women, supernatural events, or henpecked husbands. "The Ladies Fall" often accompanied verses about jilted brides and other stories of women wounded by the men who loved them.[54] Heartwell capitalizes on this history and the collective memory of his audience by making reference to the title here, substituting himself, the "Batchelor," as the object of pity. *The Poor Man's Comfort*, on the other hand, is the title of a 1684 broadside to the tune of "Fair Angel of England," the text being a dialogue between "a despairing Husband and a comfortable wife." Later, the tune title "The Poor Mans Comfort" appears on several other broadsides during the seventeenth century, including one titled *The Poor Mans Councellor,* an obvious reference to the original sheet and published the same year. This time, instead of cautionary tales and moralizing advice for women, as was the case with ballads set to "The Ladies Fall," the advice associated with this melody is directed to the bachelor on how to choose the proper wife. The ballad instructs the listener to select a spouse that is "loving and kind," but not "froward" or else she'll "lavishly spend."

The Poor Mans Comfort is also the title of a Jacobean tragicomedy by Robert Daborne originally acted at the Cockpit amphitheater around 1618 but revived in the Restoration.[55] The play depicts Gisbert, a shepherd whose daughter is abandoned by her nobleman husband. Gisbert's quest for justice leads him on a journey during which he must navigate a society filled with characters representing vice, from whores to corrupt lawyers. Congreve mines his audience's collective memory in this passage wherein Heartwell bemoans his fate as a cuckold and whose story will be accompanied by tunes known for the misfortunes of young ladies. He demonstrates that as late as 1693, his audience would have been familiar with contemporaneous dramatic works, domestic and public broadside display, ballad trade tunes, and the typical texts associated with those tunes. Congreve's allusions require the audience to recall printed ballads containing these tunes, and the kinds of ballad texts with which they were routinely paired, through a complex web of theatrical reference, musical recollection, and communal remembering.

The "lasting-pasted monuments" affixed to the walls of Tudor-Stuart homes were plastered and painted over throughout the centuries. Printed on heavy, cheap paper, these penny sheets were used for all manner of household and hygienic tasks.[56] While the late-seventeenth-century antiquarians Anthony Wood and Samuel Pepys aimed to preserve broadsides in their personal collections, they often haphazardly trimmed and cropped the original sheet to fit in their scrapbooks, and reshuffled and reordered pieces of a single broadside, further fragmenting the ostensibly fixed "material object."[57] The disintegration, dismemberment, and disregard of broadsides continued through the nineteenth century. Yet, to be "chronicled in ditty" connotes the idea of preservation—that is, Congreve's Heartwell is concerned he will be stigmatized through *song* in a lasting way. In her important study on voice and agency in early modern England, Gina Bloom challenges the definition of "the material" as visible and tangible by theorizing the relationship among voice, theatrical performance, gender, and agency: "Invisible yet substantial, ephemeral yet transferable, voice destabilizes any easy assumptions about the category of matter."[58] Considering the intertexual practices at work in the broadside trade through the lens of *ars memoriae* further complicates these ostensibly fixed categories of the material and immaterial. The standardized visual image of the broadside, coupled with the performative experience of ballads in the theater, home, street, and communal gathering spaces again destabilizes the notion of the "tangible" object and the "ephemeral" voice elegantly problematized by Bloom. Tunes were mutable—changing titles and associations with specific subject material over the century—and yet permanent enough in the collective memory of seventeenth-century ballad consumers, home audiences, and playgoers that a complex system of intertextuality and cross-reference *could* exist between these seemingly disparate theatrical spaces. The fixed, didactic nature of the *ars memoriae*, like the broadside print artifact and humanist theater, is complicated when translated to the realm of performance. The imagined *theatrum* presupposed an audience that emphasized decorum, "consistency, uniformity, and the coordination of characters with 'appropriate' and therefore expected roles," one that "responded predictably and homogeneously."[59] While humanists, and also the playwright Thomas Heywood, believed in the didactic capabilities of theater, they could not control the audience's responses and behaviors, as well as the co-optation of texts, references, and, most especially, the circulation of music beyond the "wooden O." The memory arts were similarly problematic. Though they were designed to "affix" knowledge in the mind of the practitioner, the primary metaphor for the process of imprinting information was a wax tablet, a surface that could be wiped clean and easily remolded.[60] Broadside ballads as material objects—easily recognizable and ubiquitous—were capable of extending the life of a tune, converting its acoustic properties to visual imagery, naming it on the page, and rendering it more permanent in the minds of consumers. Yet the material object eventually disintegrates and the song's memory is perpetuated through constant, mutable, and unpredictable performative references within the ballad trade and theatrical productions. Detached from their original referents, tunes will become unruly agents, possessing lives of their own as misremembered "monuments."

Notes

1. Congreve, *The Old Batchelor*, 20.
2. For more information on the standardization of the broadside ballad's visual format, see Watt, *Cheap Print*, 64–79.
3. See Puttenham, *The Arte of English Poesie*, sig. M1, and Brown, *Britannia's Pastorals*, sig. C2r for descriptions of various spaces both public and private that broadside ballads were performed.
4. See Williams, "'A Swearing and Blaspheming Wretch,'" 309–356.
5. Many recent studies in literary history and popular culture privilege ballad texts over tunes and performance issues. See, for example, Fumerton, Guerrini, and McAbee, *Ballads and Broadsides in Britain*, 1–10; Würzbach, *The Rise of the English Street Ballad*, 1–27; Shepherd,

The Broadside Ballad, 18–23; Clark, *Women and Crime*, 70–86; Dolan, *Dangerous Familiars*, 1–19. For existing studies on broadside trade tunes, see Simpson, *The British Broadside Ballad and Its Music*; Ward, "Apropos the British Broadside Ballad and Its Music," 28–86; Poulton, "The Black-Letter Broadside Ballad and Its Music," 427–437; Chappell, *The Ballad Literature*, 254–384; for more current contextual studies of the broadside and its music, see Marsh, "The Sound of Print," 171–190, and *Music and Society*, 225–327; Smith, *Acoustic World*, 168–205; Duffin, *Shakespeare's Songbook*, 15–42, and "Ballads in Shakespeare's World," 32–47.

6. For excellent texts on the memory arts in early modern Europe, see Minear, *Reverberating Song*, 1–16; Iselin, "Myth, Music, and Memory," 173–186; Cressy, "National Memory in Early Modern England," 61–73; Ivic and Williams, *Forgetting in Early Modern English Literature*, 1–17; Carruthers, *The Craft of Thought*, 7–59; Bolzoni, "The Play of Images," 16–65, and *The Gallery of Memory*, 236–259; Sherlock, *Monuments and Memory*, 197–230; Engel, *Mapping Mortality*, 1–11, and *Death and Drama*, 389–393; Hiscock, *Reading Memory*, 1–36; Wilder, *Shakespeare's Memory Theater*, 10–13, 24–58. See also the following primary sources on the memory arts and drama in early modern English culture: Puttenham, *The Arte of English Poesie*, 31–34; Agrippa, *Of the Vanitie and Uncertaintie*, sig. 24v–25r; Heywood, *An Apology for Actors*, sig. F3v.

7. Sullivan, *Memory and Forgetting*, 7. See also Yates, *The Art of Memory*, 11–12 for a more recent and particularly useful explanation of how to use a memory image and 2–4 for how to create a memory repository; Carruthers, *The Book of Memory*, 60–68. For early modern instructions on how to construct mental repositories, see Willis, *Mnemonica*, 61, 71–74; Willis, *The Art of Memory*, 1–10; D'Assigny, *The Art of Memory*, 83–90. In his preface to *Mnemonica*, Willis also describes the portion of the brain where images are stored as the "imaginative faculty" (sig. A5v). Fludd's diagram on the intellect and the functioning of the senses from *Utriusque Cosmi . . . Historiae* (217) locates this area in the rear of the brain.

8. Sullivan, *Memory and Forgetting*, 6. See also Engel, *Death and Drama*, 32.

9. Quoted in West, *Theatres and Encyclopedias*, 46.

10. Ibid., 2, 44–45.

11. See West, *Theatres and Encyclopedias*, 45, 55. See also Smith, *Acoustic World*, 206–245.

12. Fludd, *Utriusque Cosmi . . . Historiae*, 55. See Yates, *The Art of Memory*, 330–354 for an explanation of why she believes Fludd envisioned the Globe in particular.

13. Willis, *Mnemonica*, 52.

14. See 4.3.52–53. For more on the "Willow Song," see Austern, "The Music in the Play," 450–454.

15. Minear, *Reverberating Song*, 10–11.

16. See Dunn, "Ophelia's Songs," esp. 58–61.

17. See Carruthers, *The Book of Memory*, 5.

18. Heywood, *An Apology for Actors*, sig. F1v.

19. For the purposes of this study, however, I am more concerned with the act of recollection as early modern treatises on memory made the distinction between rote learning and reminiscence. See Carruthers, *The Book of Memory*, 20; Enders, "Music, Delivery, and the Rhetoric of Memory," 450–464; Busse Berger, *Medieval Music*, 1–8.

20. For more on the Guidonian hand and solfege as mnemonic aids, see Berger, "The Hand and the Art of Memory," 87–120; Busse Berger, *Medieval Music*, 92–93; and Carruthers, *The Book of Memory*, 21–22.

21. Cicero, *De Oratore*, 357–358.

22. Pepys, *Diary*, May 15, 1668, 200; Pepys, *Diary*, January 2, 1665, 2.

23. Pepys wrote of one visit to the fair wherein he heard the popular tune "Mardike" but decided it was too "silly" and so "did not write it out." This could perhaps indicate he did write out tunes he found interesting on occasion. Pepys, *Diary*, February 4, 1660, 41.

24. 3.1.71. Emphasis mine.
25. See Carruthers, *The Book of Memory*, 17–28 for the spatial nature of memory images.
26. See Minear, *Reverberating Song*, 10 and Iselin, "Myth, Music, and Memory," 180. On the relationship between performance and printed plays in the seventeenth century, see Stern, *Making Shakespeare*, 137–158, and *Documents of Performance*, 160–168.
27. For more on the visual nature of seventeenth-century popular culture, see Maravall, *Culture of the Baroque*, 96–101.
28. Brathwaite, *Whimzies*, 9–11.
29. Bownde, *Doctrine of the Sabbath*, 241.
30. Watt, *Cheap Print*, 192–195. See also Fleming, "Graffiti," 327, and Fumerton, "Not Home," 493–518. See Maravall, *Culture of the Baroque*, 97, 99, on imagery used as a psychological tool to alter and educate mass culture.
31. Saltonstall, *Picturae loquentes*, sig. E10. See also Walton, *The Complete Angler*, 49.
32. Bownde, *Doctrine of the Sabbath*, 241–242. H[olland], *A Continued Inquisition*, 4.
33. See Watt, *Cheap Print*, 75.
34. Ibid., 74.
35. Ibid., 79. See also Thompson, "The Development of the Broadside Ballad Trade," 64.
36. Watt, "Cheap Print and Religion," 107.
37. Maravall, *Culture of the Baroque*, 64–65.
38. Tessa Watt's influential study on cheap print examines how godly ballads, and in turn the "godly tunes" and woodcut imagery associated with them, were capable of shaping popular piety. See *Cheap Print*, 63–65, 150–168, and 248–250, in particular.
39. Quoted in Carruthers, *The Book of Memory*, 17.
40. D'Assigny, *The Art of Memory*, 65.
41. Willis, *Mnemonica*, sig. A5r.
42. Yates, *The Art of Memory*, 10–12. See also West, *Theatres and Encyclopedias*, 85–86, 102–106.
43. See Dolan, *Dangerous Familiars*, 20–25.
44. Musicologists have also noted a similar interplay of aural and visual learning at work in seventeenth-century emblem books containing musical allegories. Contemporary with the broadside ballad, emblem books were designed to teach lessons through cryptic but culturally significant pictures and poetic epigrams. See Austern, "The Siren," 95–138, for more information on representations of music in emblem books and their relationship to sex roles in early modern England. See also, for example, Austern, "Nature," 5–7; Simonds, *Myth, Emblem, and Music*, 13–28; Leppert, *The Sight of Sound*, 4–12.
45. *A Ballad of the Life and Deathe of Dr. Faustus, the Great Cungerer* (1589) and *The Judgment of God Shewed upon Dr. John Faustus* ([1658]).
46. For a more extensive table of broadsides set to "Bragandary," see Williams, *Damnable Practises*, 76.
47. For a lengthier discussion of "Fortune My Foe" and "Bragandary" and their histories of circulation in the seventeenth-century performative arts, see Williams, *Damnable Practises*, 65–80, and "'A Swearing and Blaspheming Wretch,'" 329–332.
48. Cavendish, *Playes*, 573. A play by Thomas May also contains a possible reference to this burden and tune. See May, *The Heire*, sig. H2r.
49. Rowley and Dekker, *The Noble Souldier*, sig. D4v.
50. For more on Cavendish's knowledge of ballad tunes in particular, see Larson, "Margaret Cavendish's Civilizing Songs," 109–134. See also Larson, "Song Performance and Spatial Production," this volume. For the transmission of ballad tunes to notated lute music, see Freeman, "The Transmission of Lute Music," this volume.

51. See *Titus Andronicus Complaint*; *The Tragical History of King Lear*, though an earlier version titled *The Tragecall Historie of Kinge* LEIR *and His Three Daughters* appears in the Stationers' Company register in 1605; *A Newe Ballad of Romeo and Juliett* was also registered with them in 1596.

52. For contemporaneous dramatic works referencing ballad sellers within the theater, see Filmer, *A Defence*, 32, and Cowley, *The Guardian*, sig. D3r. For other evidence of ballad sellers in and around amphitheaters, see Gurr, *Playgoing*, 55.

53. See West, *Theatres and Encyclopedias*, 118–121.

54. "Superannuated" could be a further satirical reference to an older woman's lament as opposed to the young women and brides referenced in broadsides set to "The Ladies Fall."

55. Daborne, *The Poor Mans Comfort*, sig. D3r.

56. These tasks included fire starters, book linings, and toilet paper; in his essay *Of the Observation and Use of Things*, Sir William Cornwallis mentions he makes use of broadsides in the "privy" wherein he employs them as "waste paper" (sig. I6–I7v).

57. For an excellent essay on the implications of these seventeenth-century collecting procedures, see Fumerton, "Remembering by Dismembering," 26–28.

58. Bloom, *Voices in Motion*, 6. See also Dunn and Jones, *Embodied Voices*, 1–13.

59. West, *Theatres and Encyclopedias*, 118.

60. See Carruthers, *The Book of Memory*, 32–33.

8.

The Challenge of Domesticity in Men's Manuscripts in Restoration England[1]

Candace Bailey

Until quite recently, scholarship on keyboard sources in late-seventeenth-century England has focused on the identification of copyists' hands, contents and concordances, and the attendant inquiries about the composers represented.[2] This research emphasizes music written specifically for a keyboard instrument, such as suites by John Blow, with modern writers using vague descriptors such as "some in arrangements" for other pieces in keyboard books.[3] Much of the other music in keyboard sources is overlooked because of several modern biases: (1) the music is not demanding; (2) the sources contain a variety of genres, including many pieces outside the solo repertory; and (3) the music does not seem to have been associated with professional music making, despite the fact that the copyists were very often what Christopher Marsh has labeled "occupational musicians."[4] And yet, scholars continue to place the sources in traditional categories and draw subsequent conclusions on the repertory based on these categorizations. Labels such as "amateur" and "domestic" result in skewed readings of this repertory because these terms are at odds with "professional."[5] In other words, twentieth-century categorization has functioned as a barrier to understanding the context of keyboard music from the late seventeenth century, and I contend that to learn more about the sources and how they were used, we must move away from modern concepts of professional, amateur, and domestic.

The difficulties in looking at seventeenth-century keyboard repertory as a whole are made apparent in John Harley's *British Harpsichord Music*, Vol. 2: History.[6] For the early period (specifically, the chapter entitled "Byrd's Successors"), the narrative proceeds by composer.⁷ In contrast, no composer receives an individual heading for the midcentury. The later period (which extends into the early eighteenth century) has both: composers, followed by topics such as "French influences."⁸ His divisions reflect the general tendency to explain these repertories by composer if the music is attributable and of a certain quality, and by function if it is not. This approach enables a certain type of examination of the period as a whole but one that is misleading if context is not considered.⁹

The historiography of the post-Restoration repertory reveals that assumptions made about English keyboard music during the twentieth century continue to cloud its interpretation.¹⁰ For example, Peter Leech asserts that "new styles of keyboard music emerged during the second half of the seventeenth century, but an understanding of their development is hampered by the lack of surviving comprehensive manuscript collections of keyboard music from this period."¹¹ "This period" is the third quarter of the seventeenth century. He continues:

> The majority of manuscripts which have come down to us are small, enigmatic "domestic" compilations drawn from diverse material. Apart from musical concordances, they offer few clues which might help scholars set them in the wider context of manuscript copying and circulation in England between 1660 and 1710. The Antoine Selosse manuscript . . . is arguably one of the more significant discoveries of Restoration keyboard music in recent years.¹²

Leech's statement raises several issues, such as how we define Restoration, and what is meant by "English music" and "English composers." Two comments relate directly to the present discussion: the supposed "lack of comprehensive manuscript collections" and the idea that "small, enigmatic '*domestic*' compilations drawn from diverse material" [italics mine] cannot "help scholars set them in the wider context of manuscript copying and circulation in England between 1660 and 1710."

Some of these problems derive from scholarly views of the midcentury, which has been described as a "transition" and a "decline" in the English keyboard tradition.¹³ The music surviving from these decades is relatively simple, often in versions arranged by the person doing the copying. The sources are usually labeled "amateur," "household," or "domestic" manuscripts, implying that the manuscripts were used by women. To be sure, several bear women's names. *Anne Cromwell's Virginal Book* is a case in point as the sparse textures and simplistic pieces (understandably) do not invite immediate appreciation.¹⁴ The result is that scholars have categorized this repertory as "domestic," recognized a few innovations (such as the beginning of the suite), and moved on. Two statements by Barry Cooper demonstrate this point of view. When discussing the "Function and Social Background" of English keyboard music from the "middle Baroque," he observes that "for most of the period music written for harpsichord served primarily for domestic use." He continues that this situation "helps to explain the small, intimate nature of so much of it. Most of the performers, too, were amateurs, so that one cannot expect, and one does not find, music of exceptional difficulty, except in rare cases.... It is also significant that most of the performers were young ladies."[15] These statements voice an underlying prejudice against simplistic music as is found in many sources and frame the discussion of the "small, intimate nature" of the music as something for the "ladies"—as if women could handle only simple music.

The keyboard repertory from the end of the century is more difficult to assess and categorize, in part because most of the manuscripts are quite large and contain a variety of pieces. Occupational musicians copied much of the surviving music.[16] They have traditionally been called "professional" musicians, which means men. Indeed, most copyists were men, but at least one woman keyboard player who was remunerated for her efforts as a keyboard player can be identified from this period: Henrietta Banister was paid for teaching Princess Anne in 1679. In contrast to the fact that most of the copyists earned their living through music, the keyboard music from this period does not evince a virtuoso, or what we recognize as "professional," keyboard tradition. The composers in these books are well known, most notably Henry Purcell, but their keyboard music usually receives only casual mention in modern literature. This dichotomy—famous composers/less-than-exciting keyboard music—has influenced research, and scholarly inquiry tends to focus on famous composers' music for media other than the solo keyboard.[17] Regardless of who copied it, scholarly literature has also associated this sparsely textured repertory with women, but the narrative is much more complex than simple demarcations of professional, amateur, or domestic.[18]

Modern uses of these words often obscure meaning and context in early modern sources. "Professional" typically means remuneration for services, but it also implies someone who earns a living through the activity.[19] Those who are not professional musicians in this sense are deemed "amateurs." These "amateurs" made music at home, but whose home? Samuel Pepys sang with friends in a number of places, and he listened to others making music in a variety of venues. Pepys often made music with "professional" or at least "occupational" musicians. How does "domestic" factor into Pepys's experience? Are sources used in such a fashion either professional or domestic? Do these terms indeed assist our understanding of the musical practice?

The word *amateur* and its attendant *domestic* constitute a significant part of the problem. These two terms have been used interchangeably to signify music making occurring somewhere other than the theater, cathedral/chapel, or court. Furthermore, the professional/domestic division exasperates research on the end of the century by boxing in what a "professional" musician did. If a "professional" copied a volume that contains simple music, scholars have felt the need to explain away the problem that the technical demands do not rise to the level of what is expected of a professional player. However, the supposition that an occupational musician required a more difficult repertory does not hold up under scrutiny, as we shall see. Context is the key to interpreting these keyboard manuscripts.

The findings of a few scholars will help clarify the problem of how our understanding of space, masculinity, and related ideas have led to misreadings of early modern English culture. Since Jürgen Habermas's recognition of the profound shift in social order and new understandings of "domesticity," several studies have examined different angles to produce a more nuanced view of this culture.[20] For example, in her work on space in British novels, Karen Lipsedge notes the rise of domestic sociability and its accompanying entertainments circa 1700, and Irene Cieraad perceives that the concept of domestic and public space develops in the West in the seventeenth century, marking the new notion of "domesticity" a powerful image related to domestic space.[21] Similarly, Amanda Vickery links the evolution of domestic sociability to the availability and popularity of tea in the early eighteenth century.[22] Heidi de Mare has demonstrated that our modern ideas of domestic meaning of the home derive from a nineteenth-century ideal, but in the seventeenth century, the physical boundary of the front door does not define the fixed borders of domestic space.[23] These carefully considered investigations of some of the terms used to describe keyboard manuscripts should be a warning against categorizing with sociological terminology.

The categorization "domestic" has yielded a false sense of purpose and context. What does the term *domestic* signify? What is the difference between domestic keyboard music and nondomestic keyboard music? Assuming that copyists prepared manuscripts for practical music making (and internal evidence suggests that most of them did), the people who used these volumes and the places where they used them is of paramount importance. Many are cast as "amateur," but I will demonstrate that they were used by occupational musicians for performance circumstances that modern observers might label "domestic" music making—a situation that places them in two seemingly contradictory categories.

GB-Och Mus. 1003 exemplifies part of the overall problem with manuscript categorization. The volume consists of three parts copied by at least four different people. The first eleven leaves contain music by earlier composers, copied from GB-Och Mus. 1113.[24] Next follow thirty-three pieces copied between 1660 and 1685 (fols. 12–29v and 52–52v [rev.]). One of the hands in this section belongs to Charles Morgan (ca. 1660–1738), who wrote "C. Morgan" and "Morgan his Booke" on the cover.[25] A chorister at Christ Church until 1677, he received a BA from Magdalen in 1681 and an MA from the same college in 1684. He remained there as a lay clerk until his death in 1738.[26] The other hand in this section is that of Henry Bowman. Little is known about Bowman, but there are several large collections of music in his hand. Peter Holman speculates that Bowman lived and worked in Oxford, and notes that he copied at least eighteen manuscripts between 1669 and 1685. Bowman styled himself "Philo-Musicus" in his *Songs for 1 2 & 3 Voyces* (published in Oxford in 1677), which suggests that he was not a professional musician.²⁷ Nonetheless, his association with numerous sources evinces a significant musical reputation. Around 1700, Richard Goodson Sr. (ca. 1655–1718, organist at Christ Church and university music professor), copied three pieces into the front of the book.²⁸ A collector, copyist, and composer, Goodson acquired several music books from Edward Lowe, the previous Heather Professor of Music at Oxford and organist at Christ Church, and added to them. These include GB-Och Mus. 1176 and GB-Och Mus. 1177.²⁹ Thus, GB-Och MS Mus 1003 is a case where one manuscript containing thirty-seven pieces can be connected directly with three different Oxford musicians from the second half of the seventeenth century. Morgan and Bowman are further connected through GB-Lbl Add. MSS 30382 and 33234, manuscripts of Italian and English music, one of which belonged to Katherine Sedley, a mistress of James II.³⁰

None of the pieces as they appear in this volume can be attributed to a public performance venue, nor are the technical demands as high as we might expect of music owned by occupational musicians. During the 1660s, Bowman entered easy keyboard settings of popular tunes, such as William Lawes's "Golden Grove" suite.³¹ The arrangements are quite simple, requiring little in the way of keyboard skill. Bowman did not copy intricate arrangements made by others—not that many exist, which is a suggestive circumstance indeed. (Whether Bowman was an occupational musician is unknown, but his hand is present in several important sources.) Scholars such as Rebecca Herissone have speculated on the meaning of such skeletal versions of Restoration pieces, noting the various circumstances under which the sources might have been copied.³² Bowman may have written down works that he liked, without bothering to make elaborate arrangements, and he probably did so to play them.³³

Morgan made most of his contributions after 1677.³⁴ Like Bowman, Morgan wrote simple accompaniments to popular songs. He also copied Draghi's music and shared it with Goodson (who eventually acquired GB-Och Mus. 1003). Morgan had significant musical training, and Bowman (the self-styled "Philo-Musicus") had at least a strong musical background. Goodson was an occupational musician. Both Bowman and Morgan appear to have used GB-Och Mus. 1003 for playing purposes, and the places where they might have used it almost certainly qualify as "domestic." Andrew Woolley proposes that Morgan and Bowman created GB-Och Mus. 1003 for practical purposes.³⁵ How else could the manuscript have been used other than in a "domestic" setting? "Small and enigmatic," and even "domestic," GB-Och Mus. 1003 offers substantial evidence of how occupational musicians in Oxford were involved with practical music in venues other than those that provided their livelihood (cathedral or chapel), how they heard and performed secular repertory, and how musicians might transmit the repertory among themselves.

Another source that demonstrates some of the issues that complicate how modern scholars read keyboard volumes is GB-Lbl Add. MS 31403, a large manuscript consisting of two distinct parts. GB-Lbl Add. MS 31403 differs from GB-Och Mus. 1003 in many ways—practically the only aspects they have in common are date and a muddled compilation history associated with occupational English musicians.[36] GB-Lbl Add. MS 31403 began life in Canterbury, where Edward Bevin copied a repertory representative of keyboard music ca. 1630.[37] At some point, it came into the possession of cathedral organist Daniel Henstridge. Elsewhere in this volume, Herissone examines Henstridge's participation in secular music activities in Canterbury, looking particularly at a small pocketbook in which he collected songs and catches.[38] He copied several manuscripts of Purcell's music and owned autograph copies of the composer's anthems. He may have taught members of the Filmer family, for his hand appears alongside those of Francis Forcer and William Turner in manuscripts associated with that household.[39] He obviously knew many important musicians, and his status as an occupational musician is undeniable. His involvement in other types of music making indicates that Henstridge also performed a different type of music than that required in his cathedral position.[40]

Such music finds its way into GB-Lbl Add. MS 31403. The portion of GB-Lbl Add. MS 31403 that Henstridge copied before 1690 includes several concordances with Goodson's personal collection (GB-Och Mus. 1177), one with GB-Och Mus. 1003, and two from a printed collection published for amateurs (*The Second Part of Musick's Hand-maid*, 1689). These pieces include simple dances by John Blow, Matthew Locke, and Francis Forcer. The concordances with *Musick's Handmaid*, a source that has been frequently described as women's music, might seem inappropriate for a "professional" musician's manuscript, but they are indeed present in GB-Lbl Add. MS 31403.

If Woolley is correct in his assessment that the various Canterbury musicians who had access to GB-Lbl Add. MS 31403 added to it for personal use, then it must have been used for private music making.[41] He includes this manuscript in his chapter on "Collecting Keyboard Music," calls it a "personal collection," and notes that these types of manuscripts are connected with "domestic" music making along with GB-Och Mus. 1177 (the Goodson volume) and *William Raylton's Virginal Book* (J-Tn, N-3/35).[42] Several of these sources are comprehensive collections and quite large: GB-Och Mus. 1177 measures 33 x 21 cm with forty-one folios, and *Raylton* is 31.5 x 21.5 cm with fifty-five folios. GB-Lbl Add. MS 31403 is even more substantial: 40.5 x 27 cm with seventy-eight folios.[43] These volumes are messy in every sense of the word: several hands (most identified as occupational musicians) often appear among their pages, some were used for almost a century, and the contents include both secular and sacred music.

One of the most fascinating aspects of later manuscripts is that sources connected with occupational men and recreational women musicians look very similar, a trend that begins during the transitional midcentury period. From about 1650 on, so-called "domestic" and "professional" manuscripts become indistinguishable, and around 1700, most keyboard sources still look alike—be they female/amateur/domestic or male/professional. One cannot easily confer a title of "professional" or "domestic" on sources such as GB-Och Mus. 1003 and 1177. We have tended to label volumes that contain simple music as amateur or domestic *unless* we know who copied them. Even then, received wisdom has been to assume that they must have been pedagogical—and some certainly were but not all of them.[44]

That musicians shared these volumes also suggests something about their personal relationships *and* the places where they played the music contained therein. This leads to more questions. If an occupational musician copies a volume or uses one in private settings, is it a "domestic" manuscript? Women's manuscripts are always labeled "domestic"—no doubt that was the context in which they were used. And certainly some of the men's manuscripts were used in liturgical settings, a situation that makes them professional. But as Woolley eloquently demonstrates, several occupational men's sources were used in domestic settings. At least two owned by Goodson fit this description.[45] Furthermore, a number of volumes changed hands, some from occupational male musician to recreational woman musician. Antoine Selosse apparently copied his manuscript around 1675, and no evidence connects it to a woman before 1710.[46] The first and only woman's name to appear in GB-Och Mus. 1003 was that of Anna Goodson, and she did not use the volume until several decades after men began it for their own use.

Nonetheless scholars tend to associate this repertory with women, and period publications suggesting women's use in the title seem to support this connection.[47] As noted above, Cooper writes that most of the secular music written in late-seventeenth-century England was intended for domestic use by women, and that the advent of public solo harpsichord performances by men in the eighteenth century brought the virtuoso repertory back again.[48] However, this scenario does not account for books that contain roughly the same repertory copied by occupational male musicians (such as GB-Och Mus. 1177) from the same period. As cathedral organists, Henstridge and Raylton were occupational keyboard players, but in technical requirements their books do not differ substantially from Elizabeth Edgeworth's (which contains music by Froberger, among others).[49]

"Amateur," "domestic," and other terms associated with women have been used to explain the English keyboard repertory of the middle and late seventeenth century. The repertory has been excused with comments that relegate it to home use, domesticity. However, many sources (such as GB-Och Mus. 1003) belonged to occupational men who transcribed simple-looking scores for their own personal use. The idea that a manuscript of simple music cannot be a book used by an occupational male musician for personal playing bespeaks another prejudice—one that elevates difficulty above simplicity and a concurrent supposed male virtuosity above female domesticity. Secular keyboard music from late-seventeenth-century England is sight-readable, and the Purcell suites are prime examples. As far back as 1937, Jack Westrup described Purcell's keyboard works as "relatively unimportant" and hinted at their being women's works by describing the harpsichord works as "little suites published by Mrs. Purcell with a dedication to Queen Anne."[50] Almost sixty years later, Curtis Price commented that this repertory, from Locke to Croft, "lacks coherency and represents a marked decline from the glories of Byrd, Bull, and Gibbons." He even posited that neither Blow nor Purcell were virtuosos.[51]

Looking at the extant music in both manuscripts and publications, such observations seem to ring true. On the other hand, period commentators praise the skill of several performers (particularly Draghi) whose compositions are no more difficult than the keyboard suites of Purcell.[52] This suggests that something has been misread, misunderstood, or misinterpreted. The notated music, as presented in both publications and manuscripts, is almost certainly deceptive. Terence Charlston's recording of the music of Albertus Bryne, ca. 1660, explores the possibilities inherent in adding to the page as written (particularly track #20).[53] Charlston's familiarity with the repertory and his willingness to experiment beyond the written page demonstrate a new approach to English keyboard music of the late seventeenth century but one whose practicality is based on experience.[54] That most versions of popular pieces differ and survive in somewhat skeletal form indicates that seventeenth-century performers were not married to the page, and it further suggests that we should not be either.[55] Considering that most keyboard players played from sparse scores to accompany, it would be a natural process for them to add to the keyboard scores as well.[56]

The companion website for this book includes an excerpt from the "Saraband" in GB-Llp MS 1040, f. 24v and five audio examples made by Charlston that demonstrate how someone trained in accompanying seventeenth-century music might apply similar principles to a simple score.[57] (See the Related Links on this book's page at http://iupress.indiana.edu.) In the first audio example, Charlston plays the first eight measures of an anonymous saraband from GB-Llp MS 1040 as they are found in the manuscript (which is possibly in the hand of Albertus Bryne, organist at St. Paul's and later Westminster Abbey). In audio example 2, Charlston alters the right-hand part with offbeat melodic delays and more extensive ornamentation. Continuo experience marks audio example 3, in which Charlston punctuates the texture sometimes with fuller chords, sometimes broken ones. Audio example 4 presents an approach full of broken chords, a sound characteristic of printed keyboard music, such as some of Purcell's preludes. The final audio example is the most extreme deviation from the manuscript version in that Charlston creates a new harmonization. Considering the lack of figures in much English music from the late seventeenth century, such a realization seems entirely plausible. These audio examples illustrate how one might use these sources.[58]

Thus, maybe it is not the visually simplistic music that is the problem but our unwillingness to experiment with playing the repertory? Substantial improvisation was part of seventeenth-century performance practice—that is how scholars explain the lack of organ music from this period.[59] It appears that this repertory comes to us in an outline form, and the issues raised here further support that idea.

Music we have labeled "domestic" is not only women's music—it also includes music performed by men who made their livings as musicians. There is merit in examining music and its place in gendered cultural aesthetics, but we must be careful that we do not categorize in generalizations that do not hold up against the evidence. English manuscripts must be examined in the context in which they were created and not solely on the exact representation of the repertory within. The line between "professional" music and "amateur" music is not as clear as we have made it out to be, and performance practice is rarely considered in the context of these sources. The issue is less whether a manuscript belonged to a man or a woman, or is domestic, amateur, household, or professional, but rather how much was done with the music therein—what happened with the music in practice? Diaries such as Pepys's tell us more about how music happened than do the sources. It is time to revisit the idea of the "work" and recognize that our idea of a composition fixed on a notated page differs significantly from the way a seventeenth-century performer considered the repertory.[60]

Few scholars have focused on these late-seventeenth-century manuscripts, partly because of their numerous contents and confusing compilation histories.[61] Hogwood even presents the possibility that "the very *domesticity* of these collections is responsible for their present neglect" [italics mine].[62] Nonetheless, sources such as GB-Och Mus. 1003 and GB-Lbl Add. MS 31403 do represent the state of keyboard music in England during the last part of the seventeenth century. We have resisted the idea of men playing "domestic" music, but they did. All the evidence in letters, diaries, and similar accounts point to men making music in spaces that we would describe as "domestic." Acknowledgment of these aspects—and a willingness to treat the "solo" repertory with the same sense of improvisation that keyboard players approach continuo performance—will enable an alternative interpretation of this music.

Notes

1. Research for this essay was made possible by a Summer Stipend from the National Endowment for the Humanities. This essay is a version of papers read at the American Musicological Society in 2010 and the Society for Seventeenth-Century Music in 2009. I would like to thank Andrew Woolley for his advice and for sharing his dissertation with me during the

early stages of the paper. I also appreciate comments and ideas from Terence Charlston and James Hume.

2. Such a focus is, of course, necessary to a degree: knowing a manuscript's provenance is a key element in being able to discuss its purpose, and so forth.

3. This phrase is used to describe two of the Oxford sources discussed below in Harley, *British Harpsichord Music*, vol. 1, 72. Details on numerous sources held in the British Library also use similar words for music in "keyboard manuscripts" that may have nonkeyboard origins, even at times for pieces for which no concordances exist.

4. Marsh, *Music and Society*, 72–73. This is a useful term and one that I will employ here.

5. In his study of political culture in early modern England, Phil Withington finds "the division between public and private—and its conflation with civic and domestic" anachronistic and deceptive. See his analysis in *The Politics of Commonwealth*, 197–198.

6. Harley, *British Harpsichord Music*, vol. 2, 3–146. The first comprehensive analysis of the early English keyboard repertory was Caldwell's *English Keyboard Music*, although several other publications supplement Caldwell's. These include Harley, *British Harpsichord Music*; Brown, "England," 22–85; Bailey, *Seventeenth-Century British Keyboard Sources*; and several dissertations: Cooper, "English Solo Keyboard Music"; Cox, "Organ Music in Restoration England"; Hodge, "English Harpsichord Repertoire"; Bailey, "English Keyboard Music"; and Woolley, "English Keyboard Sources."

7. Even this, the most conventionally described period of English keyboard music, is not without exceptions. It, too, deserves a reexamination.

8. The last decades of the seventeenth century are typically joined with the early decades of the eighteenth in several modern studies, and authors tend to take the date of Handel's arrival in England as the beginning of a new period. Hodge and Woolley begin their dissertations with "c. 1660" and continue until 1714 and 1720, respectively. Cooper includes the "middle and late Baroque" in his work, roughly dividing at about the same place.

9. It should be noted that Thurston Dart proposed a much more sophisticated categorization of English keyboard manuscripts in 1964. Dart described eight categories: (1) composer's workbooks, (2) presentation copies, (3) anthologies compiled by adult amateurs of music, (4) books prepared for (or, less usually, by) young amateur keyboardists, (5) study books prepared by (or, less usually, for) young would-be professionals under the guidance of their masters, (6) choirmen's anthologies for leisure playing, (7) books for day-to-day use by professional keyboardists, and (8) posthumous memorials. Dart, "An Early Seventeenth-Century Book," 27–28. See also Woolley, "English Keyboard Sources," xi–xii.

10. These divisions between professional and household (or "domestic") are keenest in my own *Seventeenth-Century British Keyboard Sources*, esp. 9–10.

11. Leech, *The Selosse Manuscript*, v. Leech issued a revised edition of *The Selosse Manuscript*, with different numbering systems. A guide, prepared by Terence Charlston, is available at http://homepage.ntlworld.com/terence.charlston/Selosse.htm (accessed 20 July 2015).

12. Leech, *The Selosse Manuscript*, v.

13. John Caldwell used the term *transition* in *English Keyboard Music*, 141–156, but more recently, he has also used the term *decline* (Caldwell, "Keyboard Music," 578).

14. Specifically, Cooper ("English Solo Keyboard," 22–23) finds that while earlier seventeenth-century manuscripts were compiled by men ("virtuoso virginalists"), for the second half, "most harpsichord music was written for, and played by, women." Midcentury books associated with women include *Priscilla Bunbury's Virginal Book* (privately held); see *Priscilla Bunbury's Virginal Book*; *Anne Cromwell's Virginal Book*; and lesser-known volumes, such as GB-Och Mus. 92 (see Bailey, *Seventeenth-Century British Keyboard Sources*, 87–89).

15. Cooper, "English Solo Keyboard," 21–22.

16. A reexamination of seventeenth-century ideas on music and masculinity is currently being undertaken by several scholars; see, for example, Linda Austern, "Domestic Song and the Circulation of Masculine Social Energy." Here, she examines the part informal music making played in expressing different types of masculinities, allowing for both the reaffirmation and subversion of social hierarchies.

17. Woolley's "English Keyboard Sources" is the most seriously considered investigation of these manuscripts, and my work here draws on his identification of hands and other aspects as noted.

18. Hodge uses the term "lady" in Hodge, "English Harpsichord Repertoire," vol. 1, 109. Here he draws on Cooper's similar remarks, Cooper, "English Solo Keyboard Music," 21–23.

19. Notably, it was not until 1811 that "professional" meant one who makes a profession or business from any occupation. See Wickham, Berry, and Ingram, *English Professional Theatre*, 1.

20. Habermas, *Structural Transformation of the Public Sphere*, 44–45.

21. "From the late 17th to the early 18th century, the way in which the polite élite used and conceived of their living space began to change. Central to this alteration was the rise of domestic sociability. Once the polite élite began to use the home as a setting for sociability new forms of entertainment began to evolve" (Lipsedge, *Domestic Space*, 22); Cieraad, "Introduction," 1–12, esp. 3.

22. Vickery, *Behind Closed Doors*, 14.

23. de Mare, "Domesticity in Dispute," 13–30, esp. 14–15. De Mare demonstrates that seventeenth-century meanings of these terms differ from modern ones, or, in other cases, the concepts simply didn't exist.

24. GB-Och Mus. 1113 came into the broader musicological world's attention in the 1980s, when Alexander Silbiger ("The Roman Frescobaldi Tradition," 77) addressed the puzzling Italianate works therein.

25. The names "C. Morgan," "John Morgan," "Morgan His Booke," and "J. Nordin" have all been inscribed at various places on the volume.

26. On Morgan, see Shay and Thompson, *Purcell Manuscripts*, 271.

27. Holman, "Bowman, Henry," *GMO*, accessed January 25, 2011.

28. Woolley, "English Keyboard Sources," 132.

29. This latter collection provides a further connection between Goodson and Morgan in that Goodson copied (probably in the 1680s) some works by Draghi that Morgan also entered into GB-Och Mus. 1003, (before Goodson acquired GB-Och Mus. 1003). See also Bailey, "Keyboard Music in the Hands of Edward Lowe and Richard Goodson I," 119–135.

30. Here, Morgan copied pieces by Bowman (in GB-Lbl Add. MS 30382) into GB-Lbl Add. MS 33234. For more on GB-Lbl Add. MS 30382, see Wainwright, *Musical Patronage*, 239–242.

31. William Lawes's popular suite, "The Golden Grove," appears in several seventeenth-century sources, albeit with different movements. The alman remains the same (or at least the general tune and basic harmony) in GB-Och Mus. 1236, GB-Och Mus. 1003, *Musick's Handmaide* (1663), as well as two nonkeyboard sources: *Courtly Masquing Ayres* (1662) and *Musick's Delight on the Cithren* (1666). See also Cooper, "Keyboard Suite," 312–314.

32. See especially Herissone's *Musical Creativity*. I am grateful to Herissone for sending me copies of chapters from this volume before publication. The consideration of what these sources mean is a welcome trend in recent years, but scholars still stop short of suggesting practical applications.

33. Herissone has significantly broadened our understanding of these types of keyboard scores. See specifically chapter 6 ("'His Mind Be Filled with the Materiall': Arrangement, Improvisation and the Role of Memory") in *Musical Creativity*, 315–391.

34. In some cases, additions made by Morgan physically overlap with some by Bowman. Woolley discusses these in "English Keyboard Sources," 136–138.

35. Woolley ("English Keyboard Sources," 136) suggests that Morgan "used it principally to accompany songs" and notes that there may have been a teacher-student relationship between Bowman and Morgan.

36. The latter portion of GB-Lbl Add. MS 31403 has been traditionally dated ca. 1700; however, Woolley ("English Keyboard Sources," 143–147) convincingly argues that some of the works were entered earlier based on handwriting changes in Henstridge's hand over time.

37. On the earlier portion of GB-Lbl Add. MS 31403, see Ford, "Bevins, Father and Son," 104–108. Ford identifies both Edward Bevin and Daniel Henstridge as the copyists of GB-Lbl Add. MS 31403.

38. Herissone, "Daniel Henstridge and the Aural Transmission of Music in Restoration England," this volume. See also her discussion of Henstridge in *Musical Creativity*, 89–92.

39. Woolley ("Social Context," 143) states that Henstridge was a "well-connected and influential Kentish musician." See also Robert Ford, "Henstridge, Daniel," *GMO*;, and Shaw, *The Succession of Organists*, 47–48, 121, and 235–236. See also Ford, "Minor Canons," passim.

40. Johnstone ("A New Source," 66–82) has recently identified Henstridge's hand in a teaching manuscript.

41. Woolley, "English Keyboard Sources," 147.

42. Ibid., 132–157. Herissone discusses the varied contexts of "personal file copies" in *Musical Creativity*, 98–104.

43. The unwieldy size of several volumes probably indicates that a music desk on a harpsichord was not where they were used. Such manuscripts could have been laid on the instrument or used as a memory aid (a place to jot down favorite or popular melodies). At 22 x 26 cm with fifty-two folios, GB-Och Mus. 1003 is slightly smaller, and (as with other manuscripts from Oxford) is oblong.

44. See, for example, Caldwell, *English Keyboard Music*, 175.

45. GB-Och Mus. 1003 and 1177.

46. Leech, *The Selosse Manuscript*, v.

47. See also Hodge's comments in note 18.

48. Cooper, "English Solo Keyboard," 22–23.

49. On this manuscript (B-Bc, MS XY15148), see Dart, "Elizabeth Edgeworth's Keyboard Book," 470–474.

50. Westrup, *Purcell*, 236–237.

51. Price, "Newly Discovered Autograph," 78. Cooper ("English Solo Keyboard," 21), on the other hand, asserts that Blow was an "outstanding virtuoso." I, too, had wondered about Purcell's keyboard abilities and whether the extant keyboard works represented his own mediocre skills. When I put this possibility to the late Howard Ferguson, he wrote back that he knew of no references to Purcell's keyboard abilities, "but since he was organist at Westminster Abbey they must have been considerable" (personal communication, February 1990).

52. I explored references to keyboard players in late-seventeenth-century descriptions in "Composition, Thorough Bass, Lessons, and the Meaning behind Playing a Keyboard Instrument in Restoration England," a paper given at the Society for Seventeenth-Century Music, Columbus, Ohio (March 2013).

53. *Albertus Bryne: Keyboard Music, Terence Charlston*.

54. Bruce Haynes gets to the heart of the issues of notation and "the work" (or lack thereof) in *The End of Early Music*, esp. 204–205.

55. See also Eubanks Winkler, "'Our Friend Venus Performed to a Miracle'" and Herissone, *Musical Creativity*, 209–259 and 315–391.

56. Writing about variants in lute sources and the practicality of performance, Tim Crawford ("Re-creating the Lute," 160) remarks that "any historical lute manuscript preserves a 'snapshot' of the compiler's view of a piece—the versions of a particular piece gathered from

the various sources will have a common core that one might be able to identify as the 'work,' but each will be overlaid with variants reflecting in some sense different interpretations of the work."

57. I am very grateful for his assistance. Charlston made all of the audio examples from the score featured on the website.

58. Herissone ("Daniel Henstridge and the Aural Transmission of Music in Restoration England," this volume) explores the likelihood that some scores, in her case one copied by Henstridge, do not reveal all that musicians of this period might have done with the music in front of them.

59. Caldwell, *English Keyboard Music*, 175, and Cooper, "English Solo Keyboard," 190.

60. Along these lines, see Butt's chapter, "The Seventeenth-Century Musical 'Work,'" 27–54.

61. Woolley is the obvious exception, although several other scholars have included its repertory in larger studies.

62. Hogwood, *"fitt for the Manicorde,"* iv.

9.

A Midcentury Musical Friendship: Silas Taylor and Matthew Locke

Alan Howard

This essay examines the intriguing "great friendship"[1] between the English composer Matthew Locke and the antiquarian and amateur musician Captain Silas Taylor, alias Domville, with the aim of opening a window onto the many subtleties of, and porous boundaries between, the conventionally separate categories of professional and amateur, parliamentarian and royalist, Protestant and Catholic, and their public and private expression in seventeenth-century England.[2] The contrasted confessional and political backgrounds of Locke and Taylor would seem strong barriers to social interaction: Locke apparently converted to Roman Catholicism while in the Netherlands with the exiled court in the late 1640s, later marrying Mary, daughter of Herefordshire recusant Roger Garnons; Taylor, by contrast, was the son of a "Grand Oliverian" and a former parliamentarian soldier, who served in the 1650s as Herefordshire subcommissioner for sequestration and compounding with papists and delinquents.[3]

From a biographical perspective centered upon Locke, it makes sense to gloss their well-attested friendship as "in spite of religious and political differences," casting Taylor as simply "an enthusiastic amateur musician who provided [Locke] with a house in Hereford."[4] On the other hand, any tacit assumption that Taylor's "amateur" music making had—and has—little bearing on his "official" persona could be misleading. Close attention to the music associated with Taylor reveals new evidence concerning his political proclivities, aligning him with his patron Edward Harley and former military commander Colonel Edward Massey, both of whom were increasingly estranged from the Cromwell regime during the 1650s.[5] The study of royalism during the Interregnum is already severely impeded by the difficulties of defining a clear category of representative beliefs and practices;[6] such concerns are only amplified when dealing with individuals who appear to traverse such boundaries, whether through day-to-day social interactions or a gradual realignment of political identity—or indeed, as we shall see, in cases such as Taylor's where it appears the former led to the latter over time.

As Robert C. Evans suggests in relation to the royalist poet Katherine Philips, such "difficulties and dilemmas" should certainly "discourage simplistic responses to the Interregnum as a whole."[7] Indeed, comparison between Taylor and Philips, the "matchless Orinda," is particularly instructive for the present purposes, and not just because of the superficial biographical similarities between these two ostensible Presbyterians with then-scandalous royalist connections.[8] Philips's Interregnum poetry forms part of a wider 1650s political discourse that has been widely figured in recent years as an early instance of what Habermas called the "public sphere";[9] her frequent rhetoric of domestic withdrawal—once a factor in her marginalization—has emerged as a key component of a public royalist poetic shared with other members of her coterie.[10] Similarly, Taylor's music has been largely overlooked as the work of a "competent" (read "uninteresting") amateur; yet a similar reconfiguration of the complicated relationships between apparently privately conceived and privately themed discourses on the one hand, and the fundamentally public nature of their conception, dissemination, and reception on the other, casts new light upon Taylor and his music.

"A Composer of Musick"

How Taylor, who as sequestrator was responsible for the confiscation of property and collection of fines from royalists and recusants, became acquainted with the Catholic musician Matthew Locke, who in the 1650s was on his way to recognition as the foremost English composer, is unknown, but numerous sources refer to Taylor's provision of a house during this period for Locke in Hereford.[11] Later, we find them both meeting with Samuel Pepys and one of the elder Purcells on the afternoon of Tuesday, February 21, 1660, in the aftermath of Parliament's confirmation of General Monck as commander-in-chief of the armed forces. The significance of this event in the lead-up to the Restoration was surely not lost on the group, as shown by Pepys's record of the title and nature of the composition they performed—a more apt musical representation of the promised reestablishment of rule and order could hardly be imagined:

> I met with Mr. Lock and Pursell, Maisters of Musique; and with them to the Coffee-house into a room next the Water by ourselves; where we spent an hour or two till Captain Taylor came to us. . . .
> Here we had variety of brave Italian and Spanish songs and a Canon for 8 *Voc:*, which Mr. Lock had newly made on these words: *Domine salvum fac Regem*, an admirable thing.[12]

Evidence relating to Locke in Taylor's autograph survives in his "Collection of Rules in Musicke" (GB-Lbl Add. MS 4910), dating from the later 1660s.[13] Taylor's version of John Birchensha's famous "Rules of Composition" occupies much of the manuscript, but Locke provided both a preprint version of his thoroughbass primer from *Melothesia* (1673) and a pair of canons published in Christopher Simpson's 1667 *Compendium of Practicall Musick*, the first of which is three bars longer in Taylor's version.[14] All are proudly labeled "given . . . to Silas Domville al^s Taylor" (fols. 43–44, 60), with the canons dated 1669.

Further evidence of the close association between the two men relates to a collection of thirty psalms, hymns, and other devotional songs attributed to Taylor in GB-Cfm Mu MS 163, part F (hereafter Cfm 163), which will be the focus of much of the discussion below;[15] as many as twelve of these songs are ascribed to Locke in a manuscript at Brussels Conservatoire (B-Bc MS 1035; for details see table 9.1).[16] Rosamund Harding spotted five of the Cfm 163 songs, including two with contested attributions, under Taylor's name in a University of Pittsburgh manuscript;[17] she thus considered all twelve "doubtful" at best for Locke.[18] It is clear, furthermore, that most of the Cfm 163 songs can only be associated with Taylor, and there is no sharp stylistic distinction between this majority and the twelve items attributed to Locke in Brussels: all are worthy of Locke, yet quite attainable for a skilled amateur like Taylor (see figures 9.1 and 9.2).

It seems likely that Pepys referred to this same body of works in his diary on Sunday April 16, 1665:

> By and by comes Capt. Taylor . . . that understands Musique very well and composes mighty bravely; he brought us some things of two parts to sing, very hard. But that that is the worst, he is very conceited of them; and that, though they are good, makes them troublesome to one, to see him every note commend and admire them.[19]

If this indeed refers to the Cfm 163 songs, it would be fascinating to know which passages particularly stirred Taylor's pride. Although they contain some touches of imitation, there are no passages of particularly learned counterpoint; perhaps Taylor's acute ear for chromatic intensification and assured modulations aroused the envy of the diarist, who famously failed in his attempts to master the technique of thoroughbass.[20] Also worthy of note is Taylor's use of written expression marks in two songs: the instructions *"(voce) submissè"* and *"strenué"* (both with varying diacritics; see figure 9.2) appear to indicate contrasting moods, perhaps analogous with Giulio Caccini's example illustrating *Esclamazioni*, "*languida*" or "*più viva*," in the preface to his 1602 *Le nuove musiche*.[21] Taylor's use of these Latinate terms as specific performance directions in the score is extremely unusual, though as Andrew Parrott has recently pointed out, the term *submissa voce* had long been applied to the action of singing softly.[22] This usage was evidently current in England, because Charles Butler made use of an Anglicized version in 1636, urging that "In Ditti-Mixt-Musik is alway to bee observed, that the Instruments dooe either sound Submisly, or by Turns; that the Ditti bee not obscured."[23]

Table 9.1 Cfm 163, fols. 45–72: Contents.

Item	Page (folio)	Text	Source	Comments
[1]	1 (45)	Lord to my pray'rs incline thine eare	Sandys,* 84–5: Psalm 55, stanzas 1, 4 (lines 1–34), 13 (ll. 5–6)	Attributed Locke in B-Bc MS 1035, p. 16, with small variants; Taylor in Pittsburgh MS (see Harding, 32)
2	2 (45v)	When stormes arise	Sandys, 37: Psalm 27, stanzas 4–5	Final couplet of text rewritten: see page 141 below
3	4 (46v)	My pray'rs shall with yᵉ suns uprise ascend	Sandys, 86: Psalm 55, stanzas 10–11	Attrib. Locke in B-Bc MS 1035, p. 18, with small variants (Harding, 32)
4	6 (47v)	Fraile man is dayly dyeing	Sandys, 149: Psalm 90, stanzas 2–31	
5	8 (48v)	O happie summons	Sandys, 205–6: Psalm 122, ll. 1–10	
6	9 (49)	God there shall his tribunall place	Sandys, 206: Psalm 122, ll. 11–20	
7	10 (49v)	All from the sunns uprise	Sandys, 163–64: Psalm 100, complete	
8	12 (50v)	Urbs caelestis	Hildebert†, 48: ll. 11–13, 3, 7–8	Attrib. Locke in B-Bc MS 1035, p. 20 (Harding, 33)
9	14 (51v)	Canite dominum	Buchanan‡, 250: Psalm 105, ll. 1–8	Attrib. Locke in B-Bc MS 1035, p. 14 (Harding, 32–3)
10	16 (52v)	New composed dittyes sing	Sandys, 158–59: Psalm 96, ll. 1–10, 17–18	Attrib. Locke in B-Bc MS 1035, p. 10 (Harding, 32)
11	18 (53v)	Now great Jehovah raignes	Sandys, 154: Psalm 93, complete	Attrib. Locke in B-Bc MS 1035, p. 12 (Harding, 32)
12	20 (54v)	As on Euphrates shady bankes	Sandys, 219: Psalm 137, ll. 1–16	Attrib. Locke in B-Bc MS 1035, p. 6 (Harding, 31)

Table 9.1 (Continued)

Item	Page (folio)	Text	Source	Comments
13	22 (55v)	Remember Edom Lord	Sandys, 219–20: Psalm 137, ll. 17–26	Attrib. Locke in B-Bc MS 1035, p. 8, with small variants (Harding, 31)
14	24 (56v)	You Kingdomes through ye world	Sandys, 105–8: Psalm 68, ll. 95–102, 27–28, 103–6	
15	26 (57v)	I to thy wing for refuge flye	Sandys, 112–13: Psalm 71, stanza 1 (ll. 1–3), stanza 3, stanza 4 (ll. 2–6)	Attrib. Locke in B-Bc MS 1035, p. 2 (Harding, 31)
16	28 (58v)	Now in the winter of my yeares	Sandys, 114–15: Psalm 71, stanzas 9–11	Attrib. Locke in B-Bc MS 1035, p. 4 (Harding, 31)
17	30 (59v)	You who the Lord adore	Sandys, 215: Psalm 134, complete	
18	31 (60)	Civitas amplissima populo	Tremellius: Lamentations 1, vv. 1–2	Word order altered; initial "Quomodo" omitted, and v. 2 begins "Plorans Ploravit" (as Vulgate) not "Quomodo plane flet"
19	32 (60v)	Miserere mei Deus	[See "comments"]; Psalm 51, vv. 3–4, 6, 11	V. 3 Vulgate (Ps 50); vv. 4 and 6 (last clause omitted) Tremellius; v. 11 Vulgate but begins "Averte" not "Absconde"
20	34 (61v)	Dominantur in nos servi	Tremellius: Lamentations 5, vv. 8, 16–17, 15	Word order altered in places
21	36 (62v)	Quid faciemus	Unknown	Attrib. Locke in B-Bc MS 1035, p. 22 (Harding, 33); text attrib. there to St Augustine but spurious according to Harding
22	38 (63v)	Domine caelos tuos	[See "comments"]; Psalm 144, vv. 5–9.	V. 5 Vulgate, vv. 6–8 Tremellius, v. 9 Vulgate (+Hallelujah); altered word order throughout

(Continued)

Table 9.1 (Continued)

Item	Page (folio)	Text	Source	Comments
23	40 (64v)	Candore et rubore dilectus meus	Tremellius: Song of Songs 5, vv. 9–11, 15	Word order altered; second half of v. 11 and final clause of verse 15 omitted
24	42 (65v)	Dilecto meo ostium aperui	Tremellius: Song of Songs 5, vv. 5–7	Word order altered; v. 7 replaced with Vulgate v. 8 (its direct equivalent), and some other small variants
25	44 (66v)	O Deus, mi Deus	Tremellius: Psalm 63, vv. 2–5	With small variants and changes to word order
26	46 (67v)	Incubili meo per noctes	[See "comments"]; Song of Songs 3, vv. 1–2, 5	Begins as Tremellius, but second clause onward paraphrased, importing vocabulary from Vulgate vv. 2 and 4; v. 5 as Vulgate
27	48 (68v)	Vox dilecti mei	[See "comments"]; Song of Songs 2, vv. 8, 10–12	Vv. 8, 10 & 11 as Vulgate, v. 12 from Tremellius; minor variants and altered word order throughout.
28	50 (69v)	Revertere ô Sulammittis	Vulgate: Song of Songs 6, v. 12, and 7, vv. 1 & 6	Word order altered, and occasional contamination from Tremellius
29	52 (70v)	Non habet Sion corruptelam	Hildebert, 48: ll. 9, 6, 15–18	
30	54 (71v)	Cantate Jehovah	[See "comments"]; Psalm 9, verses 12 & 6	Neither Tremellius nor Vulgate; v. 12 closer to latter and 6 to former

*George Sandys, *A Paraphrase on the Psalmes of David* (London, 1636).

†Hildebert of Lavardin (1056–1133), "De Confessione Sanctae Trinitatis", available in Interregnum England in James Ussher, *De Romanae Ecclesiae symbolo apostolico vetere aliisque fidei formulis* (London, 1647), 45–48.

‡George Buchanan, *Paraphrasis psalmorum Dauidis poetica* (London, 1580); citations given from the reprint as *Psalmorum Davidis paraphrasis poetica Georgii Buchanani Scoti* (London, 1648).

§Immanuel Tremellius, Franciscus Junius, and Théodore de Bèze, *Biblia sacra* (first London folio 1580; many reprints including London, 1640).

Figure 9.1 Silas Taylor, "Dominantur in Nos Servi." Cfm 163, fol. 61v, © The Fitzwilliam Museum, Cambridge.

Figure 9.1 (*Continued*)

Figure 9.2 Silas Taylor, "Vox Dilecti Mei" (also attributed to Matthew Locke in B-Bc MS 1035, p. 24). Cfm 163, fol. 68v, © The Fitzwilliam Museum, Cambridge.

It is surprising that Taylor's very accomplished songs have not attracted greater attention. No doubt at least partly to blame are his status as an "amateur" composer, the fact that the songs remained unpublished, and their association with "private" performance. Before examining them in more detail, we must first explore the background to Taylor's political identity and flesh out some details of the public controversy in which he became embroiled in the mid-1650s.

"Beloved by All the King's Party"

The apparent conflict in Taylor's persona most obviously exemplified by his friendship with Locke, and to be further strengthened in the reading of his devotional songs that follows, stems from an implicit assumption, I argue, that his political identity can be located primarily in the external signs of his upbringing, military service, and public appointments. Very similar assumptions (concerning her youth, education, and marriage) marked the modern reception of Katherine Philips's poetry until comparatively recently, with the additional factor of gender exacerbating the degree of her marginalization.[24] As Philips's work has been taken more seriously, however, the strength of her royalist friendships has been increasingly understood as a vehicle of empowerment in the face of traditional notions of patriarchal authority and feminine domesticity.[25] Not only did Philips's assertion of authorial autonomy per se threaten conventional notions of proper female behavior, but also her royalist associations further undermined societal assumptions that women's political identities were tied, like their legal subjecthood, to those of their husbands or fathers.

Similar lines of reasoning might arguably be applied to male contemporaries, whose lives were equally (if differently) shaped by patriarchal societal norms. In Taylor's case, the conventional account is of a promising parliamentarian soldier and administrator whose career was cut short by the Restoration: "The times turning, he was faine to disgorge all he had gott, and was ruined."[26] Yet Taylor was already a controversial figure in 1650s Hereford: his sponsorship of the Catholic royalist Locke and his music meeting were publicly denounced as politically subversive. Furthermore, even his earliest biographers hint at ambivalence toward the political milieu within which he came of age. According to Wood, his education at New Inn Hall, Oxford, from 1641 was interrupted when he was "soon after *called thence*, without the taking of a degree"; thereafter, "upon the eruption of the civil wars, he took part with the rebels *upon his father's instance*," and later "was made *by his father's endeavours* a sequestrator of the royalists in Herefordshire."[27] Silvanus Taylor Sr. also looked after his eldest son's material needs: he "setled upon him a good estate in church lands . . . and *had* the moiety of the bishop's palace in Hereford setled on him."[28] Wood's phraseology may reflect his post-Restoration standpoint, but the constant passive constructions are nevertheless striking. While there is no suggestion that Taylor followed his father's wishes under protest, the strength of his patriarchal obligation is arguably little diminished even if he did so out of genuine filial loyalty. The idea that his conscience was pulling in a different direction, meanwhile, might help explain why despite his father's beneficence, once installed at Hereford, Silas "used [his power] so civilly and obligingly, that he was beloved by all the King's party."[29]

Such disjunctions would soon impinge on both Taylor's and Philips's public lives. For Philips, the occasion was the threat to her husband, the parliamentarian administrator James Philips, referred to in "To Antenor on a paper of mine wch J. Jones threatenes to publish to his prejudice."[30] Far from conforming to expected feminine modesty and retracting, Philips's response—apart from ridiculing Jones—adopted the then-remarkable strategy of reasserting her personal autonomy: "My love and life I must confesse are thine, / But not my errours, they are only mine" (lines 7–8).[31] Yet whereas the conventional lack of female subjective autonomy ironically permitted Philips such flagrantly royalist outbursts without seriously endangering her husband's (and therefore her) position, Taylor's own brush with radicalism reveals his greater difficulty in divorcing his "amateur" pursuit of music from its public implications.

His trouble originated in a dysfunctional working relationship with his fellow Herefordshire sequestrator Captain Ben Mason, an outsider identified with a town-based, radical puritan faction (as against Taylor's association with county Presbyterian gentry). From October 1652, the two exchanged accusations concerning various abuses of office,[32] with matters coming to a head in 1653 with Mason's deposition of seventeen articles against Taylor. Not least among these were that "he associates with Papists and delinquents, owns himself their protector, and has meetings with them at taverns late at night, with music"; that "he hired a house at Hereford for a Jesuitical Papist" (presumably Locke); and that "he wanted to dismiss the clerk and put a musician in his place."[33]

Ultimately emboldened by his exoneration, Taylor counterattacked with an anonymously published pamphlet *Impostor Magnus* (1654),[34] viciously excoriating one of Mason's witnesses—the puritan divine Richard Delamain—who had testified that "the Souldiers in the Garrison of *Hereford*, upon Monday and Tuesday the 3. and 4. of January, 1652, were necessitated to keep all to their arms, by reason of a convention of Papists and Delinquents . . . occasioned by a Musick-meeting, appointed by Captain *Taylor*."[35] To parry the charge that this activity was contaminating his public office, Taylor plays down its importance, scoffing "What credit he doth the Souldiers, to be afraid of a Musick-meeting; surely [they] are *fraughted* with very unharmonious Souls, to be *frighted* with fiddles."[36] Thus, whereas Philips asserts her autonomy in spite of her sex, which protects her, Taylor opts to undermine his vulnerability, protesting in essence that "it's just Musick." In doing so, he becomes complicit in the disregarding of activities not considered part of his official or public status as described above, encouraging the assumption that his "amateur" pursuits are of minimal biographical importance.

Apparently undeterred, Delamain remains adamant, in his no-more-edifying reply *The Close Hypocrite Discovered,* that Taylor's music meeting represented a genuine threat: "The Pamphleteer himself confesses, that at one meeting there was ten men and six women; the number was not above as many more that gave the first onset, when the Parliaments forces surprized the City of *Hereford* [referring to the advance party, disguised as laborers, which opened the gates to Colonel Birch's waiting army in December 1645[37]] . . . whilst such meetings by such persons are ever to be suspected."[38] Having anticipated the charge of subversion, however, Taylor sarcastically pointed out two of Delamain's own "Croneys" among the "participants in this dangerous enterprize" of music making.[39] Remarkably, Taylor goes on to blame these individuals—George Lynn, the very "clerk" Mason alleged Taylor had sought to supplant with a musician, and Matthew Price, an innkeeper and former agent for the Committee for Compounding who had himself been investigated for misdemeanor in 1653—for his opponents' knowledge of the meeting, even as he asserts their presence as evidence for its nonpartisan nature.[40]

Taylor's portrayal of his meetings as politically neutral resembles Anthony Wood's account of William Ellis's meetings in Oxford, whose participants' "love of music superseded any political, religious, or philosophical differences."[41] Taylor himself attended these meetings in the late 1650s, as Wood tells us, though it is unclear (because Wood only started attending in 1656) whether Taylor could have been familiar with this cross-partisan musical circle while his Hereford meetings were taking place.[42] Meanwhile, and whether genuine or merely polemical, Delamain's aspersions exemplify a narrative of suspected sedition that affected clubs and societies of many kinds during the seventeenth century.[43] Some mid-century musical organizations clearly were identified strongly as royalist, including the Old Jewry "Musick-Society" associated with John Playford, which Taylor also seems to have encountered in London after 1659 and which, as Bryan White notes elsewhere in this volume, drew its membership from a broad social cross-section.[44] The music meeting held by Henry Lawes at his London house was the base for a royalist musical and literary circle heavily overlapping with Katherine Philips's coterie; two of her poems on friendship appeared in Lawes's 1655 *Second Book of Ayres, and Dialogues.*[45] We know much less about the participants and repertoire at Locke's and Taylor's Hereford meetings, though Taylor's detractors clearly felt they showed similar royalist bias; the Cfm 163 "Taylor" songs, furthermore, would have been ideal repertoire for such a meeting.

"As on Euphrates Shady Banks"

One should of course be wary of assuming that vocal music per se—even setting religious texts, and even in Latin—automatically raised suspicions of Anglicanism or even popery: Cromwell himself was apparently "most taken with" the few-voice motets by Richard Dering that John Hingeston had performed in his household,[46] and indeed Hingeston even seems to have set to music a large-scale Latin ode in honor of Cromwell—*Funde flores, thura crema*—marking the third anniversary of the protectorate, in line with what Patrick Little has suggested was an increasing use of music in a state-ceremonial context in a court setting influenced more and more by cultured civilian courtiers such as Bulstrode Whitelocke, Viscount Lisle, and Pepys's patron, Edward Mountagu.[47] Yet conversely, William Ellis's Oxford meetings do seem to have favored consort music specifically as a precaution against puritan suspicion of vocal music, on the grounds that the latter was "used in church by the prelaticall partie."[48]

What is particularly striking about the "Taylor" songs, though, is not just their psalmic texts, which after all were common to Anglicans, Presbyterians, Independents, and indeed Catholics alike, but their persistent pre-Restoration royalist outlook. Table 9.1 shows the contents of Cfm 163: seventeen songs set English texts from the 1636 *Paraphrase on the Psalmes of David* by George Sandys, the royalist courtier and poet, while a further thirteen in Latin draw mainly on psalms, the Song of Songs, and Lamentations. Sandys's poetic renderings were saturated with Laudian sensuousness and references to "divine kingship," associated in his dedication with Charles I himself, all of which would have been anathema to Taylor's enemies among the Hereford Independents.[49] Moreover, the passages chosen frequently explore themes of isolation, separation, and imposition, long-standing tropes of exile and captivity among English recusant Catholics that proved similarly germane to 1650s royalism.[50]

Among the longest of Taylor's settings is Psalm 137, with its poignant description of Jerusalem laid waste and vengeful predictions toward the Israelites' Babylonian oppressors; for Paula Loscocco, tracing the influence of this text upon an emergent 1650s royalist "psalmic poetic," this text above all "enabled writers to construct the Interregnum as an interregnum—as a period of humiliation, chastisement, disenfranchisement, patience, and silence that might extend for decades . . . but that would come to an end when God's anger at the confessed sins of God's chosen people subsided."[51] Similar themes are explored in texts from Psalm 122, Psalm 71, and two songs setting texts from the Lamentations of Jeremiah, but perhaps even more revealing are the explicit allusions to royalty and kingship such as the start of Psalm 96, "New composed Ditties sing / To our Everlasting King," or the image in "Non habet Sion" of a Zion built from walls of living stone, whose protector is the King of Joy ("cujus muri lapis vivus / cujus custos rex festivus"). "When Stormes Arise," a setting of words from Psalm 27, is particularly intriguing. The stanzas selected make good sense as a reference to the same rhetoric of enforced retirement observed in the writings of Philips and her circle; what makes Taylor's setting remarkable, however, is its rewriting of Sandys's final couplet apparently with the sole purpose of introducing a reference to "my King," doing considerable violence to the original couplet of iambic trimeter:

> When stormes arise on every side,
> He will in his Pavillion hide:
> How ever great,
> In that retreat
> I shall conceal'd and safe abide.
> He, to resist their shocke,
> Hath fixt me on a Rocke.
>
> Now is my head advanc'd, renown'd
> Above my foes, who gird me round;
> That in my Tent
> I may present
> My sacrifice with Trumpets sound:
> There will I praises sing   [*Sandys:* There I thy praise will sing,
> And Hallelujahs to my King.   Set to a well-tun'd string.][52]

Other allusions to kingship are more extended. "Revertere O Sulammittis" is one of five texts from the Song of Songs, most of which express longing for an absent lover. Like the Psalms, such texts meant different things to different people: puritan interpretations figured the "Godly" protestant church as the bride of Christ, while among some Catholic writers the Song of Songs invoked a heady allegory of the Immaculate Conception and, by extension, Charles I's bride Henrietta Maria; it could thus stand as a lament for Charles I or even an expression of his subjects' desire for the "return" of Charles II.[53] The specific text of "Revertere O Sulammittis" is more subtly allegorical: the longed-for Shulamite is a female personification of peace via the etymological connection with the word *shalom*, and similarly linked to Jerusalem, frequent code for an England in better times (as in the royalist interpretation of Psalm 137);[54] furthermore, the fact that this Shulamite is the daughter of a prince seems particularly suggestive. Perhaps most striking of all the texts set in terms of its apparent reference to the royalist condition in the 1650s, though, is the selection from Lamentations chapter 5 in "Dominantur nos servi"; these are words that hardly require interpretation as a reference to Charles I's execution and its attendant disruption of social order (given here in the 1611 King James Version; for the original text and music, see figure 9.1):

> [8] Servants have ruled over us: there is none that doeth deliver us out of their hand.
> [16] The crowne is fallen from our head: Woe unto us, that wee have sinned.
> [17] For this our heart is faint, for these things our eyes are dimme.
> [15] The joy of our heart is ceased, our daunce is turned into mourning.

The emerging picture is one of a collection of sacred songs that could have provided for shared political identity among a group of even quite disparate individuals, including perhaps both Catholics and prayer book Anglicans and Episcopalians, and both those who had remained loyal to Charles I himself and those who were more generally committed to the principle of monarchy. If so, Taylor's carefully curated texts would also encompass those who originated on the opposite side of the divide but who perhaps never supported the regicide (even if strongly opposed to the person of Charles I himself); indeed, the inclusive first-person plural of Lamentations 5 seems particularly suited to such personal identification with the causes of the Troubles. Individuals like Taylor and his Presbyterian patrons (as discussed above) may increasingly have embraced the idea of Restoration in the face of anxiety about the nature of Cromwell's government and in particular, as we see in *Impostor Magnus*, the spread of radical independent religion without state control. Without going into detail here, such a reading would be consistent with the evolution shown in Taylor's manuscript and published writings, their early antiroyalism[55] tempered from the start with the antiquarian's strong distaste for iconoclastic cultural vandalism.[56] Later, they show at least a pragmatic acceptance of the inevitable return of state religion (in Taylor's transcription of the Caroline cathedral statutes of Hereford, which he noted "may be of a manifold use; to be made out hereafter"[57]), even stretching to praise for past restored monarchies—such as that of the fifth-century King Vortiger—in his 1663 *History of Gavel-Kind*.[58]

"New Composed Dittyes Sing / To Our Everlasting King"

The large amount of instrumental music Locke composed around the time he was in Hereford could have provided comparatively uncontentious repertoire for a nonpartisan music meeting along the lines of that described by Wood in Oxford, where even known Catholics and royalist sympathizers seem to have been admitted. That Taylor's meetings instead proved so controversial might be partly explained by performance of music with the strong internal implications discussed above; and as we have seen, the participants in the meetings included individuals from Taylor's opposing faction who were well placed to relay such information to his most vocal critics. The scandal seems all the more understandable, furthermore, when contextualized within the much wider flowering of royalist devotional song in the 1650s—a conscious promotion of the genre concurrent with the literary appropriation of the metrical psalm described by Loscocco, but rather more straightforwardly linked with the popularity of *stile nuovo* liturgical and sacred music in prewar courtly circles.[59] Even aside from their textual sources, this style firmly links the "Taylor" songs with repertoire that remained rich in associations with royalist activity elsewhere: Richard Dering's Latin motets had been performed in Henrietta Maria's Catholic chapel from

1625, for example, and were apparently later adopted by the reduced Anglican Chapel Royal at Oxford. During the 1640s, George Jeffreys, who supervised the copying of some of Dering's music for that purpose, also composed both Latin and English "Mottects"; later, in the 1650s, he provided similar music for Exeter House in London, where the royalist divine Peter Gunning managed to maintain prayer-book Anglican worship.[60]

Robert Thompson has pointed out the strength of topical resonance in the words from Psalm 80 set by Jeffreys probably immediately after the 1649 regicide, using careful selection from scripture in a very similar manner to the "Taylor" songs.[61] Much the same could be said of some of the Lawes brothers' songs; indeed, in its inclusion of both English and Latin words, including texts from Sandys and from Lamentations, Henry's 1648 memorial to his brother in *Choice Psalmes* presents a striking parallel with the Cfm 163 repertoire. Yet Lawes makes the royalist agenda even more explicit, not only dedicating his book to Charles I but also observing that "much of Your Majesties present condition, is lively described by King Davids pen";[62] a conceit that was to be taken even further in the 1649 *Eikon Basilike*—and its musical adaptation, John Wilson's 1657 setting of Thomas Stanley's *Psalterium Carolinum*—in which the purported prayers of the king directly appropriated psalmic language and tone.[63] Lawes's songs, furthermore, seem to have been well known in Hereford: "The ghost of *Sandys* in *Elyzium* longs / To have his Joy encreas'd by *His-Your Songs*," wrote Clement Barksdale to his fellow Hereford vicar choral John Philips, in a poem addressing Henry Lawes and later printed on the same page as a complaint on behalf of the displaced vicars choral of Hereford, who had been ejected from their college by Colonel Birch in 1645.[64] If indeed the Cfm 163 "Taylor" songs represent a provincial contribution to this wider repertoire of royalist-themed *stile nuovo* psalm settings,[65] it seems likely that their performers could have included former vicars choral; at least one, William Broad, was certainly in touch with Locke in 1654 when he proposed to him a plainsong for a canon.[66] Taylor's meetings could even have been intended to compensate for the ejected vicars' lost facilities; in the 1630s, their college is recorded as a venue for private music making by a visiting party from Norwich, while late in the century it became the site of a regular music meeting.[67]

A series of previously mysterious rubrics observed in Cfm 163 by Harding may even suggest that the "Taylor" songs were considered for wider distribution at some (perhaps later) stage;[68] as late as 1681, for example, Playford was advertising manuscript copies of "choicest Vocal Hymns and Psalms for two and three Voyces" by a distinctly retrospective list of composers—including both Lawes brothers, Locke, Jenkins, and Rogers—testifying to the continuing popularity of recreational psalm singing in the 1660s (as described later in this volume by White) and well beyond.[69] In fact, the Cfm 163 rubrics direct the reader through an ordered sequence beginning at the all-important Psalm 137 and progressing through songs—first in English, then Latin—with successively higher keynotes, beginning at G minor (table 9.2). Comparable schemes are followed, with varying degrees of consistency, in Lawes's *Choice Psalmes* and both volumes of *Cantica Sacra*. In the absence of any obvious reason to have copied the songs out of order, it seems likely that the anonymous copyist began by following the order (of composition?) in his source but later—perhaps as early as item 14, after which the sequence is already logical—began following the rising-keynote scheme, adding instructions to the existing items to derive an ordered collection for use in a scriptorium context or even perhaps as potential printer's copy.

The friendship between Locke and Taylor with which I began this essay looks considerably less incongruous in the context of Taylor's Cfm 163 psalms and their relationship to the wider royalist genre of *stile nuovo* devotional song. Taylor's political identity is likely to remain ambiguous, but the gentle hints of Wood and Aubrey and the vicious impugning of his political enemies together suggest real divergence of Taylor's views from the political status quo by 1652–1653. Nevertheless, as with Katherine Philips, it is clear that political and religious identity, normative assumptions concerning gender and its social expression, the negotiation of public and private spaces and discourses, and even the distinction between so-called professional and amateur roles all interact in complicated ways, which are more likely than not to defy conventional oppositions. Willingness to embrace such confusion, while it may produce messier and more equivocal narratives, surely results in a richer understanding of the period and its cultural legacy.

Taylor's experiences post-1660 further illustrate the difficulties of pinning down his Interregnum persona, in light of early biographical accounts conceived against the backdrop of Restoration political realities. Notwithstanding Aubrey's reference to his ruin, Taylor was able to rely on patrons to secure him in respectable employment, first as commissary of ammunition at Dunkirk under Harley, and later as Keeper of the King's Stores at Harwich through the mathematician Sir Paul Neile;[70] the notion that his career was hampered by a reputation for fanaticism, meanwhile, seems to derive from confusion with the ship builder Captain John Taylor.[71] On the other hand, both posts left him geographically—and hence culturally—marginalized, isolated from London or Oxford and with little prospect of compensation in local cultural life. Unlike Philips, who from her new Dublin base was able to harness her Interregnum reputation, asserting an increasingly panegyric royalism in hopes of securing patronage, Taylor—having previously downplayed his musical activities—was obliged to make a volte-face in deliberately harnessing them in lieu of court- and London-based official status, as a means of gaining access to elite cultural circles.[72] His relationship with Locke must have subtly evolved with the latter's ascendancy—whereas

Table 9.2 Cfm 163, fols. 45–72: order of songs implied by manuscript rubrics.

New order	Key	Item	Page (folio)	Text	Rubric/Comments
			1 (45)	–	"As on Euphrates shady bankes ye first to be sung is in pa: 20:" (1)
1	g	12	20 (54v)	As on Euphrates shady bankes	
2	g	13	22 (55v)	Remember Edom Lord	"All from the suns uprise is in page the :10:" (23)
3	G	7	10 (49v)	All from the sunns uprise	"Frayle man is page y^e: [6]" (11)
4	G	4	6 (47v)	Fraile man is dayly dyeing	"O happie summons is in page the :8:" (7)
5	G	5	8 (48v)	O happie summons	
6	G	6	9 (49)	God there shall his tribunall place	"Lord to my prayers incline &[c] is in page the :i:" (9)
7	a	[1]	1 (45)	Lord to my pray'rs incline thine eare	Assumed missing direction to page 24
8	a	14	24 (56v)	You Kingdomes through ye world	
9	c	15	26 (57v)	I to thy wing for refuge flye	
10	c	16	28 (58v)	Now in the winter of my yeares	
11	C	17	30 (59v)	You who the Lord adore	"Now great Jehovah raignes &c is in page the (18:)" (30)
12	e	11	18 (53v)	Now great Jehovah raignes	"New composed dittyes sing &c: is on page the :16:" (19)
13	e	10	16 (52v)	New composed dittyes sing	"When Stormes arise &c: is on page the :2:" (17)
14	F	2	2 (45v)	When stormes arise	
15	F	3	4 (46v)	My pray'rs shall with ye suns uprise ascend	"Civitas amplissima populo is in page the 31" (5)

16	g	18	31 (60)	Civitas amplissima populo	
17	g	19	32 (60v)	Miserere mei Deus	
18	g	20	34 (61v)	Dominantur in nos servi	
19	G	21	36 (62v)	Quid faciemus	"Urbs caelestis is in page the :12: & folowes in order" (37)
20	G	8	12 (50v)	Urbs caelestis	"Domine caelos tuos Inclina & descende is in page the 38:" (13)
21	a	22	38 (63v)	Domine caelos tuos	
22	a	23	40 (64v)	Candore et rubore dilectus meus	
23	a	24	42 (65v)	Dilecto meo ostium aperui	"Canite dominum is in page the 14: & followes in this order" (43)
24	e	9	14 (51v)	Canite dominum	"O Deus, mi Deus tempestive &c: is in page the :44:" (15)
25	e	25	44 (66v)	O Deus, mi Deus	
26	e	26	46 (67v)	Incubili meo per noctes	
27	E	27	48 (68v)	Vox dilecti mei	
28	F	28	50 (69v)	Revertere ô Sulammittis	
29	F	29	52 (70v)	Non habet Sion corruptelam	
30	F	30	54 (71v)	Cantate Jehovah	

Taylor was essentially Locke's patron in Hereford, Wood implies that in effect the reverse was true later on:

> being well acquainted with that most admired organist to the queen, called Matthew Lock ... [Taylor] did compose several anthems ... which were sung in his majesty's chapel ... his majesty was pleased to tell the author that he liked them.[73]

Paradoxically, however, such cultural exposure and royal approbation came at the cost of undermining Taylor's aspiration to higher social rank; hence the Duke of York's belittling of Taylor's efforts to Pepys in 1668: "[he] told me that [Taylor] was a better store-keeper then Anthem-maker—and that was bad enough too."[74] The earlier breakdown of traditional hierarchies—of social standing, church music career structures, and relationships between trained professional composers and dilettante amateurs—seems to have allowed Taylor access to musical circles within which he expressed a political allegiance profoundly at odds with that suggested by the more "official" circumstances of his life. Ironically, it was the later reentrenchment of these same pre-Interregnum hierarchies that would hamper his attempts to harness his musical skill in order to compensate for his reduced social standing in the post-Restoration political climate.

Notes

1. Aubrey, *Brief Lives*, vol. 2, 254.
2. I thank Stephen Rose, organizer of the study day "Crisis, Creativity and the Self 1550–1700" (Senate House, London, Tuesday, May 14, 2013) for the opportunity to present a preliminary version of this research; and my colleague at Selwyn College, David L. Smith, for reading a later draft and drawing to my attention several further studies of relevance to the context against which the present study unfolds.
3. On Locke: Holman, "Locke, Matthew," *GMO* (accessed June 29, 2013); Thompson, "Locke, Matthew (c.1622–1677)," *DNB* (accessed July 1, 2013); Harding, *A Thematic Catalogue of the Works of Matthew Locke*, xxiii–xl. On Taylor: Westrup and Spink, "Taylor, Silas," *GMO* (accessed July 3, 2013); Whitehead, "Taylor, Silas (1624–1678)," *DNB* (accessed June 29, 2013).
4. Thompson, "Locke, Matthew"; Birchensha, *Writings on Music*, 221 n3.
5. Goodwin, rev. Whitehead, "Harley, Sir Edward (1624–1700)," *DNB* (accessed June 29, 2013); Warmington, "Massey, Sir Edward (1604x9–1674)," *DNB* (accessed July 3, 2013). For a more detailed examination of the background to Harley's position during the 1650s, see Eales, *Puritans and Roundheads*.
6. See McElligott and Smith, *Royalists and Royalism*, 10.
7. Evans, "Paradox in Poetry and Politics," 176.
8. I thank Deana Rankin for suggesting this comparison at the study day detailed above.
9. Gray, "Katherine Philips and the Post-Courtly Coterie," 426–451; Russell, "Katherine Philips as Political Playwright," 299–323.
10. Compare Mulvihill, "A Feminist Link," 71–104, with Shifflett, "'How Many Virtues Must I Hate,'" 103–135; Evans, "Paradox in Poetry and Politics," 174–185.
11. At 4*l* per year according to Webb, *Memorials of the Civil War*, vol. 2, 314 (unfortunately his source is unclear).
12. Pepys, *The Diary of Samuel Pepys*, vol. 1, 62–63 (this must be Silas Taylor as Pepys moves on to his 1663 *A History of Gavel-kind*). The canon Pepys mentions is no longer extant; Harding, *Thematic Catalogue of the Works of Matthew Locke*, 26–27.
13. Birchensha, *Writings on Music*, 217–220.
14. The *Melothesia* excerpt is on fols. 43r–44r; compare also the very similar unattributed set of "Generall Rules for a Thorough Base," fols. 61ff.
15. Taylor's other compositions include at least three anthems, and two two-part suites published by Playford in *Court-Ayres* (1655). His music is frequently confused with that of his younger brother Sylvanus. *GMO* ascribes his setting of Cowley's "The Thirsty Earth" to

both, for example; though ambiguously attributed "Mr *Syl. Taylor*" in Playford's 1667 *Catch that Catch Can*, Playford's manuscript partbooks (GB-Eu MSS R.d. 58–61) credit it to "Cap:t Silas Taylor," and a nineteenth-century sale catalog at Glasgow lists a copy of the 1667 publication inscribed from Playford to Silas Taylor (special.lib.gla.ac.uk/manuscripts/search/detail_c.cfm?ID=89515, accessed June 10, 2013). *GMO* also erroneously ascribes Sylvanus Taylor's twenty-five pieces for two trebles and bass (GB-Ob MS Mus. Sch. E. 429) to Silas, compounding the error in the Viola da Gamba Society's *Thematic Index of Music for Viols*, which conflates the two (www.vdgs.org.uk/files/thematicIndex/T.pdf, accessed June 10, 2013).

16. This is not the only cross-attribution involving Locke and Taylor. The familiar five-part anthem "Lord, Let Me Know My End," ascribed to Locke in Playford's 1674 *Cantica Sacra* (which prints a two-part version) is attributed to Taylor in sources at Durham and Ely (Harding, *Thematic Catalogue of the Works of Matthew Locke*, 3, 9–11; Crosby, "An Early Restoration Liturgical Music Manuscript," 460), while Charles Badham's copy (GB-Ob MS Mus. Sch. c. 40) very curiously credits "Silas Taylor al[ia]s Mr Locke" (p. 58). Locke's authorship seems reliable, but in terms of the confusion between the men, it is perhaps notable that both Badham and Richard Hosier, copyist of the relevant Durham manuscript, had close Hereford connections; see Spink, "Badham, Charles," *GMO* (accessed July 1, 2013); Crosby, "An Early Restoration Liturgical Music Manuscript," 462; Spink, *Restoration Cathedral Music*, 225–226; Havergal, *Fasti Herefordenses*, 95–97.

17. This manuscript is now untraceable. James P. Cassaro, head of the Finney Library at Pittsburgh, suggests that it may have been copied by Theodore M. Finney, the library's founder (personal correspondence, May 28, 2013), but this seems unlikely from Harding's descriptions (*Thematic Catalogue*, 4, 5, 24, 31–33). It is not discussed in Finney's article, "A Group of English Manuscript Volumes at the University of Pittsburgh" (detailing manuscripts later sold to the William Andrews Clark Memorial Library at UCLA and the University of Texas at Austin; see Shay and Thompson, *Purcell Manuscripts*, 223 n63).

18. Harding, *Thematic Catalogue*, 27, 30–34.

19. Pepys, *The Diary of Samuel Pepys*, vol. 6, 80–81. Very few seventeenth-century English amateur musicians were principally recognized, like Taylor, as composers (others include Sir Edward Golding, Sampson Estwick, and Henry Aldrich); see also the heading of this section, from Anthony Wood (Bellingham, "The Musical Circle of Anthony Wood," 39).

20. Emslie, "Pepys, Samuel," *GMO* (accessed June 19, 2013).

21. Caccini, *Le nuove musiche*, 49.

22. Parrott, "Falsetto Beliefs," 82.

23. Butler, *The Principles of Musik*, 98.

24. Mulvihill, "A Feminist Link," 74, 79, 81–82.

25. Chalmers, *Royalist Women Writers*, 10; Gray, "Katherine Philips and the Post-Courtly Coterie," 434.

26. Aubrey, *Brief Lives*, vol. 2, 254.

27. Wood, *Athenae Oxonienses*, vol. 2, columns 1175–1176. Emphasis mine.

28. Ibid., vol. 2, column 1176. Emphasis mine.

29. Aubrey, *Brief Lives*, vol. 2, 254.

30. On the offending "paper," see Russell, "Katherine Philips as Political Playwright," 305; Gray, "Katherine Philips and the Post-Courtly Coterie," 450.

31. Russell, "Katherine Philips as Political Playwright," 306; Limbert, "Katherine Philips," 29.

32. Green, *Calendar of the Proceedings of the Committee*, part I [hereafter *CPCC*], 613, 620–621, 637, 641, 643–661. Petty disagreements rumbled on; ibid., 682, 684, 694–695, 697, 706, 710, 718–720.

33. Green, *CPCC*, 655.

34. Webb, *Memorials of the Civil War*, vol. 2, 314.

35. [Taylor], *Impostor Magnus*, 26–27.
36. Ibid., 27.
37. Webb, *Memorials of the Civil War*, 249–255. One later account has Taylor alongside Birch among the parliamentarian forces (Dugdale, *The New British Traveller*, vol. 2, 579), though Whitelocke's (*Memorials of the English Affairs*, 190) contemporary account does not.
38. Delamain, *The Close Hypocrite Discovered*, 10.
39. [Taylor], *Impostor Magnus*, 27.
40. On George Lynn, see Green, *CPCC*, 650–651, 653; for Matthew Price see ibid., 631, 636–37.
41. Bellingham, "The Musical Circle of Anthony Wood," 32.
42. Ibid., 39.
43. See Clark, *British Clubs and Societies*, 44–46, 52–55; Raylor, *Cavaliers, Clubs, and Literary Culture*, 75–83.
44. Spink, "The Old Jewry 'Musick-Society,'" 39; see White, "Music and Merchants," this volume, also Herissone, "Daniel Henstridge," this volume.
45. Chalmers, *Royalist Women Writers*, 17–21, 59–62; Evans, *Henry Lawes*, 187–191, 202–211; Hamessley, "Henry Lawes's Setting," 115–138.
46. GB-Ob MS D.19(4), "Hingston"; on the midcentury reception of Dering's motets, see Wainwright, "Richard Dering's Few-Voice 'Concertato' Motets," 165–194 at 184.
47. Little, "Music at the Court of King Oliver," esp. 178–179.
48. Bellingham, "The Musical Circle of Anthony Wood," 18.
49. Ellison, *George Sandys*, 175–211; George Buchanan, whose Latin psalm paraphrases were also set by Taylor, was a profound influence on Sandys (ibid., 190–199).
50. Shell, *Catholicism, Controversy, and the English Literary Imagination*, 169–187; for the earlier Catholic phenomenon, see Kerman, "Music and Politics," 275–287.
51. Loscocco, "Royalist Reclamation of Psalmic Song," 500, 528. Interpretation of this text of course heavily depended on one's political persuasion, given its use by all sides as a metaphor of exile and subjugation (Hamlin, *Psalm Culture*, 251–252); Taylor in *Impostor Magnus* (p. 31) invokes Babylon in conjunction with the "prophaneness, blasphemy, heresie and hypocrisie" supported by the then-incumbent regime.
52. Cfm 163, fol. 46v; Sandys, *A Paraphrase on the Psalmes of David*, 37.
53. Clarke, *Politics, Religion and the Song of Songs*, 77–104, esp. 100 (on Marvell's "The Nymph Complaining for the Death of Her Fawn" as a response to the Troubles via Song of Songs imagery).
54. Bloch and Bloch, *The Song of Songs*, 197–198; also Chapman, *Hallelujah*, 110: the Shulamite "signified the people of *Jerusalem*, so called of *Shalem*, peace."
55. For example, in GB-Lbl MS Harley 6868; quoted in Robinson, *A History of the Castles of Herefordshire*, 144.
56. GB-Lbl MS Harley 6766, fol. 192; see Parry, *The Trophies of Time*, 17–19.
57. GB-Lbl MS Harley 6726, fol. 251.
58. Taylor, *The History of Gavel-kind*, 35–36, 40–41.
59. Loscocco, "Royalist Reclamation of Psalmic Song," esp. 517.
60. Wainwright, "Richard Dering's Few-Voice 'Concertato' Motets," 169–170, 185 (esp. n54); Wainwright, *Musical Patronage in Seventeenth-Century England*, 160–177. Jeffreys, *16 Motets*, iii–vi; Thompson, "George Jeffreys," 325.
61. Thompson, "George Jeffreys," 330–331.
62. Lawes, *Choice Psalmes*, sig. A3v ("The Epistle Dedicatorie").
63. Rivers, "Prayer-Book Devotion," 205–206; Loscocco, "Royalist Reclamation of Psalmic Song," 521–523.

64. [Barksdale], *Nympha Libethris*, 56. This presumably predates *Choice Psalmes*; Barksdale may have known Lawes's music in manuscript, and/or the simpler treble-and-bass settings in Sandys, *A Paraphrase on the Divine Poems* (1638). For a list of Hereford vicars choral, see Havergal, *Fasti Herefordenses*, 97.

65. To those titles already mentioned one might add Walter Porter's 1657 *Mottetts*, and the 1650 and 1656 reprints of William Child's 1639 *First Set of Psalms*; Milsom, "Walter Porter's *Mottetts*," 1–5; Zimmerman, "The Psalm Settings," vol. 1.

66. GB-Lbl Add. MS 17801, fols. 64[r]–64v; Harding, *Thematic Catalogue*, 89.

67. GB-Lbl Lansdowne 213, p. 333 (quoted in Havergal, *Fasti Herefordenses*, 101); Chevill, "Clergy, Music Societies," 35–53.

68. Harding, *Thematic Catalogue*, 30–34.

69. Wainwright, "Richard Dering's Few-Voice 'Concertato' Motets," 184–188; see also White, "Music and Merchants," this volume.

70. Taylor, *History of Gavel-kind*, sigs A2[r]–A3v (Harley/Dunkirk); Wood, *Athenae Oxonienses*, vol. 2, column 1176 (Neile/Harwich); also Simpson, "Neile, Sir Paul (*bap.* 1613, *d.*1682x6)," in *DNB* (accessed July 1, 2013).

71. Pepys, *Diary of Samuel Pepys*, November 4 and December 19, 1664, vol. 5, 314 and 350. A related letter confirms this Taylor as John Taylor, former master shipwright at Chatham; see Rodger, *The Command of the Ocean*, 103; Green, *Calendar of State Papers*, 68 (also the extremely useful website *The Diary of Samuel Pepys: Daily Entries from the 17th Century London Diary*, www.pepysdiary.com/diary/1664/11/04/, accessed July 2, 2013).

72. On this observation concerning Philips, see Chalmers, *Royalist Women Writers*, 83; Russell, "Katherine Philips as Political Playwright," 299, 306–310.

73. Wood, *Athenae Oxonienses*, vol. 2, column 176. Music aside, Taylor sought cultural engagement through the Royal Society, of which his patron Neile had been a founder (see, for example, Birchensha, *Writings on Music*, 219), and apparently harbored theatrical ambitions, sending a script, "The Serenade, or Disappointment," to Pepys for his opinion (*Diary of Samuel Pepys*, May 7, 1669, vol. 9, 546–547).

74. Pepys, *Diary of Samuel Pepys*, June 29, 1668, vol. 9, 251.

10.

Music and Merchants in Restoration London

Bryan White

"Business ... does not require the polite part of human understanding, or call for a liberal education" declared Daniel Defoe (1660?–1731) in the *Complete English Tradesman* of 1727.[1] Many contemporaries shared his opinion, and it certainly applied half a century earlier, in the period that is the focus of this essay. Both court and gentry were snobbish toward the "vulgarity and stigma of a manual apprenticeship," the normal route for entry into business; for Sir Thomas Baines, "the being made an apprentice according to our custom is a blott at least in every man's scutchion."[2] Old prejudices are hard to eradicate. Investigations of musical culture in London in the second half of the seventeenth century have typically turned to the nobility, gentry, and university-educated professionals to illustrate domestic music making, musical consumption, and patronage, with the country gent Roger North and the Cambridge man Samuel Pepys as leading exemplars.[3] Merchants have been neglected, in part owing to prejudices that have disassociated them from the polite arts. Such a bias has obscured their role in London musical culture of the Restoration. The business community included individuals whose passion for hearing, performing, and purchasing music was every bit as strong as that of Pepys. The musical pursuits of merchants often operated on the boundary of recreation and occupation. Many who made music together also shared commercial interests. Musical sociability fostered personal networks in a community for which the exchange of information was of crucial importance.[4] It also crossed social boundaries, offering businessmen connections with members of the gentry and professions who were potential commercial associates. Merchants crossed geographical boundaries, too, and took music with them as they did so. Their role in disseminating music from the continent helped to shape English musical culture of the period, just as that culture helped to enrich their personal and business lives.

In the second half of the seventeenth century, the term *merchant* had both specific and general meanings. Members of the great trading companies were keen to restrict its usage; according to Levant Company statutes, only those engaged in overseas trade qualified. However, a wider meaning also applied, encompassing other "men of business" engaged in trading and exchange, whether or not it was primarily international.[5] It is likewise difficult to define business solely in terms of class. Mercantile work was a favored occupation for younger sons of the gentry, as it was for sons of merchants. When John Verney, a lyra-viol player and second son of Sir Ralph Verney, was apprenticed in 1659 to a Levant merchant, he hoped that his father would find his choice "noe less satisfactory then if I had beene an Inns of Court Gentleman."[6] Fluidity in social position was not uncommon; John, for instance, pursued a successful career as a merchant until 1696 when he succeeded his father as second baronet, John's elder brother Edmund and his sons having predeceased him. Wealth was also highly variable among the merchant community. The great Levant merchant Sir John Lethieullier amassed a fortune in excess of £100,000, but most earned considerably less, and apprentices usually started work with little or no capital.[7] Nevertheless, a business community was recognized in Restoration London, which could be distinguished from the nobility, gentry, and the professions. And while a career as a merchant could be highly remunerative, perhaps much more so than the professions, it did not carry the same level of social prestige. For musical attainment, distinctions in education were important. Whereas university life offered opportunities for amateur musicians, most merchants developed their musical interests either through education at home, or through access to professional musicians as teachers, or both. For members of the business community who came to cultivate an interest in music, it provided not only a personal pleasure, but also a means of social interaction, through which one might profitably encounter persons from other walks of life.

Robert Bargrave

Brief portraits of several merchants whose musical activity can be documented illustrate the passion with which it was sometimes pursued, and the way it overlapped with business and social networks. Robert Bargrave (1628–1661) is in some ways the least representative of those merchants whose musical activities are known.[8] He was the son of Isaac Bargrave, dean of Canterbury. The Bargraves were a musical family; Sir Henry Wotton bequeathed his viola da gamba to Isaac, and Robert himself probably started his musical education at home. He entered Gray's Inn aged twelve, perhaps to take part in the masques for which it was then well known.⁹ Subsequently, he attended Clare College, Cambridge, then Corpus Christi College, Oxford; but rather than pursuing a career in law or the church, he was apprenticed to the Levant merchant James Modyford. He set out with him to Constantinople in 1647, recording his travels in a diary. Their ship set down in Majorca, where Bargrave commented on music at the cathedral, and Leghorn (Livorno), from where he traveled to Siena to visit his cousin John Bargrave. There, he was invited to play the viol in front of the musicians of Mattias de' Medici. Once in Constantinople, Bargrave wrote text and music for a masque to celebrate the wedding of Modyford to the daughter of Sir Thomas Bendish, the Levant Company consul to the Sublime Porte.¹⁰ When Modyford's "rotten Love fell fowlely off," both wedding and masque were canceled.¹¹ In September 1652, Bargrave journeyed home overland, sampling music along the way, including that of the chapel of Vasile Lupu in Jassy, Moldovia; the "musick of the Russes" in Lemberg (Lvov, Ukraine); and "the admirable skill on the base Viol" of Theodore Steffkins in Hamburg. He traveled to Spain in 1654, where he enjoyed the performance of the king's private chapel at the Escorial. Journeying on to Venice, he admired the music of the convents, and the carnival of 1656. His encounter with Venetian opera was overwhelming:

> One Opera I saw represented about 16: several times; and so farr was I from being weary of it, I would ride hundreds of miles to see the same over again: nay I must needs confess that all the pleasant things I have yet heard or seen, are inexpressibly short of the delight I had, in seeing this Venetian Opera.¹²

The opera was Cavalli's *Erismena*, a score of which he copied, putting an English text to it.¹³ Returning from Venice, Bargrave passed through Innsbruck where he met the English-born violist William Young, who promised him "his Lessons composed for that Viall [i.e., an eight-string viol played "lyra-way"] and his Aires for two Bases and a Treble which he intends to publish."¹⁴ Even though Bargrave was not a London-based merchant—spending periods between his overseas journeys in Canterbury—nor representative in terms of his university education, his musical interests show similarities to other musically minded merchants. Travel provided the opportunity to experience a diversity of musical cultures and styles. He collected music and provided a potential conduit for the dissemination of continental music in England. He performed and composed himself, and he used his musical skills both on behalf of his employer and to entertain his colleagues.

Thomas Hill and Thomas Andrews

Thomas Hill (ca. 1635–1675) was another merchant for whom travel in Italy opened up new musical horizons. One of six sons of the wealthy merchant Richard Hill, a London alderman, Thomas held a minor post as prize commissioner during the First Dutch War, but also worked in the family business for which he traveled to Italy in 1657. He subsequently became an agent for the Houblon family working for them in Lisbon.[15] A letter of Hill's to his brother Abraham written from Lucca in October 1657 offers a firsthand account of his enthusiasm for music:

> Since my arrival in Italy, I have missed few opportunities of hearing what music has been publickly performed, especially in the churches; and I wish I could give you a satisfactory account of it: I would attempt it, could I but say half so well as they can sing. I observe in general, that at home we think [sing?] better than they do. What they excel us so much in is the eunuchs, whose voices are very rare and delightful, and not to be compared but with one another: the other voices not so good as we have in England. The instrumental music is much better than I expected. The organ and violin they are masters of, but the bass viol they have not at all in use; and to supply its place they have the bass violin with four strings, and use it as we do the bass viol. In short, it would be worth any one's while, who is fond of music, to travel to Italy; he would find such sweet recompence for his trouble in it. Next month we have a concert of music, at the chusing a new prince, of forty voices with several instruments. I fancy I can procure a copy of it, as I have some interest with the master of the prince's chapel: but I know it cannot be performed in England. I am using my endeavours to collect music for a single, or two or three voices, in which I have had good success. I should be obliged to you, if Mr. Lawes has put forth a third book of airs, that you would send it me, as it will be very acceptable here.[16]

Hill had returned to London by early 1660, where he acted as executor for his father's will, which included a bequest to him of £2,000.[17] In early 1664, he encountered Samuel Pepys, on whom he made an immediate impression; Pepys described him as "a master in most sorts of Musique" and a person whose acquaintance "I should covet."[18] The two met again on April 12, 1664, the first occasion on which they performed together:

> to Mr. Pagets and there heard some musique . . . Here I also met Mr. Hill, the little merchant. And after all was done, we sung. I did well enough a psalm or two of Lawes; he I perceive hath good skill and sings well—and a friend of his sings a good bass.[19]

Over the next twenty-one months, Pepys records making music with Hill on thirty-five occasions. Most often, they met on Sundays to sing psalms, including those by Ravenscroft and Lawes, in whom both Pepys and Hill were separately interested.[20] On a majority of occasions (twenty-two times), they were joined by another merchant, Thomas Andrews (1632–1684), almost certainly the bass mentioned in the diary entry of April 12, 1664. Andrews was a victualler for Tangier, and a draper, serving as warden to the company in 1677–1678.[21] Hill also occasionally supplied victuals to Tangier, and the way in which business, particularly that relating to Tangier, and musical sociability interacted is clear in the diary. One of Pepys's earliest encounters with Hill was at the Royal Exchange, a visit to which was more or less a daily requirement for merchants: "At noon to the Change, where I met with Mr. Hill the little merchant, with whom I perceive I shall contract a musicall acquaintance."²² A few months later, a session of music making gave way to business: "and so to my office till 5 a-clock; and then came Mr. Hill and Andrews and we sung an hour or two. Then broke up and Mr. Alsop and his company came and consulted about our Tanger [i.e., Tangier]-victualling, and brought it to a good head."²³ On another occasion business, religion, and pleasure are all fitted into a Sunday:

> After dinner came Mr. Andrews, and spent that afternoon with me about our Tanger business of the victuals and then parted. And after sermon comes Mr. Hill and a gentleman, a friend of his, one Mr. Scott, that sings well also; and then comes Mr. Andrews, and we all sung and supped; and then to sing again, and passed the Sunday very pleasantly and soberly.²⁴

Pepys, Hill, and Andrews sometimes expanded their musical meetings to include professionals and other amateurs. In July 1664, Hill and Andrews brought "one slovenly and ugly fellow, Seignor Pedro" to their meeting with Pepys. This was the Italian composer Pietro Reggio (ca. 1632–1685), and although Pepys found him to be a good musician, he could not bring himself to enjoy the occasion, perhaps because he could not fully participate:

> they spent the whole evening in singing the best piece of musique [. . .] made by Seignor Charissimi [. . .]. Fine it was endeed, and too fine for me to judge of.
>   They have spoke to Pedro to meet us every week, and I fear it will grow a trouble to me if we once come to bid guests to meet us, especially idle masters—which doth a little displease me to consider.²⁵

A few days later, Reggio joined them again, to no better effect in Pepys's opinion.²⁶ Thereafter, Reggio disappears from the meetings, though reading between the lines, we may imagine that Hill and Andrews continued to see him without Pepys. Hill, having spent time in Italy was probably comfortable with Italian; Andrews may have been as well. Merchants in foreign trade had to be capable of using several languages; Italian was the lingua franca of the Mediterranean where both Hill and Andrews had business concerns.²⁷ On several occasions in the latter part of 1665, Pepys and Hill had musical evenings with other professional musicians: Edward Coleman (bap. 1622–1669), gentleman of the Chapel Royal and member of the King's Private Musick; his wife, Catherine (bap. 1623), a singer; Nicholas Lanier (1588–1666), master of the King's Musick; and the singing actress, Mrs. Knipp [Elizabeth Knepp].²⁸

Pepys and Hill also shared an interest in composition. They discussed the rules of John Birchensha, Pepys's erstwhile composition teacher, and they played their compositions to one another: "to Woolwich, and there find Mr. Hill, and he and I all the morning at Musique and a song he hath set, of three parts; methinks very good."²⁹ One gets the impression that Hill was more skilled musically than

Pepys. Not only was his own composition in three parts, something Pepys may have found difficult to execute himself, but Hill also offered criticism of Pepys's own song when the diarist showed it to him: "and then home to Mr. Hill and sang, among other things, my song of *Beauty returne* [i.e., 'Beauty retire'], which he likes; only, excepts against two notes in the bass, but likes the whole very well."[30]

From the end of 1665, Hill was in expectation of traveling to Portugal on business for James Houblon Jr. (ca. 1629-1700), merchant and close friend of Pepys and of Hill, for whom he served as executor after his death in 1675. Houblon was not particularly musical himself; he joined Pepys, Hill, and Andrews for singing on one occasion—to which Pepys purposely brought a volume of Lawes's *Ayres*—but his wife, Sarah, was a fine singer: "After dinner Mr. Hill took me with Mrs. Hubland, who is a fine gentlewoman—into another room, and there made her sing; which she doth very well—to my great content."[31] Pepys and Hill never saw each other again after parting on March 2, 1666, but they corresponded while Hill was in Lisbon. One of Hill's letters indicates that he played viol and probably violin and describes his frustration at the lack of access to new music:

> we have a little consort among us, which gives us entertainment. We have five hands for viols, and violins, three of us, use both, and all, except one, the viol, but the want of music in this country obliges us to play over, and over again, some few things I brought from home accidentally, which wears off the relish, so that we are forced to go a-begging to our friends, as I do to you, that if you have anything new, you would bestow it on us and because Mr Monteage (accountant to Messrs Houblons) intends to present me some things, it may be fit to compare compositions, that they be not duplicates.[32]

While in Lisbon, Hill encountered the guitarist Cesare Morelli (*fl.* late 1660s–1686) and recommended him to Pepys, who took him on as a household musician in 1675.

Rowland Sherman, Philip Wheak, and James Pigott

The musical interests of two Levant merchants, Rowland Sherman (ca. 1663-1748) and Philip Wheak (1661-1731), and their associate, the Blackwell Hall factor James Pigott (1657-1739), offer several points of correspondence with the merchants examined above.[33] Sherman's family was from Leicester, but he and his older brother William were in London apprenticed to the Levant merchant Gabriel Roberts (1629-1715) by the early 1680s. Much of the information on Rowland's musical interests is preserved in two letter books, the first of which he began in March 1683.[34] By that time, William was working as a factor in Smyrna. He played the recorder, but it was Rowland who was most passionate about music. He sailed for Aleppo in July 1688–taking his harpsichord with him—and his letters describe his musical activities there and shed light on musical culture in

London. In Aleppo, he made music with his fellow English factors and with those from other countries, made musical connections with local Catholic missionaries, and spent considerable time in personal practice, especially in learning to play continuo. If on arriving in Aleppo he, like Thomas Hill, lacked sufficient variety of music, he remedied the problem by collecting a library of more than one hundred titles over the next sixty years.[35]

In London, Rowland had been part of a group of musical enthusiasts he referred to as the "brothers of the string," which included two friends, Philip Wheak and James Pigott. Sherman's letters indicate Wheak was a talented amateur keyboard player and that he had traveled to Italy in 1688. In Rome, Wheak heard Bernardo Pasquini play and attended performances at the Chiesa Nuova. He collected music, some of which, including toccatas by Frescobaldi and Pasquini, he sent to Sherman in Aleppo. Other music he brought back to London, where it circulated among the "brothers of the string" and where Sherman anticipated it would "stimulate the generous soul of Mr Purcell."[36] Before his journey overseas, Rowland had known Henry Purcell and sought advice from him on continuo practice. Wheak was also personally acquainted with Purcell—and probably other prominent professional musicians—as was James Pigott. Pigott did not qualify as a merchant in the strictest sense, but he was closely associated with the Levant trade. Blackwell Hall factors, known as "packers," were middlemen selling cloth from provincial makers to members of the Levant Company who then traded it abroad. Sherman used Pigott as an agent in London, asking him to request music from Purcell and pass a letter to him, and to buy supplies for his harpsichord from the instrument maker Charles Hayward with whom Pigott and Sherman were personally acquainted.

Sherman, Wheak, and Pigott were knowledgeable about the annual London Cecilian feast held by the "Gentlemen of the Musical Society."[37] This organization of professional and amateur musicians hosted a performance of a musical ode in praise of St. Cecilia followed by a dinner at Stationers' Hall every year between 1683 and 1700 (excepting 1688–1689). Wheak was a member of the society, serving as steward to the feast in 1693; Sherman and Pigott were probably associated with it as well. In fact, Levant merchants figured prominently among stewards. John Lethieullier (1659–1737), son of Sir John, was a steward to the feast in 1686 along with Sir Thomas Bludworth (1660–1694); although it is not clear if the latter was a Levant merchant, his father, also Sir Thomas—former lord mayor of London—was a major figure in the company. The Levant merchants Leonard Wessell (after 1660–1708) and Paris Slaughter (1671–1704) were stewards in 1697. The relationship among Sherman, Wheak, Pigott, and the Lethieullier family illustrates the way in which music formed a part of the dense familial and business networks of the City of London. While traveling on the continent, Wheak arranged for three harpsichords to be exported from Antwerp to Sir John Lethieullier and Bedingfield Heigham Jr., brother of Mary, whom Wheak married in March 1689.

Sherman was responsible for delivery once the instruments arrived in London. Wheak's family probably had long-standing associations with Sir John, who lived in the parish of St. Olave, Hart Street, where Philip was christened. Philip was apprenticed to Sir John's brother, William (1646–1728). Heigham was also a Levant merchant; by the time of his marriage to Esther White in 1694, the execution of her father's estate had passed from Sir Christopher Lethieullier (1639–1690), another of Sir John's brothers, to his widow, Dame Jane. In 1699 when William Lethieullier's son John went to Aleppo to work in the Levant trade, he became partner to Rowland Sherman. In Aleppo, Rowland handled cloth for Wheak and Heigham (who themselves bought cloth through Pigott) and also recommended Pigott to potential clients.

Music was an important shared interest among Sherman, Wheak, and Pigott, and probably with Heigham and members of the Lethieullier family as well. Apart from the personal pleasure it afforded, music offered a sociable bond strengthening the ties of business, friendship, and family. Musical ability may also have played a role in apprenticeship. It has been suggested that John Verney's skill as a lyra-viol player may have been a significant factor in the decision of the Levant merchant Gabriel Roberts to take him on as apprentice in 1659.[38] This supposition seems all the more likely in light of Roberts's taking on the two musical Sherman brothers years later. Roberts's interest in music is known through two manuscripts of instrumental music, D-Hs MS ND VI 3193 and GB-Lbl Add. MS 31431, which he owned. Wheak's and Sherman's enthusiasm for Italian music was seemingly shared by Roberts; GB-Lbl Add. MS 31431 includes twenty-two Italian sonatas by Cazzati, Vitali, Colista, and Legrenzi.

The Pigott Family

A striking example of a network of professional musicians and amateur merchant musicians within the same family is the Pigotts of which James was a member.[39] His father, Francis (ca. 1630–1697), a clothworker and packer, was a member of the Old-Jewry "Musick-Society."[40] The group is known from John Playford's dedication to *The Musical Companion* of 1667, which names the following members: "Charles Pigon *Esq*; *Mr.* Tho. Tempest *Gent.*[;] *Mr.* Herbert Pelham *Gent.*[;] *Mr.* John Pelling *Citizen.*[;] *Mr* Benjamin Wallington *Citizen*[;] *Mr.* George Piggot *Gent.*[;] *Mr.* Francis Piggot *Citizen* [;] *Mr.* John Rogers *Gent.*" A set of manuscript partbooks of the collection (GB-Ge R.d.58–61) includes a basso continuo book that also names Mr. Jeremy Savile Gent and describes Pigeon as "of Grais Inn," Wallington as a goldsmith, and Pelling (1632–1689) as an apothecary. The club mixed merchants, artisans, and gentlemen; judging from the contents of *The Musical Companion*, they sang catches, rounds, and simple part-songs for two to four voices. Pepys knew and sang with most of the members of this club. He described Tempest as "a gentleman . . . who sings very well endeed and understands anything in the world at first sight."⁴¹ Pelham was a "sober citizen merchant" who sings "with great skill."⁴² Pelling, who "sings well endeed," talked with Pepys "of Musique and the musicians of the town," and brought Wallington, Pigott (whether Francis or George is not specified), Rogers, and Tempest to sing with the diarist on several occasions, including one during which the group drank Pepys's "good store of wine."⁴³ Wallington, "did sing a most excellent bass" but was "a poor fellow, a working goldsmith, that goes without gloves to his hands."⁴⁴ On the recommendation of Roger North, George Pigott was admitted clerk to the Corporation of Musick in Westminster in 1672; his relationship to Francis cannot be demonstrated.⁴⁵ John Rogers may be the lutenist brother of Benjamin Rogers, and was also a member of the Corporation of Musick.⁴⁶

While James Pigott followed his father's career, becoming a packer and amateur musician, his brother Charles (1662–1740) became a church musician, though only after a mysteriously aborted career as a businessman. He attended Merchant Taylor's School, was apprenticed to Walter Kilner, Mercer in 1677, and gained his freedom in 1685.⁴⁷ He next reenters the historical record in 1719 as "Subdiaconi" in a list of prebendaries of St. David's Cathedral, Pembroke.⁴⁸ In the same year, "Charles Piggot Junr," presumably his son, was appointed chorister there; another son, Thomas, appears with his brother as a chorister in a list dated July 27, 1720.⁴⁹ Charles Sr. is listed as vicar choral as late at 1736; he died in December of 1740 and was buried in the cathedral.⁵⁰ While it seems improbable this should be the same Charles Pigott, Mercer, his four sons to his wife Margaret—Henry Delany (ca. 1702–1746), Charles Newsham (ca. 1707–1796), Thomas (ca. 1709), and George (1710–1737)—gained the freedom of the Mercers Company in London by patrimony, basing their claim on their father's freedom, granted July 10, 1685.⁵¹ Whatever the circumstances that led Charles from a career in business to that of a vicar choral in St. David's, it seems likely that he grew up with music as an integral part of family life.

The most important musician to emerge from the Pigott family was the composer and organist Francis (1666–1704), who was probably cousin to James and Charles.⁵² He was the son of Bartholomew Pigott, an ironmonger and member of the Company of Pattenmakers, and his wife, Rachel Kinsman. The rather unusual forename Dulsibella, the name of the wife of Francis Pigott, clothworker and of Bartholomew's daughter (by his second wife, Sarah Willis), suggests a close family relationship; Francis and Bartholomew were probably brothers.⁵³ Francis the composer's connection with the family of Francis the clothworker is also implied in his marriage to Ann, the only daughter of John Pelling, member of the Old Jewry music club. Francis enjoyed a successful career, serving as organist at St. John's College and Magdalen College, Oxford; at Temple Church, London; and finally at the Chapel Royal. His son John (ca. 1690–1762) succeeded him as organist at Temple Church. Through the influence of his uncle Dr. John

Pelling (1669–1750), rector of St. Anne's, Westminster, and a canon of Windsor, he was made organist of St. George's Chapel, Windsor.[54]

Merchant Patronage

Merchants and other businessmen were important patrons of music in this period. Their largesse was sometimes expressed in an impressive gift. Goldsmith and financier Charles Duncombe (1648–1711) commissioned an organ for St. Magnus Church in 1711. Completed after his death, the instrument, made by Abraham Jordan father and son, was the first English organ with a swell; it had "four Setts of Keys, one of which is adapted to the Art of emitting Sounds by swelling the Notes, which never was in any organ before."[55] Other acts of patronage were on a smaller scale. Roger North reports that the Italian violinist Nicola Matteis (*fl.* ca. 1670–ca. 1698) found an anonymous London merchant as his first patron: "he lay obscurely in the citty, by the favour of a merchant whom he had converted to his profit."[56]

A more sustained sort of patronage can be found in relation to the Musical Society and its annual Cecilian feast. Each year, the feast was overseen by a group of stewards: four in 1684 increasing to eight by 1695 of which professional musicians always numbered two. Some or all of the stewards are known for nine of the sixteen celebrations held between 1683 and 1700. Of the thirty-nine Cecilian stewards who were not professional musicians, around ten or eleven were merchants or businessmen. Shared commercial interests may have been a factor in a businessman's decision to serve as steward. We have already seen that several were directly or indirectly associated with the Levant Company. In the year before Paris Slaughter and Leonard Wessell served as Cecilian stewards, they became owners with eight other men of the *Slaughter Galley*, bound for Scanderoon.[57] Charles Blunt (steward in 1691), an upholsterer and early stockbroker, numbered among his clients John Lethieullier (1686).[58] Another group of stewards appears to have had connections through the West Indies trade and in the army and colonial government. Archibald Hutchinson (1695) was attorney general for the Leeward Islands from 1688–1702 while Nathaniel Blackiston (1696) was lieutenant governor of Montserrat from 1689 to 1695. Both knew Col. Henry Holt (1696) who led a Regiment of Foot in the Leeward Islands from 1695. Blackiston had been a colonel of this regiment before Holt took charge of it, and Hutchinson served as an agent for the regiment, petitioning the lords of the Treasury for payments of arrears to Holt's soldiers.[59] The merchant John Jeffreys (1692) was, along with his brother and partner Jeffrey Jeffreys (1699), heavily involved in trade with the Leeward Islands and in Virginian tobacco. As one of five commissioners who managed the affairs of the Leeward Islands from 1690 to 1697, Jeffrey would have been aware of the activities of Hutchinson, Blackiston, and Holt, if he did not know them personally. The merchant John Cary (1696) was a one-time resident of

Virginia and was a major tobacco exporter. He was also involved in West Indies trade and was a distant relative of Richard Cary, a commissioner for the Leeward Islands with Jeffrey Jeffreys. It is unclear to what extent, if any, these businessmen were associated with the group of musical Levant Company merchants, but the Jeffreys brothers were probably acquainted with Sir John Lethieullier, Sir Thomas Bludworth Sr., and Sir Gabriel Roberts, because they all served as directors of the Royal Africa Company.

Several of these merchants were extremely wealthy men. Cary's estate was worth £29,358 at his death.[60] John Jeffreys's will, drafted in 1692, provided a jointure for his wife of £30,000. His brother Jeffrey's estate was said to be worth some £300,000. That of his fellow steward in 1699, Charles Duncombe, was even more substantial: approximately £400,000. The pair had been elected sheriffs of London in June 1699, and both were knighted in October. For Duncombe at least, his role as steward is likely to have been part of a larger publicity campaign in London to restore his reputation after his expulsion from the Commons in 1698, which included the donation of a clock to the parish church of St. Magnus (a decade before he commissioned its organ) and hosting around one hundred clergy on New Year's Day 1700. Social prestige was probably an important aspect of stewarding, particularly for merchants. Leonard Wessell's decision to act as steward was doubtless a feature of what his parliamentary biographer describes as a "vigorous pursuit of social acceptance and political ambition."[61] Stewarding may be seen as another act of social aspiration similar to the way in which successful businessmen sent their sons to the universities and/or the Inns of Court as did Jeffrey Jeffreys, Blunt, Lethieullier, Wessell, and Wheak, none of whom were themselves university-educated. Stewarding also offered potential contacts outside of the world of business. Meetings of the stewards and the feast itself presented opportunities to forge social ties with professionals and gentry (groups well-represented among Cecilian stewards), contacts that in other circumstances could be exploited to advance commercial interests.

Experience of the Cecilian feast was probably the inspiration for the commissioning of a large-scale musical ode by Jeremiah Clarke for the "Barbadoes Gentleman" in early 1703.[62] "No more, great rulers of the sky" is written for pairs of trumpets, oboes, and recorders; kettledrums; strings; soloists; and chorus.[63] The performance took place at Stationers' Hall at an occasion that was probably similar to the Cecilian feasts celebrated there. Even though the "Barbadoes Gentlemen" are not identified, they must have been a group of Atlantic merchants and planters, and the event a rather grand version of a "token" feast, social gatherings to drink to the health of friends on the islands.[64] Perhaps some of those Cecilian stewards noted above involved in Caribbean trade were instrumental in celebrating this occasion with elaborate music. Just as in commissioning Purcell's *Yorkshire Feast Song* the London Society of Yorkshire Gentleman appropriated the ode (a court-originated form) to at once express loyalty to the sovereign and celebrate their native county, the "Barbadoes Gentleman" used it to offer "kind equinoctial blessing" on merchants and planters of the island.

Conclusions

It is difficult to speculate on the extent to which the musical interests of the merchants discussed above are representative of the larger business community. Peter Earle found that, notwithstanding Pepys's remark on the presence of a virginal in one of every three boats used to rescue personal effects from the Great Fire, less than ten percent of the 375 inventories he inspected from this period listed a musical instrument.[65] Even within the sample presented here, the level of interest in music is difficult to gauge. Bargrave, Hill, Sherman, and Wheak maintained a passion for music and were all performers of some accomplishment. However, among those businessmen whose only known musical interest is steward at the Cecilian feast, it is impossible to determine whether social prestige, networking, or musical enthusiasm drove their support of the Musical Society. These different urges are not, of course, mutually exclusive, and it is clear from this study that musical interests often intertwined with business concerns. Networking and the exchange of information were vital to success in commerce; musical meetings provided occasions at which news could be exchanged informally and business relationships fostered by sociable ties. Another theme concerns the overseas merchant. These traders often traveled widely and maintained links with contacts scattered across Europe, a circumstance that facilitated the dissemination of music. The London merchant and grocer Obadiah Sedgwick, for instance, introduced Corelli's op. 4 to a music club in Stamford.[66] His attendance there, sometime before November 1696, is likely to have come through an association with one of its leading members, Basil Ferrar, Stamford grocer. Sedgwick joined club members in playing the op. 4 sonatas, probably on the bass viol. The music was subsequently copied and used in a Stamford Cecilian entertainment in 1696 in which movements of Corelli's sonatas were placed between movements of Purcell's Cecilian ode, "Welcome to All the Pleasures."[67] The op. 4 sonatas were published in Rome in 1694, and it seems likely that trading links played a role in Sedgwick obtaining the music so quickly after publication, just as they probably played a role in his travel to Stamford. It should also be noted that many of the businessmen examined here had direct access to London's professional musicians. This contact included teaching and performance, which suggests a blurred boundary between those who played for recreation and those who played for a living. Families of wealthier London businessmen must have been important customers for musician-teachers, just as they provided a market for published music and treatises, and an audience for London's burgeoning concert life. For a significant minority of those in the business community, music was an important consideration, despite Defoe's comments with which this chapter opened. He, of course, had interests beyond business:

> I have been a Lover of the Science [of music] from my Infancy, and in my younger days was accounted no despicable Performer on the Viol and Lute, then much in Vogue. I esteem it the most innocent Amusement in Life.[68]

Furthermore, he acknowledged:

> Our Quality, Gentry and better sort of Traders must have Diversions; and if those that are commendable be denied, they will take to worse; Now what can be more commendable than Musick, one of the seven liberal Sciences, and no mean Branch of the Mathematicks?

If not all of those traders who daily frequented the Royal Exchange went thence to a music meeting, lesson, or concert, some certainly did, and we must, therefore, recognize their place as important participants in musical culture of the Restoration period.

Notes

1. *The Complete English Tradesman*, 62.
2. Grassby, *The Business Community*, 39–40, 193.
3. Westrup, "Domestic Music under the Stuarts," 19–53; Spink, "Music and Society," 1–65.
4. Gauci, *Emporium of the World*, 60–61.
5. Grassby, *The Business Community*, 11.
6. Whyman, "Verney, John, First Viscount Fermanagh (1640–1717)," in *DNB* (accessed July 18, 2013).
7. Roseveare, "Lethieullier, Sir John (1632/3–1719)," in *DNB* (accessed July 18, 2013).
8. An extended biography appears in Bargrave, *Travel Diary*, 1–14.
9. Tilmouth, "Music on the Travels of an English Merchant," 158.
10. Ibid., 148–153.
11. Bargrave, *Travel Diary*, 99.
12. Ibid., 237.
13. It was purchased by the Bodleian Library in 2009. Beth Glixon identified Bargrave as the copyist: "Cavalli, Robert Bargrave and the English *Erismena*" (paper presented at the 15th Biennial International Conference on Baroque Music, University of Southampton, July 11–15, 2012); Cavalli, *Erismena*, forthcoming.
14. Bargrave, *Travel Diary*, 244. No publication fitting Bargrave's description is extant.
15. Pepys, *Diary*, vol. 10, 185.
16. *Familiar Letters*, 16–17. Three books of Henry Lawes's *Ayres and Dialogues* were published (1653, 1655, 1658).
17. Hill, "Thomas Hill," 128.
18. Pepys, *Diary*, January 11, 1664, vol. 5, 12.
19. Ibid., 119–120.
20. Ibid., November 27, 1664, 332. Lawes, *Choice Psalmes*; Ravenscroft, *The Whole Booke of Psalmes*.

21. Pepys, *Diary*, vol. 10, 185.
22. Pepys, *Diary*, April 15, 1664, vol. 5, 124.
23. Ibid., July 8, 1664, 199.
24. Pepys, *Diary*, May 7, 1665, vol. 9, 97–98.
25. Pepys, *Diary*, July 22, 1664, vol. 5, 217. It may have been at an occasion such as this that Daniel Henstridge encountered Reggio and transcribed one of his songs as or shortly after he performed it. See Rebecca Herissone's contribution to this volume, "Daniel Henstridge and the Aural Transmission of Music."
26. Pepys, *Diary*, July 26, 1664, 226.
27. Grassby, *The Business Community*, 181.
28. Pepys, *Diary*, October 30–31 and December 8, 1665, vol. 6, 283–284, 323–324.
29. Ibid., October 29 and September 6, 1665, 282–283, 219.
30. Ibid., December 9, 1665, 324.
31. Ibid., March 22, 1665, 64.
32. Pepys, *Letters of Samuel Pepys*, April 4/14, 1673, 96–97.
33. White, "'Brothers of the String,'" 519–581.
34. GB-TNA SP 110/16 and SP 110/21.
35. White, "'Brothers of the String,'" 573–581.
36. Ibid., 530.
37. So described in the dedication to Purcell, *A Musical Entertainment Perform'd on November XXII*.
38. Thompson, "Some Late Sources of Music by John Jenkins," 296.
39. I am grateful to Chris Pigott for sharing his research on Pigott family circles, and to Ann Taylor, a descendant of Francis Pigott, clothworker.
40. Spink, "The Old Jewry 'Musick-Society,'" 35–41. Spink is probably wrong in identifying Francis as the Francis Pigott, bapt. 1643, who attended Caius College, Cambridge (admitted 1659) and Lincoln's Inn (admitted 1661).
41. Pepys, *Diary*, February 9, 1668, vol. 9, 58.
42. Ibid., May 29, 1668, 217.
43. Ibid., July 16, 1667; September 10, 1667; and February 9, 1668, vol. 8, 340, 432; vol. 9, 58–59.
44. Ibid., September 15, 1667, 437.
45. North, *Roger North on Music*, 342, n89.
46. *BDECM*, 970–971.
47. Robinson, *A Register of the Scholars Admitted into Merchant Taylor's School* (accessed July 18, 2013). His freedom is incorrectly registered as 1635.
48. Yardley, *Menevia Sacra*, 413.
49. GB-AB SD/Ch/B28 [*Collecteanea Menevensia*, vol. 2], 185, 190. In the list of choristers made on July 27, 1720, Thomas is given in error as "Joh."
50. *Collecteanea Menevensia*, vol. 2, 209–210; *Menevia Sacra*, 332. In 1742, Delabere Pritchett, husband to Charles's daughter Elizabeth (ca. 1713–1781) was appointed a vicar choral "in the place of Charles Pygot deceased"; *Collecteanea Menevensia*, vol. 2, 215.
51. The brothers received their freedoms in the following years: Henry, 1727; George, 1733; Thomas, 1733; Charles, 1741. *Records of London's Livery Companies Online* (accessed July 18, 2013). The admission papers for all but George give their place of origin as St. David's in Pembroke. Those for Henry, Thomas, and George were signed by "James Pigot," specifically a "Clothwr. Minceing Lane" in that for Henry. In a letter of December 21, 1699, Rowland Sherman described James Pigott as a "packer," living in "Dunster Court in Mincing Lane." GB-TNA SP 110/21.
52. Holman, "Pigott, Francis," *GMO* (accessed July 18, 2013); *BDECM*, vol. 2, 894–895.
53. In his extensive genealogical research into Pigott family circles, Chris Pigott has found the name in 1656 at the marriage of Francis and Dulsibella Yealding, and thereafter only in

London and St. David's, where Elizabeth, daughter of Charles, named her daughter Katharina Dulsibella Pritchard. James Pigott named his first child Dulsibella.

54. *BDECM*, vol. 2, 894–895.
55. *The Spectator*, February 8, 1712.
56. North, *Roger North on Music*, 308, n. 60.
57. GB-TNA HCA 26/3/111; GB-TNA ADM 106/482/302.
58. Murphy, "Trading Options before Black-Scholes," 8–30, and personal communication.
59. *Calendar of Treasury Papers, Volume 1: 1556–1696*, 487; *Calendar of Treasury Papers, Volume 2: 1697–1702*, 166, http://www.british-history.ac.uk/catalogue.aspx?gid=129&type=3 (accessed July 18, 2013).
60. Woodhead, *The Rulers of London*.
61. Gauci, "Wessell, Leonard."
62. White and Woolley, "Jeremiah Clarke," 30–31. Stationers' Company accounts indicate the event at which the work was performed took place between January 20 and February 9, 1703.
63. There are three extant copies: GB-Lcm MS 1106, GB-Lbl Add. MS 31452, and GB-Ob Tenbury MS 1232. A single-sheet print of the anonymous poem "An Ode Pindarick on Barbadoes" is in the British Library: C.38.1.6(26).
64. Olson, *Making Empire Work*, 9, and Penson, *Colonial Agents*, 177.
65. Earle, *The Making of the English Middle* Class, 296, 387.
66. Woodhead, *The Rulers of London*; White, "'A Pretty Knot of Musical Friends,'" 9–44.
67. GB-Cfm Mu MS 685.
68. *Augustus Triumphans* (1728), quoted in Trowell, "Daniel Defoe's Plan," 407.

11.

Daniel Henstridge and the Aural Transmission of Music in Restoration England

Rebecca Herissone

If the Restoration musician Daniel Henstridge (ca. 1650–1736) is remembered for anything today, it is for the collection of sacred-music manuscripts he acquired during his long career as a cathedral organist at Gloucester (from 1666), Rochester (from 1674), and Canterbury (from 1698).[1] Recent research has shown that Henstridge was an unusually significant copyist of liturgical repertory not so much because of the quantity of music he produced but for its content (see the first section of table 11.1). Robert Shay and Robert Thompson have demonstrated, for example, that Henstridge copied a number of unique works by Purcell, as well as early versions of pieces that do not always survive in the main London sources of the composer's music.[2] Indeed, the extensive Flackton collection shows Henstridge to have been an important collector of music, both in terms of his own copying and in his acquisition of works from other musicians, which again include rare and unique material.

While the significance of Henstridge's manuscripts of sacred music has been acknowledged by several scholars, his copying of music in other genres has attracted little interest, a tendency that has obscured the richness and diversity of the musical interactions and collaborations he experienced during his career. As section 2 of table 11.1 shows, he may have taught members of two Kent families: the Filmers, employers of Frances Forcer and William Turner, whose hands appear alongside that of Henstridge in US-NH Filmer MS 17,[3] and the Delaunes, who owned GB-Lbl MS Mus. 1625.[4] Additionally, Henstridge was almost certainly responsible for educating the choristers at Canterbury, implied by his copy of passages on canon by Elway Bevin and Giovanni Coperario's composition rules

Table 11.1 Daniel Henstridge's Autograph and Partial Autograph Manuscripts.

Shelfmark	Description
1. Liturgical Music	
GB-CA MSS 9–11	Canterbury organbooks
GB-GL MSS 106–7, 109–12	Gloucester partbooks
GB-CA MSS 1a and GB-Lbl MS K.7.e.2	Canterbury copies of Barnard, *First Book of Selected Church Musick*, with manuscript additions including some by Henstridge
US-NH Filmer MS 21	Rochester countertenor partbook fragment
GB-Lbl Add. MSS 30931–3	Large group of loose-leaf manuscripts, mainly sacred repertory, including many in the hand of Henstridge and others apparently collected by him
US-LAuc MS fC6966/M4/A627/1700	Folio scorebook of sacred music, with some instrumental repertory at reverse end
2. Keyboard music	
GB-Lbl Add. MS 31403	Folio manuscript of keyboard music and pedagogical materials linked to Canterbury, started by Elway Bevin, and continued by Henstridge and eighteenth-century hands
GB-Lbl MS Mus. 1625	Small oblong volume of harpsichord music, mainly settings, copied by Henstridge c. 1705; rudimentary notation instructions on opening pages
US-NH Filmer MS 17	Miscellaneous oblong manuscript including vocal and keyboard music in several hands, including those of Frances Forcer and William Turner as well as Henstridge, who copied a keyboard piece and incomplete songs
3. St. Cecilia's Day odes	
GB-Lbl Add. MS 33240, fols 1–6	Henry Purcell, *Welcome to All the Pleasures*, organ part
GB-Ob T MS 1309	Henry Purcell, *Hail! Bright Cecilia*, performing parts

4. Secular songs and catches

GB-Cfm Mu MS 118	Folio manuscript of secular songs and catches, mainly copied by Henstridge; one other copyist
GB-Lbl Add. MS 29397	Oblong duodecimo manuscript containing secular songs and catches in Henstridge's hand; one piece in another hand

and solmization exercises, both later stored in GB-Lbl Add. MS 31403 among teaching materials associated with Canterbury.[5]

The third group of sources in the table, comprising performing parts for Henry Purcell's two best-known St. Cecilia's Day odes, suggests another type of music making altogether: Ford has argued convincingly that they demonstrate Henstridge's involvement in the creation of a musical society at Canterbury that predated the group that certainly did exist there from the 1720s.[6] This organization probably included a broad mix of professional musicians and members of the civic community, like the equivalent "Musical Society" in London described by Bryan White in his contribution to this volume.[7] However, it is the final pair of manuscripts, containing a large quantity of simple songs, catches, and drinking songs, that has received the least attention in the scholarly literature. They confirm Henstridge's participation in informal music making in the home and tavern, where amateur music lovers and professional musicians alike regularly gathered together to sing and play at their leisure.

Taken together, the surviving manuscripts to which Henstridge contributed provide a representative cross-section of his regular musical activities. They depict vividly the fluid boundaries within which musicians operated in the early modern period, providing material evidence not only of his activities as a cathedral musician and as an employee of private aristocratic patrons like the Filmers and Delaunes, but also showing him to have worked alongside people of the merchant classes who were involved with St. Cecilia's Day celebrations, and in all probability to have mixed with people from across all these backgrounds in the social music making implied by the contents of GB-Cfm Mu MS 118 and GB-Lbl Add. MS 29397. The neglect of these two song manuscripts in particular provides a useful parallel to the keyboard manuscripts explored by Candace Bailey in this volume, because the type of repertory they contain has consistently been dismissed for precisely the same reasons—that much of it appears to be musically undemanding and that it is associated with low-level so-called "amateur" and "domestic" performance[8]—modern categorizations which, as we shall see, are as inappropriate here as they are for Bailey's keyboard collections, and equally likely to set up false boundaries leading to misinterpretation of their contents.

Indeed, just as Bailey suggests that the notation of the keyboard manuscripts can be deceptively simple—hiding the fact that it was designed to allow an experienced player brought up in the art of improvisation the freedom to add to and adapt what was written down[9]—Henstridge's song manuscripts also mask a wealth of information on the often-intricate and highly creative performing practices of this apparently "simple" repertory, even as it was performed in the most informal of contexts.

The limited scholarly interest in GB-Cfm Mu MS 118 and GB-Lbl Add. MS 29397 seems at first entirely understandable because both manuscripts seem to have been copied from readily available contemporary printed music.[10]

Closer inspection of both volumes, however, demonstrates not only that Henstridge's main sources were not printed volumes but also that his song transcriptions include unusual and unique versions of some pieces that have hitherto gone unnoticed. Indeed, Henstridge's copying preserves strong traces of the performing traditions for which the songs were created and therefore has significant implications for our understanding of the way in which this repertory was performed in the taverns and other informal settings where it thrived. In this respect, a further parallel presents itself, this time with aural transmission cultures reflected in the early modern pedagogical lute manuscripts explored in Graham Freeman's essay in this volume. Here, too, we find transcriptions by Henstridge that blur the boundaries between music as heard and music as notated, and that challenge our assumptions about the functions and interpretation of musical notation in this period. These footprints of aural transmission are strongest in GB-Lbl Add. MS 29397, and it is on this fascinating manuscript, and the tantalizing glimpses it provides of a little-understood side of everyday musical life in seventeenth-century England, that this essay concentrates.

Even before considering its contents, GB-Lbl Add. MS 29397 is a striking source: in an unusual oblong duodecimo format, it measures just 62 mm x 156 mm. Each of the book's ninety-six main leaves is ruled with four five-line staves, which are thus only slightly smaller than those in standard quarto or even folio manuscripts. Henstridge's writing is nevertheless frequently tiny, aided by his use of a very thin nib for some entries. Many pieces contain alterations or corrections, and the copying is often untidy, giving the impression that it was completed quickly; figure 11.1, showing Robert Smith's "How Bonny and Brisk," is typical. Frequent changes of ink color and hand size additionally suggest that this was a book into which Henstridge added music gradually. This is also implied by the lack of organization of its contents, which comprise seventy pieces, including solo songs and dialogues—usually only their melody lines—as well as catches and drinking songs. Taken together, the physical characteristics of the manuscript point toward it having been Henstridge's personal musical notebook. It

Figure 11.1 Robert Smith, "How Bonny and Brisk;" GB-Lbl Add. MS 29397, fols. 11v–12r, © The British Library Board.

would appear from its repertory that the manuscript was used by Henstridge throughout most of the 1680s.[11]

There are no annotations in the book to identify either its function or its relationship to other manuscripts used by Henstridge, but remarks included in a songbook by Edward Lowe (ca. 1610–82) may well provide some clues: GB-Lbl Add. MS 29396 is a large folio manuscript containing precisely the same sort of repertory as Henstridge's book but copied over four decades from the 1640s.[12] Like GB-Lbl Add. MS 29397, Lowe's manuscript contains copies of music that differ from those in contemporary print publications, and his copying includes a number of other similarities to Henstridge's, as we shall see.[13] Significantly, Lowe twice included an annotation at the end of songs for which he had copied only the first verse of text, to indicate that "The rest of ye words are in my pocket Manuscript."[14] The implication is that Lowe had a small notebook like Henstridge's, in which he jotted down music that he later transcribed into this scorebook.

Lowe's "pocket Manuscript" no longer survives, so we cannot tell if it was similar to GB Lbl Add. MS 29397, but Henstridge's notebook seems to have been designed precisely to fit into a deep pocket—indeed its duodecimo format is shared with other types of book that were often intended to be portable, such as psalters. For example, the 1673 edition of Sternhold and Hopkins's *Whole Book of Psalms* measures 80 x 155 mm, and US-NH Filmer MS 32, a personal psalm manuscript entitled "Robert Filmer His Booke: of psalmes," is a similar sort of duodecimo.[15] Presumably, then, Henstridge carried this pocket book with him when he went to the tavern, or to music meetings, as a ready-made source of songs and catches. Whether he also transcribed them into a larger book equivalent to Lowe's manuscript is more difficult to judge: his large songbook, GB-Cfm Mu MS 118, would seem the obvious candidate, but it was not personal to Henstridge—another hand is present throughout—and the ten pieces it shares with the pocket book have a complex textual relationship to GB-Lbl Add. MS 29397. If there was a companion folio volume, it appears to have been lost.

For our purposes, the more interesting question is where and how Henstridge acquired the pieces in his pocket book. Some of his exemplars do seem to have been printed sources. About eight of the songs, and many of the catches, are sufficiently similar to the versions given in contemporary print publications to make this feasible, and one of these—his copy of Purcell's Mad Bess of Bedlam, "From Silent Shades"—certainly shows signs of a direct link with Playford's printed copy of the song published in the fourth book of *Choice Ayres, Songs and Dialogues* in 1683.[16] As Laurie notes, a misprint in Playford's edition at "Did'st thou not see my love as he pass'd by you?" (from m. 57) results in rhythmic values that do not add up.[17] The problem measure is adjusted in different ways in a number of contemporary manuscripts, including in Henstridge's pocket book, where his apparent deletion and correction of the area around the rests suggests some indecision about which possible solution to adopt.[18]

Elsewhere, it is sometimes implied strongly that Henstridge had access to versions of songs that were circulating in manuscript, independent of printed copies of the same repertory. This is likely where significant differences between his copies and the printed sources are concordant with readings in other manuscripts. For instance, Henstridge's copy of Blow's song "Alexis, Dear Alexis" matches exactly the version of the piece in the Oxford source GB-Lbl Add. MS 33235, but these manuscripts' readings differ from the song as it was printed in the 1684 edition of *Choice Ayres*, both in the patterns of repetition given for each section, and more especially in the continuo accompaniment part.[19] Another example is John Abell's ostinato song "High State and Honours," which is unusual for having a ground bass of varying lengths, sometimes five bars, sometimes six, depending on whether the closing note of the ostinato is elided with the first note of the next statement. These changing patterns of repetition differ between Henstridge's copy in GB-Lbl Add. MS 29397 and the song as it was printed in the 1683 *Choice Ayres*, with corresponding variants in the vocal line.[20] However, the structure of Henstridge's version is followed precisely in GB-Lbl Add. MS 19759, a songbook owned by Charles Campelman and dated 1681.

Thus far, Henstridge's copying in GB-Lbl Add. MS 29397 does not appear exceptional: the above examples suggest that he was collecting music through notated sources, including both print publications and manuscripts. Henstridge's versions are rarely exactly the same as other surviving notated copies, but this is not out of the ordinary: it was normal for English scribes in this period to incorporate small changes into the music they copied—features for which Alan Howard coined the useful term *background variation*, which include minor differences of rhythm, ornamentation, the register of notes in the continuo part, and so on.[21] The patterns of variants across sources of songs in particular indicate a general flexibility in the textual transmission of the repertory. But in some of the pieces in GB-Lbl Add. MS 29397, the differences between what Henstridge notated and what can be found in other surviving sources are considerably more extreme than those seen in other situations, and they hint at an entirely different method of dissemination.

One example that is particularly illuminating in this regard is Pietro Reggio's "Arise Ye Subterranean Winds" (*The Tempest*, 1674 production), which Henstridge entered on fols. 78v–77v at the reverse end of his pocket book. This transcription stands out because of the unusual nature of the text Henstridge entered below the stave (see figure 11.2).[22] Although Henstridge's thick nib and evidently hasty writing makes the text difficult to read, it can clearly be seen that he copied the text twice. His initial copying includes not only unorthodox spelling, even for the seventeenth century—such as "Aureise" for "Arise" in the opening phrase—but also many words to which an additional syllable "a" appears to have been appended. Thus he originally copied the phrase "more to distract their guilty minds" as "more-a to-a de-a-stract dear-a gilty moing." The presence of these extra syllables, together with the spelling used for particular words—"moing" for "mind," "vicha" for "which," "owl" for "howl"—imply strongly that Henstridge's first version of the text was a pseudo-phonetic transcription of a performance he had heard of a piece with which he was not already familiar, and that the singer was not a native English speaker. Indeed, the apparent mispronunciation he recorded makes it likely that the singer was Italian; it could even have been Reggio himself, despite the use of the treble clef for the melodic line.[23] Henstridge apparently entered the second set of words in order to provide a correct copy, but it is not clear from where he acquired this text: there is one variant line that I have been unable to find in any other surviving sources, including the printed playbook.[24] What is more significant is the fact that the music Henstridge copied fits with the pseudo-phonetic words, not the "corrected" text: each of the extra syllables has a note underlaid. Consequently, this version of the melodic line differs substantially from the song as Reggio himself published it in his *Songs* of 1680, in addition to which Henstridge's copy includes extensive notated ornamentation not found in other sources. It is therefore difficult to interpret his version of the piece as anything other than a literal transcription of a specific

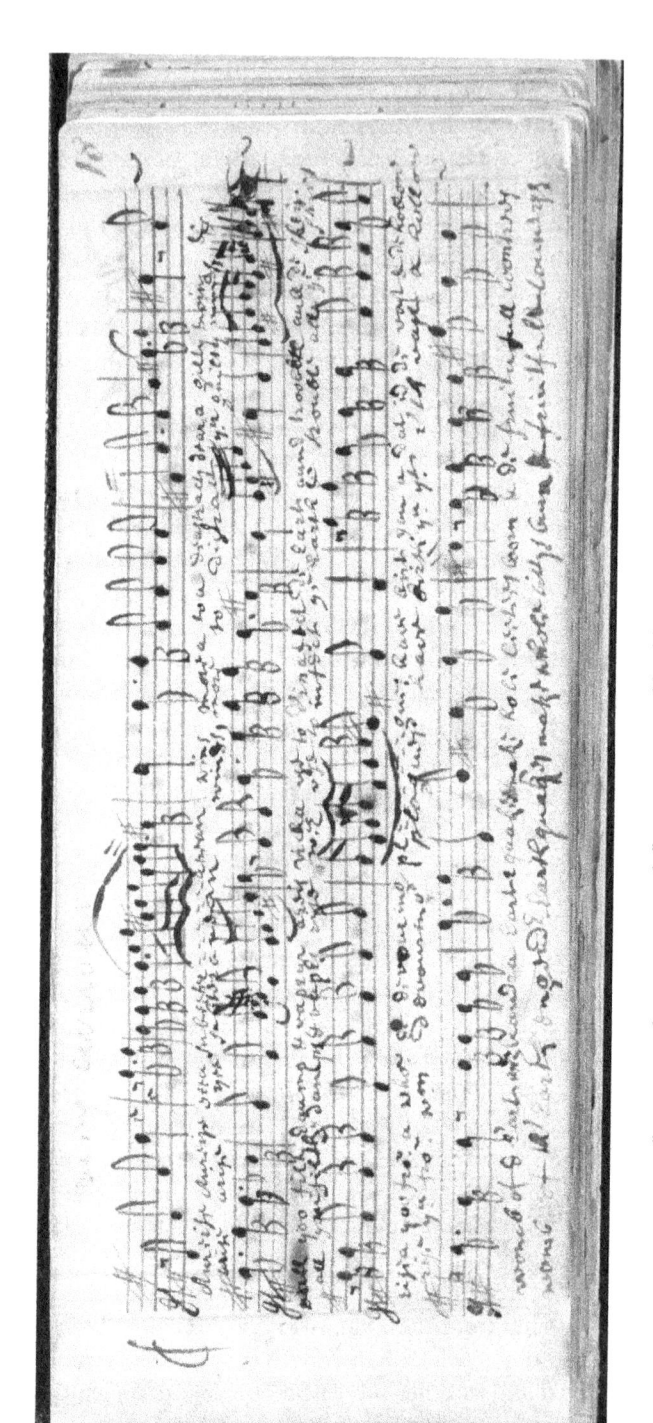

Figure 11.2 Pietro Reggio, "Arise, Ye Subterranean Winds," Opening; GB-Lbl Add. MS 29397, fol. 78v (inv.), © The British Library Board.

performance Henstridge had recently (just?) heard and wanted to preserve in his personal musical notebook, made without reference to a notated exemplar. It therefore reveals a good deal about the creative role of the performer.

Henstridge's copy suggests that the performer's interpretation resulted in radical transformation of the music in relation to the composer's authorized publication. Musical example 11.1 shows the opening three phrases of the song as notated in GB-Lbl Add. MS 29397 and in Reggio's 1680 book of songs, which was almost certainly already published by the time Henstridge copied his version.[25] Apart from the large number of repeated notes included in the pocketbook version to accommodate the extra syllables, the manuscript suggests that phrases were elongated and contracted relative to the published song: two beats are added after the initial rising arpeggio on "arise," but in the second phrase, "more to distract" enters a beat early. Substantial ornamentation results in an extra half measure on "subterranean" and one further quarter note added for a pictorial slide up to "rise" at the end of the extract. There is no accompaniment part to indicate how the continuo might have fitted against this elaboration, but it is implied in both cases that the penultimate note before each cadence resolution would have been sustained.[26] Obviously, some allowance has to be made here for the possibility that Henstridge might have transcribed either inaccurately or

Musical Example 11.1 Opening of Reggio's "Arise Ye Subterranean Winds;" (a) as copied by Daniel Henstridge in GB-Lbl Add. MS 29397, fol. 78v (inv); (b) as printed in *Songs Set by Signior Pietro Reggio* (London, 1680), 12.

approximately, and he does seem to have had some difficulty fitting the music he remembered into conventional measures, because his short second measure has two-and-a-half beats. Nevertheless, the impression given is that the singer incorporated considerably more elaborate melodic ornamentation into the music than is suggested in Reggio's own singing treatise, *The Art of Singing*, published in 1677—which included an example from "Arise Ye Subterranean Winds" for which Reggio only recommended the addition of a simple *trillo*[27]—or than would be common in a modern historically informed performance based on the printed score. Even if it was the particular context in which this copy was made that caused the singer to give an exceptionally elaborate interpretation (or even led Henstridge to exaggerate in his copying), the performance-practice implications of this copy are startling.

Although it may be difficult for us to conceive of this kind of aural transcription as a practical possibility, given the speed of working and short-term memory feats that would be required, such transmission routes were well developed in many walks of life in seventeenth-century England: Freeman's chapter in this volume highlights the evidence that sermons and poetry were often written down from memory, for example.[28] We also know from Pepys's diary that audience members sometimes tried to write down excerpts of material they heard in the theater. During a performance of *The Tempest* in 1668, Pepys attempted to transcribe the "Echo" song, "Go Thy Way," from act 3, scene 4, but had to seek the help of the actor who had performed it to complete his copy.[29]

Because Pepys had pressed John Banister to write out the music of the song for him some days earlier, we can be sure that he himself concentrated only on the text in this instance.[30] However, Freeman's assessment of the transmission of lute music from this period suggests that much of that repertory was accumulated initially through aural transmission, particularly in pedagogical contexts.[31] Moreover, Mary Chan's research on surviving manuscripts associated with music meetings held during the Commonwealth period has provided clear evidence that similar aural transmission routes were also used for precisely the genres of music preserved in Henstridge's pocket manuscript: in a note written next to a transcription in John Hilton's song manuscript GB-Lbl Add. MS 11608, the anonymous scribe remarks, "The treble I tooke & prickt downe as mr Thorpe sung it."[32] Chan also detected signs of memorized transcription in a related manuscript, GB-Lbl Egerton MS 2013, including the use of shorthand notation of texts and partial transcription of the continuo part.[33] Notably, incomplete or missing accompaniment parts are also a characteristic of Edward Lowe's folio manuscript, GB-Lbl Add. MS 29396, which, taken together with his comments about his "pocket Manuscript" cited above, may suggest that he too entered some of the material in this book via aural transcription.

Henstridge's eccentric version of Reggio's "Arise Ye Subterranean Winds" provides the clue we need to identify GB-Lbl Add. MS 29397 as a Restoration equivalent to the manuscripts Chan has found for the Commonwealth period: not only does it include repertory that was entered using "standard" textual transmission routes, but there is also material in the book that Henstridge almost certainly acquired aurally during his musical encounters with colleagues, acquaintances, and fellow professionals. While none of the other pieces sticks out quite as readily as the Reggio song, a number of the pieces Henstridge transcribed contain one or more of four main features that appear to be indicative of memorized transcription:

1. There is evidence that the scribe was relying on what he heard, and could not always fully understand the text being sung.
2. The notation shows an unusual flexibility in the interpretation of rhythm and phrase structure, mainly in declamatory songs.
3. Ornamentation is more densely notated than in printed sources, and is often included in the staff notation rather than through use of ornament signs.
4. The transmission of the melody line is privileged above that of the accompaniment, which is only partly entered, or omitted altogether.

The first of these features is clearly demonstrated by one of the four Italian songs in the book: like the Reggio song, its text must be a pseudo-phonetic transcription of the Italian (see figure 11.3). Clearly, Henstridge was no Italian scholar.[34] Beginning "Amanti fuggite" ("Amonte fougete" according to Henstridge), the song's final line should read "Quel frutto che cade, più dolce non e" (The fruit that falls is no longer sweet), but is transcribed by Henstridge as "kel fruto ke kaudi[,] Pudoulchi no na."[35] The musical setting has what I believe to be its earliest concordance in GB-Cmc MS 2591, one of the manuscripts copied for Pepys by Cesare Morelli, whom he employed as his guitar teacher probably between ca. 1679 and 1682.[36] In the "Catalogue" of the contents given on fols. 164v–165r of MS 2591, Morelli clearly identifies himself as the composer of this song, which poses interesting questions about how Henstridge may have become aware of its existence, particularly because he apparently did so in the context of its being performed.[37] What is interesting from our perspective is that, in contrast to the text there are no clues in Henstridge's notation that the music was transcribed from something other than a written source. It is clear to see why this copy should contrast so strongly with "Arise Ye Subterranean Winds": stylistically, the song is very simple and therefore the kinds of interpretative freedoms that the declamatory style of Reggio's song invited would simply not have been relevant in performance.[38] But this alerts us to the possibility that equally straightforward English dance songs in the manuscript, whose texts Henstridge could have understood without difficulty and whose notation is equally "normal" looking, might also have been transcribed without the use of a notated exemplar.

The second characteristic suggesting memorized transcription—flexibility in the interpretation of rhythm and phrase structure—is well demonstrated by

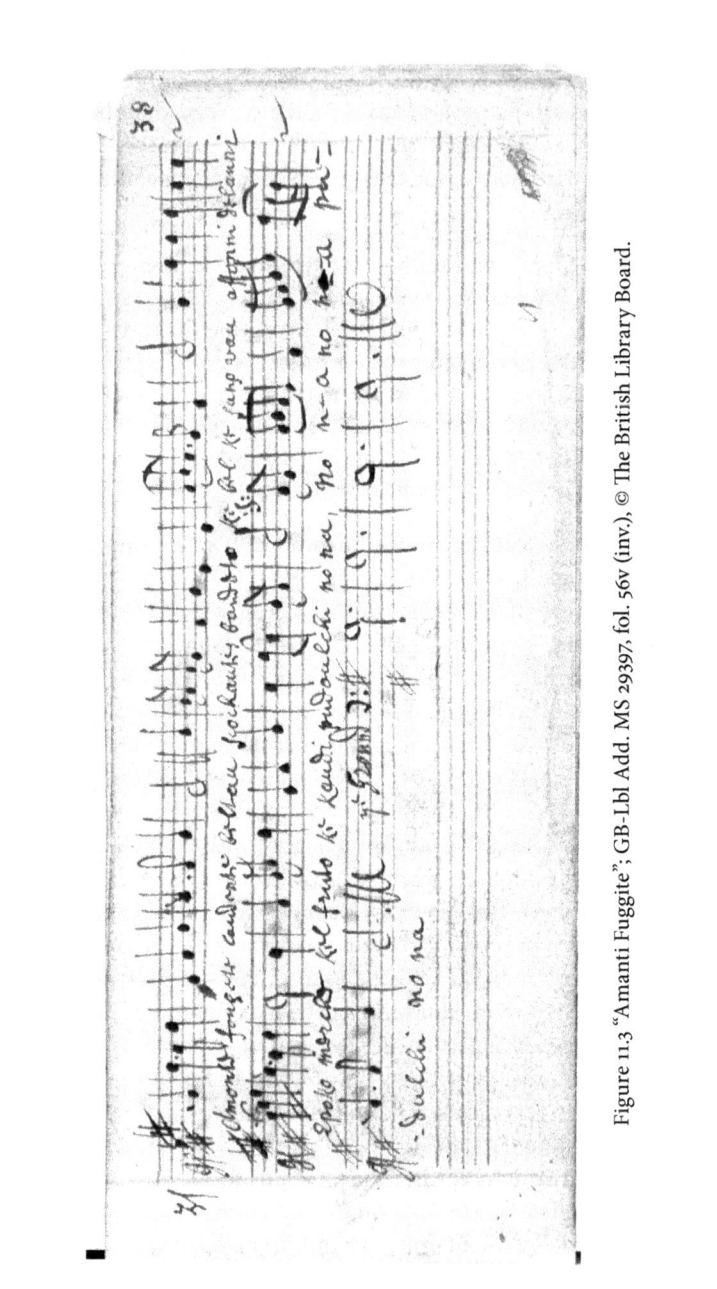

Figure 11.3 "Amanti Fuggite"; GB-Lbl Add. MS 29397, fol. 56v (inv.), © The British Library Board.

Henstridge's copy of Matthew Locke's dialogue between Thirsis and Dorinda, "When Death Shall Part Us from These Kids."[39] Although the words here do not differ from the printed version of the song, the dialogue opens in declamatory style, and there are hints of the same kinds of flexibility in interpretation as we see in his copy of "Arise Ye Subterranean Winds."[40]

As musical example 11.2 shows, the opening phrase is twice contracted in relation to the printed version of the song, while the coronas in the second and third systems imply possible expansion of the held notes at the ends of phrases; indeed, there is clear elongation of phrase openings later in the piece.[41] We also have evidence here of the third characteristic of memorized transcription, because quite substantial ornamentation is added in relation to the printed sources, seen both through the use of signs and in the notation, and mainly occurring at cadences, although the elaboration is not on the same level as for Reggio's song. The addition of the c-sharp in the phrase "is our cell Elizium?" also varies the placement and addition of accidentals in relation to the printed copy, something that features in several other parts of the piece and the manuscript as a whole, and which may suggest that incorporation of these sorts of pitch variants was considered at the time as a form of ornamentation that could be employed by performers or copyists.

As with most of the songs in the manuscript, Henstridge transcribed Locke's dialogue with only its vocal lines, omitting the continuo accompaniment part—the fourth characteristic of aural transcription identified in the list. Of all the features of this method of notation we have encountered so far, this perhaps has the most significant implications for contemporary performance practices, something that is demonstrated more clearly where Henstridge did provide some or all of a bass line apparently without using an exemplar. The "problem" of the bass seems to have been solved by Henstridge partly through his choice of pieces: an unusually high proportion of the songs in the manuscript are written over a ground bass, which Henstridge usually wrote down on a facing page or at the end of his transcription, and which would have given a transcribed melody a ready-made accompaniment. But there are indications that for non-ostinato pieces the absence of a transcribed bass part was remedied in another way: several of the songs for which bass parts are provided or partially provided show significant variants in relation to other extant sources, or are completely unrelated to them, suggesting that Henstridge created his own new bass parts, or filled in gaps where his aural transcription was incomplete.

One likely example of this is the anonymous song "Could Man His Wish Obtain," which has a bass part that imitates sections of the vocal melody, but for which only some sections of the bass were entered by Henstridge in GB-Lbl Add. MS 29397 (see figure 11.4).[42] The copy gives the impression that he was attempting to transcribe both parts aurally but lost his way in the bass during the second section of the piece. In general, the relationship between this transcription and

Musical Example 11.2 Opening of Locke's "When Death Shall Part Us from These Kids;" (a) as copied by Daniel Henstridge in GB-Lbl Add. MS 29397, fol. 18v; (b) as printed in *Choice Ayres, Songs and Dialogues . . . The Second Edition* (London, 1675), 80.

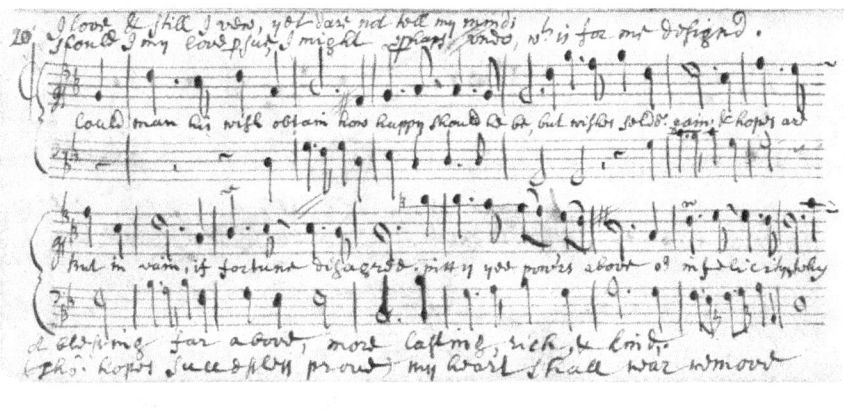

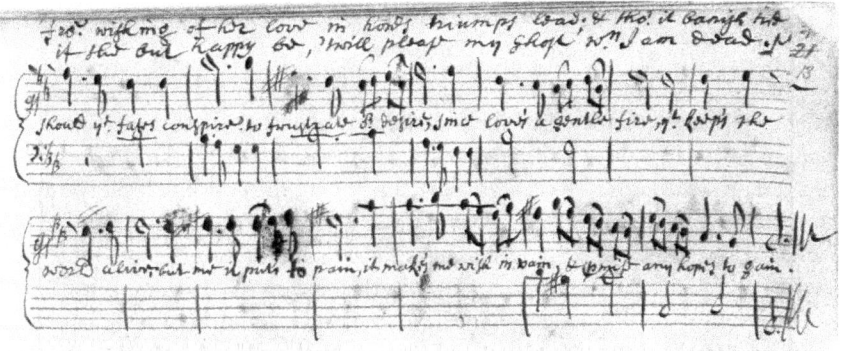

Figure 11.4 "Could Man His Wish Obtain;" GB-Lbl Add. MS 29397, fols. 12v–13r, © The British Library Board.

the printed version of the song in *Choice Ayres, Songs and Dialogues* (1683) is relatively close, but there are signs of aural transcription in the top vocal part's ornamented melodic line and some small variants in the words.[43] The relationship between the bass part and the treble is sufficiently simple that it would surely have been possible to remember much of the song with ease. However, at the point where the bass stops and reenters in the second section, Henstridge's notation does not correspond with the printed score, and the final cadence seems simply to have been added as a typical cadential formula, providing a stereotyped ending to the piece. Additionally, the bass part at the end of the first section is entirely different (see musical example 11.3), and shows a different imitative relationship with the top part: perhaps Henstridge could remember enough to know that there was imitation but not in which measure it occurred.

While this bass part seems to have originated as an aural transcription, some of the others in GB-Lbl Add. MS 29397 may well have been added independently

Musical Example 11.3 "Could Man His Wish Obtain," mm. 8–14; (a) as copied by Daniel Henstridge in GB-Lbl Add. MS 29397, fol. 12v; (b) as printed in J. Playford, *Choice Ayres, Songs and Dialogues . . . The Fourth Book*, 5.

after Henstridge completed an aural transcription of the melody line. This is perhaps most likely where the bass part is not laid out in score under the vocal line, but rather was copied as a separate part, and where the bass line itself seems not to be related to those given in other extant sources. A good example of this is "Why Is Your Faithful Slave Disdained," for which Henstridge copied the vocal line on fol. 41v of the manuscript, and then the bass on fol. 42r, a part that differs substantially from the bass as it appears in two printed sources of 1688.[44] As musical example 11.4 shows, both versions of the bass in the second half of the song include imitation again, but Henstridge's copy has the bass entering at a different point—arguably less successfully—and he also elides the end of the part into the repeat. Apart from at the formulaic cadences in mm. 10–11, there is little in common between the two bass lines.

It is entirely possible that more than one version of this piece was in circulation in Henstridge's lifetime, and that what we see here are revisions that Courteville himself carried out. However, the likelihood that Henstridge composed this bass line to go with the melody line of a song he transcribed aurally is heightened by evidence elsewhere in the manuscript that he did sometimes add in new parts of his own making. This is almost certainly the case for Michael Wise's "Old Chiron Thus," printed as a two-part song for treble and bass in *Catch that Catch Can* (1685) and in *The Second Part of the Pleasant Musical Companion* (1686), and also circulated widely in manuscript.[45] Henstridge initially copied the treble and bass parts in score on fols. 61v–58r at the reverse end of the manuscript, in a version without significant variants from the printed copies, but at its conclusion he notated an additional treble part, lying mainly under the first one, which he signed at the end "D: Hens:," as Shay and Thompson have noted.[46] Henstridge did succeed in incorporating limited additional imitation into the added part (see

Musical Example 11.4 "Why Is the Faithful Slave Disdained?" mm. 6–12; (a) as copied by Daniel Henstridge in GB-Lbl Add. MS 29397, fol. 41v–42r; (b) as printed in *The Banquet of Musick . . . The Second Book*, 5.

musical example 11.5), but he was unable to fit in all the text, and the harmony in m. 5 is uncomfortable. In general, the added part uses a fair amount of parallel motion, especially with the upper part, but it is by no means dependent on it.

Conclusions

These examples suggest that Henstridge's copying in his pocket book was not just a matter of recording what he heard and transcribing pieces he was able to access in printed and manuscript sources: in some cases he also engaged creatively with the music he encountered, perhaps partly out of necessity, when he was transcribing aurally and was unable to take down all the parts he heard, and sometimes as a method of adapting and developing the material that was available to him. Taken as a whole, Henstridge's copying in GB-Lbl Add. MS 29397 implies a number of significant adaptations to our understanding of the ways in which Restoration vocal music was performed in the period in relation to the versions of

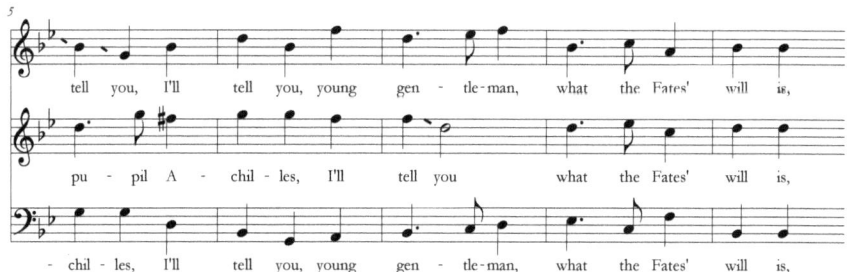

Musical Example 11.5 Opening of "Old Chiron Thus Preach'd to His Pupil Achilles," as copied by Daniel Henstridge with added middle part; GB-Lbl Add. 29397, fol. 61v (inv.) and 58r (inv.).

the music that were transmitted through print publication. First, it suggests that declamatory song may have incorporated greater flexibility of tempo than we might imagine today, particularly at the beginnings and ends of phrases, which seem to have been treated very freely. Second, ornamentation appears to have been applied much more extensively than is suggested by notated sources produced via more standard scribal transmission, particularly in declamatory styles, where such decoration was apparently allowed to disrupt meter, at least in the most dramatic music. Although the extreme ornamentation in Henstridge's copies of Purcell's Bess of Bedlam and "O Solitude" has been noted elsewhere as two isolated cases, in fact virtually every piece Henstridge transcribed is steeped in both ornamentation symbols—particularly the slide—and in decoration incorporated into the staff notation itself.[47] Third, in privileging melody lines over accompaniments when transcribing aurally, Henstridge almost certainly created his own accompaniment parts, so that some pieces were probably performed with entirely different or partially variant bass lines from those transmitted in the notated sources. For a professional organist like Henstridge, it would probably have been easy to improvise an accompaniment for most of these songs, and some other Restoration sources—including Lowe's songbook, as noted above, and Purcell's autograph manuscript GB-Lg MS Safe 3—have examples of incomplete bass parts that imply similar practices.[48] Finally, Henstridge's creative engagement with the music he copied into the manuscript is also shown by his addition of at least one extra part, which is again a trait that can be seen in other manuscripts associated with aural transcription, such as Lowe's songbook and the lute manuscripts discussed by Freeman elsewhere in this volume.[49]

Daniel Henstridge's tiny pocket manuscript thus holds a wealth of musical treasures concerning the performance of secular song in the Restoration period. The fact that it contains a good deal of material that also happens to have been printed by the Playfords in the 1680s is evidently indicative less of the sources Henstridge used when entering material into the manuscript than of the way in which the Playford prints reflect the popular repertory that was being sung in taverns and other places where musicians met together during the 1680s. Unlike these printed books, however, GB-Lbl Add. MS 29397 preserves something of the living tradition in which the music was performed, just like the group of sources that Chan was able to link to earlier music meetings in the Commonwealth period. Henstridge's manuscript therefore has the potential to assist us in bridging the ever-difficult gap between notation and practice in Restoration England, as well as helping to create a more rounded picture of the way in which the music making of cathedral musicians like Henstridge involved them in a much wider range of social interactions than their occupational activities alone would suggest.

Notes

1. For details of Henstridge's biography, see Ford, "Henstridge, Daniel," *GMO* (accessed June 30, 2012). Ford notes that Henstridge effectively retired in 1718.

2. Shay and Thompson, *Purcell Manuscripts*, 221–226. On Henstridge's London connections, see Ford, "Purcell as His Own Editor," 48–49.

3. See Ford, "The Filmer Manuscripts," 820–821, and Bailey, "The Challenge of Domesticity," this volume, 119.

4. As suggested in Johnstone, "A New Source," 67–69 and 77.

5. These begin on fol. 141 of GB-Lbl Add. MS 30933. For more on Lbl Add. MS 31403 and its possible functions, see Bailey, this volume, 118–119.

6. See Ford, "Henstridge, Daniel," and Ford, "Minor Canons at Canterbury Cathedral," 445–447.

7. See White, "Music and Merchants," this volume, 156–7 and 159–60. Some members of the London Musical Society are listed in the prefatory material to Purcell's *A Musical Entertainment* (1683) and Blow's *A Second Musical Entertainment* (1684), but White has uncovered information about many more of the individuals who were involved with this "Musical Society."

8. See Bailey, "The Challenge of Domesticity," this volume, 114. Jack Westrup's dismissal of Purcell's extensive output of catches in a single sentence is typical (*Purcell*, 169–170): "Nothing

need be said here of Purcell's numerous catches . . . they are too slight to have any permanent significance."

9. Bailey, "The Challenge of Domesticity," this volume, 121–122.

10. Shay and Thompson, *Purcell Manuscripts*, 276. The three books are Lawes, *Select Ayres* of 1669 and two books published by John Playford: *Choice Ayres . . . The Second Edition* from 1675 and *Choice Ayres . . . The Second Book*, from 1679.

11. As suggested in Shay and Thompson, *Purcell Manuscripts*, 275–276.

12. As argued in Chan, "Edward Lowe's Manuscript," 440–454.

13. Ibid., 449.

14. One example occurs on fol. 75r, at the end of the song "How Happy's That Pris'ner Who Conquers His Fate," and another at the end of the following song, "Stay, Shut the Gate," fol. 76r.

15. Ford, "The Filmer Manuscripts," 823.

16. J. Playford, *Choice Ayres . . . The Fourth Book*, 45.

17. See Purcell, *Secular Songs for Solo Voice*, 28 and 281.

18. This passage is also corrected in GB-Cfm Mu MS 118, but the copy is in the unknown scribe's hand, not Henstridge's, and the solution differs from that given in GB-Lbl Add. MS 29397. The textual relationship between the pocket book and Playford's printed edition remains complex, because Henstridge's copy also incorporates significant additional melodic ornamentation.

19. See GB-Lbl Add. MS 33235, fol. 50r, GB-Lbl Add. MS 29397, fol. 62v, and J. Playford, *Choice Ayres . . . The Fifth Book*, 60. The Oxford provenance of GB-Lbl Add. MS 33235 is noted in Shay and Thompson, *Purcell Manuscripts*, 271. The only variants between the manuscript readings comprise some absent ties in GB-Lbl Add. MS 29397 and one variant harmony note in the treble part.

20. J. Playford, *Choice Ayres . . . The Fourth Book*, 21.

21. See Howard, "Understanding Creativity," 97, and also the longer discussion of the concept in Herissone, *Musical Creativity*, 245–258.

22. The following two paragraphs are extracted from Herissone, *Musical Creativity*, 377–381.

23. In this period, songs printed in the treble clef were considered suitable for men's voices when transposed down an octave; see Herissone, *Music Theory in Seventeenth-Century England*, 110. Reggio sang bass at the court of Queen Christina in Stockholm and in the French royal choir, and John Evelyn wrote on September 23, 1680, that he "sung *admirably* to a *Guitarr* & had a perfect good tenor and base &c."; quoted in G. Rose, "Pietro Reggio," 212.

24. [Shadwell], *The Tempest or the Enchanted Island*, 30. The variant line is "engender earthquakes, make whole countries shake and stately cities into deserts turn," which Henstridge copied as "engender earthquakes, make whole cities burn and fateful countries into deserts turn."

25. The song appears in modern edition in Locke, *Dramatic Music*, 42–45, using only the printed source (see the editorial commentary in ibid., 235). In addition to Henstridge's copy, it also survives in two other contemporary manuscripts, GB-Lbl Add. MS 19759 and in GB-Lbl Add. MS 33234. Both these copies contain variants of their own, with hints of aural transcription. Their characteristics are examined in Herissone, *Musical Creativity*, 381–383.

26. Had the singer been Reggio himself, he would surely have provided his own accompaniment: Pepys noted in July 1664 that Reggio sang "to the theorbo most neatly" (quoted in G. Rose and Spencer, "Reggio, Pietro," *GMO* (accessed June 20, 2012)), and Evelyn referred to his self-accompaniment on the guitar (see note 23 above). I am grateful to Alan Howard for this observation.

27. Reggio, *The Art of Singing*, 9. As Stephen Rose has noted ("Performance Practices," 132–133), Reggio emphasized subtle dynamic shading as the principal expressive technique for

the singer, and there is only brief mention of this kind of *passaggi*-like ornamentation (in *The Art of Singing*, 15).

28. See Freeman, "The Transmission of Lute Music," this volume, 45–7.

29. Pepys, *Diary*, vol. 9, 195; quoted in Smyth, *"Profit and Delight,"* 114. Smyth suggests that this kind of transcription was probably widespread in this period, and may account for variants between copies of literary texts.

30. In the entry for May 7, 1668, he wrote that he "did get him [Banister] to prick me down the notes of the Echo in 'The Tempest,' which pleases me mightily"; Pepys, *Diary*, vol. 9, 189.

31. Freeman, "The Transmission of Lute Music," this volume, 47–50.

32. The annotation occurs on fol. 63v; as quoted in Chan, "A Mid-Seventeenth-Century Music Meeting," 233.

33. Ibid., 237.

34. Of the other three, "Dite O cieli" (Carissimi) is straightforwardly copied from the 1688 published version in Henry Playford's *The Banquet of Musick . . . The Second Book*, 22, but the origins of the other two, "Ecco l'Alba"'(also Carissimi) and "Bel tempo" (anonymous) are not yet clear. Neither appears to have been printed in England in the Restoration period.

35. I am grateful to Michael Talbot and other delegates at the Fifteenth Biennial Conference on Baroque Music, University of Southampton, July 2012, for their assistance in deciphering this text, and to an anonymous reader for assistance in its identification.

36. This is a large and extravagantly copied book with the title "Songs & other Compositions Light, Grave, & Sacred, for a Single Voice. Adjusted to the particular Compass of mine; With a Thorough-Base on ye Ghitarr by Cesare Morelli" (written in Morelli's hand rather than that of Pepys, despite the reference to the first person). Although the date 1693 is given on the front of the leather binding, Morelli left Pepys's service to return to Flanders in 1682 (see Short, "Morelli, Cesare," *GMO* (accessed June 1, 2015)). This song is found among the "Compositions Light," on pp. 21–22 (fol. 14). A transcription is given in Morelli, *Eight Songs for Samuel Pepys*, 17–26. Kyropoulos identifies the text as an extract from a cantata by the mid-seventeenth-century Roman poet and singer Margherita Costa, *Oh Dio, voi che mi dite* (see ibid., 5).

37. The song must have circulated outside the context of Morelli's employment by Pepys, because a later reference to the same text occurs in the 1701 volume of Christoph Ballard's *Meilleurs airs italiens*, although no composer is listed here. The melody as given by Morelli was later used as air no. 32 in John Gay's banned ballad opera *Polly*, act 2, scene 4, where it occurs with the replacement text "Fine women are devils." See Gay, *Polly: An Opera*, 31, and the music notation paginated separately at the end of that volume, 7; see also Gay, *The Beggar's Opera and Polly*, 118 and 180.

38. Nevertheless, the variants between Henstridge's version of the song and that notated by Morelli indicate that the singer included added and variant ornamentation, although this is on a scale similar to that given for Locke's dialogue in example 11.2, rather than being of the more extreme sort that Henstridge notated for "Arise Ye Subterranean Winds."

39. GB-Lbl Add. MS 29397, fols. 18v–21v.

40. The song first appeared in print in J. Playford, *Choice Ayres . . . The Second Edition*, 80–84. It was reprinted identically in J. Playford, *Choice Ayres . . . Newly Re-printed*, 90–93, in 1676, and also in H. Playford, *The Theater of Music . . . The Fourth and Last Book*, 78–81, in 1687, where the part of Thirsis was placed in the bass clef, and where there is one rhythmic difference and one apparent misprint in the bass, but the text is otherwise identical.

41. Dorinda's phrase "But in Elizium" begins on an eighth note in the printed copy, but on a quarter note in GB-Lbl Add. MS 29397; Thirsis's next phrase, "Oh, there is neither hope nor fear," starts on a quarter note in the printed version but a half note in Henstridge's copy.

42. GB-Lbl Add. 29397, fols. 12v–13r.

43. J. Playford, *Choice Ayres... The Fourth Book*, 5. The song was also copied by Henstridge in GB-Cfm Mu MS 118, 55, a fifth lower than the versions in GB-Lbl Add. MS 29397 and *Choice Ayres*. There is a close relationship between GB-Cfm Mu MS 118 and the print publication—thus meaning no direct link between GB-Lbl Add. MS 29397 and GB-Cfm Mu MS 118—apart from transposition and a few examples of background variation, as well as minor variants in the bass line that result from the fact that the bass as given in GB-Cfm Mu MS 118 is apparently not a vocal line, and therefore has some sustained notes that are shown separated in the print publication; the manuscript version also omits four notes of the bass part between mm. 10 and 11.

44. See H. Playford, *The Banquet of Musick... The Second Book*, 5, and H. Playford, *Vinculum Societatis... The Second Book*, 19. Henstridge attributes the song to "Mr Courteville," but it is anonymous in both printed versions.

45. J. Playford, *Catch that Catch Can*, no. 52; J. Playford, *The Second Part of the Pleasant Musical Companion... The Second Edition*, part II, no. 6.

46. Shay and Thompson, *Purcell Manuscripts*, 275–276.

47. S. Rose, "Performance Practices," 147 n161; Purcell, *Thirty Songs in Two Volumes*, vol. 1, 30–35.

48. On the evidence for memorized copying in Purcell's "Gresham" autograph, see Herissone, *Musical Creativity*, 368.

49. Lowe added parts to several songs in GB-Lbl Add. MS 29396; his addition to "The Thirsty Earth" is analyzed in ibid., 327–331.

12.

Courtly Connections: Queen Anne, Music, and the Public Stage

Amanda Eubanks Winkler

Upon the death of William III in 1702, Queen Anne took the throne without incident.[1] Unfortunately, after this smooth transfer of power, strife marked the early years of Anne's reign: the War of the Spanish Succession raged in Europe, renewed French support for the Jacobite cause threatened the stability of her realm, and partisan factions divided Parliament. To demonstrate support for the new queen and to assuage the fears of the public during difficult times, a series of musical panegyrics appeared on the London stage: Thomas D'Urfey's *The Old Mode and the New* (1703), Richard Steele's *The Lying Lover* (1704), and Peter Motteux's *Britain's Happiness* (1704), all of which feature songs in praise of Anne. In these entertainments, many of the same rhetorical strategies of praise and celebration found in court odes of this period carried over into a more public context. Even nonelite audience members would have recognized the encomiastic strategies deployed in these entertainments, as court odes were widely disseminated in printed sources. Odes were also performed in concert settings, allowing a broader audience to become conversant with the elaborate sound of monarchical praise. This essay traces the process by which courtly musical and poetic rhetoric circulated in the early eighteenth-century marketplace. As we shall see, during the early years of Anne's reign, the products of court culture were increasingly available; this was part of a larger trend that commodified and marketed what had previously been available to only a small coterie.

COURT, CONCERT, AND STAGE UNDER THE STUARTS

Recent musicological studies demonstrate how direct royal subsidy for music in public settings waned over the course of the late Stuart era.[2] Charles II had been intimately involved in the playhouse, shaping content and supplying his court musicians for lavish musical entertainments, such as the operatic revision of *The Tempest* (1674) performed at Dorset Garden Theatre.[3] The symbiosis between the courtly and the public realms was disrupted during James II's fractious and short reign, but when William and Mary took the throne in 1689, the relationship between the two was reestablished and significantly reconfigured, not by the monarchs themselves but rather by the musicians in their service. As Bruce Wood and Andrew Pinnock have shown, during the 1690s, Henry Purcell used Dorset Garden Theatre as a "job creation agency for members and former members of the Private Music," using the prestige associated with the court to "sell instruments, sheet music, tutor books and private lessons."[4] Furthermore, there were numerous "gestural or ideational" correspondences between Purcell's odes and his operas during this period, with musical ideas generally moving from the court ode to the commercial opera.[5]

After the untimely deaths of Queen Mary and Henry Purcell in 1695, the two London theater companies—the United Company and the company at Lincoln's Inn Fields—competed with each other to celebrate important milestones in William's reign.[6] For instance, Thomas Dilke included an ode honoring William in his play *The City Lady*, performed at Lincoln's Inn Fields in 1696. The playwright acknowledged that the ode did not fit well within the play, but he was willing to sacrifice dramatic coherence for panegyric musical pleasure:

> I very well know that the Ode in the third Act ["Give to the Warrior Loud and Lasting Praise"] seems to be introduc'd something unseasonably. It was made and set long since, in hopes of having it perform'd before the King, at his return from *Flanders*; and the Music being so finely compos'd by Mr. *John Eccles*, I was loath it shou'd be wholly lost to the Town.[7]

In the following year when William signed the peace treaty with Louis XIV at Ryswick, both theater companies offered public celebrations to honor the king. Thomas Morgan and other composers contributed to an entertainment celebrating the peace at Drury Lane, and Jeremiah Clarke set an ode, "Tell the World Great Caesars Come."[8] For Lincoln's Inn Fields, Eccles provided music for Peter Motteux's libretto, *Europe's Revels for the Peace* (1697), a French-style *ballet des nations*.[9] As with Dilke's insertion of the ode into *The City Lady*, the musical celebrations of William as peace broker served multiple purposes: to entertain an audience hungry for music, to prove the loyalty and patriotism of the creators, and, perhaps, to procure future preferment for the playwright and composer.

During William and Mary's reign some music of the court also began to appear regularly in print.[10] Certain publishers specialized in the conveyance of courtly propaganda: one was the aforementioned Motteux, who, after emigrating to England upon the revocation of the Edict of Nantes (1685), became a major force in designing musical entertainments in support of the Williamite cause.[11] Starting in 1692, he began publishing New Year's and birthday odes in *The Gentleman's Journal*, his short-lived but influential periodical.[12] As Margaret Ezell observed, in this magazine "one can see the process of transforming the mechanics and genres characteristic of earlier coterie literary practice to suit a wider commercial reading public."[13] Motteux's presentation of the poetic ode with its music was part of the process whereby music intended for a small, bounded audience was transformed into mass culture, the courtly commodified. John Blow also included odes in his self-published collection, *Amphion Anglicus* (1700) and Henry Purcell's widow, Frances, followed suit, publishing her husband's birthday ode for the Duke of Gloucester as well as two birthday odes for Queen Mary in the second book of *Orpheus Britannicus* (1702).

Courtly Modes of Cultural Production and the Public Sphere

By the accession of Queen Anne in 1702, there had already been a long-standing precedent for blurring the lines between courtly and public entertainments; indeed, during Anne's reign, the dissemination of courtly cultural products to a broader public only increased.[14] Yet this claim directly contradicts recent narratives of late Stuart culture; R. O. Bucholz has argued that Anne attempted "to provide a court life that was, in her terms, entertaining, inspiring, and popular, as her uncle's had been." Ultimately, she failed, because of economic exigencies, an "antiquated administrative system," and courtiers more interested in individual preferment than court culture. According to this line of argument, the center of artistic life had shifted irrevocably from the court to the "public theater and concert hall."[15]

This tale of courtly artistic decline can also be found in the work of the tremendously influential social theorist Jürgen Habermas. According to Habermas, in England a distinct public sphere after the Glorious Revolution, one in which the "middling sort," a newly empowered bourgeoisie, enjoyed "rational-critical debate and discussion" in coffee houses and via pamphlets and newspapers.[16] Habermas was careful to point out that the public sphere was "coextensive with public authority."[17] However, citing Whig historian G. M. Trevelyn for support, Habermas described a secluded court with diminished artistic influence.[18] This notion has proved tremendously persistent.[19] Although Habermas may not have intended to create a rigid separation between his public sphere and the court, his work did little to mitigate the impression that one existed.

James Winn, Estelle Murphy, and others have questioned this narrative of courtly marginalization and decline, as they have amply demonstrated the importance of Anne as a generator of culture, both at court and for a wider public.[20] In his recent comprehensive study, Winn demonstrated that Anne was an avid and knowledgeable patron of the arts. As Murphy pointed out, during Anne's reign the performance of New Year's and birthday odes were regularized and courtly discourses increasingly made their way into the public sphere.[21] Viewing this development through a Habermasian lens, we might cynically wonder if the increasingly powerful public sphere co-opted and commodified courtly cultural products, causing them to lose "their aura of extraordinariness" and "their once sacramental character," as they were "profaned" by the "private people" who could independently determine their meanings.[22] Yet, there is little historical evidence to support this assertion. Instead, in the marketplaces of the London stage, the concert room, and print culture, musical paeans to the monarch were valuable and attractive *precisely because* they were imbued with the aura of royal power.

Following the groundwork laid by Winn and Murphy, we might shape a new model that acknowledges the increased audibility of courtly musical rhetoric as well as the inherent permeability between the courtly and noncourtly spheres. Indeed, we might even question the existence of a Habermasian public sphere at all, instead thinking in terms of overlapping audiences, courtly rhetoric flowing freely into noncourtly discourses.[23] Or, as Harold Love has argued, we might consider "the existence of a considerable number of discrete publics and the fact that members of these publics were usually also members of other publics."[24] For the person who first heard an ode at court might hear it again in the theater, finally buying a printed copy for consumption and performance at home.

Poetry and Music: Odes for Queen Anne

A common encomiastic language deployed in both courtly and noncourtly musical entertainments allowed the rhetoric of the court to circulate freely among diverse publics. To understand the parameters of the panegyric mode developed for Anne, we must first turn to the texts of court odes, which, despite their artistic poverty, provide an invaluable medium for understanding the symbols and allegorical language associated with the queen between 1702, the time of her accession to the throne, and 1704, when *The Lying Lover* and *Britain's Happiness* were performed.[25]

Although poets continued to use some rhetorical strategies from odes written for William (in particular the invocation of Phoebus), the ode texts for Anne mostly forged a new path, as language was reshaped to accommodate a female monarch. In his 1703 New Year's ode, poet laureate Nahum Tate compared Anne (or Anna as she is often styled) to a goddess of spring who inspires rebirth, ushering in a golden age of peace and plenty to England.[26] Motteux pursued many of the same themes in his birthday ode from the same year. Anne's powers transcend those of the natural world, and she is aligned with the wise goddess Pallas Athena, a strategy that had been previously deployed during her coronation, when, during the singing of the coronation anthems, spectators received medals

Table 12.1 Odes for Anne, 1702–1704.

Year	Occasion	Poet	Composer	Title
1702	Coronation	Tate	Abell	*Aloud Proclaim the Cheerful Sound*
1702	Coronation	D'Urfey	Farinell	*Mars Now is Arming* (probably not performed)
1702	Coronation	Unknown	D. Purcell	*Phoebus, Monarch of the Skies* (performed in 1704)
1703	New Year	Tate	Eccles	*Hark How the Muses Call Aloud*
1703	Birthday	Motteux	Eccles	*Inspire Us, Genius of the Day*
1704	New Year	Tate (?)	Eccles	*While Anna with Victorious Arms*
1704	Birthday	Tate (?)	Eccles	*Awake, Awake, Harmonious Pow'rs*

that depicted Anne as Pallas Athena battling a Hydra-like creature.[27] In his birthday ode, Motteux also carefully defended Anne's feminine virtues: while some may "disclaim" a female monarch, Motteux averred that her critics will soon "totter." Other poets implicitly or explicitly compared Anne with her female predecessor on the throne, Elizabeth I. For example, playwright Thomas D'Urfey's coronation ode for Anne refers to the Queen as Gloriana and claims that Anne's reign will equal Eliza's in glory.[28]

In response to the ongoing English involvement in the War of the Spanish Succession, many of the odes are martial in tone. Anne brings peace, but she uses military might to secure her nation's interests. For instance, in Tate's New Year's ode of 1703, he praised the peace that will come in Anne's reign (she silences "War's Angry Voice" after quelling "Oppressors" and awing "Tyrants"). Motteux also celebrated her husband's position as "Lord High Admiral" of the navy. He is called "England's Protecting GEORGE, AND / Guardian of the Main." Motteux used a similar strategy in his 1703 birthday ode for Queen Anne. She only arms herself "to secure the World's Repose" and deploys military might to secure peace and to "Keep Europe free."

Given the fraught political circumstances of the time and very real health problems of both Anne and George, these odes were clearly more propaganda than truth. Anne, obese, gout-ridden, and female, was an unlikely candidate for warrior-monarch. George, an asthmatic with little experience in battle, would never be a respected military leader. Anne had tried to persuade her allies to appoint him commander of the forces during the War of the Spanish Succession, but the Dutch preferred the Duke of Marlborough; thus, George had to settle for the largely ceremonial title of "Lord High Admiral."[29] Nevertheless, in song, poetry, and image, a potent alternate reality was crafted, one in which George valiantly protected the seas, and Anne, Pallas-like, ruled with wisdom and might, vanquishing all strife.

COMMODIFIED ODES, 1702–1704

The propaganda found in the odes was not simply heard by a lucky few at court; to promote the message about Anne's glorious new reign, these pieces were sometimes performed in theaters and concert halls. In 1703, either the New Year's or birthday ode was performed at Lincoln's Inn Fields while Lincoln's Inn Fields singers Short, Cook, and Davis performed "Chide the Drowsy Spring" from Eccles's 1704 birthday ode as part of a benefit for Mr. Short and Mrs. Willis.[30] Also in 1704, Daniel Purcell enjoyed a long-delayed first performance of his coronation ode for Anne, *Phoebus, Monarch of the Skies*, at the Theatre Royal in Drury Lane by well-known singers Richard Leveridge, Mrs. Lyndsey, Francis Hughes, and Mrs. Campion.[31]

Odes also resonated beyond the public theaters and concert halls. They were printed in collections, putting them within the reach of a literate, book-buying public. The public undoubtedly experienced printed odes differently than performed odes. Publishers sometimes printed odes in significantly reduced form, sometimes only including the barest musical outlines, as with D'Urfey's ode in honor of the queen's coronation, printed in volume four of the 1706 *Wit and Mirth* (see figure 12.1): like other songs in *Wit and Mirth*, only the vocal line and text are given. Some consumers probably silently scanned the words and music or perhaps performed the piece a cappella by themselves or with friends, but if they wanted more information on the ground (allowing for a more elaborate performance), they would have needed to flip back a few pages to *The Kings Health*, D'Urfey's celebration of William's exploits, which had a header identifying the name of the ground used in both pieces: "Farinel's *Grounds*." "Farinel's Grounds" (a folia by French violinist and composer Michel Farinel) would have been well-known to musically educated consumers of the period, as it circulated in print, and, one must assume, in the aural tradition as a bass line designed for improvisation.[32] The musically ambitious consumer would have needed to fit the vocal line and text of the ode to the suggested ground bass—an act of composition or at least substantial arrangement.[33]

D'Urfey's ode would have required reconstruction before it was performable with accompaniment, but other song sheets altered the material to make it more accessible for domestic performance (see figure 12.2). This movement, from Nahum Tate and John Eccles's 1703 New Year's ode, *Hark How the Muses Call Aloud*, was printed as part of John Walsh's serial, *The Monthly Mask of Vocal Musick*. Practical concerns shaped the publication. Placing "They Call and Bid the Spring Appear" within the "compass of a flute" (recorder) gave purchasers some flexibility in their mode of performance. Also, choruses for this ode were omitted; they would have taken up too many pages.[34] Regardless of the musical forces consumers had available, performing these odes for or with like-minded friends could foster a community of belief—about the monarch's goodness, her benevolent stewardship of the nation, and her ability to foster fear in her foes.

Figure 12.1. Thomas D'Urfey, *Mars Now Is Arming* in *Wit and Mirth: Or Pills to Purge Melancholy*, vol. 4 (London: Printed by W. Pearson, 1706), © The Bodleian Library, University of Oxford.

First Strain.

Mars now is Arming,
The War comes on Storming;
All *Europe* is viewing,
What *England* is doing;
The flighted (1) Memorial,
In *France* and th' *Escurial*,
Has balk'd (2) Gallick *Nero*,
And *Porto* (3) *Carrero*;
Brittains cease-weeping,
For (4) *Pan* that lyes sleeping;
Tho' *Jove* us denies him,
Yet (5) *Pallas* supplyes him.
Then Sing out yet Muses,
What *Phœbus* infuses;
Divine is the occasion,
Queen *Anne's* Coronation.

(1) The French Memorial.
(2) The French K.
(3) The new K. of Spain's cheif Minister.
(4) King William.
(5) Queen Anne.

Second Strain.

Pair your hearts and joyn,
For now the rightful Line;
Has left you no Excuse,
For Jarring or abuse;
The thought of Right and Wrong,
That plagu'd ye all so long;
No more be now let in,
To raise the *Senates* Spleen;

Nor

Figure 12.1 (*Continued*)

326   *Pills to Purge Melancholy.*

Nor simple Fewds let grow,
'Twixt High Church and the Low;
But all refolve to go,
To One at leaft for fhow;
And then made happy fo,
Direct your Angers blow,
Againft the Common Foe.

Third Strain.

Divine *Gloriana*,
Now Rules the Glad nation;
  Mild Prudent and Pious,
Without Affectation;
  Sence Juftice and Pitty,
Her life ftill renewing;
  And Queen of all hearts,
E'er the Pageant of Crowning:

Fourth Strain.

All the Radiant court of Heaven have bleft Her,
Bright *Aftrea* leaves the Sky to affift Her;
Whilft on her from all,
  Revolves the Sacred praife,
    Of fam'd *Eliza*'s Days.

Sing then ye Mufes,
What Phœbus infuses;
Divine is the Occafion,
Queen Anne's Coronation.

This Cho. may be fung to Ground-Bafs.

F I N I S.

Figure 12.1 (*Continued*)

Figure 12.2 "They Call and Bid the Spring Appear," from *Hark How the Muses Call Aloud* in *The SONGS and Symphonys Perform'd before Her MAJESTY at her Palace of St. James, on New=years day . . . Published for February 1703* (London: Printed for and sold by J[ohn] Walsh, 1703), © The British Library Board.

QUEEN ANNE, MUSIC, AND THE PUBLIC STAGE 197

Figure 12.3 John Eccles, *While Anna with Victorious Arms* in John Eccles, *A Collection of Songs for One, Two, and Three Voices* (London: Printed for J[ohn] Walsh, [1704]), © The British Library Board.

Sometimes, song-sheet versions of the odes reproduced instrumental parts that stretched the bounds of the typical resources deployed in domestic music-making (see figure 12.3).[35] The New Year's ode for 1704, *While Anna with Victorious Arms* was printed in Eccles's 1704 collection of his songs. *While Anna* served a different purpose than the odes in *Wit and Mirth* or *The Monthly Mask*. As mentioned previously, *Wit and Mirth* included only the vocal line and text. On the other hand, Walsh's *Monthly Mask* was a serial, and the publisher was concerned with novelty—putting out the newest songs as quickly as possible so the target audience could play and sing the "hit tunes" at home.[36] Eccles's 1704 collection served yet another purpose. Published by subscription, this volume was expensive (18s.) and lengthy—165 pages not including the introductory material—rendering it unwieldy to use in performance.[37] Instead, Eccles's songbook was intended to be his approved, corrected collected works, an omnibus organized by key. It contains unique versions not found in earlier imprints and pieces never before issued (as is the case with *While Anna*). Eccles also retained symphonies for violins or flutes, although these resources may have been unavailable to most consumers.[38] Because of their lavish presentation, the odes in Eccles's collection signaled to the consumer the resources brought to bear at the moment of original performance and thereby served as a visual (rather than aural or performative) signifier of the queen's power. Indeed, strategically displaying a beautifully engraved ode in one's home, whether or not it was played, demonstrated the owner's musical and political proclivities, as well as his ability to afford luxury items.[39]

Panegyric Music in Plays

As the foregoing discussion makes clear, the rhetoric and music of the ode reverberated well beyond the confines of court. Given the fact that odes were available in print and were performed in the theaters, it is not surprising that playwrights who wanted to demonstrate their support for the queen would insert ode-like songs into their plays. Indeed, there is very little difference between the odes performed at court and the songs and entertainments produced to praise the queen in the theaters.

To return to the aforementioned Thomas D'Urfey, a notorious trimmer who had been writing plays since the reign of Charles II: D'Urfey had supported each successive monarch—regardless of their religion or politics—in print and song. By 1703, D'Urfey's fortunes were waning, but he tried to curry favor with Anne by penning the previously discussed ode in honor of her coronation and praising her in song in his comedy *The Old Mode and the New* (1703). The plot of *The Old Mode and the New* also engages with politics: the only virtuous male character in the play is Will Queenlove, a country gentleman and scholar, who is "moderate in Opinion, and pleas'd with the present Reign and Posture of Affairs."[40] The meaning of the name Queenlove, is, of course, abundantly obvious. D'Urfey was not a subtle man.

D'Urfey's foray into musical encomium occurs in act 2, scene 2 of the play. Musicians entertain Queenlove and his companions with the song "The Infant Blooming Spring," as they eat dinner. The text of the song, as with the court odes from around the same time, makes mention of the War of the Spanish Succession, comparing Anne to a goddess, who, in partnership with Bellona will defeat the French. D'Urfey also explicitly (and probably deliberately) echoed Tate's 1703 ode for New Year's Day. D'Urfey mentioned spring and Phoebus overcoming "the winter shade," while Tate compared Anne to the goddess of spring, who promotes rebirth in the kingdom.

After two movements, dialogue interrupts the musical performance. Queenlove and his friend Frederick ridicule their companion Major Bombast, who feels slighted because he has not yet received career advancement from the queen. To establish Bombast's loyalty to the new regime, they cajole him into toasting the queen's health with them. It is unclear in the play text whether this toast was sung, but consulting other concordant sources makes clear that the first five lines were a continuation of the "The Infant Blooming Spring" (see figure 12.4). As mentioned above, the communal performance of odes in a domestic setting could have promoted or enforced support for the queen—a possibility that D'Urfey dramatized with Queenlove, Frederick, and Bombast's boozy celebration.

"The Infant Blooming Spring"—like the court odes discussed previously—outlived the moment of original performance, for its patriotic message spread in print. Bernard Lintott published the text of D'Urfey's play, and although the music has been lost, D'Urfey printed the words to "The Infant Blooming Spring" in his collection *Songs Compleat* (1719) (see again figure 12.4). Thus, D'Urfey's celebration of Anne, like the printed odes discussed above, rearticulated the author's loyalty to the Stuarts and promoted the memory of Anne to those who purchased such wares, even years after her death.

Richard Steele, like D'Urfey, used his play *The Lying Lover*, a revision of Corneille's *Le menteur* (1642) to solidify his position with the new queen. At the time of its writing, Steele, a military officer, had been stationed at the dilapidated Landguard Fort and through a dedication to the Duke of Ormond—then raising a new regiment of dragoons—and his compliments to the queen, he hoped to secure a better position.[41] In his preface, Steele specifically appealed to "Her Most Excellent Majesty." He is pleased that she "has taken the Stage into Her consideration" and anticipated that "by Her gracious Influence on the Muses, Wit will recover from its Apostacy; and that by being encourag'd in the Interests of Virtue, 'twill strip Vice of the gay Habit in which it has too long appear'd."[42] In addition to his appeal to Anne in the preface, Steele further aligned himself with her by including encomiastic music in the final moments of the play, a song "The Rolling Years" performed by singer Richard Leveridge.

Although the music has unfortunately been lost, the text of the song recapitulates many of the themes previously discussed. The first stanza equates Anne

30 *The Old Mode and the New,* or,

Bomb. Either of 'em, good Mr.——— a-but is not a Bumper in that Glass too much, hah? [*Combwig is waiting on* Fred.

Comb. Too much, Sir; no nor twenty such Glasses neither; Powder me, de know where ye are, Sir, to ask such a Question?———Why this is the New Family, Major; you are not starving at Sir *Fumbler's* now: Come, come, try if you can find a Pearl in the bottom.

Bomb. Nay, the young Fellow has the Soul of an Emperor, that's the truth on't: For I think *Heliogabalus* himself had scarce more Variety than here has been.

Fred. That Old Fellow, *Will*— is a surly Malecontent, and meerly so, through too blind a Conceit of his own little or no Merits. He was a great Grumbler all the last Reign, choak'd himself daily, and would seek, nor take, forsooth, no Employment under the Prince of *Orange*, as he call'd him———and now not being in haste cramb'd with a Commission for Colonel, is in the same Uneasiness; thou shalt see me open him with this Brimmer, and lay his Intellects before thee.

Queen. I have met several of those fine Persons formerly, who rather than eat with t'other Party, would dine upon a piece of Loyal Bread and Cheese, in some dirty Ale-house, and fancy they deserve to be Sainted for it. Dam 'em, I hate Fellows that prefer the Service they owe their Country, to the Folly of a sullen captious Humour: If the Government were of my Mind, they should eat their Loyal Crust long enough.

Fred. Prithee observe him,———*Combwig*, give each Man his Brimmer: Come Major *Bombard*, the Queen's Health, three Go-downs, and let it be done with these Words, round her three Kingdoms.

> *In Wealth may she flow,*
> *May she* Lewis *bring low,*
> *May her Fame spread and grow,*
> *Whilst Sun shines, or Winds blow,*
> *And hang up her Foe.* [Drinks.

Bomb. Ay, *And Scoundrels also,*
That won't let her know
Where Merit lies low,
Once renown'd ———*in*———*in*

Queen. *In Crambo,* ha, ha, ha. [*they laugh.*] *Bomb.*

Figure 12.4 Comparison between *The Old Mode and the New* (1703) and *Songs Compleat* (1719), © The British Library Board.

220   Songs *Compleat*,

SONNET *Royal, Made for one Voice to Instruments.*

THE Infant blooming Spring appears,
   Sol has his way through *Aries* made;
And now this Wond'rous of all Years,
   The Prize of *Europe* muſt be play'd.

Creſted *Belona* ſhakes her Lance,
   Her Siſter *Britain* to defend;
Whilſt *Mars* of Old, in League with *France*,
   Dares proudly againſt both contend.

[*Second Movement.*]

But Rouze valiant *Britains*, and fear quite remove,
   You cannot of Victory fail;
Our Goddeſs below, and our Goddeſs above,
     By force of their Charms,
     As that of their Arms,
Have a right ſtill to conquer the Male.

[*Third Movement.*]

   March on then brave ſouls,
     You're ſure of your Pay;
   And toping full Bowls,
     Warm valours allay,
This wiſh to the *Queen*, daily chant by the way:
   In wealth may ſhe flow
   May ſhe *Lewis* bring low,
   May her Fame ſpread and grow,
   Whilſt Sun ſhines, or Wind blows,
   And Hang up Her foes.
In Wealth &c.

Engliſ

Figure 12.4 (*Continued*)

with Elizabeth, a monarch who presided over a former "female age" in which "Britain" was "happy." All the beauty of rural England is subsumed under the queen's power, and in turn she protects "Their Safety and their Pride." Although Steele's praise of Anne is not as well integrated into the plot of the play as D'Urfey's was (perhaps because Steele revised his play from a preexisting French source), his invocations of the queen's morality, power over nature, and connection with the glorious English past bookend the entertainment. From his laudatory mention of Anne in his preface to the musical finale in her honor, Steele made clear his allegiance to the new regime. Unfortunately, his panegyrics did not produce the desired effect. *The Lying Lover* was a failure, and by 1705 a frustrated Steele had left the army to pursue preferment in London.[43]

SUBSCRIPTION MUSIC AND *BRITAIN'S HAPPINESS*

Although songs and act tunes were commonplace in plays, the 1703–1704 season saw a focused effort to increase musical offerings in London. As Olive Baldwin and Thelma Wilson have discussed, two groups of noblemen sponsored subscription concerts in winter 1703–1704. The Tories organized concerts featuring Margherita de L'Epine, while prominent Whigs supported a series of ten concerts held in the London theaters.[44] The Whig concert series featured encomiastic music for Anne, including performances of the aforementioned coronation ode by Daniel Purcell and Motteux's *Britain's Happiness* set by John Weldon and Charles Dieupart. A later concert featured a performance of the same libretto, this time set by Richard Leveridge.

As mentioned previously, Motteux had written texts for court odes and entertainments such as *Europe's Revels* (1697), so he had ample experience with encomiums. From the opening of *Britain's Happiness*, Motteux used strategies that had worked in his previous endeavors, beginning with martial rhetoric as two officers incite all good Englishmen to fight to save Europe (a clear nod to the ongoing conflict). The soldiers then compare Anne to Eliza of blessed memory and suggest that just as Elizabeth quelled the aggression of Spain and France, so too shall Anne. Instead of praising her husband George (as Tate had done), Motteux celebrated Anne's own power over the seas: "she can awe the whole World who is Queen of the Main." Pallas Athena, a goddess Motteux had previously equated with Anne in his 1703 birthday ode, also makes an appearance to reconcile Neptune, threatened by Anne's nautical powers, to the naturalness of female rule.

Unfortunately, very little music from *Britain's Happiness* survives. Three songs by John Weldon appeared in the June 1705 issue of *The Monthly Mask of Vocal Musick*, while one piece by Leveridge, a setting of the raucous "Just Comeing from Sea," survives in *The Bottle Companions* (1709). From an encomiastic perspective, the most interesting surviving piece is Weldon's setting of "The Welfare of All on Blest Anna Depends." Weldon carefully deployed melismas on the words *Anna*, *Honour*, and *Awe* to ornament and emphasize Anne's powers (see figure 12.5). This musical strategy would have been evident even to the most

Figure 12.5 "The Welfare of All on Blest Anna Depends," in *The Monthly Mask of Vocal Musick . . . Publish'd for June* (London: Printed for and sold by J[ohn] Walsh and J[ohn] Hare, 1705), © The British Library Board.

casual listener in the theater, and it certainly makes a visual impact on the page. Indeed, Weldon deployed a technique found in many late-Stuart court odes: emphasizing important words, including the monarch's name, through ornamental elaboration.[45] As with the court odes, the printed song sheet, whether performed or not, provided purchasers the opportunity to prove their loyalty through the consumption of goods.

Conclusions

During the early years of Anne's reign, there was considerable cross-fertilization between the court and the public stage, and Londoners were presented with diverse opportunities to demonstrate their political allegiance through the act of consumption. By the turn of the century, many court odes were appearing in print and were performed outside the environs of court, bringing a much wider audience into contact with their musical and rhetorical style. In turn, composers and playwrights used the now-familiar language of the court ode, repurposing it for a theatrical context, deploying it publicly in a careful and calculated attempt to secure preferment with the new regime. In the case of D'Urfey's play, *The Old Mode and the New*, praise of the new monarch infiltrates many elements of the play, including the very name of the character Queenlove. On the other hand, Steele's *The Lying Lover* takes another approach. Here, the encomiastic design is relegated to the preface and conclusion of the play, perhaps because Steele adapted a French source. Finally, Motteux's *Britain's Happiness*, like *Europe's Revels* before it, is a freestanding musical entertainment. Although Neptune sounds a note of discord, the appearance of Pallas Athena, a goddess associated with Anne in her coronation and the 1703 birthday ode, quickly defuses the storminess of the sea god. In all these cases, printed songs and texts ensured a life beyond the initial performance, allowing the message to reverberate beyond the theaters, giving consumers the opportunity to buy (and perhaps even sing) songs in praise of "glorious Anna."

Notes

1. A version of this essay was presented at the American Society for Eighteenth-Century Studies conference, San Antonio, 2012. I thank James Winn for his suggestions, Olive Baldwin and Thelma Wilson for their detailed feedback, and Estelle Murphy for sharing her dissertation with me.

2. Peter Holman provided a comprehensive discussion of the relationship between the court musical establishment and the public stage in *Four and Twenty Fiddlers*, 331–355. As he observed, "by [the 1690s] the centre of London's musical life had shifted away from the court, and the theatres no longer relied on the Twenty-four Violins for their orchestras" (p. 355).

3. Ibid., 334. For a broader view of the blurred lines between courtly and public discourses during this period, see Shohet, *Reading Masques*; Jenkinson, *Culture and Politics*; and Backscheider, *Spectacular Politics*, particularly 1–66.

4. Pinnock and Wood, "Come, Ye Sons of Art—Again," 448.
5. Ibid., 449, 457.
6. For more on the development of the rival companies, see Milhous, *Thomas Betterton*, 3–77. For a musicological perspective, see Price, *Henry Purcell*, 16–17.
7. *The City Lady*, A[3r]. On this play and its music see Eccles, *Incidental Music*, 105–130.
8. On the entertainments at Drury Lane, see Lowerre, "A *ballet des nations* for English Audiences," 420.
9. On *Europe's Revels*, see ibid., 419–433.
10. Previously, some court ode texts had been disseminated without music; for example, Robert Veel printed birthday and New Year's ode texts in *New Court-Songs and Poems* (1672). For more information, see McGuinness, *English Court Odes*, 45.
11. On Motteux's musical/theatrical activities, see Hook, "Motteux and the Classical Masque," 105–115.
12. On the music in *The Gentleman's Journal*, see ibid., 107–109.
13. Ezell, "The 'Gentleman's Journal,'" 324.
14. Murphy, "The Fashioning of a Nation," particularly vol. 1, chapter 4.
15. Bucholz, *The Augustan Court*, 35.
16. Habermas, *The Structural Transformation of the Public Sphere*, 32–33.
17. Ibid., 30.
18. Ibid., 32.
19. See, for instance, Brewer, "'The Most Polite Age and the Most Vicious,'" 342–343: "[In England] culture failed to thrive as an artifact of state power, court intrigue, or religious instruction and understanding."
20. Winn, *Queen Anne*; Murphy, "The Fashioning of a Nation"; and Reverand, ed., *Queen Anne and the Arts*.
21. Murphy, "The Fashioning of a Nation," vol. 1, chapters 1 and 4.
22. Habermas, *The Structural Transformation of the Public Sphere*, 36–37.
23. This theory partially recapitulates Gerard Hauser's notion of dialogic public spheres organized around issues rather than the class identity of the population engaging in the discourse. "A public sphere, then, is a discursive space in which strangers discuss issues they perceive to be of consequence for them and their group" (Hauser, *Vernacular Voices*, 64).
24. Love, "How Music Created a Public," 259–260.
25. For recent considerations of ode texts as sources for political information, see Walkling, "Politics, Occasions, and Texts," 211–216, and Murphy, "The Fashioning of a Nation," vol. 1, chapter 3.
26. As Olive Baldwin and Thelma Wilson noted in private correspondence, Anne's birthday was February 6, so her association with the coming spring was understandable.
27. Winn, *Queen Anne*, 290–291.
28. Anne chose Elizabeth's motto, *Semper Eadem*, as her own. See Bucholz, *The Augustan Court*, 206. For more on Anne's connection to Elizabeth, see Gregg, *Queen Anne*, 152.
29. Winn, *Queen Anne*, 294.
30. Baldwin and Wilson, "Music in the Birthday Celebrations," 6.
31. For a reprint of the program from this performance, see Baldwin and Wilson, "The Subscription Musick of 1703–04," 36–39.
32. Benoit and Kocevar, "Farinel," *GMO* (accessed May 14, 2013). "Faronells Division on a Ground" was published in *The Division-Violin* (1685).
33. For similar instances in contemporary manuscripts where players were expected to fit a ground bass to a melody line, see Herissone, "Daniel Henstridge," this volume.
34. Personal communication with Olive Baldwin and Thelma Wilson. For more on the publication history of this ode, see *The Monthly Mask of Vocal Music, 1702–1711*, 5–6, 25.

35. On the usual performing forces used in domestic contexts, see Westrup, "Domestic Music under the Stuarts," 19–53; Forgeng, *Daily Life in Stuart England*, 179–181; Trillini, *The Gaze of the Listener*, 33–62. But, as Candace Bailey has recently noted, in the late seventeenth and early eighteenth century, "differences between the contents of amateur and professional manuscripts diminished" ("Blurring the Lines," 512, 515).

36. Despite the elimination of the choruses, the February 1703 *Monthly Mask* was still longer and far more costly than usual (1s. 6d.). Baldwin and Wilson suggest that this issue was not successful with the *Monthly Mask* clientele, as Walsh never again charged more than sixpence. See their edition of *The Monthly Mask of Music*, 5–6.

37. For the cost of a smaller publication from the same time period, see note 36. The scope of Eccles's volume is similar to other self-published volumes sold by subscription; see Herissone, "Playford, Purcell, and the Functions of Music Publishing," 243–290. Composers who self-published such volumes (Purcell, Blow, Eccles), bore the brunt of the cost but retained control over its production (p. 256). Many are dedicated to a noble person (in Eccles's case, Queen Anne). Herissone suggests that the dedicatee may have contributed funds to support the volume after its production (p. 262). For more on subscription publication and book prices during the period, see Hume, "The Economics of Culture in London," 487–533. As Hume notes, musical books of all kinds were fantastically expensive; he cites Eccles's collection as one of the more expensive publications (p. 531). Hume gives the price as 15s.; however, it was advertised as 18s. in *The Post Man*; see Hunter, *Opera and Song Books*, 34.

38. Walsh also retained string and flute parts in *The Monthly Mask*. The upkeep of string instruments would have been prohibitively expensive in most households; see Hume, "The Economics of Culture in London," 531–532.

39. Murphy has suggested that purchasing large volumes such as Eccles's *Collection* served as an "indicator of taste, fashion," and, given the political content in support of Anne, as a signifier of "political affiliation and loyalty" ("The Fashioning of a Nation," vol. 1, 249).

40. D'Urfey, *The Old Mode and the New*, unpaginated dramatis personae.

41. Winton, "Steele, Sir Richard (*bap.* 1672, *d.* 1729)," in *DNB* (accessed May 30, 2013).

42. Steele, *The Lying Lover*, a2r.

43. Winton, "Steele, Sir Richard."

44. Baldwin and Wilson, "The Subscription Musick of 1703–04," 29–44.

45. See, for example, Eccles's setting of *When Anna*, reproduced earlier in this essay.

13.

Disseminating and Domesticating Handel in Mid-Eighteenth-Century Britain

Suzanne Aspden

George Frideric Handel has always epitomized musical grandeur and represented music's role in, and service to, the state. A volume such as this, however, affords an opportunity to nuance that view: not only Handel's high status but also the increasing technical and social accessibility of his music in the 1730s and 1740s facilitated performance of the composer's works and appropriation of Handel himself as cultural symbol in a range of contexts removed from the traditional civic entertainments of the capital.[1] A burgeoning market for music in all forms allowed works written for Handel's aristocratic patrons to percolate into both more public and more domestic settings, seemingly opposed as those environments were becoming in this period.[2] In demonstrating this interconnection between what we would traditionally designate public and private, I will touch on the ways in which music as a cultural commodity and cooperative art not only reflected an individual's status within the broader community but also helped to reinforce the consanguinity of different aspects of social life.

On a practical level, of course, all artists had to manage their public image through private contact with members of the aristocracy and gentry. Those who provoked aristocratic ire could find themselves the butt of fierce newspaper criticism or of musical cabals.[3] Handel's perceived haughtiness toward members of the aristocracy had severe repercussions for his operatic career in the 1730s and 1740s, during which time there was, as one noble lord put it, "a Spirit got up against the Dominion of Mr. Handel."[4] On the other hand, his ability and willingness to negotiate such relationships (perhaps when greater deference was shown) is demonstrated in his cordial relations with members of the royal family, and in the affectionate correspondence of James Harris and his circle about him.⁵

For all musicians, from the exalted to the humble, the interweaving of public and private was determined by their reliance on private patronage for at least some of their livelihood; indeed, to the end of the century at least, many counted themselves fortunate to have the security that went with aristocratic patronage.⁶ In terms of music making, in a period when performance of larger-scale works outside London's (and, to some extent, other cities') public theaters and concert venues relied on the generosity and influence of local gentry who made their homes and musical resources available to others, the notion of what was public and what was private must have seemed quite arbitrary at times.⁷ Performers themselves were often keen to maintain their status by playing chiefly for private gatherings or subscription concerts in aristocratic homes. For instance, Charles Burney notes that

> [Francesco] Geminiani was seldom heard in public during his long residence in England. His compositions, scholars, and the presents he received from the great, whenever he could be prevailed upon to play at their houses, were his chief support.⁸

Wealthy patrons, on the other hand, might organize a semipublic music society, if they wanted to perform or hear a wide variety of music. For example, the well-to-do Dr. Claver Morris in the early eighteenth-century cathedral town of Wells seems to have founded the local music society, provided desks and candlesticks for their venue, acted as its administrator, and provided it with instruments and music from his own collection.⁹ Similarly, in 1730s Oxford, the Professor of Music Richard Goodson Jr. found his family's private music collection mixed with that of the Music Society, as another source for the Society's performances.¹⁰ The Wells music meetings, though comprising a set membership (and guests), teetered between what we might think of as public and private, "sometimes attracting a great appearance of Company and on occasions yielding not Hands enough for a Consort."¹¹ Morris acted as something of an impresario, bringing in musicians he went to hear in Bath (in private homes as well as in public), and putting them up in his home. Like many members of the nobility and wealthy gentry, Morris also entertained Cathedral musicians at home, with music making as part of the proceedings.¹²

The accounts of some of these musically active individuals and their associated societies reveal not only the relatively easy contact with musicians of some note but also access to composers' music independent of publication. Handel's music could be obtained by provincial societies either before it had been performed in public in London or before it was published: Morris "perform'd very justly Hendel's Oritorio [i.e., *Esther*], & some of his Anthems" in 1724, before *Esther* had been given a public performance.¹³ Donald Burrows demonstrates that Oxford musicians used a range of contacts to obtain Handel's unpublished music, to the point that Oxford became known for the performance of Handel's choral works.[14] Certainly, the *Articles of the Musical Society, in Oxford*, nominally of 1757, which contain a catalog of the Society's musical holdings, show his total dominance of their vocal music. Similarly, the scattered accounts of their early performances suggest his prominence in their concerts, even before the appointment of William Hayes (an ardent Handelian) to the Heather Professorship in 1741.[15] It seems, though, that even Hayes in 1756 had to seek Handel's permission to perform *Joshua* via an intermediary, James Harris, who in turn asked the Earl of Shaftesbury (whose copy Hayes sought to borrow), who asked the copyist Smith, who asked Handel. The answer relayed back demonstrates that Handel took a lively interest in access to his unpublished music (as he did in publication), even when the manuscript belonged to another.[16] Shaftesbury wrote:

> Smyth has been with me just now to say, there is no objection to my lending the score of Joshua to Dr Hayes. Yet this is done under a confidence of Dr Hayes's honour, that he will not suffer any copy to be taken or to get about from his having been in possession of this score. For otherwise both Handel and Smyth (his copier) will be injur'd.[17]

Societies farther afield used such access as precedent: the Edinburgh Musical Society, for whom Handel's music was a staple until the 1780s, justified its request to Handel for copies of unpublished music by noting that he had "allowed such copys to other Societys that have applyed for them."[18]

Domesticating Musical Identities

As the caution over *Joshua* shows, Handel's music seems to have excited competitive consumption, one Oxford copyist confiding to James Harris that there appeared to be "a private spirit of emulation in some people to get a larger collection scarcer or better then [*sic*] others," which inhibited the sharing of music.[19] This jockeying among individuals and music societies for access to Handel and his music suggests that the mediation between public and private music in practical terms had ideological overtones as well. Music was one marker of identity (personal, professional, national, social) in a period when, because of increasing social mobility, defining and shoring up those identities was of great importance. Establishing a sense of self for the individual was, of course, crucially bound up with questions of public and private. This was a period when, for men, personal virtue was demonstrated by public service, while concern for women's increasing idealization and withdrawal from public life into an apparently more circumscribed domestic sphere was also (paradoxically) played out publicly.[20] For all, the social performance of one's identity was articulated not only in word and action but also through varied cultural expressions that confirmed (or undermined) the individual's place within desired social networks.

The way in which music could be used to negotiate status and identity in the semipublic world of the polite domestic gathering is nicely demonstrated in Henry Carey's satirical poem "Blundrella: or, The Impertinent. A Tale" (1730). Here the eponymous antiheroine first bests "*Belinda*, blooming Fair" by forcing her to sing when Belinda's feminine modesty would enjoin silence ("The lovely Virgin tun'd her Voice, / More out of Complaisance than Choice"), and then demonstrates her apparent cultural superiority through her assured retailing of musical gossip.[21] Blundrella is only shown up as a fraud when the attractive male guest, Eugenio, arrives and sets a trap to prove she is unable to distinguish a well-known operatic tune from a nursery rhyme:

Madam, (said he) before I go,
Your dear Commands I'd gladly know.
BLUNDRELLA rear'd her Crest aloft,
And begg'd him to play something soft:
What think you, Madam, of *AL OMBRA*?
That's poor dull Stuff, do ye like *SGOMBRA*?
Si Caro, if you please, said she:
He play'd the Tune of *Children three*.
She was in Raptures, and intreated
The self same Tune might be repeated.
HE chang'd his Airs, and, to her Shame,
She took ten others for the same.
In short, *Eugenio* play'd her off,
And made her all the Circle's Scoff:
While, stupid she! ascrib'd to Wit and Sense
The Laughter rais'd by her Impertinence.[22]

"Blundrella" simultaneously demonstrates the dangers of poor understanding or taste and the desirability of cultivating discernment.[23]

The satire also reminds us that access to music could play an important role in conditioning an individual's taste: the hapless Blundrella may have cloth ears, or she may simply not have had the acquaintance with opera arias that her antagonist, Eugenio, had cultivated. After all, as a young woman she may not have been as readily able to attend the opera as he, probably requiring the company of family or a chaperone to maintain respectability. It is revealing that Eugenio plays a repertory of airs (whether English or Italian) rather than singing them: performance on the flute (or recorder) was one means by which male amateurs (but not female, for whom it was thought unseemly) could domesticate and come to know opera arias; it might have seemed a safer musical route, too, requiring less dramatic presence and therefore lessening his exposure to the accusation of frivolity that the Earl of Chesterfield, among others, leveled at male musical amateurs.[24] Eugenio might have played relatively easy tunes, like the ballad "Children Three," but even arias for virtuoso castrati were transcribed for instrumental rendition. For male auditors, therefore, access to music was less restricted than for women, just as they were less constrained than women were in performing at social gatherings.[25] Music societies were also almost invariably male.

The private (or, as we have seen, semipublic) concert, which flourished increasingly in the second half of the century, was one way in which women could take a more active role in music making—within the bounds of propriety, of course. As Michael Burden's discussion of London's concert scene shows (this volume), women—whether professional singers or aristocrats—were often promoters of concerts. Women might also perform at such occasions when they would not do so in public: the soprano Elizabeth Linley, trained as a professional singer from childhood and for a few years the darling of the oratorio circuit, was prevented from singing in public after her marriage in 1773; however, her husband (playwright R. B. Sheridan) did allow her to perform in a series of highly sought-after private concerts.[26] There, alongside renditions of Handel's airs, she effectively competed against great Italian singers of the day such as Lucrezia Aguiari and Franziska Danzi, as Charles Burney later noted: "she astonished all hearers by performing their bravura arias, extending the natural compass of her voice a fourth above the highest note of the harpsichord."[27]

For those female and male amateur (i.e., nonprofessional) singers,[28] who lacked the ability to perform (and particularly to ornament) difficult professional arias, operatic music was still available for domestic rendition:[29] the arias Blundrella praises are all minuets—"soft," lyrical and relatively simple (at least, if sung without ornamentation).[30] Perhaps the most popular parts of an opera in this period were such simple and affective arias;[31] indeed, such was the demand for this kind of piece that the minuets played at the end of overtures or in instrumental works were also appropriated: following in the tradition of the *menuet chanté*,[32] these minuets were seen as singable (though not always so) because of their use of simple, melody-dominated lines and balanced phrases. Handel's minuets were regularly supplied with English texts, almost always on pseudo-pastoral themes, to be sold as single song sheets intended for amateur performance (see figure 13.1). Such reimaginings of the operatic scene domesticated the genre in more ways than one: just as the simplicity of the music, though not always grateful to the voice in terms of melodic line, made it feasible for the less-accomplished singer, so the pastoral sentiments rendered it more appropriate for the genteel female performer than the high drama of many an operatic aria. These song sheets anticipated the practice of the *Lady's Magazine*, as described by Bonny Miller, in circumscribing a musical domain for appropriate amateur performance.[33]

Figure 13.1 [G. F. Handel], "A Song Made to a Favourite Minuet in Rodelinda," GB-Ob Harding Mus. G.O. 24 (1), © The Bodleian Library, University of Oxford.

Oratorio: A "New Thing" for "Wealthy Citizens"

Many of Handel's operatic minuets were set to English words in the 1720s and 1730s, and the packaging of Handel's English arias for domestic performance continued to be popular to the end of the century and beyond. But as the selection of Handel's music published in the *Lady's Magazine* and other similar organs suggests, the accessibility of Handel's music was enhanced through routes other than the "Englishing" of opera arias from the midcentury: the public dissemination of his oratorios and the development of musical performance in pleasure gardens, following the innovations of Vauxhall and other London gardens, were key in Handel's ascendency to the status of national composer. These two arenas saw, not paradoxically, both an increased availability of Handel's music to a broad "public" in performance and its adaptability for domestic rendition. And in both arenas, Handel played a role in the decision to bring his music to a wider audience. Indeed, contemporaries noted Handel's awareness of the value in catering for audiences beyond those of Italian opera's traditional aristocratic backers, as one observer wrote in 1736, following Handel's success with *Alexander's Feast*:

> you know wee are in a very Uncertain Climate that the sweetest Gugle of an Eunuck is soon tyresome. however Handel has gott 5 or 600 guinniys clear wch is more than the [Italian opera] Academy have yet offerd him. & he tells me he intends a New thing soon fitt for the Tast at lest[?] of the Wealthy Citizens.[34]

A man who chose to write something for the "Wealthy Citizens"—that is, for the merchant class of the City of London—was no doubt attuned to the public desire to access realms of musical privilege and domesticate them.

Handel's astuteness about the increasing public (or at least merchant-class) appetite for elite culture is most obvious in his oratorios, the success of which was underpinned by the intermarriage of exclusive and popular musical forms.[35] It is well known that Handel's first public oratorio performance in England, of *Esther* in 1732, saw the work's migration from its original private performance for the Duke of Chandos (ca. 1718) to performance in a London tavern, to Handel's production in the opera house. Handel's preparation of the oratorio for public performance entailed interpolation of festal religious music—anthems composed for the coronation of George II in 1727—into a biblical drama in operatic form. Just as he combined English and Italian musical traditions, so he also brought together the singers of those traditions, employing members of the Chapel Royal and other religious establishments alongside the King's Theatre's Italian opera cast.

The hybrid nature of the genre was made clear in the advertisements for the first public performances, which declared "The Musick to be disposed after the Manner of the Coronation Service."[36] It was evidently calculated to pique the interest of London audiences, giving a wider public access to the exclusive music of the royal coronation, which only the nobility would have attended. This in itself might remind us that the "public" was by no means a singular entity, any more than all public spaces were universally accessible. Indeed, Bernard Gates's dramatic renditions of *Esther* in the Crown and Anchor Tavern, which in turn inspired Handel's theater performances, were conducted on behalf of two (all-male) music clubs; these performances prompted Princess Anne to ask Handel to stage it at the opera house, where she (like other respectable women who could afford the entrance price) might see it.[37]

Of course, such hybridity was possible because the oratorio's biblical subject matter constituted a shared cultural property which even the lowliest in society would have known—indeed, given that it was commonplace for children to learn to read by reciting from the Bible, and that adults were enjoined to read the Bible regularly for their spiritual well-being, as well as attending church frequently, its stories and language would have been intimately familiar.[38] Such knowledge—alongside a biblically inspired typological habit of mind, whereby parallel and precedent could be sought in the Bible for any everyday event—ensured that biblical texts crossed all boundaries and permeated all orders and aspects of life.[39] The ubiquity of the sacred world (and particularly scripture) in everyday life can be illustrated by the appearance of sacred references not only in biblical ballads, chapbooks, and poetic paraphrases but also on ladies' fans of the period.[40] Eighteenth-century biblical fans featured a range of well-known biblical scenes, including some that also formed the basis for oratorios: Esther before King Ahasuerus, Delilah cutting Samson's hair, the Queen of Sheba approaching King Solomon, and so on.[41]

The oratorio's popularity also had more prosaic bases, however: the English language and religious sentiments, along with the importance of the choruses and (in many oratorios) relatively simple nature of a fair number of the solo arias, encouraged domestic and provincial production. This tendency was particularly apparent with Handel's early English-language works, *Acis and Galatea*, *Esther*, and *Alexander's Feast*, which crop up repeatedly in accounts of provincial performances.[42] Those (including students) with an interest in music and means to mount performances domestically contributed to the dissemination of these much-loved works; for example, Samuel Helier, a student at Exeter College, Oxford, in the 1750s, commissioned parts for *Alexander's Feast*, to have it performed at his Staffordshire seat, Wombourne Wodehouse.[43] The Salisbury Musical Society in early 1740 performed overtures from the operas *Arianna* and *Tamerlano*, but the vocal music came from *Esther*, *Saul*, and (principally) from *Alexander's Feast*, while at the Salisbury Festival in October 1748, *Alexander's Feast* and *Acis and Galatea* were the first works to be given in their entirety in their evening concerts.[44] Donald Burrows and Rosemary Dunhill note that most of Handel's oratorios had been performed in Salisbury by 1761.[45]

Handel Outdoors

Excerpts from Handel's oratorios appeared in still more varied settings, however, and in ways that emphasized and enacted Handel's incorporation into national public life still further. Vauxhall Gardens was particularly important in this regard.[46] Handel seems to have had some kind of connection with this pleasure garden under Jonathan Tyers's management: he may have been present at Tyers's relaunch of the Gardens in 1732,[47] and Tyers's installation of a statue of Handel in the Gardens in 1738 seems to have been linked to Handel's publication of his deluxe edition of *Alexander's Feast* that year, a volume that (like the statue itself) asserted his preeminent status in Britain's cultural life.[48] It is not known how often Handel's music was played at Vauxhall, but the odd newspaper report provides glimpses: on May 7, 1739, "Hush Ye Pretty, Warbling Choir" from *Acis and Galatea* and the "Solemn March from Saul" were "among the new pieces" played at Vauxhall Gardens.[49] Handel also seems to have composed for Vauxhall occasionally: a hornpipe in 1740, and after the defeat of the Jacobite uprising of 1745, "A Song on the Victory Obtain'd over the Rebels by His Royal Highness the Duke of Cumberland," set to words by the Gardens' publicist, John Lockman, "Sung by Mr. Lowe &c. in Vauxhall Gardens."[50] This simple strophic song with chorus was suitable both for outdoor performance and, equally, for popular adoption (see figure 13.2).

But the music provided at Vauxhall served as more than simple entertainment. Like other aspects of the Gardens, which encouraged visitors' sense of participation in the unfolding spectacle, music both helped foster the genteel ambience Tyers desired for Vauxhall and facilitated a very active engagement in culture formation on the part of auditors and viewers.[51] It has been noted that Tyers gradually turned Vauxhall Gardens into a theatrical space (following the informal, theatrical garden designs of William Kent), to which trompe l'oeil, statues, pavilions, waterfalls, and hidden musicians all contributed.[52] Pamphleteers describing the attractions of the Gardens enthused on this point. In 1741, the author of *The Turkish Paradise or Vaux-Hall Gardens: Wrote at Vaux-Hall Last Summer* (probably Tyers's publicist, John Lockman) posed the rhetorical question: "This Stage, how can it fail to move the Heart, / Where all who see the Play perform a Part."[53] Likewise, in the 1750s, the author of the *Sketch of Spring-Gardens, Vaux-Hall* (probably also Lockman) suggested that "One great Pleasure felt in this *Grove,* by an intelligent, contemplative Spectator, is for him to observe, in how beautiful a Variety the several Objects of it groop, as he moves through the different Parts of this magical Spot."[54] *The Turkish Paradise* also enlisted music in its theatricalization:

No longer ye soft soothing Lyres be mute,
O now or never touch the breathing Flute;
Raise my sunk Mind—where has my Fancy stray'd?
How wander'd in the Maze itself has made!

Figure 13.2 G. F. Handel, "A Song on the Victory Obtain'd Over the Rebels by His Royal Highness the Duke of Cumberland," [1745/6]. GB-Ob MS Mus.c.107, p. 16, © The Bodleian Library, University of Oxford.

But hark! the Organ penetrates the Air,
As if *Cecilia*'s Soul were Vocal there;
The Trumpet lives again, my Spirits wake,
And gloomy Thoughts my raptur'd Soul forsake.[55]

Seemingly, this evokes straightforward Arcadian and mythic topoi, but the instruments and images described—the lyre and flute, raising of the "sunk Mind" and straying fancy, followed by Cecilia's manifestation with the organ—clearly recall the world of *Alexander's Feast*, where just such instruments characterize Timothean music, where Timotheus is responsible for raising Alexander from torpor, and where Cecilia succeeds and surpasses the pagan musician.[56] Also implicitly evoked is the social (and martial) vigor inspired by Handel's music and associated with his statue, located in the most populous part of the Gardens, near the bandstand.[57] The long-lasting significance assigned to Handel and *Alexander's Feast* in defining the gardens' "experience" is indicated in another, seemingly more casual, poetic reference: an anonymous eulogy to one Miss Wright, who sang at Vauxhall in 1765, used lines from the prefatory address to Handel attached to the 1738 edition of *Alexander's Feast* as a way of underscoring Miss Wright's vocal powers. Just as Handel's librettist, Newburgh Hamilton, wrote of Handel: "Be ever Your's (my Friend) the God-like Art, / To calm the Passions, and improve the Heart," the author of the verses to Miss Wright apostrophized: "Yet higher tasks are for thy powers design'd, / To rouse the passions, or improve the mind."[58]

I have elsewhere described the ways in which *Alexander's Feast* would have been heard as enacting the musical effects it described, and as incorporating Handel into its mythical narrative as proxy for both Timotheus and Cecilia.[59] It is telling that this process, whereby listeners were effectively caught up in the legend as modern-day subjects of Handelian/Timothean musical power, was also invoked in *The Turkish Paradise* as part of the Vauxhall experience. Indeed, the author implicitly ennobled the perambulating auditor at Vauxhall as a modern Alexander—the enlightened listener being equivalent to the *Sketch of Spring-Gardens'* "intelligent, contemplative Spectator." Although there are no reports of *Alexander's Feast* being performed at Vauxhall at this time, Handel's Vauxhall statue graced the illustrated prints of at least two songs eulogizing the refined pleasures of London's gardens, as if the composer himself gave his blessing to their activities.[60] And it is clear from an examination of the music written for the gardens that performances there were, like the inclusion of Handel's statue, intended as an expression of London's broader cultural life: some songs demonstrated the refined pastoralism familiar to collectors of minuets, which was then being both dignified and popularized in the lavishly illustrated, serially published songs of George Bickham's *Musical Entertainer* (1737–1739). Others cultivated the fashionable musical styles of contemporary Italian opera. Both would have served to enhance the pleasure gardens' credibility (and, at the same time, marketability) as the resort of polite and fashionable society.

Such was the cultural significance of Handel's role as virtual overseer of Vauxhall's musical activities, that his figure was incorporated into other gardens, in ways that suggested his idealization as both a public figure and a personal friend. Frederick, Prince of Wales, who was Tyers's landlord and was accorded particular status at Vauxhall, invoked the association with *Alexander's Feast* again in his plan to include Timotheus and Handel among the worthies on his "Mount Parnassus" at Kew, as corresponding ancient and modern figures.[61] For Frederick, whom Handel knew well enough to tease, the composer's inclusion in the planned Kew garden nonetheless represented the civic role of musical art in British society. Such civic function could also be turned into more personal homage, as at Wombourne Wodehouse in the 1760s, when Sir Samuel Helier, having been immersed in Handel's music while at Oxford, employed the young architect, James Gandon, to create "Handel's temple" in his new gardens. The structure does not survive, but a contemporary painting shows that it included a trompe l'oeil painting of the composer modeled on Roubilliac's Westminster Abbey sculpture.[62] Helier's awareness (indeed, desire) that the country-house tourism then becoming fashionable would make his house and garden a public space (at least, for the right set), informed both his enthusiasm for the garden's design and his concern that it be ready for viewing, as a note to his steward from late April 1768 demonstrates: "As Handel's Temple is an intire new design and as Mr Gandon has drawn it and exhibited it to publick view I am very anxious to have it quite completed out of hand for which reason pray forward it with great expedition."[63]

Helier's relish for garden design was matched by his love of music: he established a significant collection of instruments and scores, including (as mentioned earlier) *Alexander's Feast*, all intended for use in Wombourne, performed by his own specially trained band of workmen. As with his garden, his musical projects were conceived as reflections of polite culture: conforming to the fashion for music on the water, he intended that his "Band" should "play when I'm in the Country to me every evening when they've left work for an hour to divert me and go sailing with me upon the water."[64] And the musical experience of the London pleasure gardens was another model: on acquiring a "fine copy" of *Messiah*, he directed his steward to "keep it quite clean and don't lend it from Wombourn. If they will not lend us the Church I will have an oratorio done in the wood," perhaps in the process invoking notions of the sublime then being associated with Handel, as much as those of Vauxhall's polite sociability.[65]

The intermingling of the public and the private in eighteenth-century musical life was, as these instances suggest, as much a matter of social ambition as of practical necessity. For Samuel Helier, desperate for the approval of "people of consequence," adhering to the models provided by London's public cultural life in his gardens and musical activities helped to ensure that he would be perceived as a man of fashion, not as one of the local "Rusticks" with whom he worried about associating.[66] Equally, for Jonathan Tyers, performances of music by composers associated with fashionable theaters—or even, in perhaps his biggest success, from a state occasion, the celebration of the Peace of Aix-la-Chapelle with Handel's Music for the Royal Fireworks—confirmed the social aspirations of his popular pleasure gardens. In some senses, then, while all aspects of life for those of a certain social standing in this period were "public," music, as an inherently collaborative art, both emphasized that fact and refined it into an expression of cultural identity.

Notes

1. As Richard Sennett (*The Fall of Public Man*, 17) notes, in the eighteenth century "The focus of this public life was the capital city."

2. The rhetorical opposition of "public and private" is visible in writings of the period (for example, Joseph Butler, *Sermons* [1726, cited in Sennett, *The Fall of Public Man*, 16] proposes that "every man is to be considered in two capacities, the private and the publick"). Sennett (*The Fall of Public Man*, 16) suggests that "By the end of the 17th Century, the opposition of 'public' and 'private' was shaded more like the way the terms are now used. 'Public' meant open to the scrutiny of anyone, whereas 'private' meant a sheltered region of life defined by one's family and friends." Such definitions nonetheless also encompassed ideas foreign to modern understanding, such as the civic humanist concept of public life as concerning "the common good and the body politic" (ibid., 16). And of course there was considerable elision between the two spheres for those dependent for their livelihood on patronage, as Ian Woodfield (*Salomon and the Burneys*, 1) notes. For the "patrons" themselves, the circle of "family and friends" in this period was often wide enough to make even private events rather public by modern standards, as later discussion will show.

3. For examples of such problems around the singers Faustina Bordoni and Francesca Cuzzoni and the composer Giovanni Bononcini, see Aspden, *The Rival Sirens*, 40–47; Lindgren, "A Bibliographic Scrutiny," 296–328.

4. Earl of Delawarr to the Duke of Richmond, June 16, 1733; cited in Deutsch, *Handel*, 303–304.

5. On Handel and Frederick, Prince of Wales, see McGeary, "Handel, Prince Frederick," 168–169. On the Harris circle, see Burrows and Dunhill, *Music and Theatre*, xxviii. Burrows and Dunhill observe that among Harris's acquaintance at least, Handel "commanded respect regardless of social niceties" (p. xxviii).

6. On the importance of patronage to the career of an artist in eighteenth-century England, see, for example, Woodfield (*Salomon and the Burneys*, 1), who notes that "A substantial element of the concert-going public still consisted of private patrons, whose support was best obtained through personal contact. . . . [S]ocial savoir-faire . . . was every bit as important as technical proficiency or musicianship in building a career." Woodfield cites as an example Leopold Mozart's promotion of his children via private soirées in London.

7. Borsay, "Concert Topography and Provincial Towns," 20–22. Michael Burden similarly notes the variety entailed in the private concert, in his essay in this volume. Surveying the use of the term *gentleman* from medieval times to the nineteenth century, Penelope J. Corfield

("The Rivals," 1–33) has suggested that its application widened beyond traditional landowners. Roz Southey ("The Role of Gentlemen Amateurs in Subscription Concerts," 116) observes that "By the eighteenth century, it was not necessary for someone to avoid trade in order to be considered a gentleman.... 'Gentleman' was always a flexible term, involving a mediation between ancestry, social standing, and personal reputation."

8. Burney, *A General History of Music*, vol. 2, 992. Cited in McVeigh, "Introduction," 9–10.
9. Johnstone, "Claver Morris," 95–96, 100.
10. Burrows, "Sources for Oxford Handel Performance," 179.
11. Claver Morris, in Johnstone, "Claver Morris," 95.
12. Ibid., 108, 104, 114–115.
13. Ibid., 117; it was performed on May 1, 1724, in Kelston, at the house of Morris's friends, the Haringtons.
14. Burrows, "Sources for Oxford Handel Performance," 183. See also Burrows and Ward Jones, "Musicians and Music Copyists," 115–139.
15. On notices of Oxford's concert life before 1753, when *Jackson's Oxford Journal* commenced publication, see Burrows and Ward Jones, "Musicians and Music Copyists," 115–117. Simon Heighes (*The Lives and Works of William and Philip Hayes*, 7) suggests that William Hayes made his name in part through early performances of Handel's large-scale vocal works in Oxford and other cathedral cities.
16. Burrows, "John Walsh and His Handel Editions," 80–88.
17. Fourth Earl of Shaftesbury to James Harris, letters of May 20 and 27, 1756, in Burrows and Dunhill, *Music and Theatre*, 313, 314.
18. Burrows, "Sources for Oxford Handel Performance," 183, 184. On the Society's performance of Handel, see Burchell, *Polite or Commercial Concerts?*, 60–83.
19. John Snow to James Harris, January 1, 1742; in Burrows and Dunhill, *Music and Theatre*, 132.
20. On masculinity and public spirit, see Pocock, *The Machiavellian Moment*, 423–552; Hundert, *The Enlightenment's Fable*. On the development of the ideology of female domesticity, see Armstrong, "The Rise of the Domestic Woman"; Jones, *Women in the Eighteenth Century*.
21. On the ideal of female passivity, see Jones, *Women in the Eighteenth Century*, 15.
22. "Blundrella: or, The Impertinent. A Tale," 8.
23. Carey was himself a liminal figure. As a singing teacher and would-be professional composer who both applauded and denigrated Italian opera and who may have aspired to social recognition as the supposed illegitimate son of the Marquis of Halifax, he must have recognized keenly the role of music in establishing identity and negotiating public status. Aspden, "Henry Carey (1687–1743)," *DNB*.
24. Leppert, *Music and Image*, 174. For Chesterfield's well-known comment, see Miller, "Education, Entertainment, Embellishment," this volume.
25. For an overview of conventions of male and female musical performance for the period, see Leppert, *Music and Image*.
26. On Linley's career, see Aspden, "Sancta Cæcilia Rediviva."
27. [Burney], "Linley, John."
28. I use amateur here as the *OED* defines it: "One who cultivates anything as a pastime, as distinguished from one who prosecutes it professionally," that definition being current in the eighteenth century.
29. In the late seventeenth or early eighteenth century, Roger North (*Roger North*, 21) commented on the enthusiasm of "ladys" for learning songs from the stage without first acquiring the "principle" by which to understand the rules of embellishment: "Ladys hear a new song, and are impatient to learne it. A master is sent for, and sings it as to a parrot, till at last with infinite difficulty the tune is gott, but with such infantine imperfect, nay broken abominable, graces, in

imitation of the good, that one would splitt to hear it. Yet *this is fine*, and the ladys goe to teaching one and other [*sic*]." On the transmission of operatic arias from stage to the domestic sphere, see Burden, "From London's Opera House."

30. Of the arias Blundrella mentions, it is possible to identify "Si caro, caro si" from Handel's *Admeto* (1727: "Let us have that which the *Faustina* / Sings when she hangs on *Senisino*"), "Ascolta o figlio" from Bononcini's *Astianatte* (1727: "There is a Song, that in the Garden, *Cuzzoni* sings unto her Son"), and "T'amo tanto, o mio tesoro" from Attilio Ariosti's *Artaserse* (1724). "Si caro, caro si" and "T'amo tanto" were two of only three Italian arias published in George Bickham's *Musical Entertainer*, vol. 1 (1737-1739), the third also being a minuet, "Dimmi cara." Of the arias Eugenio mentions, "Sgombra dell'anima" from Handel's *Siroe* (1728), is a moderately virtuosic vehicle for the soprano Faustina Bordoni.

31. For example, Giovanni Bononcini's "Ascolta o figlio," which Blundrella names as a favorite, and its accompanying minuet from *Astianatte* (1727), seem to have been the most popular pieces from that opera; see Aspden, *The Rival Sirens*, 101-103.

32. For examples, see Ballard, *Les menuets chantants*.

33. Miller, this volume. See also Ritchie, *Women Writing Music*, 81-86.

34. GB-Lbl Add. MS 27738, fols. 235v-236r, H. Corry to the Earl of Essex, March 9, 1735 [1736].

35. On patronage of the arts among the merchant classes, see, for example, Galinou, *City Merchants and the Arts, 1670-1720*.

36. Burrows, *Handel*, 168.

37. Gates's production emphasized further exclusivities: while the singers were professional choral performers, the orchestra "consist[ed] only of Gentlemen;" Dean, *Handel's Dramatic Oratorios and Masques*, 204.

38. Preston, "Biblical Criticism;" cited in Suarez, "The Mock Biblical," 15. For an earlier period, see Watt, *Cheap Print and Popular Piety*. Suarez observes that there is no equivalent study for the eighteenth century.

39. Studies demonstrating the importance of biblical typology and exegesis in everyday life in this period include Keach, *Tropologia*; Fisch, *Jerusalem and Albion*; Zwicker, *Dryden's Political Poetry*; Suarez, "Bibles, Libels, and Bute;" Korshin, *Typologies in England*; Smith, *Handel's Oratorios and Eighteenth-Century Thought*.

40. For further discussion of the ubiquity of scriptural references in British society of this period, see Suarez, "The Mock Biblical," 11-24.

41. Green, *A Collector's Guide to Fans*, color plates 24, 29, and 30, n.p.

42. See, for instance, Burrows and Ward Jones, "Musicians and Music Copyists," 115-117; Burchell, *Polite or Commercial Concerts?*, 74.

43. Burrows and Ward Jones, "Musicians and Music Copyists," 137.

44. Burrows and Dunhill, *Music and Theatre*, 90-92, 251-252.

45. Ibid., xxx.

46. How "public" Vauxhall was is open to question: its one-shilling entrance price made it cheaper than the London theaters and the opera, but as David Hunter ("Rode the 12,000?," 17) notes, "In one way, the Gardens were even more exclusive than the opera house; servants in livery were admitted to the second balcony of the King's Theatre, but they were excluded from the Gardens."

47. Chrissochoidis, "'Hee-Haw . . . llelujah,'" 221-262.

48. Aspden, "'Fam'd Handel Breathing,'" 54-58.

49. Scrapbooks of material relating to Vauxhall Gardens in the Bodleian Library, Oxford, GB-Ob G. A. Surrey c.21, Item 75/2, a handwritten note. T. Lea Southgate, writing a century ago on Handel's association with Vauxhall, said that the *Water* and *Fireworks Music* were "often performed" and that "Handel wrote for the Gardens"; no source is provided for either observation. Southgate, "Music at the Public Pleasure Gardens," 148.

50. The hornpipe is referred to (without source) in Southgate, "Music at the Public Pleasure Gardens," 148. The song is in the collection GB-Ob MS Mus.c.107, p. 16.

51. Hunt, *Vauxhall and London's Garden Theatres*.

52. Allen, "The Landscape"; Hunt, "Theatres, Gardens, and Garden-Theatres," 95–118.

53. Anon [John Lockman?], *The Turkish Paradise or Vaux-Hall Gardens: Wrote at Vaux-Hall Last Summer*, 5.

54. [Lockman,] *A Sketch of the Spring-Gardens*, 17.

55. Anon [John Lockman?], *The Turkish Paradise*, 8.

56. On these effects, see Aspden, "Fam'd Handel Breathing," 59–62.

57. The clearing around the orchestral pavilion was generally acknowledged as the "grand rendezvous" of the Gardens, and its most heavily populated area; see *A Description of Vauxhall Gardens*, 19.

58. "On hearing Miss Wright sing at Vauxhall" (n.d.), GB-Ob G. A. Surrey c.21, Item 99. Newburgh Hamilton, Preface to *Alexander's Feast* (London, 1739), cited in Deutsch, *Handel*, 399.

59. Aspden, "'Fam'd Handel Breathing,'" 55–65.

60. "The Invitation to Mira, Requesting Her Company to VauxHall Garden" and "The Pleasures of Life," in Bickham, *The Musical Entertainer*, vol. 2 (1740), 5 and 21.

61. On Tyers and Frederick, see Aspden, "Fam'd Handel Breathing," 48–49. On Frederick's choice of figures and his garden design (informal, like Vauxhall's), see Rorschach, "Frederick, Prince of Wales," 24–25, 30–31.

62. Probably not coincidentally, Gandon was a student of the architect eventually appointed after Frederick's demise to design the Kew garden. William Chambers, who, though he did not follow the prince's original plans, would certainly have been aware of them. The painting of the Wombourne Wodehouse Temple, by J. Hughes and held in the J. W. Phillips collection, is reproduced in McParland, *James Gandon*, 14. McParland says the temple itself was "no more than a routine reworking of Chambers's Temple of Bellona at Kew" (p. 15). For a fuller discussion of Helier's garden, which apparently also included a bust of Handel in the Music Room, see Barre, "Sir Samuel Hellier," 310–327.

63. Young, "The Shaw-Helier Collection," 165. Gandon's drawing of the temple had been shown at London's annual Society of Arts exhibition in either 1767 or 1768; Mulvany (*The Life of James Gandon*, 21) gives 1767; McParland (*James Gandon*, 207) gives 1768.

64. Barre, "Sir Samuel Hellier," 312. Johann Friedrich Reichardt (*Briefe eines aufmerksamen Reisenden die Musikbetreffend* [1774–6]; cited in Howard, *Gluck*, 5) attests that it was a Europe-wide phenomenon for "gentlemen" to train servants in music in order to create an in-house orchestra.

65. Young, "The Shaw-Helier Collection," 163. On Handel and the sublime, see Mainwaring, *Handel, passim*; Johnson, "'Giant Handel' and the Musical Sublime," 515–533.

66. Barre, "Sir Samuel Hellier," 311, 310.

14.

From London's Opera House to the Salon? The Favourite *(and Not So "Favourite") Songs from the King's Theatre*

Michael Burden

It is hard to imagine a more "public" piece of music than an aria performed in situ in a mid-eighteenth-century Italian opera staging. Whether in Paris, London, Rome, or Madrid, it was the focus of an opera singer's activity, encompassing issues of vocal range, vocal quality, musical style, additional ornamentation, and acting skills. These were part of a performance that encapsulated a singer's public persona. Such performances were the primary interface between a performer and the public, and were therefore under constant scrutiny, a scrutiny that led, inevitably, to the identification of abuses: Charles Burney, for example, noted that

> it is well known, that a company of singers is now reckoned good, in Italy if two or three airs and a duet deserve attention; the audience neither expecting nor attending to any thing else. And the managers, who find this custom very convenient, take care not to interrupt play or conversation by the useless and impertinent talents of the under-singers; so that the performers of the second and third class are generally below mediocrity.[1]

If the audience's attention was on gossip and gambling, then those "two or three airs," heard as individual pieces, assumed a greater importance in the aural texture of the evening, one that included talk and chitchat of all kinds. Arias, when heard in the context of an opera, were understood as a series of affects, which the Scottish Enlightenment author John Brown located as the differences between the "affections of the mind":

> The Airs are divided, by the Italians, into certain classes; these classes are originally founded on real distinctions, drawn from the nature of the various affections of the mind; but musicians, who, like other artists, are seldom philosophers, have distinguished them by names relative to the practice of their own profession.[2]

As he dryly notes, musicians, in attempting to categorize arias, took what was probably a quite sophisticated understanding of aria characteristics, and transferred it into language that lacks subtlety. Brown went on to note the musician's division of them into *aria di agilità* or *aria di bravura*; *aria di portamento*; the *cantabile*; the *mezzo carattere*; and the *aria parlante* (with its subdivisions, *aria di nota e parola, aria agitate, aria di strepito,* and *aria infuriate*).[3] Similarly, Burney, in discussing the voice and manner of castrato Giovanni Manzoli, which was "grand, and full of taste and dignity," remarked that in his

> first opera he had three songs, composed by Pescetti, entirely in different styles: *Recagli quell' acciaro*, an animated *aria parlante*; *Caro mio bene addio*, an adagio in a grand style of cantabile; and *Mi dona mi rende*, of a graceful kind, all of which he executed admirably.[4]

Burney's remarks emphasize that arias were perceived to have an individuality divorced from its position in the opera,[5] which allowed them to have a life of circulation and publication, of different ownerships and performance contexts, and of movement from the private realm to the public sphere—and back again.

The main way in which arias lived this independent life in London was through a series of publications called *The Favourite Songs*, a group of arias extracted from operas that were currently being performed at the King's Theatre.[6] While the title of each collection varied slightly, the format remained much the same: each publication contained usually three or more arias that had been included in a single work. They were not cheap—notions that such publications made the music generally accessible are fantasies—but they were portable and salable, and containing music by composers from Handel to Salieri, were brought out with regularity during the eighteenth century.

London audiences first encountered these arias during public performances at the Opera House (called, colloquially, the Opera)—which came into existence in 1705 as the Queen's Theatre and after a few years of erratic administration and programming, became the King's Theatre under George I. It had a repertory confined to Italian opera and operated with a subscriber base centered on the theater's boxes: this was an audience of the elite, who were not, of course, merely the aristocratic but included opera aficionados from across the social spectrum;[7]

there was also, too, a casual public audience of which we know little. Significantly for its health as an institution, it operated for most of its life on an annual license which allowed little forward planning, thereby building into its administration an inherent instability from which it rarely escaped. This was in marked contrast to the playhouses, which, since the Restoration, operated a duopoly under royal patent.[8]

One of the consequences of this situation was the Opera's personnel—singers, dancers, and often the composer and the musical director—had to be booked each season but could not be—or at least were not—offered a contract beyond that. London was not unique in this, and it might not have made much difference in the running of the theater were it not for the fact that in London, every performer was, by definition, foreign: The singers were primarily Italians, The Opera needing a minimum of six singers, seven or eight to be certain of a working season, and more, if they could be afforded. But whatever the numbers, substitutes in cases of emergencies were not automatically to be had; The Opera could not simply send to the next town for a replacement. The circumstances also emphasize that the performances of Italian arias, at least when those arias were heard in public, were usually the Italians themselves.

From the Singers' Suitcase to the London Public Arena: Moving Arias Around

Arias heard in London came primarily from two sources, from the pen of the composer employed by the Opera House or via him from previously composed works, and from the singer's "suitcase." In the case of previously composed works, the music could be adjusted when it did not suit the singers' voices, and in the case of new settings, these presumably would be written to suit. This is not to suggest, however, that these often work-a-day settings fall into the category of the elaborately "commissioned" pieces sometimes associated with suitcase arias, although if successful, they undoubtedly ended up in performers' portmanteaux. But if the offerings of the composer did not suit, or a performer's preference lay elsewhere, a singers' suitcase came into play, one that was both metaphorical and real. Singers arriving from the continent brought with them a collection of arias, texts that had been set for them, or arias they had sung in former productions, or just ones that they had picked up in the course of a musical career.[9] Mingotti's row with the manager Francesco Vanneschi during a production of Lampugnani's new setting of *Siroe, re di Persia*, provides evidence of the arias, and the use to which they were put:

> [W]hen *Vanneschi* heard me privately sing the Songs that were allotted me in this Opera, he found them so little to his Taste, that he begged of me as a Favour to substitute other Songs of other Masters, knowing that I had better Compositions in my Possession.[10]

Mingotti's suitcase arias not only had the advantage of improving the score, but they would also have been new to the London audience. "Newness" was a vital component in the success or failure of an opera:

> In February this year, *Signor Cassani*, another Italian opera singer from Italy arrived, who, with the new songs, first appeared in the part of Mitius in Camilla. At this time a new subscription was opened, the number of tickets at half a guinea each, not to exceed four hundred.[11]

Burney's report juxtaposed the new arias with the opening of a subscription, the latter needing the promise of the novelty of the former to succeed. Burney later attributed the failure of Giuseppe Sarti's 1786 *Giulio Sabino* to the lack of new songs, for "several of the songs, indeed, had been previously sung here at concerts, and did not appear new."[12]

Newness was primarily about the arias; the old stories in they were inserted—such as those by Pietro Metastasio, Gaetano Roccoforte, Apostolo Zeno, and so on—were tolerated, and indeed, defended on occasion:

> We could not see without surprise the Opera of *Demophoonte* disguised under the appellation of *L'Usurpator Innocente*. Such an insult, from the hand of some botching pruner, to the name of Metastasio, the first poet of the Italian stage, should not have been tolerated.[13]

The House sometimes advertised the fact that the story was old with the work of such masters as Metastasio being considered classic. Fanny Burney could casually remark:

> The opera is to be Metastasio's *Didone*, which is the very opera that Agujari sung to us 12 songs from, composed by her maestro Sig^r Colla. It is to be *half* Pasticcio, but all the recitatives by Sacchini, as well as a Cantabile for Rauzzini, & *All the part* of la Gabrielli.[14]

Didone by Metastasio was something from which she had already heard twelve songs in settings by one composer; however, she was just as keen to hear it in new settings by other composers.

The practice of aria substitution in whatever form it took was—and is—well understood, and is today generally considered to have worked counter to the quality of the eighteenth-century opera repertory. But while doubtless the insertion of arias with absolutely no reference to the affect of the preceding recitative was less than ideal, there is no doubt that the shortcuts the process offered made the staging of a season's operas easier. The extent to which those arias were actually used depended on the balance of power in the opera house at any given moment; a soprano of international standing, for example, had more clout than a singer just starting out. Another factor was the position of the composer; if he (inevitably) was either also the musical director or house composer for that season (or seasons, in the case of Handel), then clearly he was in a position of authority over the singers. And there were other reasons why arias were changed during a season:

> Is it not extraordinary that Marchesi should have been obliged, last season, to leave a song of the most superb effect only for want of a clarinet to accompany his voice?[15]

This rhetorical question, posed by Antoine Le Texier in his manifesto for reform at the London Opera House, was an attempt at a wake-up call to the casual way in which operas were altered to suit the theater for whatever performance was required.

The Arias: Who Owned the Object?

Clearly, the singer "owned" the aria as a performance, its value to the performer being in direct proportion to the public's reception of the song; if the public were not enthusiastic, then it would certainly be dropped from that singer's role. This process began during rehearsal. When, for example, the 1786 version of *Giulio Cesare* was being prepared, the journal *The World and Fashionable Advertiser* gave a hint that these rehearsals, at least for the singer Signor Gattolini, were not trouble-free:

> Gattolini, scared by preceding ridicule, sung his scouted song no more.—Like *mock oratory*, once "coughed down," to be *silent ever after*.
>
> "So should desert be crown'd"—
>
> And so much for those solicitous of the "*Salus Populi*" constitution.[16]

"Salus Populi" implies that Gattolini had performed or had attempted to perform his own aria. In this case, his "own" had one of several meanings: he could have written it himself; it could have been written for him; or he could have simply chosen it because it suited his performance. But Gattolini failed to take public ownership of an aria that he had clearly promoted as a vehicle for his own performance, and the aria was dropped.

Once the opera reached the stage, the ownership became a matter of negotiation between the singer and the public. The report of Mara's performance in the 1786 *Didone abbandonata* shows that the reception of her performances was influenced by precisely what arias were chosen:

> The pleasure with which she was heard, had a considerable increase from her choice of songs; which, being in different styles by Sacchini, Piccini, Mortellari, and Gazzaniga, were all severally encored during the run of the opera; a circumstance, which I never remember to have happened to any other singer.[17]

Attending an opera today with arias by Sacchini, Piccini, Mortellari, and Gazzaniga would be the last thing any operagoer would expect or desire, and yet here, the ability of the performer to showcase a number of composer's styles seems to have been one of things that captured her public's attention and approbation.

Once an aria was "out there" in published form, the question of ownership becomes more complex, for an appearance in the *Favourite Songs* was the point at which a singer was forced to relinquish sole ownership of the performance of those arias published. This was not itself a serious matter for the singer, for most Italian performers could be confident that few singers in London could equal them in the skill required to perform this repertory, and some that could were restricted in the manner of their performance; as Suzanne Aspden recounts elsewhere in this volume, one who did was Elizabeth Linley.[18] But publication was also the point at which the arias, ephemeral in their performance at the Opera House, now entered a more permanent type of circulation, a process that turned the music into what Richard Taruskin calls a "durable music-thing" (*The Favourite Songs*), thereby memorializing the otherwise ephemeral product of the "music-makers" (the arias as sung in the Opera House).[19]

The arias reached this stage through activities of the King's Theatre copyist: it seems that it was through his agency that the arias reached the publisher. Copyists did not, of course, make a living at just that: for example, the Opera House paid the singer Leopoldo de Micheli £150 a year, but he earned more through the "absolute and exclusive power of disposing of the Copy right thereof it being part of his salary."[20] There was a brief rebellion in 1756–57 when the songs from the operas *Alessandro*, *Antigono*, and *Il re pastore* were published not by Walsh, but by Regina Mingotti and Felice Gardini, and the "FOUR SONGS in the OPERA Call'd IL DEMOFONTE [sic] sung by *Sigra Mingotti*" could be "had at Sr de Giardini's lodgings."[21] However, the stranglehold of the theater copyists over access to these songs clearly reasserted itself after this brief interlude.

But at this point in the process, legal copyright was also an issue. In the broadest terms, the 1709 act conferred copyright on publications registered at Stationers' Hall for twenty-eight years, a provision that held until 1814.[22] But that copyright rested with the printer: it was not until 1777, in a ruling in the case of *J. C. Bach v. Longman and Lukey* that a composer was able to benefit from the copyright of his own music, and it took further judgments for it to be clear that this applied to vocal as well as instrumental music. At the Opera House, institutional control intervened. In the case of aria texts written for it by its employees, it appears that the house owned the copyright of the words; the affidavits in the case of *Storace v. Longman and Broderip* indicate that whatever was produced for the theater was regarded by the institution as its property. This would have applied to, say, the London works of Giovanni Bottarelli and to those of Carlo Badini, but obviously not to texts such as those by Metastasio, Roccaforte, or Zeno. The same appears to have applied to the composer: if the house employed him, then the music he wrote during his tenure was the property of the house. In the case of a composer employed in the manner of J. C. Bach, whose contract included the provision of a new opera, or the similar offer made by Felice Giardini to Niccolo Piccini,[23] presumably the score as composed also became the property of the theater. But it is less than clear that while the King's Theatre may have owned a version of the piece, that the composer was then entirely restricted in his use of that material elsewhere. In *Storace v. Longman and Broderip*, the court rulings and affidavits suggest that the publishers could not profit from the publication and sale of the aria in London, but that there can have been no objection to the composer using that aria in a performance in, say, Rome or Venice.

The situation articulated here relates only to works created for that institution: in the legal case of *Storace v. Longman and Broderip*, the aria had been written for the Opera House by the house composer. The conclusions previously drawn in a study of this case have suggested that any aria—which would include suitcase arias—inserted into an opera made it part of that opera, and therefore, the property of the theater.[24] But the judgment seems to have a limiting factor: such a transfer seems restricted to those occasions on which the act of copying or official insertion took place, as described by Leopoldo De Michele in his deposition: "Signora Storace gave ye Manuscript Copy of the said Song to [me] . . . to be written into the ye Music of ye House as forming part of ye said Opera of Il Re Teodora [sic]."[25] It does not seem to apply to a simple replacement, where the aria was "loose." In another case, Gertrud Mara sold the aria "Anche nel petto io sento" for her benefit to Longman and Broderip, while Leopoldo De Micheli sold an illicit copy of it to the publishers Skillern and Goulding. An action brought by Longman and Broderip against Skillern and Goulding was settled in the plaintiff's favor, suggesting that Mara's actions were upheld. Indeed, it seems wholly improbable that singers of the stature of Mara, Mingotti, and Brigida Banti would accept a situation in which their subsequent use of their own suitcase arias was restricted by the Opera House, an institution that was merely that season's employer. If the situation was otherwise, a singer could have lost his or her rights to very valuable pieces of property, always assuming the arias to have been the singer's property in the first place!

The *Favourite Songs* Collections as Objects

The individual arias, having been sold by the copyist to whichever music publisher was able to produce them, were then engraved and assembled into collections. Such a method of assemblage meant that these collections were not "sets," nor can the *Favourite Songs* be called "series," for they are not periodical publications and their content is assembled in a random manner, although it is perhaps not always quite the random one it appears to be at first glance.[26] Many of the arias in the *Favourite Songs* are, for example, grouped by the performer with whom they were associated. Thus, the three collections of *Favourite Songs* in

Didone published by Robert Bremner in 1775 contained only arias for Dido, sung by Caterina Gabrielli, and *Æneas*, sung by Venanzio Rauzzini; in such cases, the music was not necessarily limited to the output of a single composer. But other collections were limited in just such a way: for example, the *Favourite Songs* for the 1757 *Ciro Riconosciuto*, which came in two parts from John Walsh, contained music only by Gioacchino Cocchi. The implications of these approaches must be the assumption that arias associated with a well-known singer—Mara, Farinelli, Senesino, or whoever—could be expected to sell better, as also could arias set by a composer of the moment.

As far as the compilation process goes, though, whether the songs that were published were the "favorites" of anyone other than the copyist or the publisher, was something that seems to have been entirely left to chance; as Burney remarked of the songs by Abos and Lampugnani from the 1756 opera *Tito Manlio*, "the *favourite airs* of this opera were printed by Walsh, though none were favoured by the public."[27] While a publisher would undoubtedly want to bring out the popular *numbers*, getting the name of the composer on the title page, or the name of the popular *singer* on the top of the inside page was more of a priority. But it is also the case that some arias that were unpopular in the theater had a new lease of life once circulated in the *Favourite Songs* format, as the disastrous reception of *Adriano in Syria* in 1765 showed:

> The songs were printed by the elder Welcker, and many of them sung afterwards at concerts with great applause, and found, as detached airs, excellent, though they had been unfortunate in their totality.[28]

The failure, which was attributed to a range of causes including the public's high expectations of the piece, did not stop the publisher taking on the separate songs.

But who were the publishers? Starting in 1721, the collection of songs taken from Bononcini's opera *Cyrus* was published by John Walsh, and John and Joseph Hare. From 1727, the publications were produced by Walsh and Joseph Hare, and then, after 1730, by John Walsh alone until his death in 1766. Throughout this period, Walsh published collected volumes of his *Favourite Songs* under the title of *Le delizie dell'opere*, a collection that had one printed title page per volume and the original plates stamped with a second, through-numbered sequence; one such set, in nine volumes, can, for example, be found advertised in 1763 in *The Favourite Songs to Zanaida*.[29] As already mentioned, there was a small rebellion when Mingotti and Giardini published some songs themselves, and there were some pirate editions produced by the curious James Oswald. After Walsh's death in 1766, the imprint passed to William Randall and John Abell until 1768, and then Randall carried it forward on his own until his death in 1776. However, he published no new *Favourite Songs*, although after his death Elizabeth Randall capitalized on the plates and stock the firm had inherited from Walsh and published a new edition of *Le delizie dell'opere* with the subtitle, "*being a collection of all the Favourite Songs in score, collected from the operas.*" Elizabeth Randall was later succeeded by the partnership of Wright and Wilkinson in 1783.

New sets of songs continued to appear, but they were not all produced by a single publisher. The most active was the Scottish music publisher Robert Bremner; there was also Peter Welcker, John Preston, and William Napier. Peter Welcker was a long-established music seller, printer, engraver, and publisher; the business was taken on by his widow after Welcker's death in 1775. Bremner opened his shop in London in 1762, and he bought some of the *Favourite Songs* plates from John Cox, and then, on the death of Mrs. Welcker in 1779, the plates and music from her estate. This concentrated many of the later *Favourite Songs* sources in Bremner's hands. William Napier appears to have established himself as a credible publisher very quickly, for he is found from about 1772 at an address in the Strand. He published a number of sets of songs, including the collection from *Zemira e Azore*, and then moved on to other things.[30] John Preston, whose only contributions to the series were two sets of songs from the 1784 *Issipile*, was to purchase the plates and stock of Robert Bremner in 1789. He ended up with the plates of Bremner's editions and any others that Bremner had acquired through the purchases from the firms of Cox and of Welcker. Significantly, Preston does not seem to have regarded it as worthwhile to produce new editions or to continue with the sets.

Once the songs were in circulation, the public did not have to rely on buying what were, after all, expensive prints. The service of a copyist could be procured, the prints being borrowed and copied as required. De Micheli—who, as previously mentioned, was employed by the Opera House as a copyist—was also advertising his services beyond the institution, taking "the Liberty to offer his Service to the NOBILITY and GENTRY in General."[31] Such copying was also a feature of music lessons, and indeed, may have formed part of a pupil's training.

From the Public Sphere, to the Private Salon, to the Closet

The arias, having moved from the privacy of the singer's suitcase to the public realm of the theater to the publisher, had then to be made suitable for performance in other contexts. And in order to do this, the arias themselves were reinvented through arrangement to encourage general purchase. Some had just a bass line underneath the melody line; in others, there was a reduction above that, the whole making a part for an unspecified keyboard instrument; in others, this reduction was labeled in the manner of a short score, although the music on offer was often so skeletal that it cannot be convincingly referred to as such; and in still more, such as those songs from J. C. Bach's setting of *Zanaida*, the work is virtually full score. The description of the activities of William Babell, for example, give some feeling for the manner in which these were sometimes undertaken:

> This author acquired great celebrity by wire-drawing the favourite songs of the opera of *Rinaldo*, and others of the same period, into *showy* and brilliant lessons, which by mere rapidity of singer in playing single sounds, without the assistance of taste, expression, harmony, or modulation, enabled the performer to astonish ignorance, and acquire the reputation of a great player at a small expense.[32]

As it happens, Babell's "wire-drawing"—which we can interpret as spinning out to great length, with excessive detail, or over-refinement—was probably not much more elaborate than some of the flashy ornamentation added by the Italian singers in performance, although there is no evidence that he drew on actual sets of ornaments as a source for this activity. There were also arrangements with parts that enabled the orchestration to expand or contract for concert performance. When Robert Bremner took over from John Walsh, he also produced a "plan of Printing the Opera Songs [which] is chiefly intended for the Conveniency of Concerts."[33] Concert promoters may have appreciated the "conveniency," but this method of publication, which retained the original *Favourite Songs* approach, was not taken up to the extent required to make producing such sets a commercial proposition, and the format was abandoned.

The arias had now become a concert item, both at public and private concerts, and at impromptu performances. The London public concert was an important institution for the concert societies, promoters, and theaters alike: by the 1789–1790 season, there were twenty-three different concert series operating.[34] And while arias from the Italian operas would not have appeared in all of these, the style popularized by the Opera House held sway in London concerts in both vocal and instrumental music until about 1780, when the programs began to show a broadening to include the more demanding Austro-German music.[35] However, Italian arias included in the concert repertory were not those concurrently being performed at the Opera House but tended to be numbers taken from older works.[36] Obviously, there was the matter of "ownership" (who did the public think owned the performance of the aria at that moment?) and competition (would another singer really want to take on an opera star?). If true, then such a reluctance may be one of the reasons why Robert Bremner's score-and-parts publications of the *Favourite Songs* seems to have been such a short-lived format: the lack of "encouragement" from concert promoters meant that they just didn't sell.

Private concerts could be formal events with large audiences: at a concert of "forty or fifty people" in 1767, Lady Mary Coke noted:

> A natural daughter of Lord Pigot's, a Girl of nine or ten years of Age, sung several songs out of the Comic Operas, & imitated so exactly the action & manner of the two principal performers, that it was impossible to mistake who

She intended taking off, but for one of her sex & age it appear'd to me rather an extraordinary qualification than a desirable one.[37]

Walpole, writing to Sir Horace Mann on May 29, 1786, mentions the fee paid to the castrato Giovanni Rubinelli for a concert at the home of Maria Cosway, wife of the portraitist, Richard Cosway, suggesting a formal footing for these events; he heard Rubinelli sing "*one* song at the extravagant price of ten guineas, and whom for as many shillings I have heard sing half a dozen at the opera house."[38] Mrs. Fox Lane, a particular promoter of the soprano Regina Mingotti, ran her concerts in such a way that admission was limited to her "choice friends," and her events became

> the subjects of envy and obloquy to all those who were unable to obtain admission . . . and the difficulty, or rather impossibility, of hearing these professors and illustrious dilettanti any where else, stimulated curiosity so much that there was no sacrifice or mortification to which fashionable people would not submit, in order to obtain admission.[39]

Fox Lane was known for using these affairs to sell Benefit tickets to her friends' performances "as if on the road" in the manner of a highwayman.

These affairs were quite grand. Of a different order were the concerts given by Felice Giardini at his house, ones that were professional showcases that included a different sort of performance of such arias:

> After he had been here a few years, he formed a morning *academia*, or concert, at his house, composed chiefly of his scholars both vocal and instrumental, who bore a part in the performance.[40]

On the next step down (or up) in privacy, we find the impromptu concerts given by professionals in informal circumstances: one such is noted by Susan Burney, who recounted of one evening in 1779:

> After talking awhile of the Opera, & cutting up Mr Tessier very notably, we had Music—that is, Piozzi sung several songs, serious & comic like an Angel— I have not heard him to so much advantage this long time—He sung all my favourites—Infelici Dircea of Mislewecek—Non saro mai piu geloso, & Fortuna maledetta of Anfossi—Recagli quel acciaro, a charming song, full of dignity & feeling, composed by Bertoni for Guadagni, &c &c. Mr. Barry, as he understands Italian, & as to all uncultivated hearers Vocal Music had ever more effect than Instrumental seemed much delighted, & our Evening passed very agribbly.[41]

Susan Burney's remark that his performance showed him to "advantage" emphasizes just how crucial the suitability of the aria for a singer's performance was, even in a private setting. And equally, Charles Burney's remark on Benini's performance in the apparently disastrous *Giannina e Bernadoni*—"the drama was thought too long, and too full of silly Italian buffoonery"—is telling in its understanding, through performance, of the different requirements of the public stage and the private salon:

> Her voice was not powerful, but of a good quality, and perfectly in tune. Her execution surprises no more than her voice; but her taste is good, and her manner of singing extremely graceful and pleasing. If she was a dilettante and only to sing in a room, her performance would be perfect.[42]

There were, therefore, expectations of a certain style of performance when the aria was performed in the salon by an amateur, a "dilettante." A singer, who might not be able to own a performance of the aria at the Opera House, might be able to "own" it in the salon, thereby giving the aria a different life as a private piece. Lucrezia Aguiari was engaged to sing at London's Pantheon, but called on the Burneys in June 1775:

> She sung in 20 different styles. The greatest was son Regina & son[o] amante from Didone. Good God! What a song! & how sung! Then she gave us 2 or 3 *Cantabiles*, sung divinely, then she chanted some *Church Music*, in a style so nobly simple & unadorned, that it stole into one's very soul! Then she gave us a Bravura, with difficulties which seemed only possible for a Instrument in the Hands of a great master.[43]

Had she been employed by the Opera House, Aguiari would have been a success in the role:

> She also has great ideas of action—& grew so animated in singing an Aria Parlante from Didone, that she acted it through out, with great spirit & feeling.[44]

Aguiari not only adopted the arias, but laid claim to the role through her acting skills and force of personality. It was, however, definitely a private affair: "We had not a soul here but our own Family, which was her particular desire."[45]

It is Fanny's sister Susan who provides us with an example of the *Favourite Songs* in that most private of places, the closet. On August 6, 1779, Susan Burney asked for some volumes to be sent to her:

> Should no parcel be yet sent when you receive this, I beg you to encrease its size by adding to it the following books. A set of Motezuma—a set of Aprile's Duets in M.S. given me by Ly. Clarges—the set of Didone wch. contains Son Regina—the 2d. No. of Tamerlano—& Sacchini's Duets.[46]

It is clear that this collection of music consists of printed scores, extracts, and manuscript copies, possibly made by professional copyists; the music from Lady Clarges (Louisa Clarges, wife of Sir Thomas Clarges [1751–1782]), for example, seems to have been a "set," which suggests a previous grouping rather than a newly random selection by a copyist: it is possible that either set one or set two of the printed copies was the source for these.

The *Favourite Songs* printed sets also attracted those interested in private study. The operagoer Thomas Harris, on hearing Galuppi's *Il trionfo della Continenza*, commented that it was "as bad as the Italian music generally is; its made by Galuppi, & though there is I believe great difficulty to find out the favourite songs (as some there must be)."[47] Harris was writing on February 1, 1746; by February 15, his wish was gratified, with the announcement of the *Favourite Songs* in the *General Advertiser*,[48] and a second set announced on March 1.[49] Harris was not going to use them for performance, indeed, quite the opposite: his role was that of a connoisseur of music, he would like to examine the arias to see if they were as poor as he thought they were when he heard them at the Opera House. And Burney inevitably made use of the *Favourite Songs* himself while writing the *General History*:

> A very fine air from his opera of *Vologeso* was sung by Monticelli in England, and printed by Walsh among the favourite songs of the opera of *Gianguir, nell' orror di notte oscura*, to which I refer as a specimen of his serious style.[50]

Burney was referring to music by Rinaldo di Capua, and went on to recommend that "the curious will, however, do well to procure a copy" of the scene in the opera which starts with the recitative "Berenice, ove sei?": as he himself noted, the music at that time was fifty years old, and can have had no currency as performable music.

Conclusions

Italian opera arias, then, could, in performance, be public, semipublic, semiprivate, or private, each setting offering its own distinct relationship between the performer, the music, and the listener. And London's *Favourite Songs* collections were the main way in which the public accessed the Opera House repertory for private performance. But there is the possibility of what we might think of as an aria performed in public, which, by dint of circumstance, retains its "privacy." Such a possibility was hinted at in Burney's comments detailing the focus of operagoers on one or two arias; further, Le Texier described a situation generally assumed in continental opera-going, but here detailed in London:

> I know it is not to be affected that the fair sex and their admirers come to the Opera; I know that in the former the pleasure of being seen, and in the latter that of seeing.... When the pleasure of the table is over, towards nine or ten o'clock, they come to applaud a song or a ballet, and sometimes one passes unheard, and the other unseen.[51] The evening is spent in the coffee-room, with that common topic of conversation, politics and horses, there they wait till the end of the Opera brings the whole of the polite company.[52]

It might be argued that the aria, although performed in a public arena as described by Le Texier, remained private because "knowledge" of the work failed to reach its intended audience. We cannot, of course, know which arias these might have been—and speculation would be fruitless—but it should make us consider again our assumptions about the nature of the spaces that the performance of an aria occupied.

Notes

1. Burney, *A General History of Music*, vol. 4, 560.
2. Brown, *Letters upon the Poetry and Music of the Italian Opera*, 35–36.
3. Ibid., 36–40.
4. Burney, *A General History of Music*, vol. 4, 485.
5. See Burden, *London Opera Observed*, vol. 3, 85–86, for a discussion of the background to John Brown's volume.
6. There is one possible exception to this: a single set of songs by Sacchini for *Demetrio* survives in the form of the *Favourite Songs*, labeled in eighteenth-century handwriting.
7. See Hall-Witt, *Fashionable Acts*.
8. For a discussion of the patents, see Hume, "Theatre as Property in Eighteenth-Century London," 17–30.
9. As well as contemporary discussions on "suitcase arias" in the eighteenth century and their uses, see Poriss, *Changing the Score*; Strohm, *The Operas of Antonio Vivaldi*, vol. 2, 552–556; Burden, "Divas, Arias, and Acrimony," 73-88; and Butler, "From Guadagni's Suitcase," forthcoming.
10. Mingotti, *An Appeal to the Public*, 3–4; see further discussion of Mingotti's aria substitutions in Burden, *Impresario and Diva*, 42–43.
11. Burney, *A General History of Music*, vol. 4, 206.
12. Ibid., 530.
13. Quoted in Smith, *The Italian Opera and Contemporary Ballet in London*, 14.
14. Burney, *The Early Journals and Letters of Fanny Burney*, vol. 2, 160.
15. Le Texier, *Ideas on the Opera*, 5.
16. *The World and Fashionable Advertiser*, March 26, 1787.
17. Burney, *A General History of Music*, vol. 4, 524.
18. See also Kennerley, "Flippant Dolls and Serious Artists," for a discussion of the position of nonprofessional singers.
19. See Taruskin, "Text and Act," 353. Taruskin's remarks deal with the notion that the fact of the printed text was part of the music becoming a "classic."
20. The defendants' affidavit (GB-TNA C31/247/81); Storace's affidavit (GB-TNA C31/247/39); see Girdham, *English Opera in Late Eighteenth-Century London*, 89.
21. See GB-Lbl G. 201 (1*).
22. Kleiner and McFarlane, "Copyright," in *GMO* (accessed June 25, 2016).
23. Price, Milhous, and Hume, *The Impresario's Ten Commandments*, 15.
24. Price, "Unity, Originality, and the London Pasticcio," 18–25, 27.
25. Ibid., 26.
26. Burden, "Divas, Arias, and Acrimony," 73–88.
27. Burney, *A General History of Music*, vol. 4, 466.
28. Ibid., 487.

29. For a bibliographic description of the confusing results this process of grouping, re-grouping, and republication, see Smith and Humphries, *A Bibliography of the Musical Works Published by the Firm of John Walsh*, 122ff.

30. He reduced his publishing activities and established a circulating musical library in 1784, a move which was probably the reason for his bankruptcy in 1791.

31. Bottarelli, *Sophonisba, a Serious Opera*, 48.

32. Burney, *A General History of Music*, vol. 4, 648.

33. *Public Advertiser*, January 17, 1764.

34. McVeigh, *Concert Life in London*, 5.

35. Ibid., 158.

36. Ibid., 108.

37. Coke, *The Letters and Journals of Lady Mary Coke*, vol. 1, 199.

38. Walpole, *Horace Walpole's Correspondence*, vol. 25, 646.

39. Burney, *A General History of Music*, vol. 4, 671–72.

40. Ibid., 669–70.

41. S. Burney, Letter-Journal, GB-Lbl Egerton MS 3691, fols. 33[r]–33v. Fanny Burney also records this evening, *The Early Journals and Letters of Fanny Burney*, vol. 2, 77–78.

42. Burney, *A General History of Music*, vol. 4, 527.

43. Burney, *The Early Journals and Letters*, ed. Troide, vol. 2, 155.

44. Ibid.

45. Ibid.

46. Burney, Letter-Journal, fol. 10v.

47. Thomas Harris to James Harris, in Burrows and Dunhill, *Music and Theatre in Handel's World*, 222.

48. *General Advertiser*, February 15, 1746.

49. *General Advertiser*, March 1, 1746.

50. Burney, *A General History of Music*, vol. 4, 559.

51. Burden, "Eating and the Theatre," http://ora.ox.ac.uk/.

52. Le Texier, *Ideas on the Opera*, 32–33.

15.

Education, Entertainment, Embellishment: Music Publication in the Lady's Magazine

Bonny H. Miller

From its debut in August 1770, a music sheet was included every month in the London *Lady's Magazine; or Entertaining Companion for the Fair Sex*, yielding a total of some four hundred songs by 1805, when music ceased as a regular feature.[1] The *Lady's Magazine* stood at the forefront of education for women in Georgian England, and its music sheets reflected the periodical's twin goals of instruction and entertainment. As the century progressed, more works by earlier English composers appeared in addition to fashionable airs, demonstrating that the *Lady's Magazine* also served as a medium to cultivate the heritage of British song among magazine readers. The monthly periodical format provided a fluid conduit to convey musics from a range of urban venues (theater, pleasure gardens, concert stage, and men's convivial music clubs) directly into the domicile, thereby creating permeable boundaries between public and private spaces, genres, and repertoire.

On the title page of each issue, the *Lady's Magazine* listed a song among the so-called "Embellishments" in the table of contents. While "embellishments" might suggest fashion, the varied nature of the plates is evident from a title page, such as July 1779, that itemized "the following Copper-Plates, viz. 1. An accurate Whole Sheet Map of Africa. 2. A beautiful historical Picture of Omrah restored: and 3. A Song, set to Music by Mr. Hudson."[2]

At its zenith, the *Lady's Magazine* reached perhaps fifteen thousand subscribers, making it as widespread as the venerable *Gentleman's Magazine* (1731–1907), at the same price of sixpence per issue, and spanning more than a half-century before merging with rival publications.[3] Despite the extensive circulation of the

Lady's Magazine, Jenny Batchelor cites difficulty of access and unanswerable questions about readership, purchasers, authors, and anonymous editors, all of which have contributed to a lack of definitive scholarship for the periodical.[4] The "polite literature" that filled the issues was echoed by music deemed appropriate for the home, such as chaste love songs, but the magazine also circulated favorite airs and duets from English operas, occasional music, and catches from music societies. The *Lady's Magazine* printed excerpts from more than twenty of George Frideric Handel's odes and oratorios, as well as songs by many English composers of merit: Thomas Morley (ca. 1557–1602), William Boyce (1711–1779), Henry Purcell (1659–1695), Maurice Greene (1696–1755), Charles King (1687–1748), Samuel Howard (1710–1782), and Elizabeth Turner (d. 1756). The range of repertoires in the *Lady's Magazine* gives a glimpse of domestic study and music making that mixed music from public venues into private or semiprivate, nonprofessional performances along a "performative continuum" broader than just inferior amateur entertainment in the home.[5]

A Musical Tradition

The phenomenon of "magazine music" in literary periodicals for the general reader began even before the eighteenth century.[6] In 1692, Huguenot refugee Peter Anthony Motteux initiated his elegant *Gentleman's Journal, or, the Monthly Miscellany* (1692–1694), which contained a regular music supplement.[7] Motteux was familiar with publication of engraved *chansons* in the premiere French miscellany, *Le Mercure Galant* (1672–1825). He understood the potential for a monthly periodical to deliver London's culture of music and theater into the private domicile, but few entrepreneurs followed his model until 1731, when Edward Cave began publication of the *Gentleman's Magazine*.[8] Cave's literary miscellany enticed a sizable readership with news, serialized fiction, essays, gossip, and advice.[9] Cave popularized the term *magazine*, meaning a storehouse, to describe such a miscellany, but "storehouse" fails to connote the dynamic aspect of magazines to channel experience, spectacle, and fashion from Georgian London into distant towns and rural homes. Printing technologies enabled miscellanies to include illustrations of the latest buildings, monuments, celebrity portraits, theatrical scenes, and music from the stage and pleasure gardens.

Song lyrics were already staples of the "Poetical Essays" in the *Gentleman's Magazine* when the first song score appeared in October 1737.[10] The *London Magazine* (1732–1785), *Universal Magazine* (1747–1815), and other competitors soon added strophic airs and dance tunes for flute or violin to their poetry sections. These poems and song scores frequently cited both performer and venue, confirming that London literary miscellanies regularly brought music into the domicile from the theaters and pleasure gardens. Ranelagh and Vauxhall Gardens mounted nightly concerts that alternated overtures, concertos, and songs to entertain listeners as well as to provide ambiance for crowds as they strolled or chatted. Although the songs were typically genteel, their double entendre could be quite suggestive, whether in pastoral lyrics of love between shepherds and nymphs, or between Scottish lads and lasses.

THE *LADY'S MAGAZINE* EMERGES

Following the style and content of the *Gentleman's Magazine,* Irish writer Oliver Goldsmith edited the first-titled *Lady's Magazine. Or Polite Companion for the Fair Sex* (1759–1763), issued by John Coote.[11] Goldsmith's *Lady's Magazine* contained a monthly song but often duplicated those in the *Royal Magazine* (1759–1771) or James Oswald's *Musical Magazine* (1760), all produced by Coote, who attested that he was the publisher of some magazines, and the "proprietor" of others.[12] Coote finally achieved a successful blend of content, tone, and features in 1770 with a redesigned *Lady's Magazine; or, Entertaining Companion for the Fair Sex* that relied less on the look of earlier London miscellanies.[13]

Many journals of the era promised to unite amusement and information, but the *Lady's Magazine*'s pledge of "Entertainment and Instruction for the Ladies of these Kingdoms" was no idle claim.[14] The periodical encompassed lengthy travel accounts, historical essays, and biographies of famous lives to improve, as well as to entertain, the household. As in much eighteenth-century literature directed at Englishwomen, ubiquitous tutelage in conduct and morality was encoded in sentimental stories, serialized novels, and sermonizing essays. While the magazine cultivated the British woman's education, each page also presented models to construct her opinions and conduct.

Magazine music sheets were no exception. The Georgian view of music as a "metaphor for social order" embraced women's practice and study as means to regulate the potentially disorderly pleasures of music.[15] Most *Lady's Magazine* scores fall into Leslie Ritchie's three categories of women's songs: songs of love, including romantic love as well as Christian caritas; pastoral songs; and songs of British nationalism.[16] Although the majority of music was limited to numbers considered appropriate for the drawing room—not too long, not too difficult, and not too racy—the magazine introduced music from some public venues into the domestic realm but not without modifications. References to fashionable pleasure gardens disappeared. Lyrics that were too suggestive of inappropriate sentiments or behavior were revised into inoffensive pastoral verses. The music published in the *Lady's Magazine* nevertheless challenges the notions that the songs published in household periodicals were insignificant, if not "pretty terrible," and belonged to a domestic performance tradition "almost invariably judged to be of inferior or at best mediocre quality."[17]

For young women of the upper and aspiring middle classes in Britain, the ability to sing and skill at the piano were desirable accomplishments, as well as pursuits preferable to novel reading or cards.[18] "Musick," declared a 1722 conduct book, "refines the Taste, polishes the Mind; and is an Entertainment . . . that preserves [Ladies] from the Rust of Idleness, that most pernicious Enemy to Virtue."[19] The *Lady's Magazine* nurtured the musical tastes of readers with assistance from an unnamed "Music Master," who was demonstrably Robert Hudson (1732–1815), a versatile singer associated with St. Paul's Cathedral for sixty years, from choirboy to vicar choral and master of the choristers.[20]

The summary of composers with music in the *Lady's Magazine* (see appendix) reveals that more than 100 selections were by Handel, and almost 150 were songs by Hudson.[21] Most composers were British-born musicians or longtime residents such as Handel and Domenico Corri (1746–1825). In 1776, the selections reflected a mix of historical and contemporary numbers, with excerpts from Handel's *Jephtha, Semele, Samson,* and *Judas Maccabaeus,* four of Hudson's secular airs, a canzonet for two voices by Thomas Morley, an anonymous "Venetian Ballad" in Italian, and a song each by Philip Hodgson of Newcastle, Mr. Hoare of Taunton, Somerset, and an anonymous "correspondent." Over time, the magazine's musical offerings swelled to a modest storehouse of English song for the home, a collation of music primarily in English, by British composers, that accorded with English taste in current use and former practice.[22]

Magazine music inserts found a place in private collections and personal volumes of music, and song titles from the magazines often overlap with sheet music imprints in domestic collections.[23] Music selections in the *Lady's Magazine* were usually limited to one or both sides of a single loose sheet that facilitated removal to the keyboard or music stand for study or performance. The songs were not intended exclusively for female performers; some excerpts from Handel's oratorios were tenor or baritone arias in their original clefs.[24] Song texts sometimes expressed a male viewpoint, but could have been performed by either sex. While the insert usually indicated "*Lady's Magazine*," the month and year were not added until 1785, making it difficult to assign earlier song sheets with certainty. Monthly tables of contents were often no more specific than "Favorite New Song."[25]

The "Music Master"

Short communications "To our Correspondents" appeared on the reverse side of the title page in most magazine issues. In November 1772, the journal editor wrote, "The song signed Iris, is obliged to be postponed . . . we shall send it as soon as possible to our composer, to be set to music." Two months later, the musical setting "Iris," by "Mr. Hudson," appeared in the year-end supplementary issue. Another communication in March 1777 referred to him as the "Music Master." Hudson's three-decade involvement indicates that he valued his role at the *Lady's Magazine*. Music instruction constituted a major strand in Hudson's life. He served as almoner at St. Paul's, in charge of schooling eight to ten choirboys from 1773 until 1793. Music pedagogy for women was also a personal concern, since his wife and daughter were professional musicians.[26]

Hudson chose magazine songs with texts that were suitably "polite," or changed the words to reduce sensual allusions and double meanings in pastoral ballads. Through careful selection and occasional revision, he skirted around concerns voiced by Rev. John Bennett:

> Many songs are couched in such indelicate language, and convey such a train of luscious ideas, as are only calculated to foil the purity of a youthful mind.... Indeed, church music is, in itself, more delightful than any other. What can be superior to some passages of Judas Maccabaeus, or the Messiah?[27]

Hudson enacted Bennett's suggestion through oratorio selections in the magazine that embodied Christian piety and scriptural stories. Hudson's topical songs celebrated the seasons, holidays, and special occasions of royal commemoration or military victory.

While *Lady's Magazine* songs often displayed a prescriptive slant, Hudson injected more works by earlier English composers as the century progressed, interweaving the pedagogical intention of using the periodical as a vehicle to cultivate the heritage of British song for the domestic audience. With its academies and interest in "Ancient Music," England evinced a burgeoning historical consciousness that Hudson transmitted to magazine readers.[28] The historical emphasis in the *Lady's Magazine* emerged in 1775, when a canzonet by Morley and catches by Greene, King, and Travers appeared in music inserts. Numerous oratorio excerpts began in 1776, well before the first Handel commemoration of 1784, and indicate the continuing "domestication" of Handel's music that Suzanne Aspden describes in this volume. Excerpts from Hawkins's *General History of the Science and Practice of Music* and Burney's *General History of Music*, both published in 1776, soon appeared in the magazine.[29]

Nowhere did Hudson discuss the monthly music published in the magazine, but his musical tastes and values for domestic song performance have been preserved through his methodical choices. In addition to excerpts from odes and oratorios from English concert life, Hudson made selections from outstanding song collections, such as Boyce's *Lyra Britannica* (1747–1759), inserted in the magazine during 1782, or Greene's 1739 *Sonnets* to texts from Edmund Spencer's *Amoretti*, in 1794 and 1795. He balanced fashion with propriety in selecting popular songs composed by contemporaries such as William Shield (1748–1809).

A Musical Sampler

Four selections from the *Lady's Magazine*—two composed by Hudson and two that he chose from other composers—illustrate a range of repertoire streams from varied venues that comingled in the periodical: pleasure garden air; patriotic music; part-song from men's clubs; and "ancient music." Hudson knew how to write

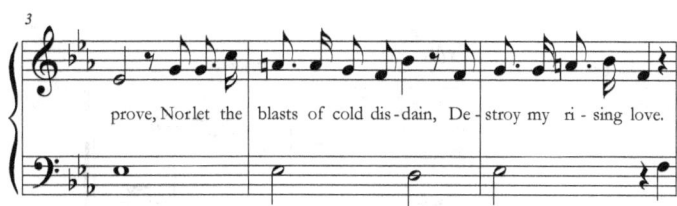

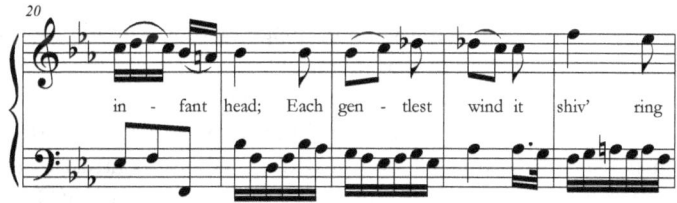

Musical Example 15.1 Hudson, "Thyrsis," *Lady's Magazine* 16 (December 1785).

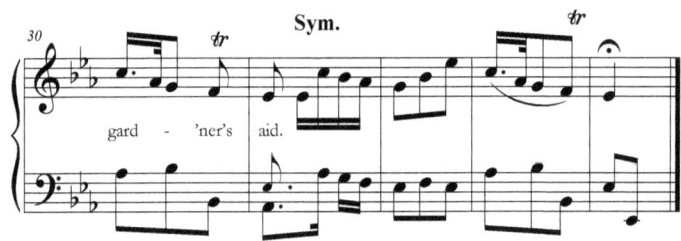

Musical Example 15.1 (*Continued*)

a pleasant tune that fit the voice and sometimes placed it within a small *scena* that suggested the metropolitan venues of the stage or garden.[30] Such a setting is "Thyrsis," a pastoral scene of unsuccessful love published in December 1785, "at the Request of several Female Correspondents" (musical example 15.1).[31] The song was already "ancient," being a revision of "Love at First Sight," the concluding song from *The Myrtle*, a collection of Hudson's airs in the pleasure garden style of the 1750s.[32] The figured bass indications were eliminated in the magazine, but the active bass line implies or completes the harmony when combined with the treble melody.[33] The ardent recitative, "When I survey thy matchless Face, sure never raptur'd Lover cou'd in a Nymph such Beauties trace," was reworded with supplication, "In pity Thyrsis to my pain, No more my heart reprove." Five strophes beseeched a "heav'nly maid" for "A Med'cine to remove / The cruel pangs . . . from unsuccessful love."[34] The overt physicality of the original verses was replaced by the image of tentative love emerging like a flower in need of care. "Thyrsis" demonstrates how Hudson prepared a song from the public gardens for the genteel space of the drawing room by replacing visceral images with less vivid pastoral metaphors that nevertheless suggested sentiments of love.

An ebullient example of Hudson's song style for public celebration is the "Song on Nelson's Glorious Victory," a shower of praise following the Battle of the Nile in August 1798.[35] This topical song provides a vibrant contrast to the polite *amour* of "Thyrsis." The sturdy tune, with its rising scales, cheers of "Huzza," and frequent unisons, seems to embody an English nation united during the glory days of the British Navy (musical example 15.2). Simple but memorable

Musical Example 15.2 Hudson, "Song on Nelson's Glorious Victory," *Lady's Magazine* 29 (October 1798).

Musical Example 15.2 (*Continued*)

melodic phrases sung in unison, such as "Let three times three ascend the sky," were a feature of Hudson's patriotic numbers in the magazine. These national and occasional songs engaged British subjects far from the centers of political or military power, and contributed to a shared sense of Englishness. If not political enfranchisement, the song at least offered recognition that women, too, shared in the national dialogue and celebration of British identity.

A departure from chaste music in the *Lady's Magazine* came from the tradition of music clubs, in which gentlemen convened for dinner, wine, and a cappella glees and catches. Women could not be members, although some clubs presented an annual "Ladies Night."[36] Hudson may have wanted to extend the practice of part-songs and canzonets to women and men at home, but catches were notorious for their naughty lyrics. "On Music," a catch by organist John Alcock Jr. (ca. 1740–1791), afforded a fresh, lively piece for domestic music making that stopped short of overstepping proprieties without altering John Oldham's 1685 ode, "For an Anniversary of Musick Kept upon St. Cecilia's Day" (musical example 15.3).[37] The first voice sings the opening twelve-measure phrase, indicated "1" ("Music does all our joys refine . . ."), then proceeds to phrase "2" ("'Tis that gives rapture . . .") as the next voice begins phrase "1," and so on. The setting could be described as a round rather than a catch, because there are no "hocketing" rests within phrases that allow humorously inappropriate words from other parts to pop up unexpectedly during silences.[38] The glees and catches in the magazine show that Hudson chose carefully to enlarge the range of acceptable domestic music with men's semiprivate club repertoire.

Elizabeth Turner was the only significant woman composer identified by name in the magazine.[39] Probably born during the 1720s, she was a soprano soloist in London concerts and oratorios from 1744 until her death in July 1756.[40] Hudson and Turner certainly knew each other by professional reputation; indeed, Turner subscribed to one of Hudson's *Myrtle* collections. They were performers well known in London venues, and they may have sung together in oratorios in the early 1750s. Turner self-published two books of songs in 1750 and 1756 with impressive lists of subscribers.[41] Although they were not entered for copyright protection at Stationers' Hall, her collections were never reprinted, nor were her works included

Musical Example 15.3 Alcock, "On Music," *Lady's Magazine* 12 (December 1781).

in eighteenth-century vocal anthologies. Between 1782 and 1797, eight of Turner's songs appeared in the *Lady's Magazine*, sometimes more than once. Her music had been out of circulation for decades when Hudson incorporated her songs into the periodical, possibly to present the example of a woman composer to the magazine's many female readers. Turner's creative voice was effectively silenced until her remarkable second life in the pages of the *Lady's Magazine*.

The songs came from Turner's 1756 *Collection of Songs with Symphonies and a Through Bass with Six Lessons for the Harpsichord*.[42] "Phillis with Her Enchant-

Musical Example 15.4 Turner, "A Song, the Words by a Lady; and Set to Music by the Late Miss E. Turner," *Lady's Magazine* 13 (July 1782), mm. 9–20.

ing Voice"—Song VI from the collection—was the first of Turner's songs published in the *Lady's Magazine*, inserted in July 1782 and again in 1786 and 1795.[43] The anonymous poetry "by a Lady" expressed typical pastoral sentiments, but Turner's setting was elegant and melodious, as seen in the phrases that begin the first stanza (musical example 15.4). With its ornamental graces for harpsichord and voice, the song was an antique in the *stile galant* of three decades earlier. Hudson omitted the figured bass indications from Turner's songs in the magazine, and the eight-measure keyboard introduction disappeared in the 1786 and 1795 reprints, but the lyrical flow of the vocal line and the smooth counterpoint between treble and bass remained intact. Her songs exemplify the English tradition of deceptively simple, tuneful melodies in repeated halves, rather than the typical da capo form of Italian opera arias.

Turner is one of the composers found most often in the periodical after Handel and Hudson. By reprinting her songs, Hudson honored and perpetuated the memory of a respected fellow musician as he did for such colleagues as Boyce and Howard.[44] Through Hudson's efforts, the *Lady's Magazine* embraced not only a range of repertoires, but also contained the most serious and historic music of any literary miscellany in eighteenth-century Britain. Hudson's replacement, William Barre Jr., didn't abandon the historical approach, but he failed to retain his predecessor's success.[45] Barre's songs were numerous in the *Lady's Magazine* during 1801 and 1802, but music publication in the *Lady's Magazine* terminated abruptly during 1805 and never resumed as a monthly feature. This change followed a trend as fashion and domestic skills eclipsed education in the magazine and as sentimental fiction replaced historical or moral essays. But new English periodicals for women—the *Ladies' Monthly Museum* (1798–1832) and *La Belle Assemblée* (1806–1837)—carried the tradition of music inserts into the Regency period after the dowager *Lady's Magazine* discontinued the practice.[46]

In an era when fashions came and went with each season, Hudson's thirty-year legacy of music in the *Lady's Magazine* was no small achievement. Through the agency of the *Lady's Magazine*, Hudson relocated selected public musics into the drawing room and allowed nonprofessional music lovers to perform some repertoire that career musicians staged in British centers of culture and privileged male amateurs enjoyed in semiprivate societies. Rarely a mere embellishment, music in the *Lady's Magazine* intertwined pleasure with pedagogy, partaking of both public and private as the magazine mingled historical with musical streams from the city venues of concert stage, theater, pleasure gardens, and recreational music clubs for the consumption and education of magazine enthusiasts and listeners.

Appendix

Named or confirmed composers of music published in Robinson's edition of *Lady's Magazine*, 1770–1805, with number of occurrences, year(s), and specific sources (oratorio, ode, opera, play, masque) as identified in the *Lady's Magazine*.

Alcock, J[ohn], younger (ca. 1740–1791)
    1: 1781

Arne, Dr. Thomas A[ugustine] (1710–1778)
    5: 1789-2 (*Alfred, Eliza*); 1802 (*Alfred*); 1804 (*As You Like It*); 1805 (*Abel*)

Baildon, Mr. [Joseph] (1727–1774)
    3: 1775-2; 1788

Barre, William, junior   (*fl.* 1790–1805)
    37: 1791; 1794; 1800-2; 1801-5; 1802-8; 1803-10; 1804-6; 1805-4

Bates, William (ca. 1720–1790)
    1: 1794

Boyce, Dr. [William] (1711–1779)
    7: 1782-4; 1789 (*Solomon*); 1797 (*The Chaplet*); 1798 (*The Chaplet*)

Brewer, Thomas (1611–ca. 1665)
    1: 1790

Chapman, Richard, of Portsmouth
    1: 1777

Chard, George (1765–1849)
    1: 1783

Corri, D[omenico] (1746–1825)
    1: 1805

Finch, Miss
    1: 1804

Ford, Thomas (ca. 1580–1648)
    1: 1789

Giardini, [Felice] (1716-1796)
    1: 1800

Gidley, C.
    1: 1775

Gluck, [Christoph Willibald von] (1714–1787)
    1: 1775 (*Iphigénie*)

Greene, Dr. [Maurice] (1696–1755)
    10: 1775; 1786; 1794-3; 1795-5

Handel, Mr. [George Frideric] (1685-1759)
    107: 1776-4 (*Jephtha, Semele, Samson, Judas Maccabaeus*); 1777-2 (*Judas Maccabaeus, Susanna*); 1778-5 (*Judas Maccabaeus, Esther, Joshua, Hercules,*

Theodora); 1779-4 (*Alexander Balus, Acis and Galatea, Occasional Oratorio*); 1781-2 (*Saul, Samson*); 1782-2 (*Choice of Hercules*-2); 1783 (*Deborah*); 1784-3 (*Messiah, Samson, Semele*); 1785-7 (*L'Allegro, il Penseroso, ed il Moderato*-2, *Deborah, Alexander Balus*-2, *Saul, Samson*); 1786-4 (*Saul, Occasional Oratorio, Susannah*-2); 1787-10 (*Deborah, Occasional Oratorio, Alexander's Feast, Hercules, Judas Maccabaeus, Saul, Susanna, Semele, Additional Oratorio, Time and Truth*); 1788-5 (*Jephtha, Alexander Balus, Messiah, Joseph*); 1789-6 (*Messiah*-2, *L'Allegro*-3, *Esther*); 1790-7 (*Messiah, Alexander's Feast, Solomon, Redemption*); 1791-7 (*Occasional Oratorio, Acis and Galatea*-2, *Semele, Esther; Theodora, Saul*); 1792-6 (*Saul*-2, *Susanna*-2, *Alexander Balus*); 1793-10 (*Susanna*-2, *Dryden's Ode, Judas Maccabaeus*-2, *Esther, Theodore, Jephtha*-2, *Saul*); 1794-5 (*Occasional Oratorio*-2, *Joshua, Semele, Saul*); 1795-2 (*Saul, Deborah*); 1797-3 (*Judas Maccabaeus, Alexander's Feast, Joshua*; 1798-6 (*Saul, Solomon, Susannah, Choice of Hercules, Occasional Oratorio*); 1799-2 *Hercules, Susanna*); 1800-2 (*Alexander Balus*); 1805-2
Hawkins
1: 1780

Hawkins, Captain A., of the North Devon Regiment
3: 1783-2; 1788

Haydn, [Franz Josef] (1732–1809)
1: 1800

Henly, Mr. Rev. [Henley, Phocion] (1728–1764)
1: 1778

Hilton, Mr. [John, younger] (ca. 1599–1657)
2: 1775-2

Hoare, Mr. R.
1: 1776

Hodgson, Mr. Philip, of Newcastle
10: 1773-3; 1774-2; 1775-2; 1776; 1777-2

Howard, Dr. [Samuel] (1718–1782)
14: 1782-2; 1793; 1796-2; 1798; 1799-8

Hudson, Mr. [Robert] (1732–1815)
142: 1770-5; 1771-14; 1772-9; 1773-7; 1774-9; 1775-6; 1776-4; 1777-4; 1778-4; 1779-6; 1780-10; 1781-8; 1782-2; 1783-4; 1784-5; 1785-4; 1786-2; 1787-2; 1788-6; 1789-1; 1790-2; 1791-2; 1792-2; 1793-1; 1795-5; 1796-7; 1797-4; 1798-5; 1799-2

Ives, Simon (1600–1662)
1: 1784

King, Mr. C[harles] (1687–1748)
    1: 1775

Laws [Lawes], William (1602–1645)
    1: 1794

Major, Joseph (1771–1829)
    1: 1804

Martini, Vincenzio [Vicente Martin y Soler] (1754–1806)
    1: 1801

Morgan, Mr.
    1: 1773

Morley, Thomas (1557–1602)
    5: 1775; 1776; 1783; 1792; 1794

Mozart, [Wolfgang Amadeus] (1756–1791)
    2: 1800-2

Pring, Joseph, late chorister of St. Paul's Cathedral
    1: 1792

Purcell, Henry (1659–1695)
    3: 1786; 1787; 1792

Ravenscroft, Mr. [Thomas] (ca. 1592–ca. 1635)
    2: 1790-2

Reichardt, [Johann Friederich] (1752–1814)
    2: 1801

Reynolds, Mr.
    1: 1797

Rogers, Dr. [Benjamin] (1614–1698)
    2: 1786; 1789

Scarlatti [sic]
    1: 1804

Shaw, Mr., of Bath
    1: 1777

Shield, Mr. J[ohn], Jr.
    4: 1780; 1781; 1784; 1791

Shield, Mr. William (1748–1809)
9: 1774-2; 1778-2; 1801; 1802; 1803; 1804; 1805

Shield, Mr. [William?]
7: 1783; 1784; 1786-2; 1800-2; 1801

Stone, J., Organist at Marlborough; Organist of Farringdon, Berks.
8: 1777; 1778; 1779-3; 1780; 1796-2

Tenducci, Seignior [sic; Giusto Ferdinando] (ca. 1735–1790)
1: 1800

Travers, John (ca. 1703–1758)
4: 1775; 1786; 1789; 1792

Turner, Miss Eliza[beth] (d. 1756)
13: 1782-2; 1783; 1784; 1785; 1786; 1788; 1795; 1796-2; 1797-3

[Weelkes, Thomas] (1576–1623)
1: 1790

Wright, T[homas], of Stockton-upon-Tees (1763–1829)
1: 1791

Notes

1. The *Lady's Magazine* adopted large, folding music inserts like those included with the *Court Miscellany* (London, 1765–1771). Since the oversize inserts were not secured in the monthly issues, the music is frequently missing or misbound in library holdings. The most satisfactory source to see music in the *Lady's Magazine* is the microfilm series *Women Advising Women*, Part 3 (1770–1800) and Part 4 (1801–1832), based on holdings from the British Library, Cambridge University, and Birmingham Central Library. While the music supplement sheets are often missing, the song inserts have been photographed in full in *Women Advising Women*. Music leaves have not been opened and scanned in the digitized volumes of *Lady's Magazine* available in the HathiTrust Digital Library, Europeana Collections, and Google Books.

2. The music sheets were not copperplate engravings, but typeset for the magazine, with frequent errors, by the London firm of Bigg & Cox. "Omrah Restored" was a short story set in the Middle East.

3. After 1832, the magazine continued as *The Lady's Magazine and Museum of Belles Lettres*, then as *The Court Magazine and Monthly Critic, and Ladies' Magazine and Museum of Belles Lettres* from 1838 to 1847.

4. Batchelor, "'Connections which Are of Service,'" 247. See also Adburgham, *Women in Print*, 128–158, and Marks, "Lady's Magazine, The." The University of Kent is conducting a research project titled "The *Lady's Magazine* (1770–1818): Understanding the Emergence of a Genre," with website http://blogs.kent.ac.uk/ladys-magazine/category/content/, accessed August 15, 2015. An index of music in the magazine prepared by me will appear as part of this project.

5. See Ritchie's chapter 2, "Women's Occasion for Music," in *Women Writing Music*, 57–86.

6. Miller, "A Mirror of Ages Past," 883–901. The term *magazine music* was in occasional use by the mid-nineteenth century, as in *Sartain's Union Magazine of Literature and Art*, 8 (1851): 133. The data on magazine music cited throughout this essay comes from the author's index of music in British monthly miscellanies to 1800, based on collections at preeminent British, Irish, and American libraries; microfilm series *English Literary Periodicals, Early British Periodicals, Women Advising Women, Early English Newspapers, History of Women*; and subscription databases *Eighteenth Century Collections Online, British Periodicals Collection I and II*, and *Eighteenth Century Journals*.

7. Laurie and Price, "Motteux, Peter Anthony," *GMO* (accessed November 27, 2013). See also "Index to the Songs and Musical Allusions in *The Gentleman's Journal*, 1692–4"; and Radice's "Henry Purcell's Contributions to *The Gentleman's Journal*, Part I," and "Henry Purcell's Contributions to *The Gentleman's Journal*, Part II."

8. Barker, "Cave, Edward (1691–1754)," *DNB* (accessed May 2, 2014). See Italia, *The Rise of Literary Journalism in the Eighteenth Century*, 110–122.

9. By contrast, the essay serial or periodical essay contained the work of one author, often with a political slant, such as Joseph Addison's and Richard Steele's *Spectator* (1711–1714). Reviewing journals such as the *Monthly Review* (1749–1844) published abstracts and excerpts of scholarly or scientific material from learned books.

10. A note below the music for "The Charmer" stated, "N.B. This SONG is inserted by Desire," presumably meaning by request of a reader, in *Gentleman's Magazine* 7 (1737): 626.

11. Few earlier serials written for or by women, such as *The Female Tatler* (1709–1710) and *The Lady's Curiosity* (1738), lasted more than a season or two. See Adburgham's chronological list in *Women in Print*, 273–281.

12. Fitzpatrick, "J. Coote," 57–65.

13. Coote sold the magazine to George Robinson and John Roberts in April 1771, without informing John Wheble, who continued to print monthly issues. The court decided for Robinson but permitted Wheble to continue his edition of the magazine, which lasted until the end of 1772. See Batchelor, http://blogs.kent.ac.uk/ladys-magazine/tag/john-wheble/ (accessed August 15, 2015).

14. Front matter, *Wheble's Lady's Magazine* 3 (1772).

15. Ritchie, *Women Writing Music*, 11.

16. Ibid., 81–86.

17. Picard, describing songs in the *Gentleman's Magazine*, in *Dr. Johnson's London*, 245; and Head, "Music for the Fair Sex," 244.

18. Opinion regarding music study by boys was codified in the Earl of Chesterfield's letter of April 19, 1749, warning his son not to play an instrument, as it was "frivolous, contemptible, and takes up a great deal of time, which might be much better employed" (Stanhope, *Letters to His Son by the Earl of Chesterfield*, vol. 1, 170).

19. Essex, *The Young Ladies Conduct*, 85.

20. The vicar choral was a layperson who chanted portions of the liturgy. Hudson was honored for his long service by internment in St. Paul's. Husk and Gifford, "Hudson, Robert," *GMO* (accessed September 17, 2007). See Spink, "Music, 1660–1800," 392–398; Dawe, *Organists of the City of London*, 5–7.

21. The appendix does not include the music sheets from April 1771 until the end of 1772 in the edition of the *Lady's Magazine* printed by Wheble (see endnote 13).

22. Many *Lady's Magazine* songs were reprinted in Alexander Hogg's pirated imitation, the *New Lady's Magazine; Or, Polite and Entertaining Companion for the Fair Sex* (London, 1786–1795). Songs in Hogg's periodical were newly typeset on regular magazine pages that are

rarely absent from library holdings; thus, the copycat magazine provides music sometimes missing from volumes of *Lady's Magazine*.

23. The Joly Collection at the National Library of Ireland and the Harvard Theatre Collection contain many song sheets taken from London miscellanies. Jane Austen's music books lack any song sheets extracted from the *Lady's Magazine*, although there is some overlap of titles by Handel (Gammie and McCulloch, *Jane Austen's Music*).

24. Examples include "Total Eclipse" from *Samson* and "Angels Ever Bright and Fair" from *Theodora*.

25. The annual "Directions to the Binder" indicate that music was to be bound in or near the poetry section, but song sheets were sometimes placed at the beginning or end of the monthly issue or annual volume.

26. Like her husband, Mrs. Hudson sang at the pleasure gardens, and their daughter, Mary Hudson (ca. 1758–1801), worked as a musician and organist in London (St. Olave Hart Street) from 1781 until her death (Dawe, *Organists of the City of London*, 4; Robins, *Catch and Glee Culture*, 49–50). Mr. Hudson and Miss Hudson were listed as chorus members for the Handel commemoration concerts in Burney's *Account of the Musical Performances in Westminster-Abbey and the Pantheon*, 19–20.

27. Bennett, *Letters to a Young Lady*, vol. 1, 151.

28. Vocal music from the sixteenth and early seventeenth centuries was cited as "ancient music" by the Academy of Vocal Musick in 1726, later called the Academy of Ancient Music. In 1776, the "Concert of Antient Music" broadened the practice to include music composed more than twenty years earlier. Tim Eggington traces the historical movement in *The Advancement of Music in Enlightenment England*.

29. Burney, "Effects of Ancient Music," *Lady's Magazine* 7 (1776): 81–84, 126–129, and 206–209. Hawkins, "Anecdotes of Mr. Handel," *Lady's Magazine* 7 (1766): 699–700. Hawkins, "On the Marvellous Power and Effects of Ancient Music," *Lady's Magazine* 9 (1778): 321–323, 510–512, and 707–711. See also Aspden, "Disseminating and Domesticating Handel," this volume.

30. Hudson also composed hymns and liturgical music, but the majority of entries in the British Library *Catalogue of Printed Music* are items located in, or extracted from, the magazine.

31. Hudson, "Thyrsis," *Lady's Magazine* 16 (1785), following p. 664 in *Women Advising Women* microfilm, Part 3, reel 8.

32. Hudson published three undated sets titled *The Myrtle*, the third of which specified, "A Collection of Songs sung at Ranelagh." "Love at First Sight" was presented in *The Myrtle*, both as a solo air, 11–12, and duetto, 13.

33. Hudson rarely included figured bass in the *Lady's Magazine* after 1790. Song sheets with figured bass had been common in literary miscellanies, and figures can be seen as late as the 1790s, as in "Urbani's Celebrated Rondeau," *Aberdeen Magazine* 4 (1791): 499–501.

34. Significant errors occur in "Thyrsis" from *Lady's Magazine* when compared to "Love at First Sight" in *The Myrtle*, digitized from GB-Lbl G.806.g.(13) in the Petrucci Music Library at www.imslp.org. The magazine imprint has A-flat in the treble in m. 14 ("when"), but "Love at First Sight" uses E-flat, as in the opening ritornello. The treble in "Thyrsis" uses A-natural in m. 28, when "Love at First Sight" has A-flat. The bass in m. 31 of "Thyrsis" begins with A-flat, resulting in parallel fifths with the treble, whereas the bass resolves upward to E-flat in "Love at First Sight."

35. Hudson, "Song on Nelson's Glorious Victory," *Lady's Magazine* 29 (1798), following p. 472 in *Women Advising Women*, Part 3, reel 14.

36. Robins, "The Catch and Glee in Provincial England," 147–148.

37. Alcock, "On Music," *Lady's Magazine* 12 (1781), following p. 664 in *Women Advising Women*, Part 3, reel 6.

38. Rubin, *English Glee in the Reign of George III*, 196.

39. The other example definitely composed by a woman was "The Negro's Complaint ... Music by a Female Correspondent—an Amateur," *Lady's Magazine* 24 (1793). The attribution in August 1804, "A Patriotic Song. By Miss Finch," could refer either to the music or to the poetic text.

40. Yelloly presents the known facts and social context in "'The Ingenious Miss Turner,'" 72–75.

41. Yelloly discusses Turner's subscribers, ibid., 68–69, as does Ritchie, *Women Writing Music*, 66–76.

42. Turner's 1756 collection can be viewed in the Petrucci Music Library at www.imslp.org.

43. Turner, "A Song," in *Lady's Magazine* 13 (1782), following p. 368 in *Women Advising Women*, Part 3, reel 6; "Song," in *Lady's Magazine* 17 (1786), following p. 380 in *Women Advising Women*, Part 3, reel 8; and "Song for the *Lady's Magazine*," in *Lady's Magazine* 26 (1795), following p. 432 in *Women Advising Women*, Part 3, reel 13. The 1795 song sheet is available in the HathiTrust Digital Library, accessed August 15, 2015.

44. While elegiac poets had stressed her beauty, voice, and virtue, Hudson included her songs without comment, thereby granting Turner the same respect that he extended to male colleagues, rather than following "the cult of the beautiful dead," described by Head in "Cultural Meanings for Women Composers," 231 and 233.

45. He was probably the William Barre who entered psalm and hymn tunes at Stationers' Hall in 1800 (Kassler, *Music Entries at Stationers' Hall*, 437 and 442).

46. *La Belle Assemblée* contained regular music sheets from 1806 and *Lady's Monthly Museum* from 1816.

Selected Bibliography

Manuscripts

B-Bc MS 1035
B-Bc MS XY 15148
D-Hs MS ND VI 3193
GB-AB Brogyntyn MS 27
GB-AB SD/Ch/B28 [*Collecteanea Menevensia*, vol. 2] http://www.llgc.org.uk/index
.php?id=collectaneamenevensia
GB-CA MSS 1a
GB-CA MSS 9–11
GB-Cfm Mu MS 118
GB-Cfm Mu MS 163, part F
GB-Cfm Mu MS 685
GB-Ckc Rowe MS 1
GB-Cmc MS 2591
GB-Cssc MS 59
GB-Cu MS Dd.2.11
GB-Cu MS Dd.5.78.3
GB-Cu MS Dd.9.33
GB-Cu MS Nn.6.36
GB-ERO MS D/DP E2/1
GB-ERO MS D/DP Z6/1
GB-Eu MSS R.d. 58–61
GB-Ge R.d.58–61
GB-GL MSS 106–7, 109–12
GB-Lbl Add. MS 4910
GB-Lbl Add. MS 11608
GB-Lbl Add. MS 17801
GB-Lbl Add. MSS 18936–9
GB-Lbl Add. MS 19759
GB-Lbl Add. MS 27738
GB-Lbl Add. MS 29396
GB-Lbl Add. MS 29397
GB-Lbl Add. MS 30382
GB-Lbl Add. MS 30931–3
GB-Lbl Add. MS 30933
GB-Lbl Add. MS 31403
GB-Lbl Add. MS 31431
GB-Lbl Add. MS 31452
GB-Lbl Add. MS 33234
GB-Lbl Add. MS 33235
GB-Lbl Add. MS 33240

GB-Lbl Egerton MS 2013
GB-Lbl Egerton MS 3691
GB-Lbl G. 201
GB-Lbl G.806.g.(13)
GB-Lbl Harley MS 6726
GB-Lbl Harley MS 6766
GB-Lbl Harley MS 6868
GB-Lbl Harley MS 6910
GB-Lbl Lansdowne MS 213
GB-Lbl Lansdowne MS 241
GB-Lbl MS Mus. 1625
GB-Lbl Roxburghe MS 1.190–191
GB-Lbl Roxburghe MS 2.367
GB-Lcm MS 1106
GB-Lcm MS 2036
GB-Lg MS Safe 3
GB-Llp MS 1040
GB-Ob Douce 280
GB-Ob G. A. Surrey c.21
GB-Ob MS D.19(4)
GB-Ob MS Mus.c.107
GB-Ob MS Mus. Sch. c. 40
GB-Ob MS Mus. Sch. E. 429
GB-Ob Mus. e. 1–5
GB-Ob Tenbury MS 1232
GB-Lbl Add. MS 33240
GB-Och Mus. 92
GB-Och Mus. 1003
GB-Och Mus. 1113
GB-Och Mus. 1176
GB-Och Mus. 1177
GB-Och Mus. 1236
GB-TNA C31/247/39
GB-TNA C31/247/81
GB-TNA ADM 106/482/302
GB-TNA HCA 26/3/111
GB-TNA SP 110/16
GB-TNA SP 110/21
GB-TNA SP 110/73
J-Tn, N-3/35
US-LAuc MS fC6966/M4/A627/1700
US-NH Filmer MS 17
US-NH Filmer MS 21
US-NH Filmer MS 32
US-NYp Drexel MS 4041
US-NYp Drexel MS 4257

PRINTED MATERIALS

Abbate, Carolyn. "Music: Drastic or Gnostic?" *Critical Inquiry* 30, no. 3 (Spring 2004): 505–536.

Aberdeen Magazine, Literary Chronicle and Review. Aberdeen: 1788–1791. In *Eighteenth Century Collections Online.* Gale. ECP.

The Accession and Coronation and Marriage of Mary Tudor as Related in Fours Manuscripts of the Escorial. Translated by C. V. Malfatti. Barcelona: C. V. Malfatti, 1956.

Adburgham, Alison. *Women in Print: Writing Women and Women's Magazines from the Restoration to the Accession of Victoria.* London: Allen and Unwin, 1972.

Agrippa von Nettesheim, Henry Cornelius. *Of the Vanitie and Uncertaintie of the Artes and Sciences.* Translated by J. Sanford. London, 1575.

Albertus Bryne: Keyboard Music, Terence Charlston: Harpsichord, Organ and Spinet. Deux-Elles Classical Recordings DXL1124, 2008.

Allen, Brian. "The Landscape." In *Vauxhall Gardens*, edited by T. J. Edelstein, 17–24. New Haven, CT: Yale Center for British Art, 1983.

Altick, Richard D. *The English Common Reader: A Social History of the Mass Reading Public, 1800–1900*, 2nd ed. Columbus: Ohio State University Press, 1998.

"Amateur, n." *OED* (accessed July 3, 2014).

Amussen, Susan Dwyer. *An Ordered Society*: Gender and Class in Early Modern England. Oxford, UK: Blackwell, 1988.

Anne Cromwell's Virginal Book, 1638, transcribed and edited by Howard Ferguson. Oxford, UK: Oxford University Press, 1974.

Anon. [John Lockman?]. *The Turkish Paradise or Vaux-Hall Gardens: Wrote at Vaux-Hall Last Summer.* London, 1741.

Arblaster, Paul. *Antwerp & the World: Richard Verstegan and the International Culture of Catholic Reformation.* Leuven, Belgium: University of Leuven, 2004.

———. "The Infanta and the English Benedictine Nuns, Mary Percy's Memories in 1634." *Recusant History* 23 (1997): 508–557.

Arendt, Hannah. *The Human Condition.* Chicago: University of Chicago Press, 1958.

Ariès, Philippe. "Introduction." In *A History of Private Life*, vol. 3: *Passions of the Renaissance*, edited by Roger Chartier and translated by Arthur Goldhammer, 1–12. Cambridge, MA: Belknap, 1989.

Armstrong, Nancy. "The Rise of the Domestic Woman." In *The Ideology of Conduct: Essays on Literature and the History of Sexuality*, edited by Nancy Armstrong and Leonard Tennenhouse, 96–139. London: Methuen, 1987.

Aspden, Suzanne. "'Fam'd Handel Breathing, though Transform'd to Stone': The Composer as Monument." *Journal of the American Musicological Society* 55 (2002): 39–90.

———. "Henry Carey (1687–1743)." *DNB* (accessed July 7, 2016).

———. *The Rival Sirens: Performance and Identity on Handel's Operatic Stage.* Cambridge, UK: Cambridge University Press, 2013.

———. "Sancta Cæcilia Rediviva." *Cambridge Opera Journal* 27, no. 3 (2015): 263–287.

Attridge, Derek. *Well-Weighed Syllables.* Cambridge, UK: Cambridge University Press, 1974.

Aubrey, John. *Brief Lives, Chiefly of Contemporaries*, edited by Andrew Clark. Oxford, UK: Clarendon, 1898.

———. *Remaines of Gentilisme and Judaisme.* London: Pub[lished] for the Folk-lore Society by W. Satchell, Peyton, 1881.
Austern, Linda Phyllis. "'Alluring the Auditorie to Effeminacie': Music and the Idea of the Feminine in Early Modern England." *Music & Letters* 74, no. 3 (1993): 343–354.
———. "Domestic Song and the Circulation of Masculine Social Energy in Early Modern England." In *Gender and Song in Early Modern England*, edited by Leslie C. Dunn and Katherine R. Larson, 123–138. Farnham, UK: Ashgate, 2014.
———. "'For, Love's a Good Musician': Performance, Audition and Erotic Disorders in Early Modern Europe." *Musical Quarterly* 82 (1998): 614–653.
———. "'For Musicke Is the Handmaid of the Lord': Women, Psalms, and Domestic Music-Making in Early Modern England." In *Psalms in the Early Modern World*, edited by Linda Phyllis Austern, Kari Boyd McBride, and David L. Orvis, 77–114. Farnham, UK: Ashgate, 2011.
———. *Music in English Children's Drama of the Later Renaissance.* Philadelphia: Gordon and Breach Science, 1992.
———. "The Music in the Play." In *The Oxford Shakespeare: Othello*, edited by Michael Neill, 445–454. Oxford, UK: Oxford University Press, 2008.
———, ed. *Music, Sensation, and Sensuality.* New York: Routledge, 2002.
———. "Nature, Culture, Myth, and the Musician in Early Modern England." *Journal of the American Musicological Society* 51 (1998): 1–47.
———. "'Sing Againe Syren': The Female Musician and Sexual Enchantment in Elizabethan Life and Literature." *Renaissance Quarterly* 42 (1989): 420–448.
———. "The Siren, the Muse, and the God of Love: Music and Gender in Seventeenth-Century English Emblem Books." *Journal of Musicological Research* 18, no. 2 (1999): 95–138.
———. "Women's Musical Voices in Sixteenth-Century England." *Early Modern Women: An Interdisciplinary Journal* 3 (2008): 127–152.
Austern, Linda, and Inna Naroditskaya, eds. *Music of the Sirens.* Bloomington: Indiana University Press, 2006.
Authentic Memoirs of that Exquisitely Villanous Jesuit, Father Richard Walpole. London: William Williams, 1733.
Bach, Carl Philipp Emanuel. *Sechs Clavier-Sonaten für Kenner und Liebhaber.* Leipzig, Germany: Im Verlag des Autors, 1779.
Backschneider, Paula. *Spectacular Politics: Theatrical Power and Mass Culture in Early Modern England.* Baltimore: Johns Hopkins University Press, 1993.
Bailey, Candace. "Blurring the Lines: *Elizabeth Rogers hir Virginall Book* in Context." *Music & Letters* 89 (2008): 510–546.
———. "English Keyboard Music, c. 1625–1680." PhD diss., Duke University, 1992.
———. "Keyboard Music in the Hands of Edward Lowe and Richard Goodson I: Oxford, Christ Church Mus. 1176 and Mus. 1177." *Royal Musical Association Research Chronicle* 32 (1999): 119–135.
———. *Seventeenth-Century British Keyboard Sources.* Warren, MI: Harmonie Park, 2003.
———. "William Ellis and the Transmission of Continental Keyboard Repertories in Early Restoration England." *Journal of Musicological Research* 20 (2001): 211–242.

Baldwin, Olive, and Thelma Wilson. "Music in the Birthday Celebrations at Court in the Reign of Queen Anne: A Documentary Calendar." *A Handbook for Studies in 18th-Century English Music* 19 (2008): 1–24.

———. "The Subscription Musick of 1703–04," *The Musical Times* 153, no. 1921 (2012): 29–44.

Bale, John. "Three Laws." In *The Complete Plays of John Bale II*, edited by Peter Happé, 65–124. Cambridge, UK: D. S. Brewer, 1986.

A Ballad of the Life and Deathe of Dr. Faustus, the Great Cungerer. London, 1589.

Ballard, Jean Baptiste Christophe. *Meilleurs airs italiens.* [Paris, 1721.]

———. *Les menuets chantants, surtous les tons*, 2 vols. [Paris, 1725.]

Ballaster, Rosalind. *Women's Worlds: Ideology, Femininity, and the Woman's Magazine.* Houndmills, UK: Macmillan, 1991.

Bargrave, Robert. *The Travel Diary of Robert Bargrave, Levant Merchant 1647–1656*, edited by Michael Brennan. London: The Hakluyt Society, 1999.

Barker, Anthony David. "Cave, Edward (1691–1754)." *DNB* (accessed May 2, 2014).

[Barksdale, Clement]. *Nympha Libethris: Or the Cotswold Muse.* Worcester, 1651.

Barley, William. *A New Booke of Tabliture.* London: William Barley, 1596.

Barre, Dianne. "Sir Samuel Hellier (1736–84) and His Garden Buildings: Part of the Midlands 'Garden Circuit' in the 1760s–70s?" *Garden History* 36 (2008): 310–327.

Batchelor, Jennie. "'Connections, which Are of Service . . . in a More Advanced Age': *The Lady's Magazine*, Community, and Women's Literary Histories." *Tulsa Studies in Women's Literature* 30, no. 2 (2011): 245–267.

Batchiler, John. *The Virgin's Pattern in the Exemplory Life and Death of Mrs Susanna Perwich.* London, 1661.

Bate, Jonathan, and Eric Rasmussen, eds. *William Shakespeare and Others: Collaborative Plays.* London: Palgrave Macmillan, 2013.

Bateson, Thomas. *The Second Set of Madrigales.* London, 1618.

Bathe, William. *A Briefe Introduction to the Skill of Song*, edited by Kevin C. Karnes. Aldershot, UK: Ashgate, 2005.

Beal, Peter. *In Praise of Scribes: Manuscripts and Their Makers in Seventeenth-Century England.* Oxford, UK: Oxford University Press, 1998.

Beales, A. C. F. *Education under Penalty: English Catholic Education from the Reformation to the Fall of James II, 1547–1689.* London: Athlone, 1963.

Beetham, Margaret. *A Magazine of Her Own: Domesticity and Desire in the Woman's Magazine, 1800–1914.* London: Routledge, 1996.

La Belle Assemblée, or Court and Fashionable Magazine. London: 1806–1832. In *Early British Periodicals.* Ann Arbor, MI: University Microfilms; also in *British Periodicals.* ProQuest. ECP.

Bellingham, Bruce. "The Musical Circle of Anthony Wood in Oxford during the Commonwealth and Restoration." *Journal of the Viola da Gamba Society of America* 39 (1982): 6–71.

Bennett, John. *Letters to a Young Lady, on a Variety of Useful and Interesting Subjects: Calculated to Improve the Heart, to Form the Manners, and Enlighten the Understanding.* London, 1789; Newburyport, MA: John Mycall, [1792]. HathiTrust Digital Archive (accessed November 21, 2013).

Bennett, John, and Pamela Willetts. "Richard Mico." *Chelys* 7 (1977): 24–46.

Benoit, Marcelle, and Éric Kocevar. "Farinel." *GMO* (accessed May 14, 2013).

Bentley, Gerald Eades Bentley. *The Jacobean and Caroline Stage*, 7 vols. Oxford, UK: Clarendon, 1941–1968.
Berger, Karol. "The Hand and the Art of Memory." *Musica Disciplina* (1981): 87–120.
Bermúdez, Egberto. "Urban Musical Life in the European Colonies: Examples from Spanish America, 1530–1650." In *Music and Musicians in Renaissance Cities and Towns*, edited by Fiona Kisby, 167–181. Cambridge, UK: Cambridge University Press, 2001.
Bevington, David. *Tudor Drama and Politics: A Critical Approach to Topical Meaning.* Cambridge, MA: Harvard University Press, 1968.
Bickham, George. *The Musical Entertainer*, 2 vols. London: Thomas Harper and J. Harper (vol. 1); London, 1739 (vol. 2).
Bicknall, Stephen. *The History of the English Organ.* Cambridge, UK: Cambridge University Press, 1996.
Bicks, Caroline. "Producing Girls on the English Stage: Performance as Pedagogy in Mary Ward's Convent Schools." In *Gender and Early Modern Constructions of Childhood*, edited by Naomi J. Miller and Naomi Yavneh, 139–153. Farnham, UK: Ashgate, 2010.
A Biographical Dictionary of English Court Musicians 1485–1714, 2 vols., edited by Andrew Ashbee and David Lasocki, assisted by Peter Holman and Fiona Kisby. Aldershot, UK: Ashgate, 1998.
Birchensha, John. *Writings on Music*, edited by Christopher D. S. Field and Benjamin Wardhaugh. Farnham, UK: Ashgate, 2010.
Black, Jeremy, ed. *Culture and Society in Britain 1660–1800.* Manchester, UK: Manchester University Press, 1997.
———. *The English Press in the Eighteenth Century.* Philadelphia: University of Pennsylvania Press, 1987.
———. *A Subject for Taste: Culture in Eighteenth-Century England.* London: Hambledon and London, 2005.
Blank, Paula. *Broken English: Dialects and the Politics of Language in Renaissance Writing.* London: Routledge, 1996.
Bloch, Ariel, and Chana Bloch. *The Song of Songs: A New Translation with an Introduction and Commentary.* New York: Random House, 1995; Berkeley: University of California Press, 1998.
Bloom, Gina. *Voices in Motion: Staging Gender, Shaping Sound in Early Modern England.* Philadelphia: University of Pennsylvania Press, 2007.
Blow, John. *A Second Musical Entertainment Perform'd on St. Cecilia's Day.* London, 1685.
Bold, John. "Privacy and the Plan." In *English Architecture Public and Private*, edited by John Bold and Edward Chaney, 107–119. London: Hambledon, 1993.
Bolzoni, Lina. *The Gallery of Memory: Literary and Iconographic Models in the Age of the Printing Press*, translated by Jeremy Parzen. Toronto: University of Toronto Press, 2001.
———. "The Play of Images: The Art of Memory from Its Origins to the Seventeenth Century." In *The Enchanted Loom: Chapters in the History of Neuroscience*, edited by Pietro Corsi, 16–65. New York: Oxford University Press, 1991.
Boorman, Stanley, et al. "Printing and Publishing of Music." *GMO* (accessed November 20, 2013).

Borsay, Peter. "Concert Topography and Provincial Towns in Eighteenth-Century England." In *Concert Life in Eighteenth-Century Britain*, edited by Susan Wollenberg and Simon McVeigh, 19–33. Aldershot, UK: Ashgate, 2004.
Bossuyt, Ignace. "The Art of Give and Take: Musical Relations between England and Flanders from the 15th to 17th Centuries." *The Low Countries: Arts and Society in Flanders and the Netherlands, a Yearbook* (1993-1994): 39–50.
Bottarelli, Giovanni Gualberto. *Sophonisba, a Serious Opera*. London, 1772.
Bownde, Nicholas. *The Doctrine of the Sabbath*. London, 1595.
Brathwaite, Richard. *Whimzies: or, a New Cast of Characters*. London, 1631.
Bray, Roger. "England I, 1485–1600." In *European Music 1520–1640*, edited by James Haar, 487–508. Woodbridge, UK: Boydell & Brewer, 2006.
———. "Sacred Music to Latin Texts." In *Music in Britain: The Sixteenth Century*, edited by Roger Bray, 46–93. Oxford, UK: Blackwell, 1995.
Brennan, Michael G. "Bargrave, Robert (1628–1661)." *DNB* (accessed July 18, 2013).
Brett, Philip. "'Blame Not the Printer': William Byrd's Publishing Drive, 1588–1591." In *A Byrd Celebration*, edited by Richard Turbet, 17–66. Richmond, VA: Church Music Association of America, 2008.
———, ed. *Consort Songs*. Musica Britannica, vol. 22. London: Stainer & Bell, 1967.
———. "Edward Paston (1550–1630): A Norfolk Gentleman and His Musical Collection." *Transactions of the Cambridge Bibliographical Society* 4 (1964): 51–69.
———, ed. *Gradualia I (1605): All Saints and Corpus Christi*. The Byrd Edition, vol. 6a. London: Stainer & Bell, 1991.
Brewer, John. "'The Most Polite Age and the Most Vicious': Attitudes toward Culture as a Commodity, 1660–1800." In *The Consumption of Culture 1600–1800: Image, Object, Text*, edited by Anne Bermingham and John Brewer, 341–361. London: Routledge, 1995.
Bridge, Frederick. *The Old Cryes of London*. London: Novello, 1921.
Brinsley, John. *Ludus literarius: or, the Grammar Schoole Shewing How to Proceede from the First Entrance into Learning, to the Highest Perfection Required in the Grammar Schooles, with Ease, Certainty and Delight both to Masters and Schollers; Onely According to Our Common Grammar, and Ordinary Classical Authours*. London, 1627.
Brokaw, Katherine Steele. "Music and Religious Compromise in John Bale's Plays." *Comparative Drama* 44, no. 3 (2010): 325–349.
Brome, Richard. *The Antipodes*, edited by Richard Cave. *Richard Brome Online* (http://www.hrionline.ac.uk/brome/).
———. *A Jovial Crew*, edited by Tiffany Stern. London: Bloomsbury, 2014.
———. *A Jovial Crew, or The Merry Beggars*, edited by Eleanor Lowe, Helen Ostovich, and Richard Cave. *Richard Brome Online* (http://www.hrionline.ac.uk/brome/).
———. *The Northern Lass*, edited by Julie Sanders. *Richard Brome Online* (http://www.hrionline.ac.uk/brome/).
Brookes, Virginia. *British Keyboard Music to c. 1660: Sources and Thematic Index*. Oxford, UK: Oxford University Press, 1996.
Brown, Alan. "England." In *Keyboard Music before 1700*, rev. ed., edited by Alexander Silbiger, 22–85. New York: Routledge, 2003.
Brown, David. "Jones, Robert (ii)." *GMO* (accessed November 21, 2013).

Brown, John. *Letters upon the Poetry and Music of the Italian Opera; Addressed to a Friend. By the Late Mr John Brown, Printer.* Edinburgh, Scotland: printed for Bell and Bradfute; London, 1789.
Brown, William. *Britannia's Pastorals. The Second Booke.* London, 1616.
Bryne, Albertus. *Keyboard Music.* Terence Charlston: Harpsichord, Organ, and Spinet. Deux-Elles Classical Recordings DXL1124, 2008, compact disc.
Bullokar, John. *An Englis[h] Expositor[:] Teaching the In[ter]pretation of the Harde[st] Words [vsed] in Our Language.* London, 1621.
———. *An English Expositour, or Compleat Dictionary.* Cambridge, UK, 1684.
Bruster, Douglas. "The Jailer's Daughter and the Politics of Madwomen's Language." *Shakespeare Quarterly* 46, no. 3 (1995): 277–300.
Buchanan, James. *Psalmorum Davidis paraphrasis poetica.* London, 1648.
Bucholz, R. O. *The Augustan Court: Queen Anne and the Decline of Court Culture.* Stanford, CA: Stanford University Press, 1993.
Burchell, Jenny. *Polite or Commercial Concerts?: Concert Management and Orchestral Repertoire in Edinburgh, Bath, Oxford, Manchester, and Newcastle, 1730–1799.* New York: Garland, 1996.
Burden, Michael. "Divas, Arias, and Acrimony: The Revolving Door of Musical Resources for London's Italian Opera." In *Theatrical Heritage: Challenges and Opportunities,* edited by Bruno Forment and Christel Stalpaert, 73–88. Leuven, Belgium: Leuven University Press, 2014.
———. "Eating and the Theatre." Oxford University Research Archive (http://ora.ox.ac.uk/objects/uuid:da693734-c18c-4330-b140-9460168529fa).
———. *Impresario and Diva: Regina Mingotti's Years at London's King's Theatre.* Royal Musical Association Monograph 22. Farnham, UK: Ashgate, 2013.
Burden, Michael, ed. *Italian Opera Aria on the London Stage 1705–1801.* http://italianaria.bodleian.ox.ac.uk.
———. *London Opera Observed 1711–1844.* 5 vols. London: Pickering & Chatto, 2013.
Burgess, Clive, and Andrew Wathey. "Mapping the Soundscape: Church Music in English Towns." *Early Music History* 19 (2000): 1–46.
Burke, Peter. "Publicizing the Private: The Rise of 'Secret History.'" In *Changing Perceptions of the Public Sphere,* edited by Christian J. Emden and David Midgley, 57–72. New York: Berghahn Books, 2012.
Burney, Charles. *An Account of the Musical Performances in Westminster-Abbey and the Pantheon, May 26th, 27th, 29th; and June the 3d, and 5th, 1784. In Commemoration of Handel.* London, 1785.
———. *A General History of Music,* 2 vols., edited by Frank Mercer. London: Foulis, 1935.
———. *A General History of Music, from the Earliest Ages to the Present Period,* 4 vols. London, 1776–1789.
———. "Linley, John [sic]." In *The Cyclopaedia,* 31 vols., edited by Abraham Rees. London: Longman, 1802–1820), vol. 21 (1812).
Burney, Frances. *The Early Journals and Letters of Fanny Burney,* edited by Lars E. Troide. Kingston, ON: McGill-Queen's University Press, 1990.
Burrows, Donald. *Handel.* Oxford, UK: Oxford University Press, 1994.
———. "John Walsh and His Handel Editions." In *Music and the Book Trade from the Sixteenth to the Twentieth Century,* edited by Robin Myers, Michael Harris, and

Giles Mandelbrote, 69–104. Newcastle, UK: Oak Knoll Press and the British Library, 2008.

———. "Sources for Oxford Handel Performance in the First Half of the Eighteenth Century." *Music & Letters* 61 (1980): 177–185.

Burrows, Donald, and Peter Ward Jones. "Musicians and Music Copyists in Mid-Eighteenth-Century Oxford." In *Concert Life in Eighteenth-Century Britain*, edited by Susan Wollenberg and Simon McVeigh, 115–139. Aldershot, UK: Ashgate, 2004.

Burrows, Donald, and Rosemary Dunhill, eds. *Music and Theatre in Handel's World: The Family Papers of James Harris, 1732–1780*. Oxford, UK: Oxford University Press, 2002.

Busse Berger, Anna Maria. *Medieval Music and the Art of Memory*. Berkeley: University of California Press, 2005.

Butler, Charles. *The Principles of Musik, in Setting and Singing*. London, 1636.

Butler, Judith. *Excitable Speech: A Politics of the Performative*. New York: Routledge, 1997.

Butler, Margaret R. "From Guadagni's Suitcase: A Primo Uomo's Signature Aria and Its Transformation," *Cambridge Opera Journal* 27, no 3 (2015): 239–262.

Butt, John. "The Seventeenth-Century Musical 'Work.'" In *The Cambridge History of Seventeenth-Century Music*, edited by Tim Carter and John Butt, 27–54. Cambridge, UK: Cambridge University Press, 2005.

Caccini, Giulio. *Le nuove musiche* [1602], edited by H. Wiley Hitchcock. Recent Researches in the Music of the Baroque Era, vol. 9. Middleton, WI: A-R Editions, 1970.

Caldwell, John. *English Keyboard Music before the Nineteenth Century*. Oxford, UK: Blackwell, 1972; New York: Dover, 1985.

———. "Keyboard Music: 1630–1700." In *New Oxford History of Music: Concert Music 1630–1750*, vol. 6, edited by Gerald Abraham, 505–589. Oxford, UK: Oxford University Press, 1986.

Calendar of the Manuscripts of the Most Honorable the Marquess of Salisbury Preserved at Hatfield House, Hertfordshire, part 17, edited by M. S. Giuseppi. Historical Manuscripts Commission, vol. 9. London: His Majesty's Stationery Office, 1938.

Calendar of State Papers Relating to English Affairs in the Archives of Venice. Volume 5: 1534–1554 (1873), edited by Rawdon Brown, 531–567. British History Online. http://www.british-history.ac.uk/report.aspx?compid=94906 (accessed April 19, 2014).

Calendar of Treasury Papers, Volume 1: 1556–1696, edited by Joseph Redington. London, 1868. British History Online. http://www.british-history.ac.uk/source.aspx?pubid=883 (accessed July 18, 2013).

Calendar of Treasury Papers, Volume 2: 1697–1702, edited by Joseph Redington. London, 1871. British History Online. http://www.british-history.ac.uk/report.aspx?compid=949906 (accessed July 18, 2013).

Calogero, Elena Laura. "'Sweet Aluring Harmony': Heavenly and Earthly Sirens in Sixteenth- and Seventeenth-Century Literary and Visual Culture." In *Music of the Sirens*, edited by Linda Phyllis Austern and Inna Naroditskaya, 140–175. Bloomington: Indiana University Press, 2006.

Campion, Thomas. *The Third and Fourth Booke of Ayres*. London, [1617?].

———. *Thomae Campiani Epigrammatum libri II. Umbra. Elgiarum liber unus*. London, 1619.

———. *Two Bookes of Ayres. The First*. London, [n.d.].

Caraman, Philip. *Henry Garnet, 1555–1606, and the Gunpowder Plot*. London: Longmans, Green, 1964.
———, ed. and trans. *John Gerard, the Autobiography of an Elizabethan*. London: Longmans, Green, 1951.
Carey, Henry. *Blundrella: or, The Impertinent. A Tale*. London, 1730.
Carlson, Marvin. *Places of Performance: The Semiotics of Theatre Architecture*. Ithaca, NY: Cornell University Press, 1989.
Carrafiello, Michael L. "English Catholicism and the Jesuit Mission of 1580–1581." *The Historical Journal* 37, no. 4 (1994): 761–774.
Carruthers, Mary. *The Book of Memory*. Cambridge, UK: Cambridge University Press, 2008.
———. *The Craft of Thought: Meditation, Rhetoric, and the Making of Images, 400–1200*. Cambridge, UK: Cambridge University Press, 1998.
Castan, Nicole. "The Public and the Private." In *A History of Private Life*, vol. 3: *Passions of the Renaissance*, edited by Roger Chartier and translated by Arthur Goldhammer, 403–446. Cambridge, MA: Belknap, 1989.
Castiglione, Baldassare. *The Courtyer of Count Baldessar Castilio*, translated by Thomas Hoby. London, 1561.
Cavendish, Margaret. *Playes*. London, 1662.
Cavendish, Michael. *14. Ayres in Tabletorie to the Lute*. London, 1598.
Census-Catalogue of Manuscript Sources of Polyphonic Music 1400–1550, 5 vols. Renaissance Manuscript Studies. Volume 2. Neuhausen-Stuttgart: AIM, 1979–1988.
Certeau, Michel de. *The Practice of Everyday Life*, translated by Steven Rendall. Berkeley: University of California Press, 1984.
Chaderton, Laurence. *An Excellent and Godly Sermon, Most Needefull for This Time, wherein We Liue in All Securitie and Sinne, to the Great Dishonour of God, and Contempt of His Holy Word. / Preached at Paules Cross the xxvi Daye of October, An. 1578. by Laurence Chaderton*. London, [1578?].
Chalmers, Hero. *Royalist Women Writers 1650–1689*. Oxford, UK: Oxford University Press, 2004.
Chan, Mary. "Edward Lowe's Manuscript British Library Add. 29396: The Case for Redating." *Music & Letters* 59 (1978): 440–454.
———. "A Mid-Seventeenth-Century Music Meeting and Playford's Publishing." In *The Well Enchanting Skill: Music, Poetry, and Drama in the Culture of the Renaissance*, edited by John Caldwell, Edward Olleson, and Susan Wollenberg, 231–244. Oxford, UK: Clarendon, 1990.
Chapman, Richard. *Hallelujah: or, King David's Shrill Trumpet, Sounding a Loude Summons to the Whole World, to Praise God*. London, 1635.
Chappell, William. *The Ballad Literature and Popular Music of the Olden Time*. New York: Dover, 1965.
Charlston, Terence. "The Selosse Manuscript." http://homepage.ntlworld.com/terence.charlston/Selosse.htm
Charlton, Kenneth. *Women, Religion and Education in Early Modern England*. London: Routledge, 1999.
Chartier, Roger. "Introduction" to "Community, State and Family: Trajectories and Tensions." In *A History of Private Life*, vol. 3: *Passions of the Renaissance*,

edited by Roger Chartier and translated by Arthur Goldhammer, 399–402. Cambridge, MA: Belknap, 1989.

———. "The Practical Impact of Writing." In *A History of Private Life*, vol. 3: *Passions of the Renaissance*, edited by Roger Chartier and translated by Arthur Goldhammer, 111–160. Cambridge, MA: Belknap, 1989.

Chedgzoy, Kate. "Women, Gender, and the Politics of Location." In *The Impact of Feminism in English Renaissance Studies*, edited by Dympna Callaghan, 137–149. Basingstoke, UK: Palgrave Macmillan, 2007.

Chevill, Elizabeth. "Clergy, Music Societies and the Development of a Musical Tradition: A Study of Music Societies in Hereford, 1690–1760." In *Concert Life in Eighteenth-Century Britain*, edited by Susan Wollenberg and Simon McVeigh, 35–53. Aldershot, UK: Ashgate, 2004.

Child, William. *The First Set of Psalms of III Voyces*. London, 1639. Reissued as *Choise Musick to the Psalmes of David for Three Voices with a Continuall Base*. London, 1650, reprinted 1656.

Chrissochoidis, Illias. "'Hee-Haw . . . llelujah': Handel among the Vauxhall Asses (1732)." *Eighteenth-Century Music* 7 (2010): 221–262.

The Chronicle of the English Augustinian Canonesses Regular of the Lateran, at St Monica's in Louvain, 1548 to 1625 [1625–1644], 2 vols., edited by Dom Adam Hamilton. Edinburgh, UK: Sands, 1904–1906.

Cicero. *De Oratore*, vol. 2, translated by E. W. Sutton. Cambridge, MA: Loeb Classical Library, 1942.

Cichy, Andrew. "Parlour, Court and Cloister: Musical Culture in English Convents during the Seventeenth Century." In *The English Convents in Exile, 1600–1800: Communities, Culture and Identity*, edited by Caroline Bowden and James E. Kelly, 175–190. Farnham, UK: Ashgate, 2013.

Cieraad, Irene. "Introduction: Anthropology at Home." In *At Home: An Anthropology of Domestic Space*, edited by Irene Cieraad, 1–12. Syracuse, NY: Syracuse University Press, 2006.

Clark, Peter. *British Clubs and Societies 1580–1800: The Origins of an Associational World*. Oxford, UK: Oxford University Press, 2000.

Clark, Sandra. "The Broadside Ballad and the Woman's Voice." In *Debating Gender in Early Modern England 1500–1700*, edited by Cristina Malcolmson and Mihoko Suzuki, 103–120. Basingstoke, UK: Palgrave Macmillan, 2002.

———. *Women and Crime in the Street Literature of Early Modern England*. London: Palgrave Macmillan, 2003.

Clarke, Elizabeth. *Politics, Religion and the Song of Songs in Seventeenth-Century England*. London: Palgrave Macmillan, 2011.

Coelho, Victor. "The Reputation of Francesco da Milano (1497–1543) and the Ricercars in the 'Cavalcanti Lute Book.'" *Revue belge de Musicologie /Belgisch Tijdschrift voor Muziekwetenschap* 50 (1996): 49–72.

Coke, Lady Mary. *The Letters and Journals of Lady Mary Coke*, 4 vols. Edinburgh, UK: D. Douglas, 1889–1896.

"Community, n." *OED*. (accessed August 03, 2015).

Congreve, William. *The Old Batchelor*. London, 1693.

Connelly, Roland. *The Women of the Catholic Resistance in England 1540–1680*. Durham, UK: Pentland, 1997.

The Constitutions of the Society of Jesus and Their Complementary Norms, edited by John W. Padberg. St. Louis, MO: The Institute of Jesuit Sources, 1996.
Cooper, B[arry] A. R. "English Solo Keyboard Music of the Middle and Late Baroque." PhD thesis, Oxford University, 1974.
———. "The Keyboard Suite in England before the Restoration." *Music & Letters* 53 (1972): 309–319.
Corfield, Penelope J. "The Rivals: Landed and Other Gentlemen." In *Land and Society in Britain, 1700–1914*, edited by N. B. Harte and R. Quinault, 1–33. Manchester, UK: Manchester University Press, 1996.
Corkine, William. *Ayres, to Sing and Play to the Lute*. London, 1610.
Cornwallis, Sir William. *Of the Observation and Use of Things*. London, 1600.
The Council of Trent, The Twenty-Fifth Session, edited and translated by J. Waterworth. London: Dolman, 1848.
The Court Magazine and Monthly Critic, and Ladies' Magazine and Museum of Belles Lettres. London: 1832–1848. In *Early British Periodicals*; also in *British Periodicals*. ECP.
Court Miscellany. Or Gentleman and Lady's New Magazine. London: 1765–1771. In *Eighteenth Century Collections Online*. Gale. ECP.
Cowley, Abraham. *The Guardian*. London, 1650.
Cox, Geoffrey. "Organ Music in Restoration England: A Study of Styles, Sources, and Influences." PhD thesis, Oxford University, 1984.
Craig-McFeely, Julia. "English Lute Manuscripts and Scribes 1530–1630." PhD thesis, Oxford University, 2000.
Crawford, Tim. "The Art of Re-Creating Lute Music." *Early Music* 34, no. 1 (2006): 160–163.
Creeth, Edmund, ed. *Tudor Plays: An Anthology of Early English Drama*. New York: Anchor Books, 1966.
Cressy, David. *Birth, Marriage, and Death: Ritual, Religion, and the Life-Cycle in Tudor and Stuart England*. Oxford, UK: Oxford University Press, 1997.
———. "National Memory in Early Modern England." In *Commemorations: The Politics of National Identity*, edited by John R. Gillis, 61–73. Princeton, NJ: Princeton University Press, 1994.
Crockett, Bryan. "'Holy Cozenage' and the Renaissance Cult of the Ear." *Sixteenth Century Journal* 24 (1993): 47–65.
Crosby, Brian. "An Early Restoration Liturgical Music Manuscript." *Music & Letters* 55 (1974): 458–464.
Culley, Thomas D., and Clement J. McNaspy. "Music and the Early Jesuits (1540–1565)." *Archivum Historicum Societatis Jesu* 40 (1971): 213–245.
Culpepper, Danielle. "'Our Particular Cloister': Ursulines and Female Education in Seventeenth-Century Parma and Piacenza." *Sixteenth Century Journal* 36, no. 4 (2005): 1017–1037.
Cunich, Peter. "The Brothers of Syon, 1420–1695." In *Syon Abbey and Its Books: Reading, Writing and Religion, c.1400–1700*, edited by E. A. Jones and A. Walsham, 39–81. Woodbridge, UK: Boydell, 2011.
Cunningham, John. "A Meeting of Amateur and Professional: Playford's 'Compendious Collection' of Two-Part Airs, *Court-Ayres* (1655)." In *Concepts of Creativity in Seventeenth-Century England*, edited by Rebecca Herissone and Alan Howard, 201–232. Woodbridge, UK: Boydell, 2013.

Daborne, Robert. *The Poor Mans Comfort*. London, 1655.
Danyel, John. *Songs for the Lute Viol and Voice*. London, [1606].
Dart, Thurston. "An Early Seventeenth-Century Book of English Organ Music for the Roman Rite." *Music & Letters* 52 (1971): 27–38.
———. "Elizabeth Edgeworth's Keyboard Book." *Music & Letters* 50 (1969): 470–474.
Darwin, Erasmus. *A Plan for the Conduct of Female Education, in Boarding Schools*. Derby, 1797. *Eighteenth Century Collections Online* (accessed November 29, 2013).
D'Assigny, Marius. *The Art of Memory*. London, 1699.
Davis, Walter R., ed. *The Works of Thomas Campion*. London: Faber, 1969.
Dawe, Donovan. *Organists of the City of London 1666–1850: A Record of One Thousand Organists, with an Annotated Index*. [Purley, UK]: D. Dawe, 1983.
Dean, Winton. *Handel's Dramatic Oratorios and Masques*. New York: Oxford University Press, 1959.
———. "'Rossane': Pasticcio or Handel Opera?" *Göttinger Händel-Beiträge* 7 (1998): 143–155.
Defoe, Daniel. *The Complete English Tradesman . . . in Two Volumes . . . the Third Edition*, vol. 2. London, 1727.
Delamain, Richard. *The Close Hypocrite Discovered; or, A True Description of the Life and Person of Cap. Taylor . . . Being a Vindication of Mr. Rich. Delamain . . . in Answer to a Scurrilous Pamphlet Entituled Impostor Magnus*. London, 1654.
Dering, Richard. *Cantica Sacra ad Duas & Tres Voces*. London, 1662.
A Description of Vaux-hall Gardens. London, 1762.
Deutsch, Otto Erich. *Handel: A Documentary Biography*. London: A. & C. Black, 1955.
[Dilke, Thomas]. *The City Lady: Or, Folly Reclaim'd*. London, 1697.
The Division-Violin: Containing a Collection of Divisions upon Several Grounds for the Treble Violin. Being the First Musick of This Kind Made Publick. The Second Edition, Much Enlarged. London, 1685.
Dolan, Frances E. *Dangerous Familiars: Representations of Domestic Crime in England 1550–1700*. Ithaca, NY: Cornell University Press, 1994.
———. "Gender and the 'Lost' Spaces of Catholicism." *The Journal of Interdisciplinary History* 32 (2002): 641–665.
Doring, Tobias. *Performances of Mourning in Shakespearean Theater and Early Modern Culture*. Basingstoke, UK: Palgrave Macmillan, 2006.
Doughtie, Edward. *Lyrics from English Ayres 1596–1622*. Cambridge, MA: Harvard University Press, 1970.
Dowland, John. *The First Booke of Songes or Ayres*. London, 1597.
Dowland, Robert. *A Musicall Banquet*. London, 1610.
———. *A Varietie of Lute-lessons*. London, 1610.
Dubrow, Heather. *The Challenges of Orpheus: Lyric Poetry and Early Modern England*. Baltimore: Johns Hopkins University Press, 2008.
Duffin, Ross. "Ballads in Shakespeare's World." In *"Noyses, Sounds and Sweet Aires": Music in Early Modern England*, edited by Jessie Ann Owens, 33–47. Washington, DC: Folger Shakespeare Library, 2006.
———. *Shakespeare's Songbook*. New York: Norton, 2004.
Duffy, Eamon. "The Conservative Voices in the English Reformation." In *Christianity and Community in the West: Essays for John Bossy*, edited by Simon Ditchfield, 87–105. Burlington, VT: Ashgate, 2001.

———. *Fires of Faith: Catholic England under Mary Tudor*. New Haven, CT: Yale University Press, 2009.

———. *The Stripping of the Altars: Traditional Religion in England 1400–1580*. New Haven, CT: Yale University Press, 1992.

Dugdale, James. *The New British Traveller, or Modern Panorama of England and Wales*. London, 1819.

Dunn, Leslie C. "Ophelia's Songs in *Hamlet*: Music, Madness, and the Feminine." In *Embodied Voices: Representing Female Vocality in Western Culture*, edited by Leslie C. Dunn and Nancy A. Jones, 50–64. New York: Cambridge University Press, 1996.

Dunn, Leslie C., and Katherine R. Larson, eds. *Gender and Song in Early Modern England*. Farnham, UK: Ashgate, 2014.

Dunn, Leslie C., and Nancy A. Jones, eds. *Embodied Voices: Representing Female Vocality in Western Culture*. New York: Cambridge University Press, 1996.

D'Urfey, Tho[mas], *The Old Mode and the New: Or, Country Miss with Her Furbeloe*. London, [1703].

———. *Songs Compleat, Pleasant and Divertive; Set to Musick by Dr. John Blow, Mr. Henry Purcell, and Other Excellent Masters of the Town*. London, 1719.

Eales, Jacqueline. *Puritans and Roundheads: The Harleys of Brampton Bryan and the Outbreak of the English Civil War*. New York: Cambridge University Press, 1990.

Earle, Peter. *The Making of the English Middle Class: Business, Society and Family Life in London 1660–1730*. London: Methuen, 1991.

The Early English Organ Project. "The Organs." http://www.rco.org.uk/eeop_organs.php.

Eccles, John. *A Collection of Songs for One, Two, and Three Voices, Together with Such Symphonies for Violins or Flutes as Were by the Author Design'd for Any of Them; and a Thorough-Bass to Each Song Figur'd for an Organ, Harpsichord, or Theorbo-Lute, etc.* London, [1704].

———. *Incidental Music, Part 1 (Plays A–F)*, edited by Amanda Eubanks Winkler. *The Works of John Eccles*, Recent Researches in the Music of the Baroque. Volume 190. Middleton, WI: A-R Editions, 2015.

Edgerton, William. "The Apostasy of Nicholas Udall." *Notes and Queries* 195 (1950): 223–226.

———. *Nicholas Udall*. New York: Twayne, 1965.

———. "Nicholas Udall in the Indexes of Prohibited Books." *The Journal of English and Germanic Philology* 55, no. 2 (1956): 247–252.

Edwards, Warwick. "The Performance of Ensemble Music in Elizabethan England." *Proceedings of the Royal Musical Association* 97 (1970–1971): 113–123.

Eikon Basilika: The Portraicture of His Sacred Majestie in His Solitudes and Sufferings. London, 1649.

Eggington, Tim. *The Advancement of Music in Enlightenment England: Benjamin Cooke and the Academy of Ancient Music*. Woodbridge, UK: Boydell, 2014.

Ellingson, Ter. "Transcription." In *Ethnomusicology*, edited by Helen Myers, 110–152. London: Macmillan, 1992.

Elliott, John R., Jr., Alan H. Nelson, Alexandra F. Johnston, and Diana Wyall, eds. *Records of Early English Drama: Oxford*. Toronto: University of Toronto Press, 2004.

Ellison, James. *George Sandys: Travel, Colonialism and Tolerance in the Seventeenth Century*. Cambridge, UK: D. S. Brewer, 2002.

Ellyot, George. *A Very True Report of the Apprehension and Taking of that Arche Papist Edmund Campion*. London, 1581.
Elshtain, Jean Bethke. *Public Man, Private Woman: Women in Social and Political Thought*. Princeton, NJ: Princeton University Press, 1981.
Elyot, Thomas. *The Boke Named the Governour*. London, 1531.
Emslie, McDonald. "Pepys, Samuel." *GMO* (accessed June 19, 2013).
Enders, Jody. "Music, Delivery, and the Rhetoric of Memory in Guillaume de Machaut's *Remède de Fortune*." *PMLA* 107, no. 3 (1992): 450–464.
Engel, William. *Death and Drama in Renaissance England: Shades of Memory*. Oxford, UK: Oxford University Press, 2002.
———. *Mapping Mortality: The Persistence of Memory and Melancholy in Early Modern England*. Amherst: University of Massachusetts Press, 1995.
English Benedictine Nuns in Flanders, 1598–1687: Annals of Their Five Communities. http://www.history.qmul.ac.uk/wwtn/pdfs/Annalsof5communitiesJan09.pdf
Essex, John. *The Young Ladies Conduct: Or, Rules for Education, under Several Heads; with Instructions upon Dress, Both before and after Marriage. and Advice to Young Wives*. London, 1722. *Eighteenth Century Collections Online* (accessed November 29, 2013).
Eubanks Winkler, Amanda. *O Let Us Howle Some Heavy Note: Music for Witches, Melancholics, and the Mad on the Seventeenth-Century English Stage*. Bloomington: Indiana University Press, 2006.
———. "'Our Friend Venus Performed to a Miracle': Anne Bracegirdle, John Eccles, and Creativity." In *Concepts of Creativity in Seventeenth-Century England*, edited by Rebecca Herissone and Alan Howard, 255–280. Woodbridge, UK: Boydell and Brewer, 2013.
European Magazine, and London Review. London: 1782–1826. In *English Literary Periodicals*; also in *British Periodicals* and *Eighteenth Century Collections Online*. Gale. ECP.
Evans, Robert C. "Paradox in Poetry and Politics: Katherine Philips in the Interregnum." In *The English Civil Wars in the Literary Imagination*, edited by Claude J. Summers and Ted-Larry Pebworth, 174–185. Columbia: University of Missouri Press, 1999.
Evans, Willa McClung. *Henry Lawes: Musician and Friend of Poets*. New York: Modern Language Association of America, 1941; reprint, New York: Klaus Reprint, 1966.
Ezell, Margaret J. M. "The 'Gentleman's Journal' and the Commercialization of Restoration Coterie Literary Practices." *Modern Philology* 89, no. 3 (1992): 323–340.
Familiar Letters which Passed between Abraham Hill, Esq. and Several Eminent and Ingenious Persons of the Last Century. London, 1767.
Farmer, John S., ed. *The Dramatic Writings of Nicholas Udall*. London: Early English Drama Society, 1906.
Fellowes, E. H., ed. *The English School of Lutenist Song Writers*. London: Stainer & Bell, 1920–1925; 1925–27; 1932.
The Female Tatler. London, 1709–1710. In *English Literary Periodicals*; also in *British Periodicals*. ECP.
Fenyo, Jane K. "Grammar and Music in Campion's *Observations in the Art of English Poesie*." *Studies in the Renaissance* 12 (1970): 46–72.

Feuillerat, Albert, ed. *Documents Relating to the Revels at Court in the Time of King Edward VI and Queen Mary: The Loseley MSS.* Vaduz, Liechtenstein: Kraus Reprint, 1963.
Filmer, Edward. *A Defence of Dramatick Poetry.* London, 1698.
Findlay, Alison. *Playing Spaces in Early Women's Drama.* Cambridge, UK: Cambridge University Press, 2007.
Finney, Theodore M. "A Group of English Manuscript Volumes at the University of Pittsburgh." In *Essays in Musicology in Honor of Dragan Plamenac on His 70th Birthday*, edited by Gustave Reese and Robert J. Snow, 21–48. Pittsburgh, PA: University of Pittsburgh Press, 1969.
Fisch, Harold. *Jerusalem and Albion: The Hebraic Factor in Seventeenth-Century Literature.* London: Routledge & K. Paul, 1964.
Fischlin, Daniel. *In Small Proportions: A Poetics of the English Ayre 1596–1622.* Detroit, MI: Wayne State University Press, 1998.
Fiske, Roger. *English Theatre Music in the Eighteenth Century*, 2nd ed. Oxford, UK: Oxford University Press, 1986.
Fitz-Geffry, Charles [Caroli FitzGeofridi]. *Affaniae: sive Epigrammatum Libri tres: Ejusdem Cenographia.* Oxford, 1601.
Fitzpatrick, Barbara Laning. "J. Coote (London: 1758–1777); J. Cooke and J. Coote (London: 1757–1758)." In *The British Literary Book Trade, 1700–1820*, edited by James K. Bracken and Joel Silver, Dictionary of Literary Biography, vol. 154, 57–65. Detroit, MI: Gale Research, 1995.
Flather, Amanda. *Gender and Space in Early Modern England.* Woodbridge, UK: Boydell, 2007.
Fleming, Juliet. "Graffiti, Grammatology, and the Age of Shakespeare." In *Renaissance Culture and the Everyday*, edited by Patricia Fumerton and Simon Hunt, 315–351. Philadelphia: University of Pennsylvania Press, 1999.
Fludd, Robert. *Utriusque Cosmi Majoris scilicet et Minoris Metaphysica, Physica atque Technica Historia*, vol. 2. Oppenheim, Germany, 1617.
Flynn, Jane Elizabeth. "The Education of Choristers in England during the Sixteenth Century." In *Institutions and Patronage in Renaissance Music*, edited by Thomas Schmidt-Beste, 141–160. Farnham, UK: Ashgate, 2012. Originally published in *English Choral Practice 1400–1650*, edited by John Morehen, 180–199. Cambridge, UK: Cambridge University Press, 1995.
———. "A Reconsideration of the Mulliner Book (British Library Add. MS 30513): Music Education in Sixteenth-Century England." PhD diss., Duke University, 1993.
———. "The *In nomine* as a Jesuit Emblem." Forthcoming.
———. "The Musical Knowledge and Practice of Expert Tudor Descanters." In *Late Medieval Liturgies Enacted: The Experience of Worship in Cathedral and Parish Church*, edited by Sally Harper, P.S. Barnwell, and Magnus Williamson, 177–189. London: Routledge, 2016. Forthcoming.
———. "To Play upon the Organs Any Man[ner] Play[n]song." *Journal of the British Institute of Organ Studies* 34 (2010): 6–51.
Folkestad, Göran. "National Identity and Music." In *Musical Identities*, edited by Raymond A. R. MacDonald, David J. Hargreaves, and Dorothy Miell, 151–162. Oxford, UK: Oxford University Press, 2002.
Ford, John. *The Lover's Melancholy.* London, 1629.
Ford, Robert. "Bevins, Father and Son." *Music Review* 43 (1982): 104–108.

———. "The Filmer Manuscripts: A Handlist." *Notes, Second Series* 34 (1978): 814–825.
———. "Henstridge, Daniel." *GMO* (accessed February 21, 2013).
———. "Minor Canons at Canterbury Cathedral: The Gostlings and Their Colleagues." PhD diss., University of California, Berkeley, 1984.
———. "Purcell as His Own Editor: The Funeral Sentences." *Journal of Musicological Research* 7 (1986): 47–67.
Ford, Thomas. *Musicke of Sundrie Kindes*. London, 1607.
Forgeng, Jeffrey. *Daily Life in Stuart England*. Westport, CT: Greenwood, 2007.
Forney, Kristine K. "A Proper Musical Education for Antwerp's Women." In *Music Education in the Middle Ages and the Renaissance*, edited by Russell E. Murray Jr., Susan Forscher Weiss, and Cynthia J. Cyrus, 84–125. Bloomington: Indiana University Press, 2010.
Foucault, Michel. "Space, Knowledge, and Power." In *The Foucault Reader*, edited by Paul Rabinow, 239–256. New York: Pantheon Books, 1984.
Fox, Adam. *Oral and Literate Culture in England 1500–1700*. Oxford, UK: Oxford University Press, 2002.
Fried, Harvey. *A Critical Edition of Brome's* The Northern Lass. New York: Garland, 1980.
Fumerton, Patricia. "Not Home: Alehouses, Ballads, and the Vagrant Husband in Early Modern England." *Journal of Medieval and Early Modern Studies* 32, no. 3 (2002): 493–518.
———. "Remembering by Dismembering: Databases, Archiving, and the Recollection of Seventeenth-Century Broadside Ballads." In *Ballads and Broadsides in Britain, 1500–1800*, edited by Patricia Fumerton, Anita Guerrini, and Kris McAbee, 13–34. Farnham, UK: Ashgate, 2010.
———. "Secret Arts: Elizabethan Miniatures and Sonnets." *Representations* 15 (1986): 57–97.
Fumerton, Patricia, Anita Guerrini, and Kris McAbee, eds. *Ballads and Broadsides in Britain, 1500–1800*. Farnham, UK: Ashgate, 2010.
Gair, Reavley. *The Children of Paul's: The Story of a Theatre Company, 1553–1608*. Cambridge, UK: Cambridge University Press, 1982.
———. "The Conditions of Appointment for Masters of Choristers at Paul's (1553–1613)." *Notes and Queries* 27, no. 2 (1980): 116–124.
Gale, Michael. "John Dowland, Celebrity Lute Teacher." *Early Music* 41, no. 2 (2013): 205–218.
Galinou, Mireille. *City Merchants and the Arts, 1670–1720*. Wetherby, UK: Oblong for the Corporation of London, 2004.
Gallagher, Lowell. "Mary Ward's 'Jesuitresses' and the Construction of a Typological Community." In *Maids and Mistresses, Cousins and Queens: Women's Alliances in Early Modern England*, edited by Susan Frye and Karen Robertson, 199–218. Oxford, UK: Oxford University Press, 1999.
Gammie, Ian, and Derek McCulloch. *Jane Austen's Music: The Musical World of Jane Austen Seen through the Manuscripts and Printed Editions Held by the Jane Austen Memorial Trust at Chawton: With Brief Histories of Contemporary Composers and a Catalogue of More Than 300 Musical Works*. St. Albans, UK: Corda Music, 1996.
Gauci, Perry. *Emporium of the World: The Merchants of London*. London: Hambledon, 2007.

———. "Wessell, Leonard (aft. 1660–1708), of London and Tadworth Court, Surr." In *The History of Parliament*. http://www.historyofparliamentonline.org/volume/1690-1715/member/wessell-leonard-1660-1708 (accessed July 18, 2013).

Gay, John. *The Beggar's Opera and Polly*, edited by Hal Gladfelder. Oxford, UK: Oxford University Press, 2013.

———. *Polly: An Opera. Being the Second Part of the Beggar's Opera*. London, 1729.

Gentleman's Journal, or, the Monthly Miscellany. London: 1692–1694. In *English Literary Periodicals*; also in *British Periodicals*. ECP.

Gentleman's Magazine: or, Monthly Intelligencer. London: 1731–1907. In *Early British Periodicals*; also in *British Periodicals*. ECP.

Gibson, Joy Leslie. *Squeaking Cleopatras: The Elizabethan Boy Player*. Stroud, UK: Sutton Press, 2000.

Gibson, Kirsten. "'How Hard an Enterprise It Is': Authorial Self-Fashioning in John Dowland's Printed Books." *Early Music History* 26 (2007): 43–89.

———. "'The Order of the Book': Materiality, Narrative, and Authorial Voice in John Dowland's *First Booke of Songes or Ayres*." *Renaissance Studies* 26, no. 1 (2012): 13–33.

———. "'So to the Wood Went I': Politicizing the Greenwood in Two Songs by John Dowland." *Journal of the Royal Musical Association* 132, no. 2 (2007): 221–251.

Giles-Watson, Maura. "The Singing 'Vice': Music and Mischief in Early English Drama." *Early Theater* 12, no. 2 (2009): 57–90.

Girdham, Jane. *English Opera in Late Eighteenth-Century London*. Oxford, UK: Clarendon, 1997.

Girourard, Mark. *Life in the English Country House: A Social and Architectural History*. New Haven, CT: Yale University Press, 1978.

Glixon, Beth. "Cavalli, Robert Bargrave and the English *Erismena*." Paper presented at the 15th Biennial International Conference on Baroque Music, University of Southampton, July 11–15, 2012.

Glushko, Robert J., ed. *The Discipline of Organizing*. Cambridge, MA: MIT Press, 2013.

Goehr, Lydia. *The Imaginary Museum of Musical Works*, rev. ed. Oxford, UK: Oxford University Press, 2007.

Goldratt, Eliyahu, and Jeff Cox. *The Goal: A Process of Ongoing Improvement*, 3rd rev. ed. Great Barrington, MA: North River Press, 2004.

Goodwin, Gordon. "Domville, alias Taylor, Silas (1624–1678)." *DNB* Archive, 1888. *DNB* (accessed June 29, 2013).

Goodwin, Gordon, and Rev. David Whitehead. "Harley, Sir Edward (1624–1700)." *DNB* (accessed June 29, 2013).

Gouk, Penelope. "Raising Spirits and Restoring Souls: Early Modern Medical Explanations for Music's Effects." In *Hearing Cultures: Essays on Sound, Listening, and Modernity*, edited by Veit Erlmann, 87–105. Oxford, UK: Berg, 2004.

———. "Some English Theories of Hearing in the Seventeenth Century." In *The Second Sense: Studies in Hearing and Musical Judgment from Antiquity to the Seventeenth Century*, edited by Charles Burnett, Michael Fend, and Penelope Gouk, 95–113. London: Warburg Institute, 1991.

Gowing, Laura. "The Freedom of the Streets: Women and Social Space, 1560–1640." In *Londinopolis: A Social and Cultural History of Early Modern London, 1500–1750*, edited by Mark S. R. Jenner and Paul Griffiths, 130–153. Manchester, UK: University of Manchester Press, 2000.

Grassby, Richard. *The Business Community of Seventeenth-Century England.* Cambridge, UK: Cambridge University Press, 1995.
Gray, Catharine. "Katherine Philips and the Post-Courtly Coterie." *English Literary Renaissance* 32 (2002): 426–451.
Green, Bertha de Vere. *A Collector's Guide to Fans over the Ages.* London: Frederick Muller, 1975.
Green, Mary Anne Everett, ed. *Calendar of the Proceedings of the Committee for Compounding, &c.: 1643–1660.* London: HMSO, 1889; reprint, Nedeln, Liechtenstein: Kraus Reprint, 1967.
———. *Calendar of State Papers, Domestic Series, of the Reign of Charles II: 1664–1665.* London: Longman, 1863.
Greer, David, ed. *Collected English Lutenist Partsongs,* vols. 53 and 54. *Musica Britannica.* London: Stainer & Bell, 2000.
———. "Five Variations on 'Farewel Dear Loue'." In *The Well Enchanting Skill: Music, Poetry, and Drama in the Culture of the Renaissance,* edited by John Caldwell, Edward Olleson, and Susan Wollenberg, 213–229. Oxford: Clarendon Press, 1990.
———. *Songs from Manuscript Sources,* 2 vols. London: Stainer & Bell, 1979.
———. "'What If a Day'—An Examination of the Words and Music." *Music and Letters* 43 (1962): 316–318.
Gregg, Edward. *Queen Anne.* London: Routledge & Kegan Paul, 1980.
Grymeston, Elizabeth. *Miscelanea. Meditations. Memoratiues.* London, 1604.
Gurr, Andrew. *Playgoing in Shakespeare's London,* 2nd ed. Cambridge, UK: Cambridge University Press, 1996.
Habermas, Jürgen. *The Structural Transformation of the Public Sphere: An Inquiry into a Category of Bourgeois Society,* translated by Thomas Burger with the assistance of Frederick Lawrence. Cambridge, MA. MIT Press, 1989; reprint, 1996.
Haigh, Christopher. *English Reformations: Religion, Politics, and Society under the Tudors.* Oxford, UK: Oxford University Press, 1993.
Hall-Witt, Jennifer. *Fashionable Acts: Opera and Elite Culture in London, 1780–1880.* Durham: University of New Hampshire Press, 2007.
Hamessley, Lydia. "Henry Lawes's Setting of Katherine Philips's Friendship Poetry in His Second Book of Ayres and Dialogues, 1655: A Musical Misreading?" In *Queering the Pitch: The New Gay and Lesbian Musicology,* edited by Philip Brett, Elizabeth Wood, and Gary C. Thomas, 115–138. New York: Routledge, 1994.
Hamlin, Hannibal. *Psalm Culture and Early Modern English Literature.* Cambridge, UK: Cambridge University Press, 2004.
Handelman, Dan. *Models and Mirrors: Towards and Anthropology of Public Events.* Cambridge, UK: Cambridge University Press, 1990.
Hanley, Andrew. "Mico and Jenkins: 'Musitians of Fame under King Charles I.'" In *John Jenkins and His Time: Studies in English Consort Music,* edited by Andrew Ashbee and Peter Holman, 161–169. New York: Oxford University Press, 1996.
Hanshall, J. H. *A History of the County Palatine of Chester.* Chester, UK: J. H. Hanshall, 1817.
Harding, Rosamond. *A Thematic Catalogue of the Works of Matthew Locke with a Calendar of the Main Events of His Life.* Oxford, UK: Rosamond Harding, 1971.
Harley, John. *British Harpsichord Music,* 2 vols. Aldershot, UK: Ashgate, 1992 and 1994.

———. *Orlando Gibbons and the Gibbons Family of Musicians*. Aldershot, UK: Ashgate, 1999.

———. *The World of William Byrd: Musicians, Merchants and Magnates*. Farnham, UK: Ashgate, 2010.

Harris, David G.T. "Musical Education in Tudor Times." *Proceedings of the Royal Musical Association* 65 (1938–1939): 108–139.

Harwood, Ian. "'A Lecture in Musick, with the Practice Thereof by Instrument in the Common Schooles,' Mathew Holmes and Music at Oxford University c. 1588–1627." *The Lute* 45 (2005): 19–20.

Hauser, Gerald A. *Vernacular Voices: The Rhetoric of Publics and Public Spheres*. Columbia: University of South Carolina Press, 1999.

Havergal, Francis T. *Fasti Herefordenses and Other Antiquarian Memorials of Hereford*. Edinburgh, Scotland: R. Clark, 1869.

Hawkins, John. *A General History of the Science and Practice of Music*, 5 vols. London, 1776.

Haynes, Bruce. *The End of Early Music: A Period Performer's History of Music for the Twenty-First Century*. New York: Oxford University Press, 2007.

Head, Matthew. "Cultural Meaning for Women Composers: Charlotte ('Minna') Brandes and the Beautiful Dead in the German Enlightenment." *Journal of the American Musicological Society* 57, no. 2 (2004): 231–284.

———. "'If the Pretty Little Hand Won't Stretch': Music for the Fair Sex in Eighteenth-Century Germany." *Journal of the American Musicological Society* 52, no. 2 (1999): 203–254.

Hegarty, Mary, and Andrew T. Scull. "Visuospatial Thinking." In *The Oxford Handbook of Thinking and Reasoning*, edited by Keith J. Holyoak and Robert G. Morrison, 606–630. Oxford, UK: Oxford University Press, 2012.

Heighes, Simon. *The Lives and Works of William and Philip Hayes*. New York: Garland, 1995.

Helms, Dietrich. "Henry VIII's Book: Teaching Music to Royal Children." *The Musical Quarterly* 92, no. 1–2 (2009): 118–135.

Herissone, Rebecca. *Music Theory in Seventeenth-Century England*. Oxford Monographs on Music. Oxford, UK: Oxford University Press, 2000.

———. *Musical Creativity in Restoration England*. Cambridge, UK: Cambridge University Press, 2013.

———. "Playford, Purcell, and the Functions of Music Publishing in Restoration England." *Journal of the American Musicological Society* 63, no. 2 (2010): 243–290.

Heywood, Thomas. *An Apology for Actors*. London, 1612.

Hill, R. H. Ernest "Thomas Hill, a London Merchant of the Seventeenth Century." *Home Counties Magazine* 6 (1904): 121–133.

Hiscock, Andrew. *Reading Memory in Early Modern Literature*. Cambridge, UK: University of Cambridge Press, 2011.

———. *The Uses of This World: Thinking Space in Shakespeare, Marlowe, Cary, and Jonson*. Cardiff: University of Wales Press, 2004.

Hodge, John Brian. "English Harpsichord Repertoire: 1660–1714." PhD thesis, University of Manchester, 1989.

Hodgetts, Michael. "The Godly Garret, 1560–1660." In *English Catholics of Parish and Town, 1558–1778: A Joint Research Project of the Catholic Record Society and Wolverhampton University*, edited by Marie B. Rowlands, 36–60. London: Catholic Record Society, 1999.

———. "Loca secretiora in 1581." *Recusant History* 19 (1989): 386–395.

Hogwood, Christopher, ed. *"fitt for the Manicorde": A Seventeenth-Century English Collection of Keyboard Music*. Launton, UK: Edition HH, 2003.

H[olland], A[braham]. *A Continued Inquisition against Paper-Persecutors*. London, 1625.

Holman, Peter. "Bowman, Henry." *GMO* (accessed January 25, 2011).

———. *Four and Twenty Fiddlers: The Violin at the English Court*. Oxford, UK: Clarendon, 1993.

———. *Life after Death: The Viola da Gamba in Britain from Purcell to Dolmetsch*. Woodbridge, UK: Boydell, 2010.

———. "Locke, Matthew." *GMO* (accessed June 29, 2013).

———. "Pigott, Francis." *GMO* (accessed July 18, 2013).

Hook, Lucyle. "Motteux and the Classical Masque." In *British Theatre and the Other Arts, 1660–1800*, edited by Shirley Strum Kenny, 105–115. Washington, DC: Folger Shakespeare Library, 1984.

Hornback, Robert. "A *Dirige* and Terence 'In the Briers': Mock-Ritual and Mock-Classicism as Iconoclastic Translation in Udall's *Ralph Roister Doister*." *Research Opportunities in Medieval and Renaissance Drama* (2009): 22–47.

Howard, Alan. "Manuscript Publishing in the Commonwealth Period: A Neglected Source of Consort Music by Golding and Locke." *Music & Letters* 90 (2008): 35–67.

———. "Sampson Estwick's Trio Sonata in A Minor: A Re-Creation." *Early Music Performer* 31 (2012): 4–15.

———. "Understanding Creativity." In *The Ashgate Research Companion to Henry Purcell*, edited by Rebecca Herissone, 65–113. Farnham, UK: Ashgate, 2012.

Howard, Patricia. *Gluck: An Eighteenth-Century Portrait in Letters and Documents*. Oxford, UK: Clarendon, 1995.

Hudson, Robert. *The Myrtle: A Collection of New English Songs for the Violin, German Flute or Harpsichord, Composed by Robert Hudson*. London, n.d.

Hughes-Hughes, Augustus. *Catalogue of Manuscript Music in the British Museum*, 3 vols. London: Trustees of the British Museum, 1906–1909.

"Humberston's Survey." *The Yorkshire Archaeological Journal* 17 (1903): 129–154.

Hume, Robert D. "The Economics of Culture in London." *Huntington Library Quarterly* 69 (2006): 487–533.

———. "Theatre as Property in Eighteenth-Century London." *Journal for Eighteenth-Century Studies* 31, no. 1 (2008): 17–30.

Hundert, E. J. *The Enlightenment's Fable: Bernard Mandeville and the Discovery of Society*. Cambridge, UK: Cambridge University Press, 1994.

Hunt, Alice. *The Drama of Coronation: Medieval Ceremony in Early Modern England*. Cambridge, UK: Cambridge University Press, 2008.

Hunt, Arnold. *The Art of Hearing: English Preachers and Their Audiences, 1590–1640*. Cambridge, UK: Cambridge University Press, 2010.

Hunt, John Dixon. "Theatres, Gardens, and Garden-Theatres." *Essays and Studies* 33 (1980): 95–118.

———. *Vauxhall and London's Garden Theatres*. Cambridge, UK: Chadwyck-Healey, 1985.

Hunter, David. *Opera and Song Books Published in England, 1703–1726: A Descriptive Bibliography*. London: Bibliographical Society, 1997.
———. "Rode the 12,000? Counting Coaches, People and Errors En Route to the Rehearsal of Handel's *Music for the Royal Fireworks* at Spring Gardens, Vauxhall in 1749." *The London Journal* 37, no. 1 (2012): 13–26.
Husk, W. H., and Gerald Gifford. "Hudson, Robert." In *The New Grove Dictionary of Music and Musicians*, edited by Stanley Sadie and John Tyrrell. New York: Grove, 2001.
Ignatius of Loyola. *The Spiritual Exercises of St. Ignatius of Loyola, Translated from the Authorised Latin: With Extracts from the Literal Version and Notes of the Rev. Father Rothaan, Father-General of the Company of Jesus*, translated by Charles Seager. London: Charles Dolman, 1847.
"Index to the Songs and Musical Allusions in *The Gentleman's Journal*, 1692–4." *Musical Antiquary* 2 (1911): 224–234.
Ingram, R. W. "Operatic Tendencies in Stuart Drama." *The Musical Quarterly* 44, no. 4 (1958): 489–502.
Iribarren, Patxi Xabier del Amo. "Anthony Poole (c. 1629–1692), the Viol and Exiled English Catholics." PhD thesis, University of Leeds, 2011.
Irigaray, Luce. *This Sex which Is Not One*, translated by Catherine Porter. Ithaca, NY: Cornell University Press, 1985.
Iselin, Pierre. "Myth, Music, and Memory in *Richard II*, *Hamlet*, and *Othello*." In *Reclamations of Shakespeare*, edited by A. J. Hoenselaars, 173–186. Amsterdam: Rodopi, 1994.
Italia, Iona. *The Rise of Literary Journalism in the Eighteenth Century: Anxious Employment*. London: Routledge, 2005.
Ivic, Christopher, and Grant Williams, eds. *Forgetting in Early Modern English Literature and Culture*. New York: Routledge, 2004.
Jeffreys, George. *16 Motets for One, Two or Three Voices*, edited by Peter Aston. York, UK: York Early Music Press, 2010.
Jenkinson, Matthew. *Culture and Politics at the Court of Charles II, 1660–1685*. Studies in Early Modern Cultural, Political, and Social History, vol. 9. Woodbridge, UK: Boydell, 2010.
Jensen, Ejner. "The Boy Actors: Plays and Playing." *Research Opportunities in Renaissance Drama* 18 (1975): 5–11.
Jocoy, Stacey. "The Role of the Catch in England's Civil War." In *Essays on Music and Culture in Honor of Herbert Kellman*, edited by Barbara Haggh, 325–334. Paris: Minerve, 2001.
Johnson, Claudia. "'Giant *Handel*' and the Musical Sublime." *Eighteenth-Century Studies* 4 (1986): 515–533.
Johnson, Matthew H. "Meanings of Polite Architecture in Sixteenth-Century England." *Historical Archaeology* 26 (1992): 45–56.
Johnson, Samuel. *A Dictionary of the English Language*. London, 1755.
Johnstone, H. Diack. "Claver Morris, an Early Eighteenth-Century English Physician and Amateur Musician Extraordinaire." *Journal of the Royal Musical Association* 133 (2008): 93–127.
———. "A New Source of Late Seventeenth- and Early Eighteenth-Century English Harpsichord Music by Barrett, Blow, Clarke, Croft, and Others." In *Essays on the History of English Music in Honour of John Caldwell: Sources, Style, Performance

and Historiography, edited by Emma Hornby and David Maw, 66–82. Woodbridge, UK: Boydell & Brewer, 2010.

———. "Ornamentation in the Keyboard Music of Henry Purcell and His Contemporaries." In *Performing the Music of Henry Purcell*, edited by Michael Burden, 82–103. Oxford, UK: Oxford University Press, 1996.

Jones, Robert. *A Musicall Dreame*. London, 1609.

———. *The Second Booke of Songs and Ayres*. [London], 1601.

Jones, Vivien, ed. *Women in the Eighteenth Century: Constructions of Femininity*. London: Routledge, 1990.

Jorgens, Elise Bickford, ed. *English Song 1600–1675: Facsimiles of Twenty-Six Manuscripts and an Edition of the Texts*, 12 vols. New York: Garland, 1986–1989.

The Judgment of God Shewed upon Dr. John Faustus. London, [1658].

Juhász-Ormsby, Ágnes. "The Books of Nicholas Udall." *Notes and Queries* 56 (2009): 507–512.

Kassler, Michael, comp. *Music Entries at Stationers' Hall, 1710–1818: From Lists Prepared for William Hawes, D. W. Krummel, and Alan Tyson and from Other Sources*. Aldershot, UK: Ashgate, 2004.

Kaufmann, R. J. *Richard Brome: Caroline Playwright*. New York: Columbia University Press, 1961.

Keach, Benjamin. *Tropologia, a Key to Open Scripture-Metaphors*. London, 1681.

Kelly, James E. "Kinship and Religious Politics among Catholic Families in England, 1570–1640." *History* 94 (2009): 328–343.

Kennedy, Thomas Frank. "Jesuits and Music: The European Tradition, 1547–1622." PhD diss., University of California, Santa Barbara, 1982.

Kennerley, David. "'Flippant Dolls' and 'Serious Artists': Professional Female Singers in Britain, c.1760–1850." DPhil. diss., University of Oxford, 2013.

Kenny, Elizabeth. "Revealing Their Hand: Lute Tablatures in Early Seventeenth Century England." *Renaissance Studies* 26, no. 1 (2012): 112–137.

Kerman, Joseph. *The Elizabethan Madrigal: A Comparative Study*. London: The AMS, 1962.

———. "Music and Politics: The Case of William Byrd (1540–1623)." *Proceedings of the American Philosophical Society* 144 (2000): 275–287.

Kerr, Jessica M. "Mary Harvey—The Lady Dering." *Music & Letters* 25 (1944): 23–30.

Kilroy, Gerard. *Edmund Campion: Memory and Transcription*. Aldershot, UK: Ashgate, 2005.

Kisby, Fiona. "Music and Musicians of Early Tudor Westminster." *Early Music* 23, no. 2 (1995): 223–242.

Kleiner, Peter, et al. "Copyright." *GMO* (accessed June 25, 2016).

Knowles, James. "'Infinite Riches in a Little Room': Marlowe and the Aesthetics of the Closet." In *Renaissance Configurations: Voices/Bodies/Spaces, 1580–1690*, edited by Gordon McMullan, 3–29. London: Macmillan; New York: St. Martin's, 1998.

Kolentsis, Alysia, and Katherine R. Larson, eds. "Gendering Time and Space in Early Modern England." Special issue, *Renaissance and Reformation/Renaissance et Réforme* 35, no. 1 (Winter 2012).

Korshin, Paul. *Typologies in England, 1650–1820*. Princeton, NJ: Princeton University Press, 1982.

Krummel, D. W. *English Music Printing 1553–1700*. London: Bibliographical Society, 1975.

——— . *The Literature of Music Bibliography: An Account of the Writings on the History of Music Printing & Publishing*. Berkeley, CA: Fallen Leaf Press, 1992.

Ladies' Monthly Museum, or, Polite Repository of Amusement and Instruction. London: 1798–1828. In *English Literary Periodicals*; also in *British Periodicals*. ECP.

Lady's Curiosity or Weekly Apollo. London, 1738 and 1752 editions. In *Women Advising Women: Advice Books, Manuals and Journals for Women, 1450–1837*, Part 1. Marlborough, UK: Adam Matthew, n.d.; also in *Eighteenth Century Collections Online*. Gale. ECP.

Lady's Magazine; or, Entertaining Companion for the Fair Sex Appropriated solely to their Use and Amusement. London, 1770–1832. In *Women Advising Women: Advice Books, Manuals and Journals for Women*, 1450-1837, Parts 3 and 4; digitized version in Eighteenth-Century Journals 5. Marlborough, Wiltshire: Adam Matthew.

Lady's Magazine. Or Polite Companion for the Fair Sex. London, 1759–1763. ECP.

Lake, Peter, and Steven Pincus. "Rethinking the Public Sphere in Early Modern England." In *The Politics of the Public Sphere in Early Modern England*, edited by Peter Lake and Steven Pincus, 1–30. Manchester, UK: Manchester University Press, 2007.

Lamb, Edel. *Performing Childhood in Early Modern Theater: The Children's Playing Companies, 1599–1613*. New York: Palgrave Macmillan, 2009.

Larson, Katherine R. "'Blest Pair of Sirens . . . Voice and Verse': Milton's Rhetoric of Song." *Milton Studies* 54 (2013): 81–106.

——— . *Early Modern Women in Conversation*. Basingstoke, UK: Palgrave Macmillan, 2011.

——— . "Margaret Cavendish's Civilizing Songs." In *The Public Intellectual and the Culture of Hope*, edited by Joel Faflak and Jason Haslam, 109–134. Toronto: University of Toronto Press, 2013.

Latham, Robert, and William Matthews, eds. *The Diary of Samuel Pepys*, 11 vols. London: Bell & Hyman, 1971–1983; reprint, London: HarperCollins, 1995.

Laurie, Margaret, and Curtis Price. "Motteux, Peter Anthony." *GMO* (accessed November 27, 2013).

Lawes, Henry. *Ayres and Dialogues*. London, 1658.

——— . *Ayres, and Dialogues, for One, Two, and Three Voices*. London, 1653.

——— . *Choice Psalmes Put into Musick*. London, 1648.

——— . *The Second Book of Ayres, and Dialogues, for One, Two, and Three Voices*. London, 1655.

——— . *Select Ayres and Dialogues . . . the Second Book*. London, 1669.

Leaver, Robin. "The Reformation and Music." In *European Music 1520–1640*, edited by James Haar, 371–400. Woodbridge, UK: Boydell & Brewer, 2006.

Leech, Peter, ed. *The Selosse Manuscript: Seventeenth Century Jesuit Keyboard Music*. Launton, UK: Edition HH, 2008.

Lefebvre, Henri. *The Production of Space*, translated by Donald Nicholson-Smith. Oxford, UK: Blackwell, 1991.

LeHuray, Peter. *Music and the Reformation in England 1549–1660*. Cambridge, UK: Cambridge University Press, 1967.

Lennam, Trevor. "The Children of Pauls, 1551–1582." *Elizabethan Theatre* 2 (1970): 20–36.

Leppert, Richard. *Music and Image: Domesticity, Ideology and Socio-Cultural Formation in Eighteenth-Century England.* Cambridge, UK: Cambridge University Press, 1988.

———. *The Sight of Sound: Music, Representation, and the History of the Body.* Berkeley: University of California Press, 1993.

Le Texier, Anthony A. *Ideas on the Opera, Offered to the Subscribers, Creditors, and Amateurs of That Theatre.* London, 1790.

Limbert, Claudia A. "Katherine Philips: Controlling a Life and Reputation." *South Atlantic Review* 56 (1991): 27–42.

Lindgren, Lowell. "A Bibliographic Scrutiny of Dramatic Works Set by Giovanni and His Brother Antonio Maria Bononcini." PhD diss., Harvard University, 1972.

———. "The Three Great Noises 'Fatal to the Interests of Bononcini.'" *Musical Quarterly* 61 (1975): 560–583.

Lindley, David. *Thomas Campion.* Leiden, the Netherlands: Brill, 1986.

———, ed. *Thomas Campion: De Puluerea Coniuratione,* with translation and additional notes by Robin Sowerby. Leeds, UK: University of Leeds, 1987.

Lipsedge, Karen. *Domestic Space in Eighteenth Century British Novels.* London: Palgrave Macmillan, 2012.

Little, Patrick. "Music at the Court of King Oliver." *The Court Historian* 12 (2007): 173–191.

Loach, Judi. "Revolutionary Pedagogues? How Jesuits Used Education to Change Society." In *The Jesuits II: Cultures, Sciences, and the Arts, 1540–1773,* edited by John W. O'Malley, Gauvin Alexander Bailey, Steven J. Harris, and T. Frank Kennedy, 66–85. Toronto: University of Toronto Press, 2006.

Loades, David. "The Personal Religion of Mary I." In *The Church of Mary Tudor,* edited by Eamon Duffy and David Loades, 1–32. Aldershot, UK: Ashgate, 2006.

———. *The Reign of Mary Tudor: Politics, Government, and Religion in England 1553–58.* London: Routledge, 1991.

Locke, Matthew. *Dramatic Music,* edited by Michael Tilmouth. *Musica Britannica,* vol. 51. London: Stainer & Bell, 1986.

———. *Melothesia.* London, 1673.

[Lockman, John.] *A Sketch of the Spring-Gardens, Vaux-Hall.* London, [1752].

Lord, Albert B. *The Singer of Tales.* Cambridge, MA: Harvard University Press, 2003.

Loscocco, Paula. "Royalist Reclamation of Psalmic Song in 1650s England." *Renaissance Quarterly* 64 (2011): 500–543.

Love, Harold. *The Culture and Commerce of Texts: Scribal Publication in Seventeenth-Century England.* Amherst: University of Massachusetts Press, 1993.

———. "How Music Created a Public." *Criticism* 46, no. 2 (2004): 257–271.

"The Lovely Northerne Lasse" (1624–1680?). British Library Ms. Roxburghe 1.190–191. English Broadside Ballad Archive (http://ebba.english.ucsb.edu).

Lowerre, Kathryn. "A *ballet des nations* for English Audiences: *Europe's Revels for the Peace of Ryswick* (1697)." *Early Music* 35, no. 3 (2007): 419–433.

Lux-Sterritt, Laurence. *Redefining Female Religious Life: French Ursulines and English Ladies in Seventeenth-Century Catholicism.* Aldershot, UK: Ashgate, 2005.

———. "'Virgo Becomes Virago': Women in the Accounts of Seventeenth-Century English Catholic Missionaries." *Recusant History* 30, no. 4 (2001): 537–553.

Machyn, Henry. *The Diary of Henry Machyn, Citizen and Merchant-Taylor of London from AD 1550 to AD 1563*, edited by J. G. Nichols. London: Camden Society, 1848.

Mackenzie, W. Mackay, ed. *Sir James Melville of Halhill Memoirs of His Own Life*. The Abbey Classics. Boston: Small, Maynard, [1918?].

Mackerness, Eric David. *A Social History of English Music*. London: Routledge and K[egan] Paul, 1964.

Mainwaring, John. *Memoirs of the Life of the Late George Frederic Handel*. London, 1760.

Maravall, José Antonio. *Culture of the Baroque: Analysis of a Historical Structure*, translated by Terry Cochran. Manchester, UK: Manchester University Press, 1986.

Marcus, Leah H. "From Oral Delivery to Print in the Speeches of Elizabeth I." In *Print, Manuscript, & Performance*, edited by Arthur F. Marotti and Michael D. Bristol, 33–48. Columbus: Ohio State University Press, 2000.

Mare, Heidi de. "Domesticity in Dispute: A Reconsideration of the Sources." In *An Anthropology of Domestic Space*, edited by Irene Cieraad, 13–30. Syracuse, NY: Syracuse University Press, 2006.

Marks, Patricia. "Lady's Magazine, The." In *British Literary Magazines [1]: The Augustan Age and the Age of Johnson, 1698–1788*, edited by Alvin Sullivan, 183–188. Westport, CT: Greenwood, 1983.

Marotti, Arthur. *Manuscript, Print, and the English Renaissance Lyric*. Ithaca, NY: Cornell University Press, 1995.

———. *Religious Ideology & Cultural Fantasy: Catholic and Anti-Catholic Discourses in Early Modern England*. Notre Dame, IN: University of Notre Dame Press, 2005.

Marsh, Christopher. "'At It Ding Dong': Recreation and Religion in the English Belfry, 1580–1640." In *Worship and the Parish Church in Early Modern Britain*, edited by Natalie Mears and Alec Ryrie, 151–172. Farnham, UK: Ashgate, 2013.

———. *Music and Society in Early Modern England*. Cambridge, UK: Cambridge University Press, 2010.

———. "The Sound of Print in Early Modern England: The Broadside Ballad as Song." In *The Uses of Script and Print, 1300–1700*, edited by Julia C. Crick and Alexandra Walsham, 171–190. Cambridge, UK: Cambridge University Press, 2004.

Marshall, Dorothy. *Dr. Johnson's London*. New York: Wiley, 1968.

Marshall, Peter. "Confessionalization, Confessionalism, and Confusion in the English Reformation." In *Reformation Reformation*, edited by Thomas F. Mayer, 43–64. Farnham, UK: Ashgate, 2012.

———. "The Reformation, Lollardy, and Catholicism." In *A Companion to Tudor Literature*, edited by Kent Cartwright, 15–30. Oxford, UK: Wiley-Blackwell, 2010.

Martin, Cheryl. "The Music Collection of Thomas Baker of Farnham, Surrey." *RMA Research Chronicle* 44 (2013): 19–54.

Mateer, David. "William Byrd, John Petre and Oxford, Bodleian MS Mus. Sch. E. 423." *Royal Musical Association Research Chronicle* 29 (1996): 21–46.

Mateer, David, and Elizabeth New. "'In nomine Jesu': Robert Fayrfax and the Guild of Holy Name in St Paul's Cathedral." *Music & Letters* 81 (2000): 507–519.

May, Thomas. *The Heire*. London, 1622.

Maynard, John. *The XII. Wonders of the World.* London, 1611.
Mazzio, Carla. *The Inarticulate Renaissance: Language Trouble in an Age of Eloquence.* Philadelphia: University of Pennsylvania Press, 2009.
Mazzola, Elizabeth, and Corinne S. Abate. "Introduction: 'Indistinguished Space.'" In *Privacy, Domesticity, and Women in Early Modern England*, edited by Corinne S. Abate, 1–20. Aldershot, UK: Ashgate, 2003.
McBride, Kari Boyd. "Recusant Sisters: English Catholic Women and the Bond of Learning." In *Sibling Relations and Gender in the Early Modern World*, edited by Naomi J. Miller and Naomi Yavneh, 28–39. Aldershot, UK: Ashgate, 2006.
McCarthy, Jeanne. "Disciplining 'Unexpert People': Children's Dramatic Practices and Page/Stage Tensions in Early English Theatre." *The International Shakespeare Yearbook* 10 (2010): 143–164.
McCarthy, Kerry. "Byrd's Patrons at Prayer." *Music & Letters* 89, no. 4 (2008): 499–509.
———. *Liturgy and Contemplation in Byrd's Gradualia.* New York: Routledge, 2007.
———. "The Sanctuarie Is Become a Plaiers Stage: Chapel Stagings and Tudor 'Secular' Drama." *Medieval and Renaissance Drama in England* 21 (2008): 56–86.
McCoog, Thomas M. *The Society of Jesus in Ireland, Scotland, and England, 1541–1588: 'Our Way of Proceeding?'* Leiden, the Netherlands: Brill, 1996.
McElligott, Jason, and David L. Smith, ed. *Royalists and Royalism during the Interregnum.* Manchester, UK: Manchester University Press, 2010.
McGeary, Thomas. "Handel, Prince Frederick, and the Opera of the Nobility Reconsidered." *Göttinger Händel-Beiträge* 7 (1998): 156–178.
McGrath, Patrick, and Joy Rowe. "The Elizabethan Priests: Their Harbourers and Helpers." *Recusant History* 19 (1989): 209–233.
McGuinness, Rosamond. *English Court Odes.* Oxford Monographs on Music. Oxford, UK: Clarendon, 1971.
———. "Music and the Press: Songs for Sale." In special issue *English Culture at the End of the Seventeenth Century*, edited by Robert P. Maccubbin and David F. Morrill. *Eighteenth-Century Life* 12 (November 1988): 139–148.
McKeon, Michael. *The Secret History of Domesticity.* Baltimore: Johns Hopkins University Press, 2005.
McLuhan, Marshall. *The Gutenberg Galaxy: The Making of Typographic Man.* Toronto: University of Toronto Press, 1966.
McMullan, Gordon. "Preface: Renaissance Configurations." In *Renaissance Configurations: Voices/Bodies/Spaces, 1580–1690*, edited by Gordon McMullan, xv–xxiii. London: Macmillan; New York: St. Martin's, 1998.
———, ed. *Renaissance Configurations: Voices, Bodies, Spaces, 1580–1690.* Basingstoke, UK: Palgrave Macmillan, 2001.
McParland, Edward. *James Gandon: Vitruvius Hibernicus.* London: A. Zwemmer, 1985.
McVeigh, Simon. *Concert Life in London from Mozart to Haydn.* Cambridge, UK: Cambridge University Press, 1993.
———. "Introduction." In *Concert Life in Eighteenth-Century Britain*, edited by Susan Wollenberg and Simon McVeigh, 1–15. Aldershot, UK: Ashgate, 2004.
———. "The Professional Concert and Rival Subscription Series in London, 1783–1793." *Royal Musical Association Research Chronicle* 22 (1989): 1–135.
Mellers, Wilfrid. "Words and Music in Elizabethan England." In *The Age of Shakespeare*, Pelican Guide to English Literature, vol. 2, edited by Boris Ford, 386–415. Harmondsworth, UK: Penguin, 1955.

Meres, Francis. *Palladis Tamia Wits Treasury*. London, 1598.
Mertes, Kate. *English Noble Household, 1250–1600: Good Governance and Politic Rule*. Oxford, UK: Blackwell, 1988.
Metastasio, Pietro. *Nitteti*. London, 1774.
Miles, Theodore. "Place-Realism in a Group of Caroline Plays." *Review of English Studies* 18, no. 4 (1942): 428–440.
Milhous, Judith. *Thomas Betterton and the Management of Lincoln's Inn Fields*. Carbondale: Southern Illinois University Press, 1979.
Miller, Bonny H. "Ladies' Companion, Ladies' Canon? Women Composers in American Magazines from *Godey's* to the *Ladies' Home Journal*." In *Cecilia Reclaimed: Feminist Perspectives on Gender and Music*, edited by Susan C. Cook and Judy S. Tsou, 156–182. Urbana: University of Illinois Press, 1994.
———. "A Mirror of Ages Past: The Publication of Music in Domestic Periodicals." *Notes* 50 (1994): 883–901.
Miller, E. H. *The Professional Writers in Elizabethan England*. Cambridge, MA: Harvard University Press, 1959.
Miller, Edwin Shephard. "*Roister Doister*'s 'Funeralls.'" *Studies in Philology* 43, no. 1 (1946): 42–58.
Milsom, John. *Christ Church Music Catalogue Online*. http://library.chch.ox.ac.uk/music/.
———. "Cries of Durham." *Early Music* 17 (1989): 147–160.
———. "Songs and Society in Early Tudor London." *Early Music History* 16 (1997): 235–293.
———. "Walter Porter's *Mottetts* and the 'Duplicity of Duplicates.'" *Christ Church Library Newsletter* 8 (2011–2012): 1–5. http://www.chch.ox.ac.uk/sites/default/files/lib-newsletter-2011-12.pdf (accessed June 28, 2013).
———. "William Mundy's 'Vox Patris Caelestis' and the Accession of Mary Tudor." *Music & Letters* 91, no. 1 (2010): 1–38.
Minear, Erin. *Reverberating Song in Shakespeare and Milton: Language, Memory, and Musical Representation*. Farnham, UK: Ashgate Press, 2011.
Mingotti, Regina. *An Appeal to the Public*. London, [1756].
Monson, Craig. "Thomas Weelkes: A New Fa-la." *The Musical Times* 113 (1972): 133–135.
———. *Voices and Viols in England, 1600–1650: The Sources and the Music*. Ann Arbor, MI: UMI Research Press, 1982.
Monta, Susannah Brietz. "Anne Dacre Howard, Countess of Arundel, and Catholic Patronage." In *English Women, Religion, and Textual Production, 1500–1625*, edited by Micheline White, 59–82. Farnham, UK: Ashgate, 2011.
The Monthly Mask of Vocal Musick, 1702–1711, facsimile edition by Olive Baldwin and Thelma Wilson. Aldershot, UK: Ashgate, 2007.
The Monthly Mask of Vocal Musick or the New-est Songs Made for the Theatre's & Other Occasions Publish'd for June. London, 1705.
Monumenta Angliae I: English and Welsh Jesuits: Catalogue (1555–1629), edited by Thomas M. McCoog. Rome: Institutum Historicum Societatis Iesu, 1992.
Morehen, John. "English Church Music." In *Music in Britain: The Sixteenth Century*, edited by Roger Bray, 94–146. Oxford, UK: Blackwell, 1995.
Morehen, John, and David Mateer, eds. *Thomas Ravenscroft: Rounds, Canons and Songs from Printed Sources*. Musica Britannica, vol. 93. London: Stainer & Bell, 2012.

Morelli, Cesare. *Eight Songs for Samuel Pepys (1680): Light, Grave, and Sacred, for Bass and Guitar*, edited by Dionysios Kyropoulos. Richmond, UK: Green Man Press, [2014].
Morley, Thomas. *The First Booke of Ayres*. London, 1600.
———. *A Plaine and Easie Introduction to Practicall Musicke*. London, 1597.
[Motteux, Peter]. *The Gentleman's Journal*, January 1692.
Mulvany, Thomas J. *The Life of James Gandon, Esq*. Dublin: Hodges and Smith, 1846.
Mulvihill, Maureen E. "A Feminist Link in the Old Boys' Network: The Cosseting of Katherine Philips." In *Curtain Calls: British and American Women and the Theater, 1660–1820*, edited by Mary Anne Schofield and Cecilia Macheski, 71–104. Athens: Ohio University Press, 1991.
Murphy, Anne L. "Trading Options before Black-Scholes: A Study of the Market in Late Seventeenth-Century London." *The Economic History Review* 62 (2009): 8–30.
Murphy, Emilie K. M. "Music and Post-Reformation English Catholics: Place, Sociability, and Space, 1570–1640." PhD thesis, University of York, 2014.
Murphy, Estelle. "The Fashioning of a Nation: The Court Ode in the Later Stuart Period." PhD diss., University College Cork, 2012.
Murray, John Tucker. *English Dramatic Companies, 1558–1642*. London: Constable, 1910.
Murray, Tessa. *Thomas Morley: Elizabethan Music Publisher*. Woodbridge, UK: Boydell, 2014.
Nelson, Katie. "Love in the Music Room: Thomas Whythorne and the Private Affairs of Tudor Music Tutors." *Early Music* 40 (2012): 15–26.
Neuman, Daniel. *The Life of Music in North India: The Organization of an Artistic Tradition*. Chicago: University of Chicago Press, 1990.
New Lady's Magazine; Or, Polite and Entertaining Companion for the Fair Sex. London, 1786–1795. In *History of Women. Periodicals*. New Haven, CT: Research Publications, 1979; also in Hathitrust Digital Library. ECP.
Norland, Howard B. *Drama in Early Tudor Britain 1485–1558*. Lincoln: University of Nebraska Press, 1995.
North, Roger. *Roger North on Music*, edited by John Wilson. London: Novello, 1959.
"The Northern Lasses Lamentation" (1675?). British Library Ms. Roxburghe 2.367. English Broadside Ballad Archive (http://ebba.english.ucsb.edu).
An Ode Pindarick on the Barbadoes. [London, 1703].
Olson, Alison Gilbert. *Making Empire Work: London and American Interest Groups, 1690–1700*. Cambridge, MA: Harvard University Press, 1992.
Ó'Mathúna, Seán. "William Bathe, S.J., Recusant Scholar, 1564–1614: 'Weary of the Heresy.'" *Recusant History* 19 (1988): 47–61.
Ong, Walter. *Orality and Literacy*, 2nd ed. New York: Routledge, 2002.
Orlin, Lena Cowin. *Locating Privacy in Tudor London*. Oxford, UK: Oxford University Press, 2007.
Ortiz, Joseph M. *Broken Harmony: Shakespeare and the Politics of Music*. Ithaca, NY: Cornell University Press, 2011.
Page, Daniel Bennett. "Uniform and Catholic: Church Music in the Reign of Mary Tudor (1553–8)." PhD diss., Brandeis University, 1996.
"Parody, n.2." *OED* (accessed September 30, 2015).

Parrott, Andrew. "Falsetto Beliefs: The 'Countertenor' Cross-Examined." *Early Music* 43 (2015): 79–110.
Parry, Graham. *The Trophies of Time: English Antiquarians of the Seventeenth Century*. Oxford, UK: Oxford University Press, 2007.
Pattison, Bruce. "Notes on Early Music Printing." *The Library*, 4th series 19 (1939): 378–418.
Payne, Ian. "The Provision of Teaching on Viols at Some English Cathedral Churches, c.1594–c.1645: Archival Evidence." *Chelys* 19 (1990): 3–15.
Pearson, Jacqueline. *Women's Reading in Britain 1750–1835: A Dangerous Recreation*. Cambridge, UK: Cambridge University Press, 1999.
Peery, William. "A Prayer for the Queen in *Roister Doister*." *University of Texas Studies in English* 17 (1948): 222–223.
———. "Udall as Timeserver I." *Notes and Queries* 194, no. 6 (1949): 119–121.
———. "Udall as Timeserver II." *Notes and Queries* 194, no. 7 (1949): 138–141.
Penson, Lilian Margery. *The Colonial Agents of the British West Indies*. London: Cass, 1971.
Pepys, Samuel. *The Diary of Samuel Pepys*, 11 vols., edited by Robert Latham and William Matthews. London: Bell & Hyman, 1970–1983.
———. *The Diary of Samuel Pepys: Daily Entries from the 17th Century London Diary*. www.pepysdiary.com/diary/1664/11/04/ (accessed July 2, 2013).
———. *The Letters of Samuel Pepys: 1656–1703*, edited by Guy de la Bédoyère. Woodbridge, UK: Boydell & Brewer, 2006.
Peters, Henriette. *Mary Ward: A World in Contemplation*. Leominster, UK: Gracewing, 1994.
Petti, Anthony G., ed. *Recusant Documents from the Ellesmere Manuscripts*. Catholic Record Society 60 (1968).
Philpot, John. *A Trew Report of the Dysputacyon Had & Begonne in the Convocacyon Hows at London among the Clargye There Assembled the xvii. Daye of October in the Yeare of Our Lord MDLIIII*. London, 1553.
Picard, Liza. *Dr Johnson's London: Coffee-Houses and Climbing Boys, Medicine, Toothpaste and Gin, Poverty and Press-Gangs, Freakshows and Female Education*. New York: St. Martin's, 2000.
Pinnock, Andrew, and Bruce Wood. "Come, Ye Sons of Art—Again: Court Cross-Subsidy for Purcell's Opera Orchestra, 1690–1695." *Early Music* 37, no. 3 (2009): 445–466.
Pinto, David. Booklet notes for Theatre of Voices and Fretwork, *The Cries of London*. Harmonia Mundi HMU 907214, compact disc, 2005.
Playford, Henry. *The Banquet of Musick . . . The Second Book*. London, 1688.
———. *The Lady's Entertainment, The Sixth and Last Book*. London, 1691–92.
———. *The Theater of Music*. [London], 1685
———. *The Theater of Music . . . The Fourth and Last Book*. London, 1687.
———. *Vinculum Societatis . . . The Second Book*. London, 1688.
Playford, John. *Cantica Sacra Containing Hymns and Anthems for Two Voices to the Organ . . . The Second Sett*. London, 1674.
———. *Catch that Catch Can: or the Musical Companion*. London, 1667.
———. *Catch that Catch Can: Or the Second Part of the Pleasant Musical Companion*. London, 1685.

———. *Choice Ayres, Songs and Dialogues . . . Newly Re-printed with Large Additions.* London, 1676.
———. *Choice Ayres, Songs and Dialogues . . . The Fifth Book.* London, 1684.
———. *Choice Ayres, Songs and Dialogues . . . The Fourth Book.* London, 1683.
———. *Choice Ayres, Songs and Dialogues . . . The Second Book.* London, 1679.
———. *Choice Ayres, Songs and Dialogues . . . The Second Edition.* London, 1675.
———. *Choice Songs and Ayres for One Voyce: To Sing to a Theorbo-Lute or Bass-Viol: Being Most of the Newest Songs Sung at Court, and at the Publick Theatres.* London, 1673–1684.
———. *Court-Ayres.* London, 1655.
———. *The Second Part of the Pleasant Musical Companion . . . The Second Edition.* London, 1686.
Pocock, J. G. A. *The Machiavellian Moment: Florentine Political Thought and the Atlantic Republican Tradition.* Princeton, NJ: Princeton University Press, 1975.
Pollack, Linda. "'Living on the Stage of the World': The Concept of Privacy in the Elite of Early Modern England." In *Rethinking Social History*, edited by Adrian Wilson, 21–41. Manchester, UK: Manchester University Press, 1993.
The Poor Mans Comfort. London, 1684.
The Poor Mans Councellor. London, 1684.
Poriss, Hilary. *Changing the Score: Arias, Prima Donnas, and the Authority of Performance.* "New York and Oxford: Oxford University Press, 2009.
Porter, Walter. *Mottetts of Two Voyces for Treble or Tenor and Bass with the Continued Bass or Score.* London, 1657.
Poulton, Diana. "The Black-Letter Broadside Ballad and Its Music." *Early Music* 9 (1981): 427–437.
———. *John Dowland*, 2nd ed. London: Faber & Faber, 1982.
Price, Curtis. *Henry Purcell and the London Stage.* Cambridge, UK: Cambridge University Press, 1984.
———. "Newly Discovered Autograph Keyboard Music of Purcell and Draghi." *Journal of the Royal Musical Association* 120, no. 1 (1995): 77–111.
———. "Unity, Originality, and the London Pasticcio." *Harvard Library Bulletin*, New Series 2, no. 4 (1991): 18–25.
Price, Curtis, Judith Milhous, and Robert D. Hume. *The Impresario's Ten Commandments: Continental Recruitment for Italian Opera in London, 1763–64.* London: Royal Musical Association, 1992.
———. *Italian Opera in Late Eighteenth-Century: I: The King's Theatre, Haymarket, 1778–1791.* Oxford, UK: Clarendon, 1995.
Price, David C. *Patrons and Musicians of the English Renaissance.* Cambridge, UK: Cambridge University Press, 1981.
Price, John. *An Historical Account of the City of Hereford.* Hereford, 1796.
Priscilla Bunbury's Virginal Book, transcribed and edited by Virginia Brookes. Albany, CA: PRB Productions, 1993.
"Private, adj.1, adv., and n." *OED* (accessed May 13, 2014).
"†Private, adj.2." *OED* (accessed May 13, 2014).
Purcell, Henry. *A Musical Entertainment Perform'd on November XXII, 1683 It Being the Festival of St. Cecilia.* London, 1684.

———. *Orpheus Britannicus, A Collection of All the Choicest Songs for One, Two, and Three Voices.* London, 1698.
———. *Secular Songs for Solo Voice,* edited by Margaret Laurie. *The Works of Henry Purcell,* vol. 25. Borough Green, UK: Novello, 1985.
———. *Thirty Songs in Two Volumes,* 2 vols., edited by Timothy Roberts. Oxford, UK: Oxford University Press, 1995.
[Puttenham, George; or Puttenham, Richard?]. *The Arte of English Poesie.* London, 1589.
Quintrell, Brian. "Weston, Richard, First Earl of Portland (*bap.* 1577, *d.* 1635)." *DNB* (accessed November 21, 2013).
Radice, Mark A. "Henry Purcell's Contributions to The Gentleman's Journal, Part I." *BACH: The Journal of the Riemenschneider Bach Institute* 9 (1978): 25–30.
———. "Henry Purcell's Contributions to The Gentleman's Journal, Part II." *BACH: The Journal of the Riemenschneider Bach Institute* 10 (1979): 26–31.
Rambuss, Richard. *Closet Devotions.* Durham, NC: Duke University Press, 1998.
Ratio atque institutio studiorum per sex patres ad id iussu R. P. Praepositi Generalis deputatos conscripta. Rome, 1586.
Ravenscroft, Thomas. *Thomas Ravenscroft: Rounds, Canons and Songs from Printed Sources,* edited by John Morehen and David Mateer, *Musica Britannica,* vol. 93. London: Stainer and Bell, 2012.
———. *The Whole Booke of Psalmes . . . Composed into 4.* London, 1633.
Raylor, Timothy. *Cavaliers, Clubs, and Literary Culture: Sir John Mennes, James Smith, and the Order of the Fancy.* Newark: University of Delaware Press, 1994.
Raymond, Joad, ed. *The Oxford History of Popular Print Culture,* vol. 1. Oxford, UK: Clarendon Press, 2011.
Records of London's Livery Companies Online: Apprentices and Freemen 1400–1900. (accessed July 6, 2014) http://www.londonroll.org.
Rees, Owen. "Luisa de Carvajal y Mendosa and Music in an English Catholic House in 1605." In *Essays on the History of English Music in Honour of John Caldwell: Sources, Style, Performance, Historiography,* edited by Emma Hornby and David Maw, 270–280. Woodbridge, UK: Boydell, 2010.
Reggio, Pietro. *The Art of Singing, or A Treatise, wherein Is Shown How to Sing Well Any Song Whatsoever.* Oxford, 1677.
———. *Songs Set by Signior Pietro Reggio.* London, 1680.
Reverand, Cedric D., ed. *Queen Anne and the Arts.* Lewisburg, PA: Bucknell University Press, 2014.
Rhodes, Elizabeth. "Join the Jesuits, See the World: Early Modern Women in Spain and the Society of Jesus." In *The Jesuits II: Cultures, Sciences, and the Arts, 1540–1773,* edited by John W. O'Malley, Gauvin Alexander Bailey, Steven J. Harris, and T. Frank Kennedy, 33–49. Toronto: University of Toronto Press, 2006.
Ribadeneira, Pedro. *Life of B. Father Ignatius of Loyola. Translated out of Spanish into English, by W. M.* [Michael Walpole] *of the Same Society.* Saint-Omer, 1616.
Richards, Judith M. *Mary Tudor.* London: Routledge, 2008.
Ritchie, Leslie. *Women Writing Music in Late Eighteenth-Century England: Social Harmony in Literature and Performance.* Performance in the Long Eighteenth Century: Studies in Theatre, Music, Dance. Aldershot, UK: Ashgate, 2008.

Rivers, Isabel. "Prayer-Book Devotion: The Literature of the Proscribed Episcopal Church." In *The Cambridge Companion to Writing of the English Revolution*, edited by N. H. Keeble, 198–214. Cambridge, UK: Cambridge University Press, 2001.

Robins, Brian. *Catch and Glee Culture in Eighteenth-Century England*. Woodbridge, UK: Boydell, 2006.

———. "The Catch and Glee in Provincial England." In *Concert Life in Eighteenth-Century Britain*, edited by Susan Wollenberg and Simon McVeigh, 141–160. Aldershot, UK: Ashgate, 2004.

Robinson, Charles J. *A History of the Castles of Herefordshire and Their Lords*. London: Longman, 1869.

———. *A Register of the Scholars Admitted into Merchant Taylor's School: From A.D. 1562 to 1874*. Lewes, England: printed by Farncombe, 1882.

Rodger, N. A. M. *The Command of the Ocean: A Naval History of Britain 1649–1815*. London: Norton, 2004.

Rogers, Everett M. *Diffusion of Innovations*, 3rd ed. London: Free Press, 1983.

Rorschach, Kimerly. "Frederick, Prince of Wales (1707–51), as Collector and Patron." *The Walpole Society* 55 (1989/90): 1–76.

Rose, Gloria. "Pietro Reggio: A Wandering Musician." *Music & Letters* 46 (1965): 207–216.

Rose, Gloria, and Robert Spencer. "Reggio, Pietro." *GMO* (accessed June 20, 2012).

Rose, Stephen. "Performance Practices." In *The Ashgate Research Companion to Henry Purcell*, edited by Rebecca Herissone, 115–164. Farnham, UK: Ashgate, 2012.

Roseveare, H. G. "Lethieullier, Sir John (1632/3–1719)." *DNB* (accessed July 18, 2013).

Rosseter, Philip. *A Booke of Ayres, Set Foorth to Be Song to the Lute*. London, 1601.

Rowlands, Marie B. "Recusant Women, 1560–1640." In *Women in English Society 1500–1800*, edited by Mary Prior, 149–180. London: Methuen, 1985.

Rowley, Samuel, and Thomas Dekker. *The Noble Souldier*. London, 1634.

Rubin, Emanuel. *The English Glee in the Reign of George III: Participatory Art Music for an Urban Society*. Warren, MI: Harmonie Park, 2003.

Ruff, Lillian M., and Arnold A. Wilson. "The Madrigal, the Lute Song and Elizabethan Politics." *Past and Present* 44 (1969): 3–51.

Russell, Anne. "Katherine Philips as Political Playwright: 'The Songs between the Acts' in *Pompey*." *Comparative Drama* 44 (2010): 299–323.

Les Sacqueboutiers. *The Cries of London*, booklet notes by Philippe Canguilhem. Ambroisie AMB 9965. Recorded in 2004.

Saltonstall, Wye. *Picturae loquentes*. London, 1631.

Sanders, Julie. *Caroline Drama: The Plays of Massinger, Ford, Shirley, and Brome*. Plymouth, UK: Northcote House, 1999.

———. *The Cultural Geography of Early Modern Drama, 1620–1650*. Cambridge, UK: Cambridge University Press, 2011.

———. "Introduction to *The Northern Lass*." *Richard Brome Online* http://www.hrionline.ac.uk/brome (accessed June 22, 2014).

Sandys, George. *A Paraphrase on the Divine Poems*. London, 1638.

———. *A Paraphrase on the Psalmes of David*. London, 1636.

Sargent, Brian. *Oyez! Elizabethan and Jacobean Street Cries*. Huntingdon, UK: King's Music, 1992.

Saunders, J. W. *The Profession of English Letters*. London: Routledge and Kegan Paul, 1964.

Scarisbrick, J. J. *The Reformation and the English People*. Oxford, UK: Blackwell, 1984.
Scheurweghs, G., ed. *Materials for the Study of the Old English Drama*. Vaduz, Liechtenstein: Kraus Reprint, 1963.
Schwegler, Robert. "Oral Tradition and Print: Domestic Performance in Renaissance England." *The Journal of American Folklore* 93, no. 370 (1980): 435–441.
Scully, Robert E. "Trickle Down Spirituality? Dilemmas of the Elizabethan Mission." In *The Formation of Clerical and Confessional Identities in Early Modern Europe*, edited by Wim Janse and Barbara Pitkin, 285–299. Leiden, the Netherlands: Brill, 2006.
Seeger, Charles. "Prescriptive and Descriptive Music-Writing." *Musical Quarterly* 44, no. 2 (1958): 184–195.
Sennett, Richard. *The Fall of Public Man*. London: Faber, 1977.
Sequera, Hector. "House Music for Recusants in Elizabethan England: Performance Practice in the Music Collection of Edward Paston (1550–1630)." PhD thesis, University of Birmingham, 2010.
Shadwell, Thomas. *The Tempest or the Enchanted Island. A Comedy. As It Is Now Acted at His Highness the Duke of York's Theatre*. London, 1674.
Shapiro, I. A. "Thomas Campion's Medical Degree." *Notes and Queries* 117 (1957): 495.
Shapiro, Michael. *Children of the Revels: The Boy Companies of Shakespeare's Time and Their Plays*. New York: Columbia University Press, 1977.
———. "Early Boy Companies and Their Acting Venues." In *The Oxford Handbook of Early Modern Theater*, edited by Richard Dutton, 121–135. Oxford, UK: Oxford University Press, 2011.
Sharp, A. Mary. *The History of Ufton Court*. London: Elliot Stock, 1892.
Shaw, Catherine M. *Richard Brome*. Boston: Twayne, 1980.
Shaw, H. Watkins. *The Succession of Organists of the Chapel Royal and the Cathedrals of England and Wales from c.1538*. Oxford, UK: Clarendon, 1991.
Shay, Robert. "'Naturalizing' Palestrina and Carissimi in Late Seventeenth-Century Oxford: Henry Aldrich and His Recompositions." *Music & Letters* 77 (1996): 368–400.
Shay, Robert, and Robert Thompson. *Purcell Manuscripts: The Principal Musical Sources*. Cambridge, UK: Cambridge University Press, 2000.
Shell, Alison, *Catholicism, Controversy and the English Literary Imagination, 1558–1660*. Cambridge, UK: Cambridge University Press, 2006.
———. *Oral Culture and Catholicism in Early Modern England*. Cambridge, UK: Cambridge University Press, 2007.
Shepard, Alexandra, and Phil Worthington. "Introduction: Communities in Early Modern England." In *Communities in Early Modern England: Networks, Place, Rhetoric*, edited by Alexandra Shepard and Phil Worthington, 1–17. Manchester, UK: Manchester University Press, 2000.
Shepherd, Leslie. *The Broadside Ballad: A Study in Origins and Meanings*. London: Herbert Jenkins, 1962.
Sherlock, Peter. *Monuments and Memory in Early Modern England*. Aldershot, UK: Ashgate, 2008.
Sherman, William H. *Used Books: Marking Readers in Renaissance England*. Philadelphia: University of Pennsylvania Press, 2008.
Shesgreen, Sean, and Bywaters, David. "The First London Cries for Children." *Princeton University Library Chronicle* 59 (1998): 223–250.

Shevelow, Kathryn. *Women and Print Culture: The Construction of Femininity in the Early Periodical.* London: Routledge, 1989.
Shifflett, Andrew. "'How Many Virtues Must I Hate': Katherine Philips and the Politics of Clemency." *Studies in Philology* 94 (1997): 103–135.
Shohet, Lauren. *Reading Masques: The English Masque and Public Culture in the Seventeenth Century.* Oxford, UK: Oxford University Press, 2010.
Short, Roger. "Morelli, Cesare." *GMO* (accessed June 1, 2015).
Silbiger, Alexander. "The Roman Frescobaldi Tradition: 1640–1670." *Journal of the American Musicological Society* 33 (1980): 42–87.
Simmonds, Gemma. "Women Jesuits?" In *The Cambridge Companion to the Jesuits*, edited by Thomas Worcester, 120–135. Cambridge, UK: Cambridge University Press, 2008.
Simonds, Peggy Muñoz. *Myth, Emblem, and Music in Shakespeare's "Cymbeline."* Newark: University of Delaware Press, 1992.
Simpson, A. D. C. "Neile, Sir Paul (*bap.* 1613, *d.*1682x6)." *DNB* (accessed July 1, 2013).
Simpson, Christopher. *A Compendium of Practicall Musick.* London, 1667.
Simpson, Claude. *The British Broadside Ballad and Its Music.* New Brunswick, NJ: Rutgers University Press, 1966.
Simpson, James. "John Bale, *Three Laws.*" In *The Oxford Handbook of Tudor Drama*, edited by Thomas Betteridge and Greg Walker, 109–122. Oxford, UK: Oxford University Press, 2012.
Smith, Bruce R. *The Acoustic World of Early Modern England.* Chicago: University of Chicago Press, 1999.
———. "Female Impersonation in Early Modern Ballads." In *Women Players in England, 1500–1660: Beyond the All-Male Stage*, edited by Pamela Allen Brown and Peter Parolin, 284–301. Aldershot, UK: Ashgate, 2008.
Smith, Jeremy. *Thomas East and Music Publishing in Renaissance England.* Oxford, UK: Oxford University Press, 2003.
Smith, Peter J. "The Instrumental Music of Peter Philips: Its Sources, Dissemination, and Style." PhD thesis, Oxford University, 1993.
Smith, Ruth. *Handel's Oratorios and Eighteenth-Century Thought.* Cambridge, UK: Cambridge University Press, 1995.
Smith, William C. *The Italian Opera and Contemporary Ballet in London, 1789–1820; A Record of Performances and Players, with Reports from the Journals of the Time.* London: Society for Theatre Research, 1955.
Smith, William C., and Charles Humphries. *A Bibliography of the Musical Works Published by the Firm of John Walsh during the Years 1721–1766.* London: Bibliographical Society, 1968.
Smyth, Adam, *"Profit and Delight": Printed Miscellanies in England, 1640–1682.* Detroit, MI: Wayne State University Press, 2004.
Snook, Edith. *Women, Reading, and the Cultural Politics of Early Modern England.* Aldershot, UK: Ashgate, 2005.
Solitudes and Sufferings, Rendred in Verse. London, 1657.
The Songs and Symphonys Perform'd before Her Majesty at Her Palace of St. James, on New-Years Day . . . Published for February 1703. London, [1703].
Southern, A. C., ed. *An Elizabethan Recusant House: Comprising the Life of Lady Magdalen Viscountess Montague.* London: Sands, 1954.

Southey, Roz. "The Role of Gentlemen Amateurs in Subscription Concerts." In *Music in the British Provinces, 1690–1914*, edited by Rachel Holman and Peter Holman, 115–128. Aldershot, UK: Ashgate, 2007.
Southgate, T. Lea. "Music at the Public Pleasure Gardens of the Eighteenth Century." *Proceedings of the Musical Association*, 38th Session (1911–1912): 141–159.
Southwell, Robert. *An Epistle of Comfort*. [London,] 1587.
———. *Saint Peters Complaint, with Other Poems*. London, 1595.
Spacks, Patricia Meyer. *Privacy: Concealing the Eighteenth-Century Self*. Chicago: University of Chicago Press, 2003.
Sperontes. *Singende Muse an der Pleisse*. Leipzig, 1736; facsimile reprint, Leipzig: VEB Deutscher Verlag für Musik, 1964.
Spierling, Karen E., and Michael J. Halvorson. "Introduction: Definitions of Community in Early Modern Europe." In *Defining Community in Early Modern Europe*, edited by Michael J. Halvorson and Karen E. Spierling, 1–23. Aldershot, UK: Ashgate, 2008.
Spink, Ian. "Badham, Charles." *GMO* (accessed July 1, 2013).
———. *Henry Lawes, Cavalier Songwriter*. Oxford, UK: Oxford University Press, 2000.
———. "Music and Society." In *The Blackwell History of Music in Britain: The Seventeenth Century*, edited by Ian Spink, 1–65. Oxford, UK: Blackwell, 1992.
———. "The Old Jewry 'Musick-Society': A 17th-Century Catch Club." *Musicology* 2 (1965–67): 35–41.
———. *Restoration Cathedral Music 1660–1714*. Oxford, UK: Oxford University Press, 1995.
Spring, Matthew. *The Lute in Britain: A History of the Instrument and Its Music*. Oxford, UK: Oxford University Press, 2001.
Stanhope, Philip Dormer. *Letters to His Son by the Earl of Chesterfield on the Fine Art of Becoming a Man of the World and a Gentleman*, 2 vols., edited by Oliver H. G. Leigh. London: Navarre Society, 1926.
Starr, Pamela F. "Music Education and the Conduct of Life in Early Modern England: A Review of the Sources." In *Music Education in the Middle Ages and the Renaissance*, edited by Russell E. Murray Jr., Susan Forscher Weiss, and Cynthia J. Cyrus, 193–206. Bloomington: Indiana University Press, 2010.
Steele, [Richard]. *The Lying Lover: Or, the Ladies Friendship*. London, 1704.
Steele, Robert. *The Earliest English Music Printing*. London: Bibliographical Society, 1903.
Steggle, Matthew. *Richard Brome: Place and Politics on the Caroline Stage*. Manchester, UK: Manchester University Press, 2004.
Stern, Tiffany. *Documents of Performance in Early Modern England*. Cambridge, UK: Cambridge University Press, 2009.
———, ed. *A Jovial Crew, or The Merry Beggars. By Richard Brome*. London: Bloomsbury Arden Shakespeare, 2014.
———. *Making Shakespeare: From Stage to Page*. London: Routledge, 2004.
Sternfeld, F. W., and David Greer, eds. *English Madrigal Verse*. Oxford, UK: Clarendon, 1967.
Sternhold, Thomas, and John Hopkins. *The Whole Book of Psalmes: Collected into English Meeter*. London, 1673.
Stevens, John. *Music and Poetry in the Early Tudor Court*. London: Methuen, 1961.

Stokes, Martin. *Ethnicity, Identity, and Music: The Musical Construction of Place.* Oxford, UK: Berg, 1994.
Stone, Lawrence. *The Family, Sex and Marriage in England 1500–1800.* London: Weidenfeld & Nicolson, 1977.
Streitberger, W. R. *Court Revels, 1485–1559.* Toronto: University of Toronto Press, 1994.
Strohm, Reinhard. *Dramma per Musica: Italian Opera Seria of the Eighteenth Century.* New Haven, CT: Yale University Press, 1997.
———. *The Operas of Antonio Vivaldi.* Fondazione "Giorgio Cini" Istituto italiano Antonio Vivaldi, 2008.
Strype, John. *Annals of the Reformation and Establishment of Religion . . . during Queen Elizabeth's Happy Reign,* new ed., volume 3, part 2. Oxford, UK: Clarendon, 1824.
———. *The History of the Life and Acts of . . . Edmund Grindal.* Oxford, UK: Clarendon, 1821.
Suarez, Michael F., SJ. "Bibles, Libels, and Bute: The Development of Scriptural Satire in the Eighteenth-Century Political Print." *The Age of Johnson, a Scholarly Annual* 5 (1992): 341–389.
———. "The Mock Biblical: A Study in English Satire from the Popish Plot to the Pretender's Crisis, 1678–1747." DPhil diss., University of Oxford, 1999.
Sullivan, Alvin, ed. *British Literary Magazines [1]: The Augustan Age and the Age of Johnson, 1698–1788.* Westport, CT: Greenwood, 1983.
Sullivan, Alvin, ed. *British Literary Magazines [2]: The Romantic Age, 1789 –1836.* Westport, CT: Greenwood, 1983.
Sullivan, Garrett. *Memory and Forgetting in English Renaissance Drama: Shakespeare, Marlowe, and Webster.* Cambridge, UK: Cambridge University Press, 2005.
Swaim, Kathleen M. "Matching the 'Matchless Orinda' to Her Times." In *1650–1850: Ideas, Aesthetics, and Inquiries in the Early Modern Era,* vol. 3, edited by Kevin L. Cope, 77–108. New York: AMS, 1997.
Taruskin, Richard. *Text and Act: Essays on Music and Performance.* New York: Oxford University Press, 1995.
Taverner, Richard. *An Oration Gradulatory Made upon the Joyfull Proclayming of the Moste Noble Princes Quene Mary Quene of Englande.* London, 1553.
Taylor, Silas. *The History of Gavel-Kind with the Etymology Thereof.* London, 1663.
———. *Impostor Magnus, or the Legerdemain of Richard Delamain Now Preacher in the City of Hereford.* London, 1654.
———. "Of the Way of Killing Ratle-Snakes." *Philosophical Transactions* 1 (1665): 43.
Temperley, Nicholas. "'If Any of You Be Mery Let Hym Synge Psalmes': The Culture of Psalms in Church and Home." In *"Noyses, Sounds and Sweet Aires": Music in Early Modern England,* edited by Jessie Ann Owens, 90–99. Washington, DC: Folger Shakespeare Library, 2006.
———. *The Music of the English Parish Church,* vol. 1. Cambridge, UK: Cambridge University Press, 1979.
The Testament of William Bel. Gentleman. Left Written in His Owne Hand. Sett ovt above 33. Yeares after His Death. With Annotations at the End, and Sentences, out of the H. Scripture, Fathers, &c. By his Sonne Francis Bel, of the Order of Freers Minors. Douay, France, 1632.

Theatre of Voices and Fretwork. *The Cries of London*, booklet notes by David Pinto. Harmonia Mundi HMU 907214, compact disc, 2005.

Thompson, Robert. "George Jeffreys and the 'Stile Nuovo' in English Sacred Music: A New Date for His Autograph Score, British Library Add. MS 10338." *Music & Letters* 70 (1989): 317–341.

——. "Locke, Matthew (c.1622–1677)." *DNB* (accessed June 29, 2013).

——. "Manuscript Music in Purcell's London." *Early Music* 23, no. 4 (1995): 613–616.

——. "Some Late Sources of Music by John Jenkins." In *John Jenkins and His Time: Studies in English Consort Music*, edited by Andrew Ashbee and Peter Holman, 271–308. Oxford, UK: Clarendon, 1996.

——. "Sources and Transmission." In *The Ashgate Research Companion to Henry Purcell*, edited by Rebecca Herissone, 13–63. Farnham, UK: Ashgate, 2012.

Thomson, Robert S. "The Development of the Broadside Ballad Trade and Its Influence upon the Transmission of English Folksongs." PhD thesis, University of Cambridge, 1974.

Thurley, Simon. *The Royal Palaces of Tudor England*. New Haven, CT: Yale University Press, 1993.

Tilmouth, Michael. "Calendar of References to Music in Newspapers." *RMA Research Chronicle* 1 (1961): 1–107.

——. "Music on the Travels of an English Merchant: Robert Bargrave (1628–61)." *Music & Letters* 53 (1972): 143–159.

Titus Andronicus Complaint. London, 1624.

The Tragical History of King Lear. London, [1700].

Tremellius, Immanuel, Franciscus Junius, and Théodore de Bèze. *Biblia sacra*. London, 1640.

Tribble, Evelyn. "Distributing Cognition in the Globe." *Shakespeare Quarterly* 56, no. 2 (2005): 135–155.

Trillini, Regula Hohl. *The Gaze of the Listener: English Representations of Domestic Music-Making*. Amsterdam: Rodopi, 2008.

Trowell, Brian. "Daniel Defoe's Plan for an Academy of Music at Christ's Hospital, with Some Notes on His Attitude to Music." In *Source Materials and the Interpretation of Music: A Memorial Volume to Thurston Dart*, edited by Ian Bent, 403–427. London: Stainer & Bell, 1981.

Trull, Mary. *Performing Privacy and Gender in Early Modern Literature*. Basingstoke, UK: Palgrave Macmillan, 2013.

Tudor Royal Proclamations, vol. 2, edited by Paul L. Hughes and James F. Larkin. New Haven, CT: Yale University Press, 1969.

Turino, Thomas. *Music as Social Life: The Politics of Participation*. Chicago: University of Chicago Press, 2008.

Turner, Elizabeth. *A Collection of Songs with Symphonies and a Through Bass with Six Lessons for the Harpsichord. Compos'd by Miss Eliza: Turner*. London: Elizabeth Turner, 1756. *Eighteenth Century Collections Online*. Gale (accessed July 1, 2014). Also republished in *English Music in Facsimile*. Alston, UK: J. P. H. Publications, 1999.

Turner, Elizabeth. *Twelve Songs with Symphonies and a Thorough Bass for the Harpsicord*. London, 1750. In HathiTrust Digital Library (accessed August 15, 2015).

Turner, William. *Jewel of Joye*. London, 1550[?].

———. *A Worke Entytled Of Ye Olde God & the Newe*. London, [1534].
Udall, Nicholas. "Ralph Roister Doister." In *The Dramatic Writings of Nicholas Udall*, edited by John S. Farmer, 1–112. London: Early English Drama Society, 1906.
———. "Ralph Roister Doister." In *Materials for the Study of the Old English Drama*, vol. 16, edited by G. Scheurweghs. Vaduz, Liechtenstein: Kraus Reprint, 1963.
———. "Royster Doyster." In *Tudor Plays: An Anthology of Early English Drama*, edited by Edmund Creeth, 215–314. New York: Anchor Books, 1966.
Ussher, James. *De Romanae Ecclesiae symbolo apostolico vetere aliisque fidei formulis*. London, 1647.
Van Orden, Kate. *Music, Authorship, and the Book in the First Century of Print*. Oakland: University of California Press, 2013.
V[eel], R[obert]. *New Court-Songs and Poems*. London, 1672.
[Verstegan, Richard]. *Odes in Imitation of the Seaven Penitential Psalmes, with Sundry Other Poems and Ditties Tending to Devotion and Pietie*. [Antwerp], 1601.
Vickery, Amanda. *Behind Closed Doors: At Home in Georgian England*. New Haven, CT: Yale University Press, 2009.
———. "Golden Age to Separate Spheres? A Review of the Categories and Chronology of English Women's History." *The Historical Journal* 36 (1993): 383–414.
Viola da Gamba Society. *Thematic Index of Music for Viols*. http://www.vdgs.org.uk/files/thematicIndex (accessed June 10, 2013).
Vivian, Percival, ed. *Campion's Works*. Oxford, UK: Clarendon, 1909.
Wainwright, Jonathan P. *Musical Patronage in Seventeenth-Century England: Christopher, First Baron Hatton (1605–1670)*. Aldershot, UK: Scholar Press, Ashgate, 1997.
———. "Richard Dering's Few-Voice 'Concertato' Motets." *Music & Letters* 89 (2008): 165–194.
Wales, Katie. *Northern English: A Cultural and Social History*. Cambridge, UK: Cambridge University Press, 2006.
Walker, Claire. "Continuity and Isolation: The Bridgettines of Syon in the Sixteenth and Seventeenth Centuries." In *Syon Abbey and Its Books: Reading, Writing and Religion, c.1400–1700*, edited by E. A. Jones and A. Walsham, 155–176. Woodbridge, UK: Boydell, 2011.
Walker, Greg. *The Politics of Performance in Early Renaissance Drama*. Cambridge, UK: Cambridge University Press, 1998.
Walkling, Andrew. "Politics, Occasions, and Texts." In *Ashgate Research Companion to Henry Purcell*, edited by Rebecca Herissone, 201–267. Farnham, UK: Ashgate, 2012.
Wallace, Charles William. "The Children of the Chapel at Blackfriars, 1597–1603." *University Studies (University of Nebraska, Lincoln Campus)* 8, no. 2–3 (1908): xii–207.
Walpole, Horace. *Horace Walpole's Correspondence*, 48 vols., edited by W. S. Lewis. New Haven, CT: Yale University Press, 1937–1983. Volume 25: *Horace Walpole's Correspondence with Sir Horace Mann and Sir Horace Mann the Younger*, edited by W. S. Lewis, Warren Hunting Smith, and George L. Lam. New Haven, CT: Yale University Press, 1973.
Walsham, Alexandra. "Translating Trent? English Catholicism and the Counter Reformation." *Historical Research* 78 (2005): 288–310.

Walton, Izaak. *The Complete Angler; or, The Contemplative Man's Recreation*. London, 1653.
Ward, John. "Apropos the British Broadside Ballad and Its Music." *Journal of the American Musicological Society* 20 (1967): 28–86.
———. "A Dowland Miscellany." *Journal of the Lute Society of America* 10 (1977): 5–153.
———. "The Osborn Commonplace-Book." In *Music for Elizabethan Lutes*, edited by John Ward, 22–36. Oxford, UK Oxford University Press, 1992.
———. "Sprightly & Cheerful Musick." *Lute Society Journal* 21 (1979–1981): 1–234.
Warlock, Peter. *The English Ayre*. London: Oxford University Press, 1926.
Warmington, Andrew. "Massey, Sir Edward (1604x9–1674)." *DNB* (accessed July 3, 2013).
A Warning for Wives. London, 1629.
Watkins, John. "Moralities, Interludes, and Protestant Drama." In *The Cambridge History of Medieval English Literature*, edited by David Wallace, 767–792. Cambridge, UK: Cambridge University Press, 1999.
Watson, William. *A Decacordon of Ten Quodlibeticall Questions concerning Religion and State*. [London], 1602.
Watt, Tessa. *Cheap Print and Popular Piety 1550–1640*. Cambridge, UK: Cambridge University Press, 1991.
———. "Cheap Print and Religion, c. 1550 to 1640." PhD diss., University of Cambridge, 1988.
Webb, John. *Memorials of the Civil War between King Charles I and the Parliament of England as It Affected Herefordshire and the Adjacent Counties*, 2 vols., edited by Thomas W. Webb. London: Longmans, Green, 1879.
West, Susie. "Social Space and the English Country House." In *The Familiar Past? Archaeologies of Later Historical Britain*, edited by Sarah Tarlow and Susie West, 103–122. London: Routledge, 1999.
West, William N. *Theatres and Encyclopedias in Early Modern Europe*. Cambridge, UK: Cambridge University Press, 2002.
Westfall, Suzanne. *Patrons and Performance: Early Tudor Household Revels*. Oxford, UK: Clarendon, 1990.
Weston, William. *The Autobiography of an Elizabethan*, edited and translated by Philip Caraman. London: Longmans, Green, 1955.
West-Pavlov, Russell. *Bodies and Their Spaces: System, Crisis and Transformation in Early Modern Theatre*. Amsterdam: Rodopi, 2006.
Westrup, J. A. "Domestic Music under the Stuarts." *Proceedings of the Royal Musical Association* 68 (1941–1942): 19–53.
———. *Purcell*. The Master Musicians. London: Dent; New York: Dutton, 1937.
———. *Purcell*. The Master Musicians. Rev. ed. with a new Foreword by Curtis Price. Oxford and New York: Oxford University Press, 1995; first published London: Dent, 1937.
Westrup, J. A., and Ian Spink. "Taylor, Silas." *GMO* (accessed June 29, 2013).
Wheble's Lady's Magazine. London, 1770–1772. Eighteenth Century Collections Online. Gale. ECP.
White, Bryan. "'Brothers of the String': Henry Purcell and the Letter-Books of Rowland Sherman." *Music & Letters* 92 (2011): 519–581.

———. "Mixing 'Britain's Orpheus' with 'Corelli's Heights': A Cecilian Entertainment in Stamford." Paper presented at the 14th Biennial International Conference on Baroque Music, Queen's University Belfast, June 30–July 4, 2010.
———. "'A Pretty Knot of Musical Friends': The Ferrar Brothers and a Stamford Music Club in the 1690s." In *Music in the British Provinces, 1690–1914*, edited by Rachel Cowgill and Peter Holman, 9–44. Aldershot, UK: Ashgate, 2007.
White, Bryan, and Andrew Woolley. "Jeremiah Clarke (c. 1674–1707): A Tercentenary Tribute." *Early Music Performer* 21 (2007): 25–36.
White, Paul Whitfield. *Theater and Reformation: Protestantism, Patronage , and Playing in Tudor England*. Cambridge, UK: Cambridge University Press, 1993.
Whitehead, David. "Taylor, Silas (1624–1678)." *DNB* (accessed June 29, 2013).
Whitehead, Maurice. "'To Provide for the Ediface of Learning': Researching 450 Years of Jesuit Educational and Cultural History, with Particular Reference to the British Jesuits." *History of Education* 36, no. 1 (2007): 109–143.
Whitelock, Anna. *Mary Tudor: Princess, Bastard, Queen*. New York: Random House, 2009.
Whitelocke, Bulstrode. *Memorials of the English Affairs*. London, 1682.
Whitney, Geffrey. *A Choice of Emblemes, and Other Deuises*. Leiden, 1636.
Whyman, Susan E. "Verney, John, First Viscount Fermanagh (1640–1717)." *DNB* (accessed July 18, 2013).
Whythorne, Thomas. *The Autobiography of Thomas Whythorne*, edited by James M. Osborn. Oxford, UK: Clarendon, 1961.
Wickham, Glynne, Herbert Berry, and William Ingram, eds. *English Professional Theatre, 1530–1660*. Cambridge, UK: Cambridge University Press, 2000.
Wilder, Lina Perkins. *Shakespeare's Memory Theater*. Cambridge, UK: Cambridge University Press, 2010.
Williams, Sarah F. "'A Swearing and Blaspheming Wretch': Representations of Witchcraft and Excess in Early Modern English Broadside Balladry and Popular Song." *Journal of Musicological Research* 30, no. 4 (2011): 309–356.
———. *Damnable Practises: Witches, Dangerous Women, and Music in Seventeenth-Century English Broadside Ballads*. Farnham, UK: Ashgate Press, 2015.
Willis, Jonathan. *The Art of Memory*. London, 1621.
———. *Mnemonica*. London, 1661.
Willis, Jonathan P. *Church Music and Protestantism in Post-Reformation England: Discourses, Sites, and Identities*. Aldershot, UK: Ashgate, 2010.
Wilson, Christopher R. "Campion, Thomas." *GMO* (accessed August 15, 2015).
———. *"A New Way of Making Fowre Parts in Counterpoint" by Thomas Campion and "Rules How to Compose" by Giovanni Coprario*. Music Theory in Britain, 1500–1700. Critical Editions. Aldershot, UK: Ashgate, 2003.
———. "Thomas Campion's 'Ayres Filled with Parts' Reconsidered." *The Lute: Journal of the Lute Society* 23, no. 2 (1983): 3–12.
———. "'Words and Notes Coupled Lovingly Together': Thomas Campion, a Critical Study*. New York: Garland, 1989.
W[ilson], R[obert]. *A Right Excellent and Famous Comoedy Called the Three Ladies of London*. London: Roger Warde, 1584.
Winn, James Anderson. *Queen Anne: Patroness of Arts*. Oxford, UK: Oxford University Press, 2014.

Winton, Calhoun. "Steele, Sir Richard (bap. 1672, d. 1729)." *DNB* (accessed May 30, 2013).
Wit and Mirth: Or Pills to Purge Melancholy, vol. 4. London: printed by W. Pearson, 1706.
Withington, Phil. *The Politics of Commonwealth: Citizens and Freemen in Early Modern England*. Cambridge, UK: Cambridge University Press, 2005.
Witzenmann, Wolfgang. "Marazzoli, Marco [Marco dell'Arpa]." *GMO* (accessed June 1, 2015).
Wood, Anthony. *Athenae Oxonienses: An Exact History of All the Writers and Bishops Who Have Had Their Education in the University of Oxford*, 3rd ed., edited by Philip Bliss. London: F. C. and J. Rivington and twelve others, 1817.
Woodfield, Ian. *The Early History of the Viol*. Cambridge, UK: Cambridge University Press, 1988.
———. *Salomon and the Burneys: Private Patronage and a Public Career*. Aldershot, UK: Ashgate, 2003.
Woodhead, J. R. *The Rulers of London 1660-1689: A Biographical Record of the Aldermen and Common Councilmen of the City of London*. London: London & Middlesex Archaeological Society, 1965.
Wooding, Lucy. "The Marian Restoration and the Mass." In *The Church of Mary Tudor*, edited by Eamon Duffy and David Loades, 227–257. Aldershot, UK: Ashgate, 2006.
Woolley, Andrew Lawrence. "English Keyboard Sources and Their Contexts, c. 1660–c. 1720." PhD thesis, University of Leeds, 2008.
Wong, Katrine K. *Music and Gender in English Renaissance Drama*. New York: Routledge, 2013.
Wriothesley, Charles. *A Chronicle of England during the Reigns of the Tudors*, edited by William Douglas Hamilton. London: Camden Society, 1875.
Würzbach, Natascha. *The Rise of the English Street Ballad, 1550–1650*, translated by Gayna Walls. Cambridge, UK: Cambridge University Press, 1990.
Yardley, Edward. *Menevia Sacra (1746)*, edited by Francis Green. London: Bedford Press, 1927.
Yates, Frances. *The Art of Memory*. Chicago: University of Chicago Press, 1966.
Yelloly, Margaret. "'The Ingenious Miss Turner': Elizabeth Turner (d 1756), Singer, Harpsichordist and Composer." *Early Music* 33 (February 2005): 65–79.
Young, Percy. "The Shaw-Helier Collection." In *Handel Collections and Their History*, edited by Terence Best, 158–170. Oxford, UK: Clarendon, 1993.
Zagorin, Perez. *Ways of Lying: Dissimulation, Persecution, and Conformity in Early Modern Europe*. Cambridge, MA: Harvard University Press, 1990.
Zimmerman, Joe Melvin. "The Psalm Settings and Anthems of William Child (1606–1697)." PhD diss., Indiana University, 1971.
Zwicker, Steven. *Dryden's Political Poetry: The Typology of King and Nation*. Providence, RI: Brown University Press, [1972].

List of Contributors

Suzanne Aspden is Associate Professor in the Faculty of Music, Oxford, and Fellow of Jesus College, Oxford. Her research interests center on eighteenth-century opera and issues of performance and identity; she has published widely in these areas, including in the *Journal of the American Musicological Association, Journal of the Royal Music Association, Musical Quarterly, Cambridge Opera Journal, Music and Letters*, and elsewhere. Her recent book, *The Rival Sirens*, concerns the rivalry of the singers Faustina Bordoni and Francesca Cuzzoni in 1720s London. Her current book project examines opera and national identity in eighteenth-century Britain. She also has edited volumes in progress on the English version of Cavalli's Erismena (with Michael Burden) and on opera and cultural geography.

Linda Phyllis Austern is Associate Professor of Musicology at Northwestern University where she specializes in the music of early modern Europe, especially in relation to literature, drama, the history of medicine, and the visual arts. Her books include *Music in English Children's Drama of the Later Renaissance* as well as the edited/coedited volumes *Music of the Sirens* (Indiana University Press, 2006), *Music, Sensation and Sensuality*, and *Psalms in the Early Modern World*. She has published more than thirty articles on topics ranging from music in the Jacobean theater to musical cures for erotic illness to gendered practices of early modern music in such journals as the *Journal of the American Musicological Society, Music and Letters, The Musical Quarterly*, and *Renaissance Quarterly*, and in edited collections.

Candace Bailey is Professor of Music History at North Carolina Central University. She is the author of *Music and the Southern Belle: From Accomplished Lady to Confederate Composer, Seventeenth-Century British Keyboard Sources*, as well as several articles on and two editions of English keyboard music of the seventeenth century. Bailey has presented numerous papers on keyboard music and gender of both the seventeenth and nineteenth century at scholarly conferences in the United States and Europe. She is active in a number of societies and has previously served as president of the North American British Music Association. Two forthcoming monographs on women and music have been made possible by a Faculty Award from the National Endowment for the Humanities.

Katherine Steele Brokaw is Assistant Professor of English at the University of California, Merced, where she teaches medieval and early modern literature. She is author of *Staging Harmony: Music and Religious Change in Late Medieval and Early Modern English Drama* and articles on drama and music in *Comparative Drama* and *Shakespeare Bulletin*.

MICHAEL BURDEN is Professor in Opera Studies at Oxford University and Chair of the Faculty of Music; he is also Fellow in Music at New College, where he is London dean. His published research is on the stage music of Henry Purcell, and on aspects of dance and theater in the seventeenth, eighteenth, and nineteenth centuries. He is currently completing a volume on the staging of opera in London between 1660 and 1860. He is the author of a five-volume collection of opera documents, *London Opera Observed*; a study of the London years of the soprano Regina Mingotti; and, edited with Jennifer Thorp, *The Works of Monsieur Noverre Translated from the French: Noverre, His Circle, and the English Lettres sur la Danse*. He is the past president of the British Society for Eighteenth-Century Studies and Director of Productions of New Chamber Opera (www.newchamberopera.co.uk).

AMANDA EUBANKS WINKLER is Associate Professor of Music History and Cultures and Director of Undergraduate Studies in the Department of Art and Music Histories at Syracuse University. Her research focuses on English theater music from the sixteenth century to the present day. She has published numerous essays and articles on topics ranging from didactic masques in the seventeenth century to Andrew Lloyd Webber's *The Phantom of the Opera* and has edited two volumes of music for the Restoration stage—*Music for Macbeth* and *John Eccles, Incidental Music, Part I: Plays A–F*. Research for her book, *O Let Us Howle Some Heavy Note: Music for Witches, the Melancholic, and the Mad on the Seventeenth-Century English Stage* (Indiana University Press, 2006), was supported by a long-term National Endowment for the Humanities fellowship at the Folger Shakespeare Library. Eubanks Winkler is currently completing a book on music, theater, and dance in early modern English schools.

JANE FLYNN is Visiting Fellow in the School of History, University of Leeds, United Kingdom, and a freelance organist and music teacher. Her research focuses on music education during the Tudor period, and her publications include "The Education of Choristers in England during the Sixteenth Century," in *English Choral Practice, c. 1400–c. 1650*, ed. J. Morehen, reprinted in *Institutions and Patronage in Renaissance Music*, ed. T. Schmidt-Beste; "Thomas Mulliner: An Apprentice of John Heywood?" in *Young Choristers, 650–1700*, ed. S. Boyton and E. Rice; and "Tudor Organ Versets: Echoes of an Improvised Tradition," *Journal of the Royal College of Organists*. Her blog "How to play 'divers ways upon the Plainsong *Miserere*'" can be found at tudorimprovisation.net.

List of Contributors

GRAHAM FREEMAN is an independent scholar and technical writer in Toronto, Canada. He received his PhD in musicology from the University of Toronto in 2008. He has worked on the folksong collections of Percy Grainger, the music of Alfred Schnittke, and theories of organizing systems in music. His work has appeared in *Music and Letters*, *The Folk Music Journal*, and *Grainger Studies*.

REBECCA HERISSONE is Professor of Musicology at the University of Manchester and a coeditor of *Music & Letters*. She is the author of *Music Theory in Seventeenth-Century England* and *"To Fill, Forbear, or Adorne": The Organ Accompaniment of Restoration Sacred Music*. Her article on the scoring of Purcell's *Come ye Sons of Art* won the Westrup Prize for 2007, and she has also written extensively on approaches to composition in late-seventeenth-century English music. Her four-year research project, "Musical Creativity in Restoration England," was funded by the Arts and Humanities Research Council, and resulted in a monograph, which was awarded the Diana McVeagh Prize by the North American British Music Studies Association in 2015, and a volume of interdisciplinary essays, *Concepts of Creativity in Seventeenth-Century England*, coedited with Alan Howard.

ALAN HOWARD is Lecturer and Director of Studies in Music at Selwyn College, Cambridge, and Director of Studies in Music at Queens' College. A committee member of the Purcell Society and general editor of The Works of John Eccles, his research focuses on the music of Henry Purcell and his contemporaries from the perspectives of source studies and contextualized musical analysis. He is currently working on a book on compositional artifice in Purcell's music, and critical editions for A-R and *Musica Britannica*; he is also coeditor of the leading Oxford University Press periodical *Early Music*.

KATHERINE R. LARSON is Associate Professor of English at the University of Toronto. Her research and teaching center on sixteenth- and seventeenth-century English literature and culture, with particular interests in early modern women's writing, gender and language, rhetoric and embodiment, and music (especially opera and song). She is the author of *Early Modern Women in Conversation* and the coeditor of *Gender and Song in Early Modern England* and *Re-Reading Mary Wroth*. Her work has also appeared in journals including *English Literary Renaissance*, *Milton Studies*, *Early Modern Women: An Interdisciplinary Journal*, the *Sidney Journal*, and the *University of Toronto Quarterly*. She is currently writing a monograph that integrates her training as a singer in its exploration of women's song performance in the early modern context.

BONNY HOUGH MILLER earned her PhD from Washington University in St. Louis. She has performed widely as a pianist and accompanist in addition to teaching piano and music history in universities in Missouri, Georgia, Florida, Virginia, and Louisiana. Her publications have appeared in the *Journal of the Society for American Music, Journal of the Arnold Schoenberg Institute, Notes of the Music Library Association, Fontes artes musicae, Bulletin of the Society for American Music, Piano Quarterly, Journal of Singing*, and *Cecilia Reclaimed: Feminist Perspectives on Gender and Music*. Her research focuses on music included in popular press periodicals such as literary journals and household magazines. She received the American Musicological Society Janet Levy Award for independent scholars to support research on British periodicals. Her index of music sheets is planned for the website "The Lady's Magazine (1770–1818): Understanding the Emergence of a Genre."

JOHN MILSOM is Professorial Fellow in Music at Liverpool Hope University, United Kingdom. He has published widely on Tudor topics, Josquin Desprez, and the analysis of sixteenth-century vocal polyphony. His interests in the history of the book and in compositional method are especially evident in his critical edition of Thomas Tallis and William Byrd's *Cantiones . . . sacrae* (1575). In collaboration with Jessie Ann Owens, he is currently preparing a new critical edition of Thomas Morley's *A Plaine and Easie Introduction to Practicall Musicke* (1597). He has created and continues to curate the online *Christ Church Library Music Catalogue*, a major research resource relating to the contents and provenance history of the internationally important music collections at Christ Church, Oxford.

BRYAN WHITE is Senior Lecturer in Music at the University of Leeds where he is a member of Leeds University Centre for English Music (LUCEM). He is also a member of the Purcell Society for whom he has edited Louis Grabu's opera *Albion and Albanius* and G. B. Draghi's *From Harmony, from Heav'nly Harmony*. He has published articles on English Restoration music in *Music & Letters, The Musical Times, Early Music*, and *Early Music Performer*, along with a number of book chapters. He is currently working on a book exploring music for St. Cecilia's Day in Britain from Purcell to Handel.

SARAH F. WILLIAMS is Associate Professor of Music History at the University of South Carolina. Her book, *Damnable Practises: Witches, Dangerous Women, and Music in Seventeenth-Century English Broadside Ballads* (Ashgate, 2015), explores the connections broadside ballads and their music created between various degrees of female crime, the supernatural, and cautionary tales for and about women. Her publications on the seventeenth-century musical representations of female transgression and expressions of masculinity in

American punk rock have appeared in the *Journal of Musicological Research*, the *Journal of Seventeenth-Century Music*, and a number of essay collections. She is an advisory board member of the English Broadside Ballad Archive (EBBA), and her scholarly work has been supported in part by the National Endowment for the Humanities and the American Musicological Society.

CHRISTOPHER R. WILSON holds the established Chair in Music at the University of Hull. He has published widely on early modern, nineteenth-, and twentieth-century English music with words. He has written two books and a number of articles on Thomas Campion. He is also a specialist in Shakespeare music. He was the UK research associate for the magisterial five-volume *Shakespeare Music Catalogue*, has published two books and a number of articles and book chapters, and compiled the database www.shakespeare-music.hull.ac.uk with funding from the British Academy. He was a music consultant for the permanent exhibition at The Globe theater in London. www2.hull.ac.uk/fass/music/staff/christopher-r-wilson.aspx.

Index

Note: Italicized page numbers indicate anywhere figures appear in the text.

Abell, John, 170, 230–231
accompaniment, 24n1, 37, 192; Henstridge's copies, 170, 173–174, 175, 177, 182–183, 184n26; keyboard notation, 118, 121; lute ayres, 55, 64n8
actors: choirboys, 14–16, 18, 24, 25n21, 70, 75–76, 77n13; as intermediaries, 101; memorization, 46, 102
Adriano in Syria (Metastasio), 230
Aguiari, Lucrezia, 211, 234
ahistorical categories, 15, 24n6, 52n27
aides-mémoire, 48
Albertus Magnus, 104
Alcock, John Jr., 246, *247*
Alexander's Feast (Handel), 213, 214, 215, 217
"Alexis, Dear Alexis" (Blow), 170
amateur, concept of, 1–3, 9, 11n35, 68, 167–168, 206n35, 220n28; men's manuscripts, 114–117, 119–120, 122
Amphion Anglicus (Blow), 189
"ancient music," 242–244, *243–244*, 255n28
Andrews, Thomas, 153–155
Anne, Princess, 116, 214
Anne, Queen, 7, 187–204; courtly modes of cultural production and, 189–190; odes for, 190–198, *191, 193–197*; Pallas Athena compared with, 190–191, 202, 204; panegyrics for in plays, 198–202, *200, 201*; subscription music and *Britain's Happiness*, 202–204, *203*
Anne Cromwell's Virginal Book, 115
Apology for Actors (Heywood), 101
apprenticeships, 150, 157
Aquaviva, Claudio, 35–36
architecture, 4–5, 79, 82; memory scheme/theater, 99–100, 102. *See also* spatial production
Arendt, Hannah, 2
Ariès, Philippe, 3
"Arise Ye Subterranean Winds" (Reggio), 171–175, *172, 173*, 177
ars memoriae (memory arts), 99–100, 102, 109–110
The Art of Singing (Reggio), 174
Articles of the Musical Society, in Oxford, 209

Aspden, Suzanne, 228, 242
Attey, John, 54
Aubrey, John, 6, 143
audience, 3–4, 6, 174, 242; coterie, 187, 189; for "Cries of London," 67–69, 73–76; for Handel's music, 213–214; for lute music, 47, 55–56, 59, 65n45; memory and broadside ballads, 99–101, 108–110; for *The Northern Lass*, 83–85, 87, 90–92; odes and, 187–190, 198, 204; Opera House, 224–226; for Udall's plays, 14–17, 19, 21
aural transmission, 8, 9, 42–53, 168, 175; cognition and organizing systems, 43, 45–47; maps, 46–49; memorized transcription, 175–181
Austern, Linda, 81–82, 124n16
ayres. *See* Campion, Thomas; lute ayres
Ayres, To Sing and Play to the Lute (Corkine), 56, 59

Babell, William, 231–232
Bach, J. C., 228–229, 231
background variation, 171
Bailey, Candace, 167–168, 206n35
Baines, Thomas, 150
Baldwin, Olive, 202
ballad partners, 104
ballad production, 45
ballads: gender and, 82; lute music, 47. *See also* broadside ballads
ballet des nations, 188
Ballet lutebook, 47
Banister, Henrietta, 116
Banister, John, 174
"Barbadoes Gentleman" (Clarke), 160–161
Bargrave, Isaac, 151
Bargrave, Robert, 151–152
Barksdale, Clement, 142
Barley, William, 42, 54
Barre, William Jr., 249
bass line (ground bass), 170, 177, 183, 192, 244
Batcheler, Daniel, 43
Batchelor, Jenny, 239
Bathe, William, 33
Bell, William, 31–32

306　INDEX

bells, 21
Bendish, Thomas, 152
Benedictine Convent at Brussels, 34
Bevin, Edward, 119
Bevin, Elway, 165
Bianca *(Taming of the Shrew)*, 102–103
biblical subject matter, 214
binaries, 1–2, 4, 9
Birch, Colonel, 138, 142
Birchensha, John, 129, 154
Blackfriars Theatre, 7, 79
Blackiston, Nathaniel, 159
Blackwell Hall factors, 155, 156
Blow, John, 114, 119, 121, 125n51; "Alexis, Dear Alexis," 170; *Amphion Anglicus,* 189
Bludworth, Thomas, 156, 160
"Blundrella: or, The Impertinent. A Tale" (Carey), 210–211
Blunt, Charles, 159
Board, Margaret, 47
Board lutebook, 47
body as instrument, 80–81, 85, 88
Bold, Jane (Mordaunt), 35
Bold, Richard, 35
Bolt, John, 31, 34
Bononcini, Giovanni, 230
A Book of Ayres (Rosseter), 59
Book of Common Prayer (1552), 15, 20, 24n1, 26n30
The Bottle Companions, 202
boundary crossing, 1–9, 238; "amateur" and "professional" musicians, 115–120, 167–168, 206n35; broadsides mediate, 99; commercial reading public, 189–190, 192; coteries and commercial reading public, 189, 192; "Cries of London," 67–69, 76; drama and music, 100–102; between faiths, 35; gender and, 28–30, 80–82, 85; Habermasian concepts, 3, 117, 128, 189–190; Handel, appropriation of, 207, 218–219; *Lady's Magazine,* 239, 249; merchants and gentry, 150–151, 161–162, 167–168; musicians and patronage, 208–209; song performance, 79–82, 85; spiritual recreation and liturgy, 37; Stuart era, 187–189, 204; theater as locus, 100, 102–103; transformative encounters, 5–6. *See also* domestic sphere; public sphere; public/private distinctions
bourgeoisie, 189
Bowman, Henry, 117–118
Bownde, Nicholas, 103
Boyce, William, 242
Brathwaite, Richard, 103, 105

Bremner, Robert, 230, 231, 232
Brett, Philip, 68–73
Briefe Introduction to the Skill of Song (Bathe), 33
A Briefe Introductione to the True Art of Musicke (Bathe), 33
Britain's Happiness (Motteux), 187, 190, 202, 204
British Harpsichord Music, Vol. 2: History I (Harley), 114–115
Britton, Thomas, 6
Broad, William, 142
broadside ballads, 8; commercial aspects, 104, 106; forms, 96; as images, 103–105; intertexuality, 99, 105–110; standardization, 103–104, 110; theater, interaction with, 102, 106–107; tune titles, 104, 105–106; as wall decorations, 103, 109; Titles:: *The Poor Man's Councellor,* 109; *A Warning for Wives,* 97–98, 105; Tunes:: "The Batchelors Fall," 96, 108; "Bragandary" ("Monstrous Women"; "O Folly Desperate Folly"), 97–98, 106, *107*; "Doctor Faustus," 106–108; "Fair Angel of England," 109; "Fortune My Foe," 106, 108; "The Ladies Fall," 108; "The Poor Man's Comfort," 108; "The Superanuated Maidens Comfort," 96, 108. *See also* memory
Brokaw, Katherine Steele, 29, 91
Brome, Richard, 79–95; musical spaces of, 82–84; Works:: *The Antipodes,* 82; *A Jovial Crew,* 82. *See also The Northern Lass* (Brome)
Brookesby, Eleanor (Vaux), 30, 31, 36
Brown, John, 224
Bryne, Albertus, 121
Bucholz, R. O., 189
Bullokar, John, 7
Burden, Michael, 211, 219n7
Burney, Charles, 208, 211, 223, 224, 226, 233–234
Burney, Fanny, 226, 234
Burney, Susan, 233, 234
Burrows, Donald, 208–209, 214
business. *See* merchants and businessmen
Butler, Charles, 129
Butler, Charlotte, 92
Butler, Judith, 80, 93n7
Byrd, William, 33, 34, 35, 54, 56; patent for printing music, 43, 51n2, 51n8, 63n6; Works:: *Cantiones sacrae,* 32; *Gradualia I,* 36

Caccini, Giulio, 129
Campelman, Charles, 170
Campion, Edmund, 30, 31, 36
Campion, Thomas, 54–66; composer of lyrics and music, 62; Latin poetry, 54, 57, 59–61; Lord

Hayes masque, 57; *Works:: Ad Thamesin*, 59; "Blame Not My Cheeks," 63; *A Booke of Ayres*, 57, 61; *De puluerea conjuratione*, 60; *Epigrammatum liber primus*, 60, 66n55; *Epigrammatum liber secundus*, 60, 66n56; *The Fourth Booke of Ayres*, 59; *Fragmentum Umbrae*, 59; "A Hymn in Praise of Neptune," 63; "The Man of Life Upright," 63; *Observations in the Art of English Poesie*, 59; *Poemata*, 59; *Songs of Mourning: Bewailing the Untimely Death of Prince Henry*, 61–62; *Tho. Campiani Epigrammatum Libri II Umbra Elegiarum liber unus*, 60; "Thou Art Not Faire, for All Thy Red and White," 63; "Thrice Tosse These Oaken Ashes in the Ayre," 63; *Two Bookes of Ayres*, 58, 59; "What If a Day," 63; "When to Her Lute Corinna Sings," 63. *See also* lute ayres
Canguilhem, Philippe, 69
Canterbury, 119, 165
Cantica Sacra (Lawes), 142
Cantiones sacrae (Byrd), 34
Capua, Rinaldo di, 235
Carey, Henry, 210–211, 220n3
Caroline period, 79, 82
Carvajal, Luisa de, 36, 37
Cary, John, 159–160
Cary, Richard, 160
Castiglione, Baldassare, 81
cathedral musicians, 6, 118–120
Catholicism/Catholic recusants, 3, 6, 13–14, 127; Office of the Dead, 18–19; tropes of exile and captivity, 139. *See also* education; Jesuits (Society of Jesus)
Cavendish, Margaret, 106–107
Cavendish, Michael, 56
Cecilian feast, 156, 159–161, 167; Purcell's odes, 166, 167
Chaderton, Laurence, 45
Chan, Mary, 174–175, 183
Chapel Royal, 21, 70, 77n13, 142, 154, 158, 213
Chappell, William, 47
Charles I, 139, 140, 142
Charles II, 140, 188, 198
Charlston, Terence, 121
Chichester Cathedral, 70
"Chide the Drowsy Spring" (Eccles), 192
Chiesa Nuova, 156
Children of the Chapel, 18
Children of the Revells of the Queene, 57
chirography, 45
Choice Ayres, Songs and Dialogues, 170, 179, *180*
Choice Psalmes (Lawes), 142, 143

choirboys/choir schools, 13, 29; actors, 14–16, 18, 24, 25n21, 70, 75–76, 77n13; "Cries of London" and, 70, 72, 75–76; decline in education, 33
Christ Church, 44, 117, 118
Cicero, 102
Cieraad, Irene, 117
Ciro Riconosciuto (Walsh), 230
The City Lady (Dilke), 188
Clarges, Louisa, 234
Clarges, Thomas, 234
Clark, Sandra, 82
Clarke, Jeremiah, 160–161, 188
Classical thinkers, 99–100
Clifford, Henry Lord, 58
The Close Hypocrite Discovered (Delamain), 138
Cobbold, William, 69
Cocchi, Gioacchino, 230
Coke, Lady Mary, 232–233
Coleman, Catherine, 154
Coleman, Edward, 154
"Collection of Rules in Musicke" (Taylor), 128
Collection of Songs with Symphonies and a Through Bass with Six Lessons for the Harpsichord (Turner), 247–248
collective memory, 99, 105–110
The Comical Hash (Cavendish), 106–107
commercial reading public, 189, 192
commonplace books, 44, 46, 63
community, 7–8; harmony and social concord, 17, 22–23, 29, 91
community of belief, 192
Compendium of Practicall Musick (Simpson), 129
Complete English Tradesman (Defoe), 150
composers: copyright, 228–229; famous composers/less-than-exciting keyboard music, 116. *See also individual composers*
concerts, 2, 4, 8, 202, 211, 231–237; women as promoters, 211, 232–233
Congreve, William, 96, 99
Consort Songs (Brett), 68–70
continuo parts, 121–122, 170–171, 173–174, 177
Cooper, Barry, 115–116, 120
Coote, John, 240, 254n13
Coperario, Giovanni, 165–166
Coprario, John, 54
copyists, 7, 9, 116; opera arias and, 228, 231; performing traditions captured by, 168, 171–174, *172*, *173*, 182. *See also* Henstridge, Daniel
copyright, 228–229, 246
Corelli, Archangelo, 161
Corkine, William, 56, 58–59
coronation services, 13–14, 190–192, *191*, 213–214

Corporation of Musick (Westminster), 158
Corpus Christi Mass, 36
Corri, Domenico, 241
Cosway, Richard, 233
coterie literary practice, 187, 189
"Could Man His Wish Obtain," 177–180, *179*, *180*
"Country Cries" (Dering), 75
courtly modes of cultural production, 6–7, 189–190
Cox, John, 231
Craig-McFeely, Julia, 42, 43, 47, 48
Cranmer, Thomas, 20
"Cries of London," 7, 67–78; Aldhouse, 71; Anon/Weelkes, 69, 70–71; audiences for, 68–69, 73–75; "Chandler insert," 72; Dering, 67, 69, 70, 75; Gibbons, 69–70, 72–73; Long Weelkes, 69–70, 75–76; medleys, 67, 70, 71; modern performances, 68–69; *In nomine* cantus firmus, 69, 70, 72–73; polyphonic textures, 71; Short Weelkes, 69–70, 75; Weelkes's, 68; "Winter Cries," 70, 73–75
Cromwell, Oliver, 138–139, 141
Cromwell, Thomas, 14
cultural memory, 99
Cupids Muster (ballad), 84

Daborne, Robert, 109
dance, gendered space and, 90–91
Danyel, John, 58
Danzi, Franziska, 211
d'Arezzo, Guido, 102
Dart, Thurston, 123n9
D'Assigny, Marius, 104
Davis, Walter R., 60, 65n35
Davison, Francis, 63
de Mare, Heidi, 117
De Oratore (Cicero), 102
declamatory style, 175, 177, 182
decorations, printed music as, 103, 109, 198
defensive tropes, 54
Defoe, Daniel, 150, 162
Dekker, Thomas, 107–108
Delamain, Richard, 137–138
Delaune family, 165
Dering, Richard, 67, 69, 70, 75, 139, 141–142
descants, 33
descriptive notation, 48
devotional songs, 29, 33–34, 136
Didone abbandonata (Metastasio), 226, 227, 230, 234
Dieupart, Charles, 202
Dilke, Thomas, 188

domestic sociability, 117, 124n21
domestic sphere: Catholic liturgies in, 29, 35–37; definitions, 117; keyboard music attributed to, 114–116, 119–120, 167–168; musical identities and, 209–212; professional/domestic division, 2, 8–9, 115–117; public performance of, 23, 209; residential architecture, 4–5; song performance reconfigures, 80–82, 88; state, analogy with, 85, 87
Dorset Garden Theatre, 188
Dowland, John, 42, 43, 44, 47, 53n48, 54; book of 1597, 55; education, 55, 56, 64n16; professional aspirations, 55; Works:: *First Booke of Songes or Ayres*, 55–56, 62; *Lachrimae*, 44; *A Musicall Banquet. Furnished with Varietie of Delicious Ayres*, 56; *Varietie of Lute Lessons*, 42, 50
Dowland, Robert, 42, 50
Draghi, Giovanni Battista, 6
Draycott, Helen, 35, 40n68
Dubrow, Heather, 91
Duncombe, Charles, 159
Dunhill, Rosemary, 214
Dunn, Leslie, 101
D'Urfey, Thomas, 187, 191, *191*; "The Infant Blooming Spring," 199, *201*; *The Kings Health*, 192; *Mars Now Is Arming* in *Wit and Mirth: Or Pills to Purge Melancholy*, 193–195; *The Old Mode and the New*, 187, 198–199, *200*; *Songs Compleat*, 199, *201*

Earle, Peter, 161
Eccles, John, 188, *191*, 192; 1704 collection of songs, 198, 206n37; "Chide the Drowsy Spring," 192; *Hark How the Muses Call Aloud*, 192; "They Call and Bid the Spring Appear," 192, *196*; *While Anna with Victorious Arms*, *197*, 198
Edgeworth, Elizabeth, 120
Edict of Nantes, 189
Edinburgh Musical Society, 209
education, 28–29; for Catholic children, 31–32; choir schools, 29, 33; in Latin and music, 31–33; music instruction, Catholic, 32–33; women's use of music for spiritual instruction and recreation, 33–35
Edward VI, 7, 13–15, 19–21
Eikon Basilike (Lawes), 142
Elegeia I (Fitz-Geffry), 60
Elizabeth I, 20, 31, 43, 62, 191, 202
Ellis, William, 138, 139
emblem books, 112n44
English ayres. *See* Campion, Thomas

INDEX

The English Ayre (Warlock), 55
English Lute Manuscripts and Scribes 1530-1630 (Craig-McFeely), 42
Epicoene (Jonson), 92
Epigrammata (More), 60
Erismena (Cavalli), 152
ethnomusicology, 48
Europe's Revels for the Peace (Motteux), 188, 202
Evans, Robert C., 128
Exeter House, 142
Ezell, Margaret, 189

fantasias, 71
Farinel, Michael, *191*, 192
"Farinel's Grounds," 192
The Favourite Songs to Zanaida, 230
The Favourite Songs, 224, 228-232, 235
Fellowes, Edmund, 55
Ferrar, Basil, 161
Fides ex auditu ("faith by hearing"), 45
Filmer, Robert, 170
Filmer family, 119, 165
The First Booke of Ayres (Attey), 54
The First Booke of Ayres (Morley), 58
The First Booke of Songes or Ayres (Jones), 57
The First Booke of Songes or Ayres (Dowland), 55-56, 62
Fischlin, Daniel, 61
Fitz-Geffry, Charles, 60
Flackton collection, 165
"Flat Pavan" (Johnson), 48
Fludd, Robert, 99, 100, 102
Folger MS, 48
folio books, 54-55
Forcer, Francis, 119, 165
Ford, Robert, 167
Ford, Thomas, 56, 58
Foucault, Michel, 5
14. Ayres in Tabletorie to the Lute (Cavendish), 56
Fox Lane, Mrs., 233
Francis, Earl of Cumberland, 58, 62
Frederick, Prince of Wales, 218
Freeman, Graham, 63n6, 168, 174, 183
Fretwork (recording), 68, 69, 70, 72, 75, 76
friendships, musical, 8, 127-128, 136, 138, 143, 145-146. *See also* Locke, Matthew; Taylor, Silas (Domville)
Funde flores, thura crema (Hingeston), 139

Gabrielli, Caterina, 230
Gandon, James, 218, 222n62
gardens, 213, 215-219, 239-240

Garnet, Henry, 30, 36
Garnons, Roger, 127
Gates, Bernard, 214
Gattolini, Signor, 227
Geminiani, Francesco, 208
gender, 79; "amateur" and "professional" musicians, 115-116; categorization of "domestic" keyboard music, 116, 119-120; female body as instrument, 80-81, 85, 88; hierarchy of difficulty, 120-121; identity and, 209; marginalization due to, 128, 136; music and space, 85; musical identities and, 210-211; patriarchal societal norms, 136-137, 143; silencing of women, 91-92; song performance and, 83-84, 88, 90; spatial considerations, 4, 81-82; vocal genres, 81-82; voice as marker of location and identity, 83, 90-93; women as concert promoters, 211, 232-233. *See also* women
General History of Music (Burney), 242
General History of the Science and Practice of Music (Hawkins), 242
The Gentleman's Journal, 189
Gentleman's Magazine, 238, 239
Gentlemen of the Musical Society, 156
George I, 224
George II, 213
George of Denmark, 191
Georgian view of music, 240-241
Gerard, John, 30, 31, 36, 37
Giannina e Bernadoni (Cimarosa), 233-234
Giardini, Felice, 228, 229, 233
Gibbons, Orlando, 67, 69-70, 72-73
Gibbons, William, 73
Gibson, Kirsten, 42
Giulio Cesare (Handel), 227
Giulio Sabino (Sarti), 226
Globe Theatre, 7, 46, 79, 100
Glorious Revolution, 189
Glushko, Robert J., 46
"Golden Grove" suite (Lawes), 118, 124n31
Goldsmith, Oliver, 240
Goodson, Anna, 120
Goodson, Richard, 118, 119, 120
Goodson, Richard Jr., 208
Gradualia I (Byrd), 36
Gray's Inn, 151-152
Grene, Sir William, 58
Grymeston, Elizabeth (Bernye), 34, 39n53
guided culture, 104
Guidonian hand, 102
Gunning, Peter, 142
Gunpowder Plot, 60, 62

Habermas, Jürgen, 3, 117, 128, 189–190
Hamilton, Newburgh, 217
Hamlet (Shakespeare), 101
Handel, George Frideric, 207–222; aristocracy, relations with, 207–208; in *Lady's Magazine,* 239, 241; oratorio, 213–214; outdoor performances of, 215–219; unpublished music obtained by music societies, 208–209; Works:: *Acis and Galatea,* 214; *Alexander's Feast,* 213, 214, 215, 217; *Esther,* 208, 213–214; *Giulio Cesare,* 227; *Joshua,* 209; *Messiah,* 218; Music for the Royal Fireworks, 219; *Rinaldo,* 232; "A Song Made to a Favourite Minuet in Rodelinda," 212; "A Song on the Victory Obtain'd Over the Rebels by His Royal Highness the Duke of Cumberland," 216
Handel's Temple, 218
Harding, Rosamund, 129, 142
Hardy, Sir William, 56
Hare, John, 230
Hare, Joseph, 230
Hark How the Muses Call Aloud (Tate and Eccles), 192
Harley, Edward, 127, 143
Harley, John, 114–115
harmony: matches meaning, 85; polyphonic compositions, 17–18; social concord signified by, 17, 22–23, 29, 91
harpsichord, 37, 50, 120, 155–157
Harris, James, 208, 209
Harris, Thomas, 235
Hauser, Gerard, 205n23
Hayes, William, 209, 220n15
Hayward, Charles, 156
Heigham, Bedingfield Jr., 156
Heigham, Mary, 156
Helier, Samuel, 214, 218–219, 222n62
Henrietta Maria, 140, 141
Henry VIII, 14, 23, 24n7
Henstridge, Daniel, 8, 9, 119, 120, 163n25, 165–184; autograph and partial autograph manuscripts, 166–167; informal music making, 167; Copies: "Could Man His Wish Obtain," 177–180, *179, 180;* "Old Chiron Thus," 180–181, *182;* transcription of "Amanti fuggite," 175–176, *176;* "Why Is Your Faithful Slave Disdained," 180, *181*
Herbert, Sir Edward, 56, 64n25
Hereford, 136–139, 141, 142
Hereford Independents, 139
Herissone, Rebecca, 118, 119, 124n32, 124n33, 126n58, 206n37
Heywood, Thomas, 101, 110

"High State and Honours" (Abell), 170
Hill, Gregory, 32, 35
Hill, Richard, 152
Hill, Thomas, 152–155, 156
Hilton, John, 174
Hingeston, John, 139
History of Gavel-Kind (King Vortinger), 141
Hogwood, Christopher, 122
Holford, Richard, 92
Holland, Abraham, 103
Holman, Peter, 117
Holmes, Mathew, 44
Holt, Henry, 159
Houblon, James Jr., 155
Houblon, Sarah, 155
"How Bonny and Brisk" (Smith), 168, *169*
Howard, Alan, 171
Howard, Anne, 31, 38n28
Hudson, Robert, 241–249, *243–244*
humanist thinkers, 100, 108, 110
Hunt, Arnold, 46
Hutchinson, Archibald, 159

identities, musical, 209–212
Ignatius, 29, 30
image, 102, 103–105
Impostor Magnus (Taylor), 137, 141
improvisation, 168; keyboard music, 121–122; lute music, 47, 48
In nomine cantus firmus, 69, 70, 72–73
incipit, 35
"The Infant Blooming Spring" (D'Urfey), 199, *201*
innovation, 49–50, 53n45
Interregnum, 127–128, 136–138; recreational psalm singing, 142–143
Issipile (Metastasio), 231
Italian performers, 225, 228

J. C. Bach v. Longman and Lukey, 228
Jacob, John, 32
James I, 31, 60
James II, 118, 188
Jeffreys, George, 142
Jeffreys, Jeffrey, 159, 160
Jeffreys, John, 159, 160
Jesuits (Society of Jesus), 28–41; aliases, 30, 32; household performances of festal liturgies, 35–37; importance of education and music to, 29–31; martyrdom, 30, 31. See also Catholicism; education
Jesus Psalter (Whitford), 31
Johnson, John, 43, 48

Johnson, Samuel, 8
Jones, Robert, 54, 56–57
Jonson, Ben, 19, 82, 92
Jordan, Abraham (father and son), 159

Kenny, Elizabeth, 42, 48
Kent, William, 215
Kew garden, 218
keyboard music, mid-seventeenth century, 114–126; categorized as "domestic," 114–116, 119–120, 167–168; gendered hierarchy of difficulty, 120–121; practical purposes, 118; recreational women musicians, 119–120; Selosse manuscript, 115, 120; sources, 117–119
The Kings Health (D'Urfey), 192
King's Men, 79
King's Private Musick, 154, 188
King's Theatre, 7, 213, 224, 228–229
Kinsman, Rachel, 158
Knepp, Elizabeth, 154

Lachrimae (Dowland), 44
Lady's Magazine; or Entertaining Companion for the Fair Sex, 8, 211, 213, 238–256; composers, 249–253; emergence of, 240–241; music inserts, 241, 253n1; "Music Master," 241–242; song texts, 240–242
Lampert, Anna, 3
Lampugnani, Giovanni Battista, 225
Lanier, Nicholas, 154
Lawes, Henry, 138, 142–143
Lawes, William, 118, 124n31, 142, 143
Le delizie dell'opere, 230–231
Le nuove musiche (Caccini), 129
Le Texier, Antoine, 227, 235
Leech, Peter, 115
L'Epine, Margherita de, 202
Les Sacqueboutiers (recording), 68, 69, 70, 72, 75, 76
Lethieullier, Christopher, 156
Lethieullier, John (son), 156, 159
Lethieullier, Sir John, 151, 156–157, 160
Lethieullier, William, 157
Levant Company, 151, 155–156, 159, 160
Leveridge, Richard, 199, 202
Ligny, Charles de, 36
Lincoln's Inn Fields, 188, 192
Lindley, David, 60, 62
Lingam, George, 32
Linley, Elizabeth, 211, 228
Lipsedge, Karen, 117
literacy, 45

Little, Patrick, 139
Little Trinity church (City of London), 74
Loades, David, 23
Locke, Matthew, 119; instrumental music, 141–146; Taylor's compositions attributed to, 128, 129, *130–131*, *135*, 147n16; Taylor's support of, 127–128, 137; Works:: *Melothesia*, 129; "When Death Shall Part Us from These Kids," 177, *178*
locus (place), 99–103
Longman and Broderip, 228, 229
Loscocco, Paula, 139, 141
Love, Harold, 2–3, 43, 190
"Love at First Sight" (Hudson), 244
Lowe, Edward, 118, 169, 174
lute ayres: dedications, 55–58; "Farewell Deare Loue," 57; folio books, 54–55; introspection, 61; move from private to public consumption, 58–59; patrons, 56, 57–58; public songs, 61–62; read without music, 62–63. *See also* Campion, Thomas; lute music
lute culture, 49–50
The Lute in Britain: A History of the Instrument and Its Music (Spring), 42
lute music, 9, 42–53, 54, 174; aurality, cognition, and organizing systems, 43, 45–47; Ballet lutebook, 47; Board lutebook, 47; Brogyntyn lutebook, 51n18; concordances, 43, 48; French, 43, 50; improvised, 47, 48; Mynshall lutebook, 48; pedagogy, 47–49; sources in early Modern England, 43–45; transmission in early modern England, 47–50; versions, 44; working methods, 43, 49. *See also* lute ayres; manuscripts
lute performance iconography, 47
The Lutes Apology for Her Excellency (Mathew), 50
The Lying Lover (Steele), 187, 190, 199, 202
Lynn, George, 138
Lyra Britannica (Boyce), 242

Mace, Thomas, 50
madrigals, 55, 64n10
"magazine music," 239–240, 254n6. *See also* *Lady's Magazine; or Entertaining Companion for the Fair Sex*
Mann, Horace, 233
manuscripts, 8–9, 54; duodecimo format, 169–170; "Mathew Holmes Lutebooks," 44; miscellanies, 43, 48; owned by merchants, 157; pocket manuscripts, 119, 169–170, 174, 183; printed sources, 168, 170, 171, 179; scribal editions, 43–44; sources for lute music, 43–45; visuospatial cognition, 46, 49. *See also* keyboard music, mid-seventeenth century; lute music

Manzoli, Giovanni, 224
Mara, Gertrud, 227, 229
Maravall, José Antonio, 104
Marsh, Christopher, 90, 114
Mary I, 7, 13–22
Mary II, 188
Mason, Ben, 137
masques, 57, 61
Massey, Edward, 127
material, the, 109–110
material media, 8
Mathew, Richard, 50
"Mathew Holmes Lutebooks," 44
Matteis, Nicola, 159
Maynard, John, 58
Mazzio, Carla, 19
Medici, Mattias de', 152
mementos, 99
memoria (mental faculty), 99
memory, 9, 51n5; *ars memoriae*, 99–100, 102, 109–110; audience and, 99–101, 108–110; auditory, 104; collective, 99–101, 105–110, 106–107; place and, 99–103; transcription, 175–181; visuospatial cognition, 46, 49. *See also* broadside ballads
memory theater, 99, 100, 102
men's manuscripts. *See* keyboard music, mid-seventeenth century
menuet chanté, 211
mercantile gentry, 8, 56
Mercers Company, 158
merchant, as term, 151
merchants and businessmen, 150–164, 213; Bargrave, 151–152; dissemination of continental music, 150–151; Hill and Andrews, 152–155; patronage, 159–161; Sherman, Wheak and Pigott, 155–157
Meres, Francis, 59–60
Metastasio, Pietro, 226, 227, 230–231, 234
Micheli, Leopoldo de, 228, 229, 231
Mico, Richard, 34–35
Miller, Bonny, 211
Milsom, John, 43, 51n8
Minear, Erin, 101
Mingotti, Regina, 225–226, 228, 233
minuets, 211, *212*
Miscelanea (Grymeston), 34
miscellanies, 43, 48, 51n9, 63
Mnemonica (Willis), 100, 104–105, 111n7
mnemonics, 53n43, 99–102
modern scholarship, 1; on keyboard music, 114–115, 118–119; merchants and businessmen neglected, 150

Modyford, James, 152
The Monthly Mask of Vocal Musick, 192, 198, 202, 206n36
monuments, 100, 102, 103
More, Thomas, 60
Morelli, Cesare, 155, 175, 185n37
Morgan, Charles, 117, 118
Morgan, Thomas, 188
Morley, Thomas, 33, 54, 56, 63n6, 81
Morris, Claver, 208
motets, Latin, 141–142
Motteux, Peter, 187, 188–189, 190, 191, 202, 204
Mounson, John, 57
Mounson, Thomas, 57, 59, 65n35
Murphy, Estelle, 189–190
music clubs, 158, 161, 214, 238, 246, 249
music meetings, 8, 136–138, 141, 170, 174, 182, 206, 208–209
Music Society (Oxford), 208–209
The Musical Companion of 1667, 157
Musical Magazine, 240
Musical Society, 159, 167
A Musicall Banquet. Furnished with Varietie of Delicious Ayres (Dowland), 56
A Musicall Dreame (Jones), 57
Musicke of Sundrie Kindes (Ford), 56, 58
Musick's Hand-maid, 119
Musick's Monument (Mace), 50
Mychelburnes, Laurence, Edward, and Thomas, 60
The Myrtle (Hudson), 244, 246

Napier, William, 231
national identity, 8, 83
A New Booke of Tabliture (Barley), 42, 54, 55
The Noble Souldier (Rowley and Dekker), 107–108
non-Western musical cultures, 48, 53n43
North, Roger, 150, 159, 220n29
The Northern Lass (Brome), 79–95; affinities between two Constances, 88; "As I Was Gathering Aprill Flowers," 88; female singing body, 81, 85, 88; gender and song performance, 83–84; "Hee that marries a Scold," 91; "place" as term in, 85; plot, 79–80; popularity, 79–80, 83; publication in print, 92–93; relocating song in, 84–93; "Some Say My Love Is Butt a Man," 84–85, *86*; staging, 88, 91–92, 95n41
notation, 48, 70, 168, 175, 177, 179, 183; pitch and duration, 102

"O cujus genio *Romana* Elegia debet," 60
Observations in the Art of English Poesie (Campion), 59

occupational musicians, 114, 116–119
odes, 160–161, 187, 204; commodified, 1702-1704, 192–198, *193–197*; for Queen Anne, 190–198, *191*, *193–197*
Odes in Imitation of the Seaven Penitential Psalmes (Verstegan), 34
Office of the Dead, 18–19
The Old Batchelor (Congreve), 96, 99
"Old Chiron Thus" (Wise), 180–181, *182*
Old Jewry "Musick-Society," 138
The Old Mode and the New (D'Urfey), 187, 198–199, *200*
"On Music" (Alcock), 246, *247*
opera arias, 7, 210–211, *212*; as affects, 223–224; copyright, 228–229; *The Favourite Songs*, 224, 228, 229–231; London audiences, 224–225; move from public to private, 231–235; newness required, 225–226; as objects, 229–231; "ownership," 227–231, 232; sources, 225; suitcase arias, 225–227
Opera House (London), 224–225, 227, 232
Ophelia *(Hamlet)*, 101
oratorio, 211, 213–214, 218, 242
organ playing, 13, 32–33
organizing systems, 43, 45–47, 53n44
organs, 29, 34–35, 39n53, 41n82, 159; banned, 15; portable, 36–37
ornamentation: in memorized transcription, 171, 173, 174, 175, 177, 182; in Stuart-era odes, 202–204, *203*
Orpheus Britannicus (Purcell), 189
Oswald, James, 240
Othello (Shakespeare), 101

Paget, Thomas, 32
Palladis Tamia, Wits Treasury (Meres), 59–60
panegyric mode, 187, 188, 190; odes for Queen Anne, 190–198, *191*, *193–197*; in plays, 198–202; subscription music, 202, 204
Paraphrase on the Psalmes of David (Sandys), 139
parody, 18–21
Parr, Catherine, 14, 23
Parrott, Andrew, 129
Pasquini, Bernardo, 156
Paston, Edward, 35
Paston, Margaret (Berney), 35
pastoral sentiments, 211, 217, 240, 242, 244, 248–249
patriarchal societal norms, 136–137, 143
patronage, 14, 56, 58, 143, 208; by merchants and businessmen, 159–161
Paul V, 30

Pavier, Thomas, 104
pedagogy, 9, 47–49. *See also* education; memory
Pelling, John, 158–159
penny sheets, 103, 109
Pepys, Samuel, 81, 96, 102, 109, 116, 122, 150; on audience copying, 174; *Beauty returne* (composition), 155; compositions, 154–155; on Great Fire, 161; Hill and, 153–154; on Locke and Taylor, 128, 129, 146; merchants and, 153–154, 157–158
Percy, Mary, 34, 40n58
permanence, musical, 99, 105, 110
Persons, Robert, 30, 31, 32
Petre, Catherine, 34
Petrucci (publisher), 42
Philips, James, 137
Philips, John, 142
Philips, Katherine, 128, 136, 137, 138, 143
Philips, Peter, 33
"Phillis with Her Enchanting Voice" (Turner), 247–249, *248*
Phoebus, Monarch of the Skies (D. Purcell), *191*, 192, 202
Pigott, Bartholomew, 158
Pigott, Charles, 158
Pigott, Francis, 157, 158
Pigott, George, 157, 158
Pigott, James, 155–157
Pigott, John, 158–159
Pigott family, 157–159
Pinnock, Andrew, 188
Pinto, David, 69, 72
pitch, spatial representation of, 102–103
place, memory, music, and theater as, 99–103. *See also* space
Placebo dilexi, 18–19
"place-realism" vogue, 82
A Plaine and Easie Introduction to Practicall Musicke (Morley), 33, 81
plainsong, 29, 33, 72–73
Playford, John, 138, 142, 157, 170, 183
playhouse, 102
plots, 46
pocket manuscripts, 119, 169–170, 174, 183
Poetical Rapsody (Davison), 63
The Poor Mans Comfort (Daborne), 109
Porter, Walter, 64n10
Poulton, Diana, 55–56
prescriptive music writing, 48
preservation, 109
Preston, John, 231
Price, Curtis, 121

Price, David, 56, 65n45
Price, Matthew, 138
pricksong, 33
printed music, 2, 7–8, 42, 58; ballad production, 45; odes, 192–198, *193–196*; opera arias, 224, 228–232; *Ralph Roister Doister*, 17; songs from *The Northern Lass*, 80
privacy, 3–5, 20, 44, 63. *See also* domestic sphere; public/private distinctions
professional/domestic division, 2, 8–9, 115–117
Protestants, 15, 23–24, 24n6, 25n12; aurality, importance to, 45, 52n25
psalms, 33–34, 80, 170; royalist use of, *130, 131, 139–143, 144*
Psalterium Carolinum (Stanley), 142
public, as term, 3
public sphere, 3–4, 23, 127–128, 137 138, 205n23, 219n2; concerts, 231–235; courtly cultural production and, 189–190; domestic performance of, 23, 209; odes and, 187–190, 192, 204; opera arias and, 224–225; singers and, 223, 225, 227–228
public/private distinctions, 1–9, 16, 117, 143, 219n2; broadside ballad and, 103–104, 106, 108–109; Catholic recusants and, 23–24, 28–29, 36–37; Handel's music and, 207–209, 213–215, 218–219; lute music and social hierarchy, 55, 57–63; magazines and, 239–240, 245, 249; memory and, 81, 99–100; move from private to public consumption, 58–59; professional/domestic division, 2, 8–9, 115–117. *See also* amateur, concept of; domestic sphere; public sphere; spatial production
Purcell, Daniel, *191*, 192, 202
Purcell, Frances, 189
Purcell, Henry, 116, 119, 121, 125n47, 125n51, 156; Dorset Garden Theatre and, 188; Henstridge's copies, 165, 182; Works:: *Hail! Bright Cecilia, 166*; "Welcome to All the Pleasures," 161, *166*; *Yorkshire Feast Song*, 160–161

Ralph Roister Doister (Udall), 13–27; audience, 14–17, 19, 21; choirboy actors, 14, 15, 16, 18, 24, 25n21; funeral parody, 18–21; multivalent performance context, 14–15; music as unproductive, 17; religious and musical pedagogy in, 18
Ramsey, John, 56
Randall, Elizabeth, 230–231
Randall, William, 230–231
Rauzzini, Venanzio, 230
Raylton, William, 119, 120
recollection, 99, 101

Rees, Owen, 36
Reggio, Pietro, 154, 184nn26–27; "Arise Ye Subterranean Winds," 171–175, *172, 173*, 177
religion: 1552 prayer book, 15, 20, 24n1, 26n30; denominational hybridity, 14, 20, 140; polyphonic compositions, 17–18
repository, 100
residences, 5, 6
Respublica (Udall), 13, 18
Restoration, 6, 8, 50, 109, 128, 136, 141; business community, 151
"Revealing Their Hand: Lute Tablatures in Early Seventeenth-Century England" (Kenny), 42
Rinaldo (Handel), 232
Ritchie, Leslie, 240
"Robert Filmer His Booke: of psalmes," 170
Roberts, Gabriel, 155, 157, 160
Rogers, Benjamin, 158
Rogers, John, 158
"The Rolling Years" (Steele), 199
Rosseter, Philip, 56, 57, 59
Rowley, Samuel, 107–108
Royal Africa Company, 160
Royal Exchange, 153–154
Royal Magazine, 240
royalism, 127–128, 136; motets, Latin, 141–142; poetic, 128, 139, 141; "psalmic poetic," 139, 141; in Taylor's texts, 139
Rubinelli, Giovanni, 233
"Rules of Composition" (Birchensha), 129
Russell, Elizabeth, 32

Saint Peters Complaint (Southwell), 31, 34
Salisbury Musical Society, 214
salons, 6, 233–234
Sanders, Julie, 91
Sanderson, John, 63
Sandys, George, 139, 142
Sarti, Giuseppe, 226
satire, 19
scribal publication, 43–44
Second Book of Ayres, and Dialogues (Lawes), 138
The Second Part of Musick's Hand-maid (Goodson), 119
The Second Part of the Pleasant Musical Companion, 180
Second Booke of Songs and Ayres (Jones), 58
Sedgwick, Obadiah, 161
Sedley, Katherine, 118
Seeger, Charles, 48
Selosse, Antoine, 115, 120

serials, 192, 198
sermons, 45–46
Seymour, Jane, 23
Shakespeare, William: *Hamlet*, 101; *Othello*, 101; *Taming of the Shrew*, 102–103; *The Tempest*, 171–175, *172, 173,* 188; *Twelfth Night*, 57
Shay, Robert, 165, 180
Sheldon, Edward, 32
Sheldon, Ralph, 32
Sheppard, John, 18
Sheridan, R. B., 211
Sherman, Rowland, 155–157
Sherman, William, 155
Simpson, Christopher, 129
singers, 223–237; ownership and, 227–229; suitcase, 225–227
"Sir John Harrington's Poems, Written in the reign of Queen Elizabeth," 63
Siroe, re di Persia (Lampugnani), 225
Sketch of Spring-Gardens, Vaux-Hall (attr. Lockman), 215, 217
Skillern and Goulding, 229
Slaughter, Paris, 156, 159
Slaughter Galley, 159
Smith, Bruce, 82
Smith, Robert, 168, *169*
social order, 240–241
social sphere, 3–4, 82
sol-faing songs, 35
Somerset, Edward, 34
song, 79–80; as marker of location and identity, 81–83; melancholy, association with, 85, 87–88, 91, 94n32; as privileged mode of self-expression, 84; social relationships constructed by, 80, 82. *See also* vocal music
"Song on Nelson's Glorious Victory" (Hudson), 244–246, *245–246*
song performance, 79; affective impact, 81, 82, 92; cultural ambivalence about, 80–81, 83; elides boundaries, 79, 85–88; gender and, 83–84, 88, 90
Songs Compleat (D'Urfey), 199, 201
Songs for 1 2 & 3 Voyces (Bowman), 117–118
Songs for the Lute Viol and Voice (Danyel), 58
Songs of Mourning: Bewailing the Untimely Death of Prince Henry (Campion), 61–62
sound, space and, 80–82, 92
Southwell, Robert, 30, 31, 34, 35–36, 38n28
space, 2, 5–6, 14; location and type of music performed, 81–82; misinterpretation of, 84–85, 87, 92; sound, relationship with, 80–82, 92. *See also* place

spatial production, 79–95; gendered function, 81–82, 88, 90–91; house-state analogy, 85, 87; musical-spatial interplay, 82–84; of Other, 83; pitch and duration, 102–103; visuospatial cognition, 46, 49. *See also* architecture
Spiritual Exercises (Ignatius), 28, 29
Spring, Matthew, 42
St. John's College, Oxford, 74, 75
St. Omer school, 32–33, 37
St. Paul's Cathedral, 18, 25n19, 32, 33
Stanley, Thomas, 142
state, 4–5; household compared with, 85, 87
Stationers' Company, 104
Steele, Richard, 187, 199, 202
Steggle, Matthew, 88, 90
stile galant, 249
stile nuovo, 141
Storace v. Longman and Broderip, 228, 229
Stuart, Lady Arabella, 56, 64n21
Stuart era, 187–189. *See also* Anne, Queen
subscription music, 202, 204
symbols, 104

Tallis, Thomas, 43, 51n2, 51n8
Taming of the Shrew (Shakespeare), 102–103
Taruskin, Richard, 228
Tate, Nahum, 190, *191*, 192
taverns, inns, and alehouses, 103, 167; oratorios in, 213, 214
Taylor, John (shipbuilder), 143
Taylor, Silas (Domville), 127–149; aspirations undermined, 143, 145–146; as composer, 128–136, *130–135*; as controversial figure, 137–138; GB-Cfm Mu MS 163 (Cfm 163), 129, *130–132*, 139; political identity, 136–141; portrays music meetings as neutral, 137–138; Works:: "Dominantur in Nos Servi," *131, 133–134*, 140, *145*; Lamentations in works of, *131*, 139, 140–142; "Non habet Sion," 139; Psalm 96, 139; Psalm 137, *130, 131*, 139, 140, 143; "Revertere O Sulammittis," *132*, 140, *145*; Song of Songs in works of, *132*, 139, 140; "Vox Dilecti Mei," *135*; "When Stormes Arise" (Psalm 27), *130*, 139–140, *144*; Writings:: "Collection of Rules in Musicke," 128; *Impostor Magnus*, 137, 141
Taylor, Silvanus Sr., 136
Taylor, Sylvanus, 146n15
"Tell the World Great Caesars Come" (Clarke), 188
Temperley, Nicholas, 15
Tempest, Thomas, 157–158
The Tempest (Shakespeare), 171–175, *172, 173,* 188

theater, 2, 5–6; as ideological construct, 100; illusions, 90–92; as memory, 101; as monument, 100, 102; panegyric music in plays, 198–202; as place (locus), 100, 102–103; post-play musical entertainments, 92–93; privacy, production of, 88; Queen Anne era, 187–204; silent women, depictions of, 91–92. *See also* memory
theatre, as term, 7
Theatre Royal (Drury Lane), 192
theatrum, 102, 110
theatrum mundi, 100
theorbo, 50
theory, 100
"They Call and Bid the Spring Appear" (Tate and Eccles), 192, *196*
Tho. Campiani Epigrammatum Libri II Umbra Elegiarum liber unus (Campion), 60
Thompson, Robert, 142, 165, 180
thoroughbass technique, 129
Thynne, Joan, 58
"Thyrsis" (Hudson), *243–244*
Timothean music, 217
Topcliffe, Richard, 32
Tory concert series, 202
trading companies, 151
transcription, 48; bass part, *179*, 179–180, *180*, *183*; memorized, 175–181; ornamentation, 171, 173, 174, 175, 177, 182; pseudo-phonetic, 171, 175
Trevelyn, G. M., 189
Tribble, Evelyn, 46
Tridentine decrees, 30, 37
Tudor era: audiences, 14–15; courtly modes of cultural production, 189–190
The Turkish Paradise or Vaux-Hall Gardens: Wrote at Vaux-Hall Last Summer (attr. Lockman), 215, 217
Turner, Elizabeth, 246–249, 256n44
Turner, William, 119, 165
Twelfth Night (Shakespeare), 57
Twelfth Night 1603, 74
The XII. Wonders of the World (Maynard), 58
Two Bookes of Ayres (Campion), 58, 59
Tyers, Jonathan, 219

Udall, Nicholas, 13–78; *Respublica*, 13, 18; as spokesman for religion, 23; as timeserver, 14, 19, 23. *See also Ralph Roister Doister*
United Company, 188
urban space, 5–7
Urban VIII, 37

Vanneschi, Francesco, 225
Varietie of Lute Lessons (Dowland), 42, 50
Vaux, Anne, 30, 31, 36
Vaux, Elizabeth (Roper), 30, 31
Vauxhall Gardens, 213, 215, 217–218, 221n46
Venetian opera, 152
Verney, John, 151, 157
Verney, Ralph, 151
Verstegan, Richard, 34
vice characters, 17
Vickery, Amanda, 117
viols, 33, 37
virginals, 34–35, 37
visuality, 102–103
Vivian, Percival, 59
vocal music: political implications, 138–139, 141; recreational psalm singing, 142–143, 153. *See also* singers; song; song performance
voice: as marker of location and identity, 83, 90–93; materiality and, 109–110
Vortiger, King, 141

waits, 7, 43, 68, 73–76
Walker, Greg, 15
Wallington, Benjamin, 157, 158
Walpole, Henry, 31, 233
Walpole, Michael, 30
Walsh, John, 192, 198, 230–231, 232
War of the Spanish Succession, 187, 191
Ward, Mary, 30, 32, 39n38
Ward's Institute, 32, 37, 39n38
Warlock, Peter, 55
A Warning for Wives (broadside), 97–98, 105
Watson, William, 31, 36
wax tablet metaphor, 110
Weelkes, Thomas, 67, 68
Welcker, Peter, 231
"Welcome to All the Pleasures" (Purcell), 161, *166*
Weldon, John, 202, *203*, 204
"The Welfare of All on Blest Anna Depends" (Weldon), 202, *203*, 204
Wells music meetings, 208
Wessell, Leonard, 156, 159, 160
Westcott, Sebastian, 31, 32
Westminster Abbey, 44
Westrup, Jack, 121
"What If a Day" (Campion), 63
Wheak, Philip, 155–157
"When Death Shall Part Us from These Kids" (Locke), 177, *178*
Whig concert series, 202

While Anna with Victorious Arms (Eccles), *197*, 198
Whimzies: or, a New Cast of Characters (Brathwaite), 103, 105
White, Bryan, 138, 167, 183n7
White, Esther, 157
White Webbs house, 30, 36
Whitford, Richard, 31
Whole Booke of Psalmes (Sternhold and Hopkins), 34, 170
Whole Psalmes in Foure Parts, 34
Whythorne, Thomas, 33
William and Mary, 188–189
William III, 187, 188–189
William Raylton's Virginal Book, 119
Willis, Jonathan, 100, 104–105, 111n7
"Willow Song" *(Othello),* 101
Wilson, John, 80, 85, *86*, 142
Wilson, Thelma, 202
Winchester College, 70
Winn, James, 189–190
Wise, Michael, 180
Wiseman, Jane (Vaughan), 31
Wiseman, William, 31
Wit and Mirth, 192, 198
Wombourne Wodehouse, 214, 218
women: female servants, music instruction for, 34; Jesuits and, 28–41; as musicians, 31, 34–37; silent, depictions of, 91–92; Tridentine decrees, 30; as tutors, 32; use of music for spiritual instruction and recreation, 33–35. *See also* gender
Wood, Anthony, 96, 109, 136, 138, 145
Wood, Bruce, 188
woodblock prints, 104
Woolley, Andrew, 118, 119, 120
Wotton, Henry, 151
Wright and Wilkinson, 231
Wriothesley, Charles, 19–20

Yorkshire Feast Song (Purcell), 160–161
Young, William, 152

Zanaida (Bach), 231
Zemira e Azore (Verazzi), 231

www.ingramcontent.com/pod-product-compliance
Lightning Source LLC
Chambersburg PA
CBHW071735150426
43191CB00010B/1582